# FIGHTING MEANS KILLING

# *Fighting Means Killing*

Civil War Soldiers and

the Nature of Combat

JONATHAN M. STEPLYK

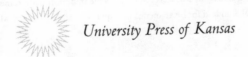

University Press of Kansas

Published by the University Press of Kansas (Lawrence, Kansas 66045), which was
organized by the Kansas Board of Regents and is operated and funded by Emporia State
University, Fort Hays State University, Kansas State University, Pittsburg State University,
the University of Kansas, and Wichita State University

Library of Congress Cataloging-in-Publication Data

Names: Steplyk, Jonathan M., author.
Title: Fighting means killing : Civil War soldiers and the nature of combat / Jonathan M.
Steplyk.
Description: Lawrence : University Press of Kansas, 2018. | Includes bibliographical
references and index.
Identifiers: LCCN 2018004096
ISBN 9780700626281 (hardback)
ISBN 9780700631865 (paperback)
ISBN 9780700626298 (ebook)
Subjects: LCSH: United States—History—Civil War, 1861–1865—Moral and ethical
aspects. | United States—History—Civil War, 1861–1865—Psychological aspects. |
Combat—Psychological aspects—History—19th century. | Soldiers—United States—
Psychology—History—19th century. | BISAC: HISTORY / United States / Civil War
Period (1850–1877). | HISTORY / United States / 19th Century. | HISTORY / Military /
General.
Classification: LCC E468.9 .S857 2018 | DDC 973.7/1—dc23.
LC record available at https://lccn.loc.gov/2018004096.

British Library Cataloguing-in-Publication Data is available.

Printed in the United States of America

10 9 8 7 6 5 4 3 2 1

*To my mother and father,*
*for their boundless love*
*and tireless support*

No bastard ever won a war by dying for his country. You won it by making the other poor dumb bastard die for his country.
—*Lieutenant General George S. Patton Jr. (May 31, 1944)*


Thee wants to go out and fight, give thy life for what thee believes. Any of us here I'm sure is ready to do that. But that's not what thee'll be asked to do. . . . What thee'll be asked to do now . . . is to kill.
—Friendly Persuasion *(1956)*


Once Chamberlain had memorized a speech from Shakespeare and gave it proudly, the old man listening but not looking, and Chamberlain remembered it still: "What a piece of work is man . . . in action how like an angel!" And the old man, grinning, had scratched his head and then said stiffly, "Well, boy, if he's an angel, he's sure a murderin' angel." And Chamberlain had gone on to school to make an oration on the subject: Man, the Killer Angel.
—*Michael Shaara,* The Killer Angels *(1974)*

# CONTENTS

Acknowledgments, *ix*

Prologue, *1*

Introduction, *5*

1 The Things They Carried: Influences on Civil War Soldiers and Killing, *13*

2 Seeing the Elephant: Killing and the Face of Battle, *41*

3 Good Execution: The Language of Killing, *76*

4 With Bayonet and Clubbed Musket: Killing in Hand-to-Hand Combat, *90*

5 Hunters of Men: Sharpshooters and Killing, *119*

6 Murder and Mercy: The Extremes of Killing, *152*

7 Killing in Black and White: Race, Combat, and Hate, *189*

Epilogue, *226*

Notes, *235*

Bibliography, *261*

Index, *279*

*An illustration gallery follows page 141.*

ACKNOWLEDGMENTS

This is my humble effort to give not only credit but warmest thanks where they are due. My thanks go out to the many individuals—colleagues, friends, family—who helped make this book possible.

I would like to thank Editor Joyce Harrison and her talented colleagues at the University Press of Kansas for their assistance, patience, and enthusiasm. They have not only made this book possible but have made the experience a rewarding one as well.

I owe special thanks to the numerous archivists and librarians who assisted me throughout my research. The staffs of the Abraham Lincoln Presidential Library, Gettysburg National Military Park, Vicksburg National Military Park, the US Army Heritage and Education Center, the Wisconsin Historical Society, Kenosha's Civil War Museum, the Lake County History Archives, and the Mary Couts Burnett Library at Texas Christian University (TCU)—to name but a few—all helped immensely in securing invaluable resources.

Generous grants and awards also made this project possible. I was privileged and honored to receive a General and Mrs. Matthew B. Ridgway Military History Research Grant from the US Army Heritage and Education Center and a Wisconsin Veterans Museum research grant. A fellowship from the TCU History Department helped me complete the initial manuscript that became this volume.

Throughout my academic career, three very special professors shaped the journey that led to this book. My undergraduate advisor, Russell Blake, confirmed my decision to study at Ripon College, inspired me in the classroom, and helped launch my graduate career. Carol Reardon guided me in my master's program at Pennsylvania State University, and it was during her exceptional military history seminar that I first read *On Killing,* which directly inspired this book. Finally, Steven Woodworth, my doctoral advisor at TCU, was truly the indispensable man throughout this process. Dr. Woodworth not only oversaw this project from start to finish but also continues to inspire me as an educator, researcher, writer, role model, mentor, and friend.

Ably serving alongside Dr. Woodworth on my committee were Todd Kerstetter, Gene Smith, and Kenneth Stevens. I am indebted to each of these scholars for helping refine my work thanks to their time, advice, insights, and encouragement.

Just as Civil War historians enjoy an embarrassment of riches in terms of sources, I have been richly blessed by the friendships I have enjoyed throughout my academic career. My Penn State friends James Adam Rogers, Megyn Dixon, Alfred Wallace, Will Bryan, and Tim and Laura Orr were among the first to hear about my inspiration to explore Civil War soldiers and killing. Enriching the journey with their fellowship and advice were TCU friends Matthew Arendt, Mike Burns, Shawn Devaney, Stephen Edwards, Blake Hill, and Miles Smith. Very special thanks go to Jonathan Engel, Mitchell Klingenberg, and Justin Solonick for sharing treasures from their own research for this book.

I am also grateful to another circle of friends, those in the living history community. Sharing this wonderful hobby with them has not only offered me remarkable insights and hands-on knowledge about the past that have shaped this book but has also created some of my warmest memories. It is impossible to name all the men and women who have made this possible, but I wish to thank especially my friends Chris Bryant, Steve Corey, Luetta Coonrod, and Bob Winter.

Finally, I offer my heartfelt thanks to my family for all their unconditional and unwavering love and support. They have fostered my journey from history buff to historian in countless ways. I am especially blessed to be part of a family with a passion for its own history and our American heritage. My grandparents, Dale and Mona Awick, were among the first to nurture my fascination with the past. Although Grandma Mona did not live to see me pursue history in higher education, I have it on good authority that she was the first to predict I would become a historian. Grandpa Dale, who still inspires me with his knowledge and storytelling, can now enjoy this accomplishment on behalf of them both. I am grateful, too, to my brother, Matthew, who shared in family trips to historic sites and remains one of my proudest supporters. Last, I wish to thank my parents, Michael and Kathy Steplyk, for a lifetime of love and support. Throughout this project, that support has gone beyond simple encouragement. Their enthusiasm for history and travel inspired them to join me on road trips to various libraries and archives. My mother, a talented genealogist, even volunteered to help comb through boxes and files of documents, relishing the treasures she found. I have truly been blessed by them and cannot thank them enough for making this all possible.

# Prologue

On May 24, 1861, Americans knew they faced civil war, but to many in the North and South, it seemed that the war would prove a quick one, with relatively little bloodshed. Even during the bombardment of Fort Sumter that had inaugurated the war, not a man in either the Federal garrison or the secessionists ringing Charleston Harbor had been killed or wounded. The weeks since had seen only a smattering of fighting, with both the US government and the rival Confederate government having just begun raising the armies that would march to battle in the coming summer. Little blood had been shed to arrest the attention of Americans at war with one another. All that would change on May 24. By the end of the day, North and South would have heroes to mourn and celebrate. Each would celebrate a man who had been killed and a man who had killed, the slain and the slayer. For the defenders of the Union, they would have two heroes to celebrate: a martyr and his avenger. For supporters of the Confederacy, their hero martyr would be one and the same.

The previous day, Virginia had formally ratified its articles of secession, so on May 24, President Lincoln ordered Federal troops in Washington to cross the Potomac and occupy the city of Alexandria. The force included men from the 11th New York Volunteer Infantry Regiment, known as the Fire Zouaves. Now their colonel, Elmer E. Ellsworth, accompanied by the regimental chaplain, a lieutenant, a newspaperman, and four enlisted men, entered the Marshall House hotel. A large Rebel flag flew defiantly from atop the hotel, large enough to be seen from the White House. Ellsworth

wanted the flag down. Not only did the impudent banner offend his patriotic soul but also the colonel feared that his Fire Zouaves, recruited from
rowdy New York City firemen, might turn unruly and destructive at the
sight of the flag.[1]

Inside the hotel, which was really a glorified tavern, Ellsworth and his
party met a startled man in the hallway, dressed only in trousers and shirtsleeves. "Who put that flag up?" Ellsworth snapped at him. "Are you the
proprietor?" The colonel, at five feet six inches, stood at least half a foot
shorter than the disheveled man, yet the commanding tone came easily,
and not solely because he was backed up by Fire Zouaves with fixed bayonets. The twenty-four-year-old Elmer Ellsworth had studied law in Illinois,
where in 1860 he met and befriended Abraham Lincoln. In addition to his
legal studies, Ellsworth pursued his passion for all things military, eventually raising a crack militia outfit, the United States Zouave Cadets, with
whom he had toured the East Coast, dazzling crowds with the Zouave Cadets' flashy uniforms and highly acrobatic military drill.[2]

The civilian told Ellsworth he was only a boarder and knew nothing
about the flag, and so the party continued their way upstairs. What the
colonel did not know was that James W. Jackson, perhaps thirty-seven years
old, did in fact own the Marshall House. Moreover, Jackson was an ardent
secessionist and defender of slavery. In 1859, he had ridden off to Harpers
Ferry to help put down John Brown's raid, but he arrived too late to take
part in the fighting. The Stars and Bars that flew over his establishment was his pride and joy. Made for him by local seamstresses, he had
them add a star to the blue field with each state that seceded.[3]

On the roof of the Marshall House, Ellsworth cut down the flag and,
carrying the captured banner over his shoulder, headed downstairs with his
seven companions. As they descended the stairs to the second-floor landing, with Private Francis E. Brownell in the lead, James Jackson stepped out
of the shadows and aimed a double-barreled shotgun at Ellsworth. Seeing
the threat, Brownell tried to deflect the shotgun with his rifle, but he lost
his footing on the stairs. Jackson fired a blast into Ellsworth's chest, the
load also driving a medal he was wearing into his body. As Ellsworth tum-
bled to the floor, killed instantly, Jackson turned his attention to the soldier.
Brownell, having regained his footing, parried the shotgun upward, the second shot passing safely over his head. The Fire Zouave leveled his rifle and
shot Jackson square in the face, then, still fueled by adrenaline, stabbed the
proprietor "through and through the body" with a twenty-two-inch saber
bayonet before he could even fall to the floor.[4]

Ellsworth's death made him the first Union officer killed in the Civil

War. Already one of the most famous military figures in the United States, he was mourned and commemorated across the North as a national martyr, memorialized in prose, verse, artwork, and music. One song honored him as "our gallant Zouave; / Who tore down the banner of Treason, / And perished our Union to save." Northern print media condemned the killing of Ellsworth by Jackson, a civilian, as "murder" and "assassination." E. H. House, the *New York Tribune* reporter who had accompanied Ellsworth and witnessed the shooting, wrote that Jackson's face, mangled by Brownell's bullet, still bore "the most revolting expression of rage and hatred I ever saw." Northerners also celebrated their still living hero, Francis Brownell, who in killing Jackson had provided "instantaneous" retribution for his fallen colonel. He posed for several photographs, including a full-length portrait in which he stood with rifle and bayonet, one foot atop the captured Rebel flag. Numerous patriotic envelopes and stationery depicted the deadly encounter, usually prominently featuring Brownell shooting or stabbing the assassin. Beneath one such image, in which Jackson bled copious red ink from his wounds, the envelope featured Brownell's message home: "Father—Col. Ellsworth was shot dead this morning. I killed his murderer. FRANK." A poem in one newspaper suggested that the best way to honor Ellsworth was to follow Brownell's example, exhorting readers, "Don't shed a tear for him! / Mourn him in blood. / Quick-dropping bullets / Shall work him most good."[5]

Just as partisan political differences divided North and South, Union partisans hailed Ellsworth and Brownell as heroes and condemned Jackson as the villain, while Confederate partisans recast the narrative with James Jackson as a Southern hero. In a short biography of the Virginian, copies of which were sold to benefit his family, the title page hailed Jackson as "the slayer of Ellsworth" and "the first martyr in the cause of Southern Independence." The biographer lauded him as a passionate Confederate patriot devoted to his country and flag, both of which he defended with "terrible determination." Whether the innkeeper had encountered Ellsworth when the soldiers first entered the Marshall House, the biographer professed uncertainty. What Confederate sympathizers did know was that Jackson had awakened to find his home "overrun by insolent trespassers," led by a glory hound of a colonel. The Alexandrian had manfully defended his home and flag and bravely lost his life in the process. Like Ellsworth's admirers in the North, Southerners commemorated their own hero in verse as well as prose. A poem from South Carolina celebrated Jackson as both slayer and martyr, boasting that the innkeeper had exacted an "Ells-worth" from the Yankees before he died. The last stanza declared:

"Down with your flag!" the spoilers cry.
Oh, how his brave pulsations bound!
Did he obey? His shots reply—
He brings his foeman to the ground.
But he fell too. For country's sake,
He on her altar bleeding lies.

While the North found two heroes in the Marshall House incident, the martyr and his avenger, Southern Rebels found in James W. Jackson a hero who embodied both roles.[6]

The altercation in Alexandria offered an allegory for the political stakes over which Americans North and South were preparing to fight. Ellsworth and Jackson had died over more than simply a flag. Their deaths centered on the question of which flag would fly over not just the Marshall House but over all Virginia and the other secessionist states: the Stars and Stripes for which Elmer Ellsworth fought, or James Jackson's Stars and Bars. Would the United States be preserved as one nation, or would the new Confederate States manage to tear themselves away to begin their own rival American republic? Similarly, the altercation reflected the military means that would decide those questions. Just as Abraham Lincoln had vowed to put down the rebellion with Federal troops and state volunteers, he ordered those forces to occupy Alexandria, and Colonel Ellsworth had on a still smaller scale entered the Marshall House to haul down a flag symbolizing that rebellion. Had Ellsworth acted the patriot, dying to quash an unlawful rebellion and remove a treasonous banner? Or had Jackson acted justly, defending his city, home, and property from an oppressive invader? The central question of slavery had not played a direct role in the incident (excepting that Jackson owned slaves and zealously defended the institution), yet nevertheless the killings spoke directly to some of the most immediate political concerns of white Northerners and Southerners in the opening months of the Civil War.

The actions of Ellsworth, Jackson, and Brownell, as well as the attitudes of their supporters, reflected not only the conflict between Americans in 1861 but also realities about the nature of war itself. Americans loyal to the Union honored both the fallen leader and the soldier who avenged Ellsworth's death by dispatching his killer. Those siding with the Confederacy hailed the man who had slain his foe but had lost his own life in so doing. Americans on each side found heroes in both the slain and the slayer. They recognized and affirmed that war could mean both dying and killing for a country and for a cause.

# Introduction

"War means fighting, and fighting means killing," Confederate cavalry commander Nathan Bedford Forrest famously declared. At its core, the Civil War involved Americans killing Americans. Regardless of the moral lens through which one views the conflict, that truth remains. If we emphasize the tragedy of the hundreds of thousands of lives lost, that tragedy is further emphasized by the fact that the combat deaths resulted from Americans slaying one another, Federals and Confederates engaging in a kind of national fratricide. If we emphasize the good that the war achieved—preservation of the American experiment in constitutional self-government and destruction of chattel slavery in the United States—then killing on the battlefield provided one of the primary means to that end. Despite that reality, Americans tend to gloss over that truth in remembering the Civil War. We speak plainly about Union and Confederate soldiers dying for their cause and country, but we more euphemistically describe them as fighting for those things. The dying resulted from Americans fighting one another. Plainly stated, Billy Yanks and Johnny Rebs killed one another.

That we are sometimes reticent about this truth is hardly surprising, for the nature of killing in war is a sensitive subject. In interviews and question-and-answer sessions with veterans, members of the public are often enjoined to avoid bluntly asking, "Did you kill anybody?" We advise against the question not only because it may prove painful or embarrassing to the veteran but also because the question is so common, especially among children and young adults, because it is a question many of us deeply want to ask. For nonveterans, especially Americans living in the peace and security amid twenty-first-century prosperity, war—and killing in war—poses a great mystery.

Historical novelist Bernard Cornwell, speaking of mankind's fascination with war throughout history, helps explain why the violence in war enthralls us:

> War, at its sharp end, is a place where the rules that govern human behavior cease to exist. We lead our ordinary lives surrounded by rules. Thou shall not kill, steal, covet, or kidnap, and our society has constructed a framework of police, courts, and laws to enforce those rules which serve to make our lives tolerably safe. Yet in war we are encouraged to kill, to plunder the enemy, and to capture his territory, families, and wealth. I suspect that many of us are fascinated by this reversal of normality and wonder how we would behave in a world where the rules that govern our safety have been abandoned.[1]

For others, killing in war repels rather than captivates. The controversy over the 2014 film *American Sniper*, depicting the life of US Navy SEAL Chris Kyle, America's deadliest sniper, illustrates the conflicting attitudes toward killing in war. The film's release and popularity prompted some public figures, generally outspoken opponents of the wars in Afghanistan and Iraq, to criticize Kyle and his military service, describing him as a coward, mass murderer, and "American psycho." Ironically, many antiwar leaders and movements of the post-9/11 world have been praised for generally focusing on criticizing political and military policy while still vocally supporting the troops themselves, partly a lesson learned from the pain and public backlash stirred by the more vociferous antimilitary sentiments voiced by some opponents of the Vietnam War. However, the popular celebration of Chris Kyle and his deadly sniping skills seemed to touch a nerve among those who preferred to think of members of the military as victims of war rather than effective, unapologetic warriors skilled at killing the enemy.[2]

This study examines Union and Confederates at the "sharp end" of the Civil War. It explores their attitudes to and experiences of killing in combat. One of my goals was to document the spectrum of these attitudes and experiences as recorded by the soldiers. As many as three million men combined served under arms for the United States and the Confederacy, and, as one historian reminds us, "enormous diversity . . . prevailed within Civil War America and the armies that it raised."[3] Drawing conclusions about the mind-set of three million individuals—and as American citizen-soldiers, Federals and Confederates most certainly saw themselves as individuals—

would seem daunting for a subject as complex and personal as killing in battle. However, merely documenting what soldiers wrote would offer only reportage, and it would detract from the value of my project if I withheld my analysis and conclusions as a historian. On the basis of the evidence, I contend that the majority of Union and Confederate soldiers positively affirmed and accepted killing the enemy as part of their military duty and a necessity for their respective causes to prevail. Conversely, a significant minority harbored doubts about or outright objected to killing in war, but even among the ambivalent combatants, most tended to fight just as purposefully (and potentially lethally) as their more bellicose comrades.

The nature of killing in the Civil War was not a simple dichotomy between killing and not killing. Rather, soldiers' attitudes and behavior fell along a spectrum of readiness, willingness, and enthusiasm, from the most prolific killers to reluctant killers to those who actively tried not to kill in battle. From the soldiers' accounts, most Civil War fighting men fell somewhere along the spectrum in which they found themselves able to fight against the enemy as effectively as they could. Perhaps most remarkably, Union and Confederate soldiers in prolonged contact with one another often alternated with surprising ease and fluidity between peaceful coexistence and actively trying to kill.

A number of factors enabled the Civil War soldier to kill, or try to kill, willingly in battle. The system of command and control exercised on the soldiers and the tactics in which they were trained may or may not have brought success on the battlefield, but it worked remarkably effectively in enforcing their combat roles and increased the likelihood that they would fight as lethally as possible. The nature of Civil War battlefields often shielded Federals and Confederates from the potential trauma of killing in combat. Poor visibility in battle, especially as a result of the smoke produced by black powder weaponry, diminished soldiers' abilities to know whether they personally had killed anyone. Evidence also suggests that a substantial majority of Civil War soldiers were strongly motivated by political ideology, which gave purpose and meaning to killing on the battlefield. Furthermore, the society that produced them and for which they fought strongly affirmed and legitimized killing the enemy—even an enemy who was a fellow American.

These fundamental conclusions diverge in key ways from those advanced in the previous historical literature. After World War II, US Army combat historian S. L. A. Marshall controversially suggested that only 15 to 25 percent of American combat infantrymen during the conflict had fired their weapons in battle. Less controversial than Marshall's actual findings was his explanation for this behavior; he noted, "The average and normally healthy individual—the man who can endure the mental and physical stresses of combat—still has such an inner and usually unrealized resistance toward killing a fellow man that he will not of his own volition take life if it is possible to turn away from the responsibility." Dave Grossman, a retired army officer and West Point psychology professor, accepts Marshall's findings and affirms his rationale in *On Killing*, perhaps the most influential book for establishing killing in combat as a subject for serious scholarly scrutiny. He posits that the prospect of killing in battle acts as great a stressor for men in battle as does fear of being killed. Grossman's book directly motivated my decision to undertake a "killology," as Grossman terms the field, of the American Civil War, as well as incorporate much of his scholarly framework and many of his arguments. Nevertheless, while I do not necessarily dispute Grossman's central argument as it pertains to twentieth-century soldiers, from whom he derives his most direct findings, I do challenge how accurately his conclusions describe the experiences of Civil War soldiers. From my own research, I contend that Federal and Confederate combat forces displayed greater willingness in their attitudes and behavior to kill in battle than previously supposed.

This work represents the first monograph treatment of the nature of killing in Civil War combat. It also represents a continuation of the study of the lives of Civil War soldiers, a field pioneered by Bell I. Wiley in the 1940s and 1950s and enriched in recent memory in works by Reid Mitchell, James M. McPherson, Earl J. Hess, and Drew Gilpin Faust. Each of these historians' contributions addresses the subject of killing as part of Civil War soldiers' experience of battle. Their findings and the sources they uncovered provided an intellectual foundation and stimulus to undertake a study focused entirely on killing in the Civil War as its subject. This project has undeniably benefited from standing on the scholastic shoulders of these giants among Civil War historians.

This work enters the historiographic discourse in the tradition of the genre of new military history. While the older school of military history focuses on the course and conduct of war in military, political, and diplomatic terms, new military history emphasizes subjects such as the psychology of military personnel and their relationship to the cultures and societies from which they emerge, both subjects with which this work deals directly. Nevertheless, this project does not represent a rejection of "old" military history. Instead, it stands as an example of bridging the two camps. For one, study of soldier life in the Civil War predates the rise of the new school, not only in terms of Wiley's midcentury work but also in treatments by the veterans themselves written to document soldier life. Furthermore, in my research I have availed myself of traditional battle studies and original tactical manuals, sources theoretically pertaining to the old school, which I believe have invaluably strengthened my attempts to reconstruct the human experience of combat in the Civil War.

As with other studies of soldier life in the Civil War, my work relies heavily on the wartime letters and diaries and the postwar reminiscences of the soldiers and veterans. When first undertaking this project, I was unsure how descriptive and forthcoming soldier accounts would be in providing the kind of details I sought. Although to date I have not found a Civil War combatant who devoted an entire letter or article to discoursing in depth on the subject of killing, a handful did episodically offer insightful glimpses into their mind-sets. Moreover, a great many of the sources I consulted provided key bits of information that contributed to the larger picture. Rarely did a particular resource, especially the longest and most complete diaries, letter collections, and memoirs, fail to provide any useful insights.

Certain factors limited the extent to which soldiers wrote about killing. Some men, for instance, wrote more deeply than others. Civil War accounts offer a rich treasure trove because many participants wrote eloquently and thoughtfully, but some men contented themselves with recording events and reporting on the health and welfare of themselves and their comrades. I am convinced that most Civil War soldiers focused far more attention on their own lives, health, and safety, as well as that of their comrades, than they did on damage they did to the enemy, especially in writing for the benefit of family and friends at home. Some men chose to omit or merely hint at the most graphic and disturbing aspects of battle, especially when writing for a female audience, and for some the experience of killing fell into this delicate area. However, the fact that so many Federals and Confederates wrote candidly about battle, even killing, and in missives that female readers would see, strongly suggests the extent to which both soldiers and their civilian supporters affirmed killing as part of their war.

I suggest another reason why Civil War soldiers did not write more extensively about killing, especially as deeply as historians would wish, is that they did not explore their psyches in writing in the same fashion as individuals in our own age do. That is not to say Civil War soldiers did not think or write introspectively—far from it. Americans in the Civil War era could discourse deeply and feelingly, with great emotion and passion. Their introspection, however, tended to work within their own familiar framework, usually expressed in terms of character, morality, and their relationship with God. Separated as we are from the generation that fought the Civil

War not only by 150 years but also by the rise of psychology as a discipline, I suspect that today we are inclined to psychoanalyze ourselves in ways that would be unfamiliar to our ancestors. Americans in the Civil War thought and felt as deeply (or as shallowly) about themselves as we do, but they did not frame those thoughts using the tools or language we now use.

With these obstacles in mind, I cast my research net as wide as possible. I did not limit my search to soldiers from one state, army, theater, or side in the conflict. Both Union and Confederate voices receive representation here. In terms of their basic attitudes and experiences of killing, I found no discernible differences among these rival forces of American citizen-soldiers. In keeping with that conclusion, when citing evidence of a particular behavior or mind-set, I often deliberately pair or group together examples from Federals and Confederates in my discussion. In terms of killing, only two major differences separated the blue and the gray. First, the sense of their homeland being invaded by enemy armies and the fighting motivation it provided disproportionately applied to Confederate soldiers. Second, the Confederacy's soldiers, who were products and defenders of a slave society, bore tremendous racial hostility toward black Union soldiers and often killed those opponents with a vengeance, even to the point of outright atrocities. Many white Federals thought of African Americans in unabashedly racist terms, and some harbored their own propensity for cruelty toward their enemies, yet little in their experience of combat could compare to the vicious conflict that played out between black soldiers in Union blue and white Southerners in Confederate gray.

Inclusive as I tried to make my approach, there are some exceptions. The navies of the United States and Confederacy played critical roles in the Civil War, but as this study examines soldiers, sailors and marines make only the most fleeting appearances. Soldiers from the eastern and western theaters receive ample representation, but those fighting in the trans-Mississippi theater appear much less often. Infantry from the two sides dominates this study, a circumstance that reflects that infantrymen made up 75 to 80 percent of Civil War armies and that the infantry, as the queen of battle, did much of the fighting, dying, and killing in the Civil War. Nevertheless, soldiers in the cavalry and artillery are hardly absent; they come on the scene in their own right, especially in cases where the nature of their service differentiated their experience of battle from other soldiers. I also confined my study largely to soldiers fighting in a regular, rather than irregular, capacity. Bands of irregulars, often not wearing uniforms and rarely accountable to any authority higher than themselves, fought their own vicious and bloody war. While irregular guerrillas feature in the chapter dealing with atrocities, otherwise this work focuses solely on the soldiers who fought the Civil War and experienced battle in the conventional sense.

In reconstructing Civil War soldiers' experiences of combat, this work incorporates both wartime and postwar accounts. Similar projects have confined themselves to only wartime accounts. Perhaps most notably, James McPherson in *For Cause and Comrades* relied primarily on wartime sources to explore soldier motivations, seeking to avoid later accounts potentially affected by hindsight, faulty memory, and intentionally writing for a public audience. As sound as his rationale is, and as important as it is to bear these factors in mind when reading postwar writings, my own work does not follow that model. To not include certain published accounts would have meant leaving out a great number of remarkable and incisive details regarding killing and other aspects of Civil War soldiering. Moreover, the inclusion of postwar remembrances contributes to the principal argument of the book. That many Civil War veterans could write candidly and unashamedly about killing offers further evidence of soldiers who affirmed or accepted killing in combat, as well as suggesting a confidence that they could express such attitudes without fearing censure by their society at large.

In presenting the words of Civil War soldiers, I have followed the convention of quoting them with as little editing or alteration as possible. Their writings appear as originally written, sometimes with great creativity in spelling, punctuation, and grammar. I have only added corrections in brackets in cases where that creativity with the English language might confuse the reader.

This study deals with its subject thematically, and the chapters are organized on that basis. Chapter 1 examines the cultural and societal factors that influenced soldiers' attitudes toward killing before and during the war. I examine the various ways soldiers experienced killing in battle in Chapter 2, especially focusing on the infantry firefight. In Chapter 3, I address killing in hand-to-hand combat, one of the rarer but most dramatic and challenging scenarios in which Civil War soldiers experienced killing. Chapter 4 explores the language of killing—the terms and turns of phrase that soldiers used to describe killing in combat. Chapter 5 deals with sharpshooters and killing, including how they and other soldiers perceived this particular form of warfare. In Chapter 6, I discuss what I describe as the extremes of killing, specifically killing that transgressed the laws of war as well as actions by which soldiers withheld from killing. I consider in Chapter 7 the impact of race and racial attitudes on killing in the Civil War. Finally, the Epilogue addresses themes dealing with the war's end and aftermath, as well as offering concluding remarks.

I trust that this project can genuinely appeal to and benefit both fellow scholars and general readers. Most directly it seeks to contribute to scholarship in Civil War and military history by helping expand the depth and authenticity of our understanding of the lives of Civil War soldiers and the nature of war. The ideas and stories in this work are in their own way timeless as well. Americans today have arguably never before been as concerned with and committed to the health and well-being of past and current members of the military, and the complex nature of killing in battle represents a key element in these matters. The study of men at war, especially the complex and enigmatic subject of killing, speaks not only to American and military history but also to fundamental aspects of the human condition. In addition to the timeless value of the subject, killing in the Civil War speaks directly to one of the most pivotal moments in American history. The Civil War represents an American *Iliad* and an American tragedy, and many readers, both academic and popular, still try to understand the how and why of the United States' bloodiest of all wars, in which Americans killed Americans. By exploring this key element of soldiers' experience of the Civil War, I hope my findings will help expand our understanding of such momentous subjects.

# I

## The Things They Carried
*Influences on Civil War Soldiers and Killing*

Men from North and South did not come as blank slates when they mustered to go to war. Before they would be asked to kill in battle, recruits had been steeped in numerous ideological, cultural, and societal influences that informed their attitudes toward the war at hand. While the reality of killing another human being was a great unknown to most of these men, many of these influences had in fact disposed them in ways large and small toward an ability and willingness to kill in combat. "We are not enemies, but friends. We must not be enemies," a newly inaugurated Abraham Lincoln pleaded with the fracturing nation in 1861. "Though passion may have strained it must not break our bonds of affection." Passion indeed had strained those bonds, and after decades of bitter sectional rivalry, many Americans did see their Northern or Southern rivals as enemies—enemies that soon must be fought, and if need be killed, for a greater purpose. In addition, various factors from antebellum culture, including the recruits' relationships with death, violence, firearms, and hunting, combined in varying degrees to prepare them for the task of killing. Of all these influences, one of the most powerful and influential they experienced—religion— also fostered the most variable attitudes toward killing. Religious belief and ethics both helped persuade or dissuade, encourage or distress, when it came to debating the morality of killing as a soldier. A complex and varied interplay of these forces would work on the hearts and minds of prospective soldiers as they prepared for the prospect of civil war.

A popular rule of etiquette admonishes us not to discuss politics or religion in polite conversation. At its heart, the maxim recognizes that political ideology and religious faith—two key components of a person's worldview—cut to the very heart of who we are and what we believe. As such, political and religious disputes can quickly turn acrimonious and ugly. One of the earliest appearances of the maxim, in a piece from 1840 by Canadian humorist Thomas Chandler Haliburton, aptly encapsulates its rationale: "Never discuss religion or politics with those who hold opinions opposite to yours; they are subjects that heat in handling until they burn your fingers."[1] Many Americans in the same era would scarcely credit following such advice, for to them religion and politics were meat and drink. Yet the political debates over the future of slavery and the American republic did burn in the handling—not just burning fingers but erupting in a great conflagration between North and South. Political animosity sparked the Civil War and helped drive Americans to kill one another on the battlefield, and as much as spiritual matters infused antebellum politics, religion would play its own complex role.

"A civil war is the worst of all wars," Edward, duke of Windsor, wrote in 1951, explaining his decision to abdicate the United Kingdom's throne, ending a short but controversial reign. "Its passions soar highest, its hatreds last longest."[2] Wars in which countrymen and even family members elect to fight and kill one another release particularly intense passions and hatreds, more so than limited wars between rival nations fighting for territory, resources, or influence. A civil war by its very nature threatens the existence of a nation and the future of its people. Moreover, the grievances that ignite a civil war take the bonds of love and fellowship that unite a country and twist them into hatred and resentment. In a war of rebellion, as the Federal government termed what is conventionally known as the American Civil War, the rebelling side typically claims that an abuse of power requires separation, while the loyalist side denies such claims and insists that no schism can be tolerated. In a war of rebellion, enemies are to one another either cruel oppressors or renegades and rebels.

Americans North and South did not learn to hate one another overnight, nor was Fort Sumter the first occasion in which Americans had fired on Americans. A sectional crisis had been brewing in fits and starts at least since the 1820s, primarily driven by the status of slavery in the western territories. In referring to his own national crisis of 1936, the erstwhile Edward VIII spoke of "a [civil] war . . . fought in words and not in blood."[3] North and South waged a virulent war of words during the antebellum period— but one punctuated by actual bloodshed as well.

In 1856, five years before Fort Sumter, proslavery and antislavery factions battled one another to decide the political future of Kansas in a kind of demi–civil war known to history as Bleeding Kansas. On May 22, the day after proslavery Border Ruffians had destroyed the fortified Free State Hotel in Lawrence, Kansas, sectional violence erupted in the halls of Congress. Representative Preston Brooks of South Carolina strode into the Senate chamber and, in retaliation for insults to his family and the South, brutally caned Charles Sumner of Massachusetts to within an inch of his life. In the aftermath of this outrage, and as political debate turned increasingly venomous, Congress truly became an armed camp. "The only persons who do not have a revolver and a knife are those who have two revolvers," noted South Carolina senator and slavery apologist James Henry Hammond.[4] With the sectional crisis tearing America asunder, senators and congressmen seemed the people's representatives in word and deed.

On October 16, 1859, political violence came to Harpers Ferry, Virginia. Abolitionist zealot John Brown, a hardened veteran of Bleeding Kansas, led twenty-one white and black followers in an attack on the US Armory and Arsenal, ostensibly for the purpose of securing arms and creating a staging point for a momentous slave rebellion. Within two days, a combination of armed citizens, militiamen from both sides of the Potomac, and US Marines scotched the attack. John Brown's raid left in its wake ten raiders, four townsfolk, two slaves, and one marine killed. Anger and fear swept the slave states in the raid's aftermath and rejuvenated the militia system in the South as an increasingly militarized population girded themselves to resist subsequent expected assaults from Northern abolitionists.

Sixty miles east of Harpers Ferry, the citizens of Baltimore experienced their own share of political violence in 1861. Baltimore was "a strongly pro-Southern city with a long reputation for street violence," notes one Lincoln biographer. Weeks before Lincoln's March 4 inauguration, his advisors learned of seemingly credible intelligence regarding a plot to assassinate him in Baltimore and so persuaded the president-elect to discreetly make his way through the city at night. During the daylight hours of April 19, less than a week after Fort Sumter, the 6th Massachusetts experienced a far less peaceful passage. Traveling between the train stations in horse-drawn cars, the Bay Staters were met by angry Baltimoreans eager to block their passage. The crowd began to rain stones, bricks, brickbats, bottles, and other missiles down on the troops. One soldier was struck in the head and fell to the street, then was brutally beaten to death by the mob. The Massachusetts men fired volleys into their attackers in self-defense, and those among the tormenters carrying or able to find firearms began returning fire. By day's end, four soldiers and perhaps a dozen Baltimoreans lay dead or dying.[5]

What had begun with soldiers making their way through a hostile crowd had devolved into urban warfare against a mob of armed secessionist insurgents. American citizens had done their best to murder US volunteers, and the soldiers had defended themselves with lethal force. Men of the 6th Massachusetts experienced killing in combat as real in the streets of Baltimore as they could on a conventional battlefield. Private Edwin F. Spofford's experience of killing perhaps characterized that of many subsequent Civil War soldiers. Having just seen a comrade next to him shot and killed by a rioter, Spofford leveled his own weapon and pulled the trigger. "The man who shot him fell dead by my rifle," the newly enlisted soldier recalled. "I felt bad at first when I saw what I had done, but it soon passed off, and as I had done my duty and was not the aggressor, I was soon able to fire again and again." Of Spofford's account, Drew Gilpin Faust observes, "Duty and self-defense released him from an initial sense of guilt and helped him to do the work of a soldier. . . . Spofford came to kill almost as a reflex, as a response to what he saw as the murder of the comrade beside him."[6]

Once the Civil War came, thousands of recruits were ready to fight—and kill—for the sake of politics, precisely because the war would decide political questions with momentous consequences. Would the union of states persevere, or would it be split asunder by the advent of a Southern confederacy? Would slavery, an institution that affected the lives of millions of Americans both black and white, survive, or would it be cast onto the ash heap of history? A number of scholars within the last century have underestimated the extent to which political ideology motivated Civil War soldiers. In the 1940s and 1950s, Bell I. Wiley assumed Federals and Confederates were basically as nonideological as had been American soldiers in World War II. In the 1980s, Gerald Linderman suggested that idealistic belief in values like courage motivated soldiers, after which the cruel reality of the "experience of combat frustrated their attempts to fight the war as an expression of their values and generated in them a harsh disillusionment." More recent scholarship, most notably James M. McPherson's *For Cause and Comrades*, has offered compelling evidence that political ideology strongly motivated and sustained the blue and gray. Out of a large sample of soldiers' accounts, McPherson finds that an impressive 66 to 68 percent of combatants expressly asserted "patriotic motives for fighting."[7]

President Lincoln's resolve to use Federal forces to put down the rebellion promised an invasion of the seceded states, and the prospect of invading Yankees filled thousands of Confederate recruits with a viscerally felt motive to kill those who threatened their homes and homeland. At the close of 1861, one grateful Confederate soldier wrote with relief that the "plunder seeking Vandals of the North have been met on every point on land with success and our home and firesides have been defended from devastation and their polluting torches." Confederate invasion rhetoric imagined a host of calamities that would befall the South at Yankee hands, from the destruction of their homes to outrages against Southern womanhood. A poem called "The Guerrillas," written by a Confederate prisoner of war and published in a Richmond newspaper, luridly made these very charges, then concluded:

> Let every man swear on his blade,
> That he will not sheathe or stay it,
> Till from point to hilt it glow
> With the flush of Almighty vengeance,
> In the blood of the felon foe.

Texas veteran William Fletcher expressed the justification he and many of his comrades felt in taking up arms against the Yankees, even in the aftermath of the Confederacy's defeat. "We knew we had committed no wrong, for self-preservation born in man is one of his strongest traits," Fletcher wrote in his memoirs, "and if killing an invader in one's country is not self-preservation, please define."[8]

Just as the Confederate cause rested on the cornerstone of slavery, protection of slavery played its own role in motivating Confederate soldiers to kill their enemies. Many Confederate soldiers tipped their hands by deprecatingly labeling their enemies as "abolitionists," sometimes using the term so often as to seem almost synonymous with "Union" or "Yankee." In June 1861, Private Robert A. More of the 17th Mississippi confidently predicted in his diary that his unit would "do some execution should they meet Lincoln's abolition cohorts on Via. soil or if need be on that of any other state." The racial ideology that undergirded the South's slave society also gave rise to paranoid fears that Abraham Lincoln and his forces sought not only the destruction of slavery but also to expose white women to the purported animal lusts of black men and to impose miscegenation on Southern society. When soldiers of the 25th Wisconsin asked Rebel prisoners why they were fighting, the Badgers were understandably bewildered when told, "You Yanks want us to marry our daughters to the niggers."[9]

Preservation of the Union was a more abstract ideological motive than Confederates' purpose of defending their own land, yet thousands of Federal volunteers were prepared to kill and be killed for their cause all the same. "My country has been assailed and my country's flag has been insulted and it matters not to me whether it is by foes within or without, it is all the same to me," James L. Welsh wrote from Illinois to his brother in Virginia's Shenandoah Valley. James warned his secessionist brother, John, just how seriously he took his loyalty to the American nation: "I would strike down my own brother if he dare to raise a hand to destroy that flag." Thousands of defenders of the Union recognized that the insult to the flag at Fort Sumter threatened to destroy not simply a banner but the Union and Constitution for which it stood. Volunteers who imagined the consequences of secession and disunion found tangible reasons why the Rebels had to be defeated. Michigan soldier Saxon DeWolf insisted that "if the union is split up the government is distroid and we will be a Rewind [ruined] nation." To the Union's defenders, disunion threatened every noble ideal and virtue that the American experiment represented—liberty, self-government, rule of law—and fight that threat they would.[10]

Far more Union soldiers fought to preserve the Union rather than to free slaves, although many came to see rooting out slavery as a means to that end. For those Federals of truly abolitionist sentiments, however, hatred of slavery and desire to liberate their fellow man could strengthen the desire to slay slavery's defenders. A captain from Massachusetts declared, "I want to sing 'John Brown' in the streets of Charleston, and ram red-hot abolitionism down their unwilling throats at the point of the bayonet." Wisconsin recruit Chauncey Cooke knew he was in a distinct minority of Union soldiers for whom emancipation trumped the Union cause. Cooke harkened to the admonition his father gave him before he left for war: "If you ever get a chance, my boy, take good aim and shoot twice to free the black while shooting once for the Union."[11]

One particular way Civil War soldiers' intense political animosities manifested was in the hatred many expressed for each side's president. As the commanders in chief of rival American republics, Abraham Lincoln and Jefferson Davis became natural lightning rods on whom politically motivated soldiers could focus their hostility. It was the former's electoral victory in 1860 that set off the first wave of secession. The coming to power of Lincoln and his Republican Party (known as Black Republicans to their proslavery rivals) represented the Confederacy's original casus belli. His pledge to bar slavery from spreading into the western territories threatened the South's peculiar institution and consequently its entire way of life. In the proslavery mind, Lincoln sought not merely to contain slavery but to subjugate Southern whites entirely and would gladly trample the Constitution underfoot in the process. Once Lincoln had committed to using Federal forces to end the rebellion, he became to newly minted Confederates the leader of the invading Yankee hordes. Conversely, to fervent defenders of the Union, Jefferson Davis stood as the archrebel and archtraitor. In their eyes, the former soldier, secretary of war, and senator had violated his multiple oaths to the Constitution by accepting the presidency of the slaveholders' republic, fomenting a schism that threatened to dissolve the Union for which the document had been drafted.

Many Union and Confederate soldiers loudly voiced desires to kill Jefferson Davis and Abraham Lincoln, respectively. Confederate soldiers could be vociferous in their hatred of the Illinois rail splitter. While most volunteer companies adopted conventional military names, such as Rifles, Guards, or Legion, one Georgia outfit boldly dubbed itself the Cherokee Lincoln Killers. Wheat's Tigers, a rowdy unit out of New Orleans described as "so villainous that every commander desired to be rid of it," went to war with various bellicose slogans emblazoned on their hatbands, one of the most popular being "Lincoln's Life or a Tiger's Death." In 1864, a Confederate picket sent a note to his Union counterpart advising him not to vote Lincoln to a second term, adding, "If he is elected again, I will go to Washington and kill him." Nor were Lincoln's mortal enemies limited to those wearing Rebel uniforms, for plenty of Southern sympathizers behind the lines also dreamed of taking his life. On the basis of reported assassination plots, Lincoln as president-elect had allowed himself to be spirited clandestinely through the streets of Baltimore in order to change trains on his way to Washington. Lincoln made it to the capital alive and well, but at the cost of humiliation in the press for his surreptitious journey. As a consequence, one of the most at-risk presidents in US history subsequently took a cavalier, even reckless, approach to his safety, ultimately at the cost of his life.[12]

Union soldiers equaled their Confederate opponents in their hatred and death wishes for the enemy president. Thousands gleefully sang, "We'll hang Jeff Davis from a sour apple tree" as part of a stanza to "John Brown's Body," a song guaranteed to raise the hackles of rebellious Southerners. "In the year 1862, the US Army used up 16 tons of bullets," read a brief report in the New York Sunday Mercury, a popular venue for Union soldiers to submit accounts from the war. "What a pity one didn't hit Jeff Davis." Some defenders of the Union wished not only for Jefferson Davis's death but also for his eternal punishment. One Wisconsin soldier, eager to see the rebellion subdued so he could go home, wrote in early 1864, "I wish old Jeff and all his gang were in the regions of the low lands where sinners go." Perhaps the most grandiloquent curse against the Confederate president can be found in the graffiti carved by Union prisoners during their incarceration in the courthouse of Winchester, Virginia:

```
            TO JEFF DAVIS
            MAY HE BE SET AFLOAT ON A
            BOAT WITHOUT COMPASS OR RUDDER
            THEN THAT ANY CONTENTS BE SWALLOWED
            BY A SHARK THE SHARK BY A WHALE
            WHALE IN THE DEVILS BELLY AND THE
            DEVIL IN HELL THE GATES LOCKED THE KEY LOST
            AND FURTHER
            MAY HE BE PUT IN THE NORTHWEST
            CORNER WITH A SOUTH EAST WIND BLOWING
            ASHES IN HIS EYES FOR ALL
                        ETERNITY
```

For Union soldiers frustrated by the fortunes of war and with plenty of time on their hands, the carving represented a defiant expression of their utter contempt for Jefferson Davis and his Rebel republic.[13]

Besides politics, the other emotionally loaded subject on which Civil War–era Americans thrived was religion. While modern polls show greater religiosity among Americans than other developed nations, it pales in comparison to the extent that religious worldviews and ethics, most significantly those of Protestant Christianity, infused antebellum culture. "By 1860," observes Mark Noll, "religion had reached a higher point of public influence than at any previous time in American history."[14] Religion played a decisive role in the nature of killing in the American Civil War because it presented believers with a source of ultimate authority, a moral worldview by which to live and abide, and strong credence in ideas of good and evil. While most of the influences mentioned in this chapter contributed to enabling a Civil War soldier to kill in battle, Christianity and the Bible could either persuade or dissuade a soldier from killing based on his convictions and interpretations. In fact, soldiers' accounts reflect that religious ethics offered the most significant source for objections to killing in combat.

A minority of American Christians belonged to pacifist sects such as the Quakers, Mennonites, and Brethren, who rejected violence and forbade their congregants from military service. A number of these denominations had established themselves a century or more before the Civil War in the Shenandoah Valley, where Confederate authorities tried with great difficulty to press them into service. Even among pacifist Christians who were induced or coerced into the army, many still refused to shoot to kill in battle. After one engagement, a captain in a Virginia regiment questioned one of his soldiers why he had not fired his weapon. Did he not "see all those Yankees over there?" "No, they're people," the soldier, a Mennonite, replied; "we don't shoot people."[15]

Historically a number of biblical verses had been cited to support pacifist positions, but no part of Scripture troubled the consciences of prospective soldiers in Civil War America more than the Sixth Commandment (Exodus 20:13), famously rendered in the King James Bible as "Thou shalt not kill." Biblical scholarship tells us that the word the King James Version identifies as *kill* is more accurately translated from Hebrew as "murder," a rendering that most modern biblical translations use. The change in meaning based on that one word could scarcely be more drastic. The KJV's use of "kill" seemingly proscribes any taking of life, while "murder" would apply only to unlawful taking of life and would not necessarily apply to killing in war. Centuries of Christian theologians had recognized this distinction. Major figures such as Augustine and Aquinas had contributed to a tradition of just war theory that weighed the circumstances under which waging war was permissible. British minister Matthew Henry published his *Exposition of the Old and New Testaments* in the early eighteenth century, one of the earliest printed commentaries on the Bible. Henry judged that the verse specifically prohibited killing "unjustly," observing, "It does not forbid killing in lawful war, or in our own necessary defense, nor the magistrate's putting offenders to death, for those things tend to the preserving of life."[16]

How were American Christians expected to interpret the Sixth Commandment? Protestant Christianity encouraged believers to read the Scriptures diligently and to be able to interpret their teachings according to their own consciences, wisdom, and discernment. A familiarity with the Bible as a whole enabled some believers to harmonize its teachings and come to an understanding that did not consider all killing to be inherently sinful. Scripture deals numerous times with eating meat and sacrificing animals; therefore, killing beasts was not prohibited. As for killing people, Old Testament history and law affirmed capital punishment, lethal use of self-defense, and wartime killing in numerous instances. It recorded how God had given the land of Canaan to the Israelites through military conquest and had granted them subsequent victories over their enemies as a reward for their faithfulness. David famously slew the Philistine champion Goliath and had gone on to become both a warrior king and psalmist, described as "a man after [God's] own heart" (Acts 13:22 [KJV]).

Among New Testament teachings, pacifists pointed to Jesus's admonition to love one's enemies and his rebuke to Peter that "all they that take the sword shall perish with the sword" (Matthew 26:52) after Peter had wounded a servant in the crowd come to arrest Jesus. Only hours before the incident, however, Jesus had instructed the apostles to arm themselves for their own personal protection in their future ministry: "He that hath no sword, let him sell his garment, and buy one" (Luke 22:36). Moreover, Jesus in His own ministry had condemned the sinfulness or corruption in various professions, but on meeting a pious Roman centurion, a professional soldier, Jesus did not gainsay the man's profession but praised him, declaring, "Verily I say unto you, I have not found so great faith, no, not in Israel" (Matthew 8:10). In a biblical context, it would seem, a tradition of Christian orthodoxy did not categorically condemn war or lethal force.

Despite the scriptural evidence that seemed to point to the "murder" interpretation of the Sixth Commandment, the King James Bible's austere use of "kill" troubled the consciences of soldiers who interpreted the 1611 translation of the verse literally. One Illinoisan aptly summed up the potential moral dilemma, reflecting, "I think it is a hard job to learn to fight, and to be a Christian at the same time." Patriotically named Confederate soldier Liberty Independence Nixon struggled with reconciling his reading of the Sixth Commandment with his military duty. Marching into his first battle with his fellow Alabamans at Shiloh, Nixon reflected, "Well . . . here I am ready to take the life of my fellow man when the Scriptures of eternal truth positively declare 'Thou shalt not kill.'"[17]

For Lieutenant Colonel George W. Lennard of the 57th Indiana, it was the apparent conflict between the New Testament and killing that deeply distressed him. "I say, how can a soldier be a Christian?" the Hoosier officer wrote to his wife. "Read all Christ's teaching, and then tell me whether *one engaged in maiming and butchering men*—men made in the express image of God himself—*can be saved* under the Gospel. Clear my mind on this subject and you will do me a world of good."[18]

Certainly religion does not alone account for Civil War soldiers who agonized over killing or refused to kill. Not all men who wore the blue or gray were Christians, devout or otherwise; nor did religious influences operate in a vacuum. American society in general treated the taking of human life as a truly grave matter. Beyond the context of nineteenth-century America, scholars remind us that a taboo against taking human life transcends many cultures. John Keegan in his landmark work *The Face of Battle* remarks with dry understatement, "Killing people, *qua* killing and *qua* people, is not an activity which seems to carry widespread approval." More pointedly, Dave Grossman suggests that this aversion to taking human life is perhaps hardwired into our psychology, arguing that there exists "a powerful, innate human resistance toward killing one's own species."[19]

While Christian teachings do not single-handedly account for reservations about killing among Civil War soldiers, it is hard to overestimate just how thoroughly religious belief informed these reservations. This is hardly surprising, considering that, as James McPherson suggests, "Civil War armies were, arguably, the most religious in American history."[20] Moreover, Civil War soldiers who expressed resistance to killing overwhelmingly attributed their misgivings to biblical influences, almost to the exclusion of any other factor. Certainly multiple factors contributed to reluctance or refusal to kill among Federals and Confederates, but no single factor shaped such attitudes as decisively as did religious convictions.

While some soldiers agonized over the spiritual implications of killing, a number of scholars surmise that the majority of professing Christians in Civil War armies believed that killing in war was sanctioned by their faith, not proscribed. Focusing on Northern Christians, David W. Rolfs concludes that most "had little difficulty reconciling their wartime experiences with their faith," leaving "a small but significant minority who struggled to reconcile their religious values with their military duties." Evidence suggests that the same applies to the bulk of religious Confederates. A soldier from the 12th Virginia recalled one of his comrades on the battle line "praying and firing at the same time," a man "who expected to be killed in every fight, yet never missed one." How individual soldiers arrived at this reconciliation varied from man to man. Many likely understood, either consciously or unconsciously, that the body of Scripture seemed to allow going to war. Moreover, those convinced of the justness of their cause could conclude that fighting for that cause was not sinful. Even among believers who harbored misgivings about killing, many found themselves following orders and actively engaging in combat, regardless of whether they had come to terms with their consciences. At Shiloh, Private Nixon decided that the morality of battle aside, his life was in God's hands, and he thus "became resigned to my fate let it be what it might. My nerve seemed to steady as if I was shooting at a beast and continued so during the fight."[21]

Surely one of the most decisive influences that religiously affirmed the propriety of soldiering was that both Northern and Southern society overwhelmingly endorsed the war in spiritual terms. Many clergy and laity on both sides insisted that not only was fighting for their respective causes not sinful but that God was in fact on their side. "Both read the same Bible and pray to the same God," Lincoln famously observed in his second inaugural address, "and each invokes His aid against the other." Ministers who invoked divine sanction for their nation's cause sometimes implicitly or explicitly included killing the enemy as part of that mission. In June 1861, a North Carolina minister preached that the seceding states sought only a peaceful separation, but if Northerners, motivated by "iniquitous and hellish sentiment," would force war on them, concluded, "In God's name let us meet our opposing foe with a steady arm and determined blow." A chaplain in a New York regiment likened the conflict to the wars of the Old Testament and "compared the loyal people of the United States with the Israelites, as the chosen people of God, and the secession rebels with the Amalekites, and others, whom they were ordered to make war upon." Perhaps the bluntest affirmation of killing came from Reverend Horace Bushnell, a Connecticut Congregationalist who wholeheartedly preached the divine purpose of the Union. Meeting George Metcalf, one of his congregants, home from the army on furlough, the minster asked if he had killed any Rebels. Metcalf, an artillery lieutenant, replied that he had not. "Time you had," Bushnell told him. "That's what you went out for."[22]

In addition to religious instruction from the pulpit, soldiers also looked to the actions of pious warriors among their leaders for spiritual role models who found fighting consistent with their faith. For Confederates, Thomas J. "Stonewall" Jackson was renowned for his fierce piety, exemplifying Old Testament zeal both for serving God and smiting the enemy. Val Giles of the Texas Brigade recalled one of Jackson's soldiers, standing outside a church where the general was worshipping, joke, "Old Stonewall is going to tell us how to save souls and shoot Yankees."[23]

Regimental chaplains offered soldiers obvious examples of Christian warriors to emulate. Most chaplains acted in noncombatant roles in action, often ministering to souls and wounds. Some soldiers believed this was the proper role for a man of God on the battlefield, as did New York infantryman Simon Bolivar Hulbert: "A chaplain is to preach to the men & not kill & slay them." Other soldiers, however, reveled in the exploits of a handful of "fighting parsons" who did in fact help them slay the enemy. Perhaps the most famous of these was Lorenzo Barber, chaplain of the 2nd US Sharpshooters. Fighting alongside the men with his telescopic rifle, he was reckoned one of the best shots among them. "Chaplain Barber shot as he prayed," extolled a sergeant in his regiment, "or in other words he helped to answer his own prayers by doing all he could to put down the rebellion." Outside the regiment, a published letter from a soldier in the 14th Brooklyn sang the Sharpshooters' praises, especially their chaplain, who "is a regular fighting minister, as well as preaching" and "fought like a hero himself."[24]

In addition to politics and religion, other elements of antebellum society influenced Civil War soldiers' ability and willingness to kill in combat. Paradoxically, while Americans pointedly rejected European militarism, citizens of the young republic gloried in their military prowess and past battlefield victories. From their forbears they had inherited English Whigs' belief that large professional standing armies threatened the people's liberties. Many Americans distrusted the United States Military Academy at West Point, suspecting that it would foster an imperious, antirepublican class of gentlemen officers. Culturally, Americans rejected military professionalism and instead trusted in the ability of virtuous citizen-soldiers to defeat professionals. The American nation had been born in the Revolutionary War, which first gave rise to the cherished myth of the embattled farmers who bested the finest soldiers that Britain could send against them.

In their wars during the four score years before the Civil War, Americans had demonstrated relatively little compunction about killing in war. In practically all the conflicts in the republic's short history, the enemy had always possessed some quality of otherness that morally and psychologically distanced them from Americans. In the Mexican War, race provided a key difference, as had Mexico's Catholicism, widely distrusted by Protestant America. Perennial wars with America's various Indian tribes provided the nation its most alien enemies. Indians differed from white America drastically in racial, religious, and cultural terms. Most of the nation deemed the Indians' way of life savage, pagan, and primitive. Americans shared tremendous common ground with Britain, the mother country and America's two-time enemy, but in both the Revolutionary War and the War of 1812 they had vilified the redcoats as the cruel hirelings of a tyrannical king. Confederates, inaugurating their own war of independence, deliberately echoed this legacy by labeling their Yankee foes as Lincoln's hirelings.

Aside from its peace churches, America had experienced little in the way of an antiwar movement based on the categorical rejection of violence. Instead, opposition to past wars had largely been based on differences in politics and policy, rather than a rejection of warfare itself. Opposition to the War of 1812 had come mostly from New Englanders who valued their region's economic and cultural ties to Britain. Opponents of slavery had resisted "Mr. Polk's War" with Mexico in 1846, seeing it as a land grab to expand Southern slavery, while many Whig partisans rejected the territorial ambitions of the Democratic administration. Antebellum Americans maintained their desire to live at peace with all nations; but for lack of the major influence of Christian ethics proscribing the unjust taking of human life, they would experience little in the way of societal taboo against killing an enemy they had resolved to fight on the battlefield.

What were antebellum American attitudes toward violence in general? In broad terms, American culture in the early Victorian era might be thought of as transitioning between two major societal forces from its history, from the wild and untamed spirit of the frontier West to the ordered and restrained civilizing mission of the East. Just as the frontier line, with its potentially violent state-of-nature existence, marched westward, miles behind it followed a more pacific and domestic civil society as settlements transformed into communities and established farms. The process, however, did not always play out with the West giving way to the East. Two frontier heroes only a few generations removed from the Civil War reflected the cultural interplay between the frontier and civilization. Daniel Boone as the soft-spoken trailblazer brought civilization to the West in the age of Enlightenment, but decades later, boisterous canebrake congressman David Crockett brought the spirit of the frontier to the East in the age of Jackson.

This tension between the forceful (sometimes violent) frontier and the order and restraint of civilization can be seen in action in the Civil War. The concept of honor dominated Southern culture, and a readiness to defend that honor defined white Southern manhood. Southerners were notorious for their willingness to resort to violence in honor's defense, whether in duels, feuds, or brawls. The notoriety of Southern honor and violence has led to the caricature of fiery, hypermasculine cavaliers and backcountry-men, contrasted with mild-mannered, genteel Yankees. Although Northerners often defined themselves against what they saw as the extremes of Southern culture, the North's population included its own violent element, generally known as roughs, men who defined their manhood in terms of honor and "violent displays of physical prowess." Northern roughs could be found both in the Old Northwest, not far removed from the frontier experience, as well as in the cities of the East. Northerners who lived according to standards of gentility and morality contrasted with the roughs not necessarily because they lacked physical prowess or rejected violence, but because they esteemed restraint and self-control, which they believed roughs and hotheaded Southerners lacked. As such, while the South carried the reputation for greater proclivity for violence, Northern society did not categorically eschew the use of force. "Restrained men expected a gentleman to harness his passion," Lorien Foote explains in her study of Union soldiers' ideas of manhood, "yet instinctively they understood that it was not manly to submit to the aggression of another."[25]

While some Northerners labored under the apprehension that they lacked the martial prowess of Southerners, especially after their embarrassing defeat at Bull Run, others dismissed the notion. Abraham Lincoln upheld the abilities of his fellow Westerners in the wake of their capture of Fort Donelson, remarking, "I cannot speak so confidently about the fighting qualities of the Eastern men, or what are called Yankees—not knowing myself particularly to whom the appellation belongs—but this I do know— if the Southerners think that man for man they are better than our Illinois men, or western men generally, they will discover themselves in a grievous mistake."[26]

The antebellum years coincide with the early phase of the Victorian age, and no discussion of Victorian culture can ignore this era's attitudes toward death. Civil War soldiers, after all, would not only risk their own deaths but potentially inflict enemy deaths. Even in peacetime, Victorian Americans encountered death more frequently and intimately than their descendants today. Modern observers tend to see the Victorians as preoccupied with death, but conversely, they did not deny the reality of death, as some critics have charged modern society. Separated from us by a century and a half of medical knowledge and advances, they experienced higher infant mortality rates and shorter life expectancies, and thus they could expect to lose parents, spouses, siblings, children, and other kith and kin sooner and more suddenly than in our time. Accepting this reality, they did not distance themselves from death. Victorians emphasized the concept of making a "good death," important elements of which often included dying peacefully at home, surrounded by one's family. Family members usually took the responsibility of washing and dressing the deceased. Wakes often took place in the home with the body laid out in the parlor.

Death was a more familiar and less foreign reality to Civil War soldiers than to subsequent generations. While that familiarity could never fully prepare them for the violent deaths and carnage they would encounter on the battlefield, much less the experience of actually inflicting death, it likely prepared and strengthened them more than lacking such awareness would have. As Mark S. Schantz notes, "Americans came to fight the Civil War in the midst of a wider cultural world that sent them messages about death that made it easier to kill and to be killed."[27]

For many citizen-soldiers from North and South, familiarity with and affinity for firearms provided a head start in preparing them for war. As with gun ownership today, antebellum Americans primarily used their rifles and shotguns for hunting game and target shooting rather than as weapons against their fellow man, yet their ownership of—and for many fascination with—such arms suggests that on some level many must have been morally agreeable to their use as weapons. Many histories tend to emphasize those Civil War soldiers who knew little or nothing about guns when they joined the army. Certainly there was no shortage of recruits lacking experience with firearms. Some men, unfamiliar with the workings of a muzzle-loading rifle, decided that because the bullet was the most important part of their ammunition, they should ram it down the barrel first, then pour the gunpowder on top. In his examination of the gun culture of Civil War soldiers, historian Earl Hess describes a spectrum of proficiency between "crack shots and gun-inept soldiers" but straightforwardly concludes, "A significant number of Union and Confederate soldiers were intimately familiar with firearms and extraordinarily interested in the quality and performance of their weapons."[28]

Firearms, especially rifles, had been absolutely essential tools of survival, both for hunting and protection, for early American settlers. Many of these settlers used these tools out of necessity, but they also derived enjoyment from them. Rifle matches provided one of the most popular forms of diversion and competition on the frontier. In his memoir of frontier life, an Indiana minister wrote, "Reader, were you ever *fired* with the love of rifle shooting? If so, the confidence now reposed in your honor will not be abused, when told my love for that noble art is unabated." Such sentiments ensured that a strong gun culture remained even after the frontier line moved westward, beyond developing communities where firearms became less critical for sustenance and self-defense. Moreover, many Civil War soldiers were scarcely removed from the frontier experience. While the frontier had advanced beyond the Mississippi River, numerous young men in the states beyond the Appalachians—the Old Northwest and Old Southwest—had experienced pioneer life or were only a generation removed. Raised on the Wisconsin frontier, Chauncey Cooke reminisced in one of his letters home about a time his father had been away and his mother had "put the gun at the head of the bed . . . ready to use if Indians should come or wild animals attack the cattle." Cooke assured his mother, "I remember these things . . . and under all circumstances I shall never forget that my father and mother were brave people."[29]

Although numerous volunteers brought their own weapons to war, the majority soon realized they would be relying primarily on sturdier, standardized arms issued to them. Confederate soldier Washington Ives left his trusty rifle back in Florida, writing his father, "Take good care of my rifle and when danger comes she'll not deceive you." Some men formed similar attachment to the army-issue weapons that faithfully served them through their battles and campaigns. Helping carry off a wounded comrade at Shiloh, Ohio soldier John Cockerill reluctantly abandoned "my Enfield rifle, with its beautiful curly stock."[30]

At war's end, Confederate enlisted men were compelled to surrender their weapons. Many outgoing Union veterans also faced the prospect of turning in the arms they had carried so long. "How soon the soldier ceased to be a soldier without a gun!" wrote the regimental historian of the 72nd Indiana, part of the elite Lightning Brigade armed with state-of-the-art Spencer repeating rifles. "Here was another separation of long united friends, and we had learned, too, to trust our Spencers as we could never trust a friend." Not all members of the brigade, however, were forced to leave their repeaters behind: "Many of our boys had become so attached to them that they desired to retain them and on the intervention of our officers were permitted to do so on the payment of $10.00 apiece for them." Ulysses Grant observed "that great numbers of soldiers going out of service are very desirous of retaining their arms," and the Federal government, in the interest of defraying costs and disposing of surplus weapons, allowed soldiers to keep their muskets for the price of $6. One New York veteran happy to take advantage of this policy wrote, "To the veteran volunteer the value will be greater than the highest work of art America ever produced." Among the approximately one million men in the Union army in April 1865, they purchased 138,000 long arms and 20,000 pistols.[31]

Most Civil War soldiers had no say in the weapons they were issued, but that did not prevent them from critically appraising them. Both the Federal and Confederate governments at times had to scrape the bottom of the barrel to arm the largest armies yet raised in US history, and sometimes this left recruits with antiquated weapons or the leavings of European arsenals. Of course, a soldier did not have to be a gun expert to complain if his musket was hopelessly inaccurate or threatened to knock him off his feet with its recoil. Nevertheless, soldiers' commentary about their firearms shows that quite a few of them did so as knowledgeable, discriminating critics. When the 31st Iowa was issued its weapons, the two flank companies received British-made Enfields, the finest rifle musket of the age (alongside the American-made Springfield). The other eight companies, however, received decrepit Prussian smoothbores, prompting one Iowan to grouse, "Our arms are old muskets and in the worst kind of order. A great many of them are not fit for service at all. The boys blame our Col. for allowing such arms to be sent to his men. Some of the Coms. [companies] would not take them at first—but—finally knuckled under." Even more disgruntled were the recruits in Berdan's Sharpshooters, many of whom had been enticed by Colonel Hiram Berdan's promise to arm them with Sharps breechloaders. When the Sharps rifles proved difficult to obtain, Berdan issued them Colt revolving rifles, which required the shooter to hold it with a loaded cylinder pointing at his hand. Berdan's men raised Cain, complaining to their congressmen and threatening to mutiny, and were only cowed by threats of harsh military punishments. Berdan's Sharpshooters took the Colts, even using them to good effect on the Peninsula, but they finally did receive their long-sought Sharps rifles.[32]

Civil War soldiers could also be effusive in their praise when their issue weapons met their high standards. Washington Ives wrote his father in summer 1864 that his brigade were issued "beautiful new Enfield rifles" just before the Union assaults on Kennesaw Mountain, but "the boys were disappointed in not getting to shoot." Opposing Ives and his comrades, the men of the 34th Illinois shared their enthusiasm for new weapons. Earlier in the summer they had exchanged their Enfields for brand-new Springfields, and, according to Sergeant Lyman Widney, "some of our boys want to fight right away just to try the new guns."[33]

No weapons were more highly coveted and prized than the new breech-loading rifles being produced in the North, especially the multishot repeating rifles. Several thousand Union soldiers paid out of their own pockets to arm themselves with the latest firearm technology, investing in increasing their own firepower in combat. Theodore Upson and his comrades in the 100th Indiana began to enviously eye the new weapons appearing on the scene: "I wish we had Henrys (as the 16 shooters that the 97 Ind have are called). The 46 Ohio have been armed with the Spencer rifle—a 7 shot gun. Ours are single muzzle loaders. Our boys are rather disappointed we did not get more improved arms." Subsequently Upson managed to buy a Henry repeater from a wounded soldier for $35, "all the money I had," but a real bargain for a rifle retailing for $50 or more. John Tenyson, a pilot in the US Navy's Mississippi Squadron, described how he and his shipmates competed with one another in shooting matches and against Rebel sharpshooters, insisting that "my pet, as I call the Henry, can beat them all in distance and accuracy."[34]

A number of soldiers expressly recognized that better weapons meant better means of killing the enemy. Sharpshooter George H. Lewis proudly wrote to his sister of the arrival of their Sharps rifles and minced no words in telling her that "we are sure of killing a man at least 100 rods [550 yards] and further if the time comes for us to shoot farther for they are good rifles and the boys all like them a lot." Colonel John T. Wilder, commander of the Spencer-armed Lightning Brigade, enthusiastically reported, "My men feel as if it is impossible to be whipped, and the confidence inspired by these arms added to their terribly destructive capacity, *fully* QUADRUPLES *the effectiveness of my command.*"[35]

However, most Civil War accounts did not emphasize the "terribly destructive capacity" of this advanced weaponry. Instead, most men seemed to focus on the weapons' defensive power, the ability of the well-armed soldier carrying one to better protect himself, even if this translated into making him a deadlier warrior. For instance, one prominent advertisement for the Henry repeater boldly promised, "A resolute man, armed with one of these Rifles, particularly on horseback, CANNOT BE CAPTURED." Proud Henry owner Theodore Upson explained, "I am glad I could get it. They are good shooters and I like to think I have so many shots in reserve," adding later, "I feel a good deal more confidence in myself with a 16 shooter in my hands than I used to with a single shot." The 7th Illinois used their sixteen-shooters to good effect in defense of Allatoona Pass, with one of their officers insisting, "What saved us that day was the fact that we had a number of Henry rifles," recalling how one company "sprang to the parapet and poured out such a multiplied, rapid, and deadly fire that no man could stay in front of it." Did this emphasis on the weapons' defensive benefits rather than their killing power reflect a reticence about discussing killing? That possibility cannot be ruled out. However, the more apparent answer that presents itself is that for the soldiers armed with these rapid-firing weapons, the foremost benefit they saw was increasing their chances of coming through battle alive and safe.[36]

Ultimately, the most critical component of familiarity with firearms came down to being able to shoot accurately in combat. Just as North and South each asserted their own superiority over the other in terms of politics, culture, and just about every other aspect of the sectional crisis, partisans for both sides argued that their portion of the country produced the best marksmen. Because more Southerners per capita lived in rural settings where firearms were an especially familiar part of everyday life, many gave themselves the edge over their Northern brethren. Confederate veteran William Fletcher, having grown up on the frontier in Louisiana and Texas, remembered how on the eve of war his neighbors confidently boasted, "One Southerner with his superior marksmanship could shoot down the D—— Bluebellies as fast as they would come in sight." Colonel James Cooper Nisbet of Georgia insisted in his memoirs that the war's early battles "demonstrated that as an untrained soldier the Southerner was a better fighter than the Northerner. . . . His early environments made him self-reliant and dominating, a practiced horseman and skilled in the use of firearms."[37]

Northerners were quick to uphold their own shooting prowess. Colonel William Ripley of the 1st US Sharpshooters acknowledged that many Union regiments included men "who had never even fired a gun of any description" before enlisting, but as he pointed out, "On the other hand, there were known to be scattered throughout the loyal states, a great number of men who had made rifle shooting a study, and who, by practice on the target ground and at the country shooting matches, had gained a skill equal to that of the men of the South in any kind of shooting, and in long range practice a much greater degree of excellency." Another Sharpshooter officer, Captain William Aschmann, credited his fellow Switzers and other German speakers with helping revive American interest in marksmanship, claiming, "There were many who lacked experience in marksmanship which at that time was not widely practiced in America." (One wonders if Ripley and Aschmann found time to debate the respective merits of American-born and Swiss riflemen and the state of shooting sports in America.) Hundreds of thousands of Germanic immigrants arrived in America in the decades before the Civil War, settling mostly in the North, and many brought their own rich culture of hunting and target shooting.[38]

Claims as to whether North or South produced the best marksmen reflected more than just sectional rivalry. Partisans for their countrymen's shooting prowess fundamentally believed that the better fighters would be the better shooters because the better shooters would be the better killers on the battlefield. On some level they agreed with Voltaire that "God is not on the side of the big battalions, but on the side of the best shots," and many supporters of the Union and Confederacy believed (or wanted to believe) that their side would prove the best shots.

If familiarity with firearms offered some preparation for shooting to kill on the battlefield, then experience hunting brought them yet another step closer in readiness for that reality. Proficiency in hunting would provide a number of useful skills to a soldier, but none was more significant than shooting accurately—and shooting to kill. A British sniper trainer in World War II described how he prized recruits who possessed a hunter's discipline and ability to kill purposefully: "The man I wanted was of cold precision, the peace-time hunter who had no hatred for his quarry but just a great interest in the stalk and in the kill." Writing some eighty years earlier, William Nugent of Mississippi would likely have enthusiastically agreed that hunting fitted a man well for war. In a letter to his wife, Nellie, Nugent found himself digressing into a "homily on hunting," asserting, "It is a manly art. Develops the muscles, and associates us with scenes of danger and bloodshed."[39]

As with proficiency with firearms in general, popular opinion then and now has credited the South with producing more hunters. A simplistic reading of history casts the agrarian South as populated entirely with wily backwoodsmen and sport-hunting planters, with the industrial North inhabited by shopkeepers and factory-worker immigrants untutored in the use of arms. While Confederate ranks probably included more experienced hunters per capita than Federal forces, this oversimplification minimizes the extent of farming throughout the North and the culture of farming that complemented it. Men from the rich farmlands of the Old Northwest and the more rugged regions of the eastern seaboard shared much in common culturally with their Southern brethren, including a strong hunting tradition. A brigade of sharpshooting Pennsylvanians became known as the Bucktails because they wore the tails of whitetail deer on their hats as proof of their prowess, while the 66th Illinois, the Western Sharpshooters, somewhat less decorously, wore squirrel tails for the same reason. Chauncey Cooke's letters home alluded several times to hunting, including reference to the news that while he was away, the faithful family dog had saved his father from a charging bear. While stationed in Minnesota, Cooke wrote to his mother, "We have bear and dear close to this place but . . . I would dearly like to be with father in his hunts, long enough at least to help him kill two or three fat bears."[40]

Of course, killing game could not offer a perfect psychological analogue to killing in battle. A number of Civil War soldiers commented on the fact that bringing down squirrels, deer, or even bears could not entirely prepare them for taking the life of a fellow human being. Sergeant Lyman Widney noted that several months into their enlistment, his fellow Illinois soldiers had seen captured Rebels ("tame Confederates"), "but have not yet been able to see any in a wild state." His comrades were "quite anxious to go on a hunt for this kind of game," but he wryly suggested, "perhaps we shall not be so eager when the game begins to hunt us. We may yet experience the feeling of the hunter who is treed by a bear." Samuel Hankins of the 2nd Mississippi realized that not all hunters turned out to be effective killers in battle: "Some crack shots at home who always returned from the woods with a dozen squirrels, all shot in the head, when in battle could not hit a 'barn door' through excitement." Hankins's observation begs the question whether moral qualms against killing human beings may also have affected their accuracy, although the Mississippian specifically attributed their misses to excitement. The accuracy of his assessment is at least open to speculation.[41]

Nevertheless, many Federals and Confederates did find parallels between hunting and shooting to kill in battle. Numerous soldiers who found that they could aim and fire coolly and deliberately in combat likened the experience to shooting game. In a letter to the *Atlanta Southern Confederacy,* a soldier-correspondent from Georgia signing himself only as Soldier Jim wrote that at First Manassas, "when the shot was showering at us thick as hail, we loaded and fired at them as though we were shooting squirrels." George W. Squier of the 44th Indiana used the same analogy. Having "stood fire" at Shiloh, the Hoosier discovered that he "was a cool and composed as if sitting down for a chat or shooting squirrels." Men who applied the hunting analogy to their experience in battle did so to describe the purposeful, almost lighthearted way they felt. Notably, both Soldier Jim and Squier, as well as other soldiers who left similar accounts, made their observations after their first battle. Thoughts of how they would behave in the test of battle preoccupied many Civil War soldiers, and both accounts suggest more than a little pride—and perhaps surprise—that they could conduct themselves so dispassionately in the great trial.[42]

The hunting comparison was not lost on veterans either. During the stealthy night march that set up the Confederate surprise attack at Cedar Creek, Captain Samuel D. Buck of the 13th Virginia realized they were traversing "familiar ground" where both he and his wife had been raised. The significance was not lost on Buck, an officer in the habit of borrowing a rifle and pitching in during a battle. Creeping up on a Union army more than double the size of his, the Shenandoah Valley native thought to himself, "Where I used to hunt squirrels and birds I now hunt men and the game is plentiful."[43]

The prevalence of agriculture in antebellum America exposed future citizen-soldiers to death and bloodshed in ways besides hunting. Americans in the Civil War era knew much more about where their food came from than their modern descendants. Farming included slaughtering and butchering livestock for their meat and hides. Dave Grossman observes that "the slaughter of animals has been a vital ritual of daily and seasonal activity for most people until this last half century of human existence." Statistical evidence suggests that about 48 percent of Union soldiers and more than 60 percent of Confederate soldiers worked in agriculture in civilian life. Furthermore, other nineteenth-century professions, both rural and urban, shared some of the grislier aspects of farming. Famously, Ulysses Grant in his boyhood was disgusted by the sights and smells of the bloody hides in his father's tannery, to the extent that later in life he could not stand being served any meat that was not thoroughly cooked, if not burned. Presumably America's ranks of farmers, butchers, and tanners developed stronger stomachs and greater comfort levels if they were able to strive and thrive in their occupations.[44]

Could exposure to slaughtering and butchering livestock have better prepared Civil War recruits for death and killing on the battlefield? As with hunting, a moral and psychological gulf certainly existed between animal slaughter under routine, controlled settings and the sudden death and dismemberment of fellow human beings, especially at one's own hands. Civil War soldiers palpably reacted to the sight of gruesome deaths and wounds on the battlefield, particularly the first they witnessed. Still, experience with animal slaughter offered another potential analogue that could fortify them against—even desensitize them to—death and killing in combat. The parallels went beyond the competing technical and figurative ways we use such terms as "slaughter" and "butchery." Again, as with hunting, Civil War soldiers drew the parallels themselves. During the Antietam Campaign, Confederate soldiers were marching through a largely Unionist town in Maryland where a local lady pointed out the campaign-worn uniform of one "ragged, dirty rebel." The ragged Rebel wryly replied, "Madam, we always put on our old clothes when we go out to kill hogs."[45]

To understand Civil War soldiers' attitudes toward killing, it is critical to consider how they understood their duty as soldiers. What exactly did it mean to fight for a country or cause? Was it their duty to risk their lives and possibly be killed? Or was it to take other lives by killing the enemy? Few men expressed the latter point of view as memorably as General George S. Patton, himself the grandson and namesake of a Confederate colonel mortally wounded at the Third Battle of Winchester. "No bastard ever won a war by dying for his country," Patton colorfully told his GIs in 1944. "You won it by making the other poor dumb bastard die for his country." What Civil War accounts can do is illustrate how Union and Confederate soldiers understood their duty. They reveal a diversity of opinion, men who embraced visions of military duty as sacrifice, killing, or both.

Americans who experienced the Civil War were no strangers to the language of sacrifice, of giving up one's life for a higher purpose. In helping dedicate a national cemetery at Gettysburg, Abraham Lincoln honored "those who here gave their lives" that the nation might live. Lincoln's countrymen especially understood the idea of redemptive sacrifice, in large part because the biblical Christianity that many of them espoused declared that Christ's death on the cross had served as a sacrifice that atoned for the sins of mankind. Numerous Americans on both sides of the Civil War infused their rival national causes with divine purpose, which included sanctifying the death of a soldier in battle. No source did so more explicitly than Julia Ward Howe's "Battle Hymn of the Republic" (a title that itself blended sacred and secular), in which the song's penultimate stanza declared, "As He died to make men holy, let us die to make men free."

Many Civil War soldiers themselves adopted the belief in the sacredness of sacrificing one's life in battle for cause and country. Numerous accounts spoke of sacrificing one's life "upon the altar of my country," language that, like Howe's song title, expressly linked spiritual and temporal institutions. Soldiers also seized on the imagery of blood and bloodshed in speaking of sacrifice. This reflected a biblical influence; throughout the New Testament, verses refer to the sanctifying power of "the precious blood of Christ," its power to "redeem" man and "cleanse" him of sin. Hoosier soldier George Squier adopted such language wholesale and explicitly applied it to dying for the Union in a poem he authored:

> The blood that flows for freedom is God's blood;
> Who dies for man's redemption dies with Christ
> . . .
> So fall our saviors on the bloody field;
> And with their blood they wash the nation clean
> And furnish expiation for the sin
> That those that slay them have been guilty of.

Other soldiers spoke of sacrifice in terms of shedding one's own blood, but in a general and less theological sense, such as William Pitt Chambers, who paid tribute to the Confederacy's "thousands of slain and maimed heroes who have already poured out their blood as water."[46]

Other soldiers thought of their duty in more Pattonesque terms and emphasized killing the enemy. Soldier Jim from Georgia, though wounded at First Manassas, matter-of-factly reported, "I killed some very large Yankees, and feel as though I have discharged my duty." The Union ranks also included men who believed it their duty to make the other fellow die for his country, such as the Berdan's Sharpshooter who unequivocally wrote, *"We have got to kill this Southern army."* Perhaps no common soldier came as close to sounding like Patton as Robert Burdette of the 47th Illinois, who concluded, "Killing is the object of war." Burdette also bluntly stated, "We are the best killers. . . . That decides the righteousness of any cause," expressing a cynicism that would have shocked those of his comrades more idealistically motivated.[47]

When I began my research, I imagined finding numerous soldiers primarily referring to duty as risking their own lives and offering passive accounts of their role in battle. Both of these practices would have offered soldiers coping mechanisms if they were unsettled by the prospect of killing. This would have emphasized what happened to them in battle instead what they might be called upon to do—namely, to kill. I did in fact find men who spoke of duty in terms of self-sacrifice and those who described battle in passive terms. Also, I would still argue both of these offered a source of emotional and psychological sanctuary to men who were reluctant to kill. More striking, however, were how many men on both sides spoke of their duty in terms of both dying and killing. It is perhaps unsurprising that some soldiers would recognize both risking their lives and taking enemy lives as elements of their military duty, yet significantly, those who did so suggested that they were able to embrace both roles, rather than choosing to downplay killing.

Among the notable examples, a significant number of soldiers offered dual visions of duty—risking life and taking life—in the same breath (or statement). Sergeant John Hill Ferguson of the 10th Illinois merged notions of dying and killing for one's country. "Some of us will undoubtedly fall in the struggle, but those whose fate it may be, will die an honorable and glorious death," he recorded in his diary at the outset of the Atlanta Campaign. "And the survivers will rush a head, revenge there deaths and gain the victory, as we know no other way to end a bloody fight." A Wisconsin soldier in the Army of the Potomac expressed similar sentiments, writing to a New York paper that if he fell in battle, "I have the consolation of knowing that I die in a glorious cause." He added, "I hope, however, that I shall be spared to send a few messengers of death into the hearts of those who have made all this trouble." North Carolina veteran Preston Lafayette Ledford included in his reminiscences examples of poetic verse hailing the soldier who would bravely "imperil ones life his country to save" but also featured lines that boasted, "Let us charge the Yankees and let them know / We can shoot them down and over their dead bodies go" and "Give them no quarter—we ask for none— / Shoot them down as fast as they come."[48]

A final factor worth considering in regard to influences on Civil War soldiers is their actual attitudes early in the war toward the prospect of killing. Reconstructing such a personal and specific part of Union and Confederate soldiers' outlooks offers a more challenging task than it does for modern warriors. Buoyed by the rise of the social sciences, militaries in the twentieth and twenty-first centuries have taken greater interest than ever before in evaluating such factors as the intelligence, psychology, and mind-sets of their personnel. In World War II, for instance, the US Army polled recruits to gauge their willingness to kill Axis soldiers.[49] No such poll exists for Civil War soldiers, yet a survey of Federal and Confederate accounts can at least identify individuals who volunteered their answers to such questions.

Quite a few Confederates echoed the sentiments of the song "The Southern Soldier," the first stanza of which declared,

I'll place my knapsack on my back
My rifle on my shoulder
I'll march away to the firing line
And kill that Yankee soldier

Early in the war, when both sides expected only a brief conflict, many re-cruits feared they would miss the action entirely, including their chance to fight against and perhaps even kill one of the enemy. Stationed on the Flor-ida coast, artilleryman S. H. Dent was grateful that his battery had had the chance to trade shots with a Federal warship, for "I did not want to go home and say that I had not fired a gun at the enemy." John O. Casler of the Stonewall Brigade remembered how his comrades had been "very keen for a fight" and "very anxious to get a shot at the 'bluecoats.'" Georgia private James T. Thompson wrote home, "All i want is a crack at a Yankee boy." Even into 1862, newly raised troops expressed similar sentiments, along with fears of missed opportunities. Eagerly awaiting weapons for his cav-alry company, Florida planter Winston Stephens told his wife, "I . . . hope to have one chance before the War ends as I do want to shoot a Yankee."[50]

Among the Yankees themselves, some men likewise voiced their enthusi-asm for killing their Confederate foes. "My motive for inlisten was to shute rebels and did to the best of my ability," 1st Wisconsin veteran Thomas Morgan plainly stated in his postwar reminiscences. In November 1861, a school superintendent in Elyria, Ohio, complained that war fever was dis-tracting the young men in his charge from their studies, remarking, "Most of them are 'spoiling for a fight' and are as public as they are emphatic in expressing an earnest desire each 'to shoot a rebel.'" A month later, soldiers in the 7th Wisconsin fought one another in a specially staged mock battle using blank cartridges, but this "regular performance of a battle" failed to satisfy the martial ardor of at least one Badger. "I wish we had had balls in our guns and the rebels standing before us and then see them fall, but they were not there may be we will have a chance after a while at lest I hope so," William Ray wrote his sisters. "I think I can fight some—if we see a battle you will never be ashamed of the way I behave in it," Captain Luther H. Cowan of the 45th Illinois wrote to his wife in February 1862. "I intend to kill at least one secesh. God being my helper."[51]

For some soldiers, this eagerness to try their hand at killing the enemy did not last long after their first battle. "You know I have often wished a chance at the Yankees," James Branscomb wrote his sister back in Alabama in the aftermath of the Peninsula Campaign. "I am satisfied now after a weeks fight. . . . I don't care now if I never hear another boom or ball." For other men, however, especially the most ideologically motivated, experiencing the reality of combat did not dim their fervor. Having "seen the horrors of war, in all its blood and terror" at First Manassas, First Sergeant A. Campbell McPherson of the 7th Georgia wrote, "My curiosity is satisfied; but I am as anxious to again brave its perils to defend our country and repel her invaders." For Confederate cavalryman James Womack, repelling the invaders most certainly meant killing them. "I intend to fight them to the last," he wrote his wife in the Shenandoah Valley. "I will kill them as long as I live even if peace is made I will never get done with them."[52]

Because no pollster asked Civil War soldiers how they felt about the prospect of killing in war, the available evidence is biased in favor of the most adamant and enthusiastic participants. Men who dreaded the prospect of having to take another man's life or who felt ambivalent may have been less willing to voice their feelings. A noteworthy exception was Mississippi cavalryman William L. Nugent, who in a letter to his wife, Nellie, described the conflict he felt between his Confederate partisanship and the spiritual concerns of his conscience. "I feel that I would like to shoot a Yankee," he wrote in August 1861, "and yet I know that this would not be in harmony with the Spirit of Christianity, that teaches us to love our enemies & and do good to them that despitefully use us and entreat us." Eventually Nugent seems to have harmonized his warlike desire and his spiritual convictions. Although he did not expressly describe how he worked out the conflict, Federal forces' threat to the Confederate home front—to despitefully use its people and resources—seems to have played a key role in persuading Nugent that it was permissible to shoot Yankees. By May 1862, Union incursions into his home state convinced him that it was the duty of every Mississippian to help destroy the foe: "Kill, slay & murder them. Give them no peace; for unless we do; we do not deserve God's mercy."[53]

Soldiers who voiced their readiness to kill in battle inform us not only of their personal attitudes toward killing but also their comfort level with discussing the subject. Their candid remarks appeared in documents both private and public—letters to family, public letters to newspapers, postwar reminiscences—suggesting that many of them did not feel a strong taboo against speaking of killing the enemy. Many of these declarations can be found in correspondence addressed to female relations, the most likely individuals one might imagine Victorian Americans might want to shield from talk of killing. Many of these accounts indicate that willingness—even eagerness—to kill the enemy was a sentiment seen as socially acceptable, perhaps even praiseworthy.

A host of ideas and influences contributed to Civil War soldiers' attitudes toward killing in combat. Collectively, these influences legitimized and pushed them toward readiness to kill in battle rather than stigmatizing it. For many, political ideology convinced them of the justness of fighting for the Union or the Confederacy, even if it meant taking the lives of their erstwhile countrymen. Christian teachings and ethics provided the single strongest roadblock to that surety, yet at the same time substantial evidence suggests that for men whose faith influenced their attitude toward war, the majority found that it permitted and even reinforced the lethal duty of a soldier. In addition, before these citizen-soldiers received their formal military training, various aspects of antebellum culture prepared and fitted them in varying degrees for that duty, whether it was exposure to firearms and hunting or simply a familiarity with death. At the same time, this chapter repeated a refrain that these analogues for killing in battle offered only shadows of that experience and could only partially prepare them for the actual test of battle. Still, even before Fort Sumter, the culture of antebellum America had provided many future Federal and Confederate fighting men with what one Revolutionary War veteran called their military "priming." Under arms and in battle, they would take on "the whole coat of paint for a soldier."[54]

# 2

## *Seeing the Elephant*
### *Killing and the Face of Battle*

Civil War soldiers called experiencing battle "seeing the elephant."
The expression aptly captured for mid-nineteenth-century Americans the idea of encountering something incredible, extraordinary, unfamiliar, larger than life, and potentially dangerous. Battle
represented the supreme test for Civil War soldiers. The ordeal of
combat challenged not only whether citizen-soldiers from North
and South could stand fire and risk being killed or maimed but also
whether they could kill. Just as most Federals and Confederates
found that they could overcome their fear and enter the storm of
battle, most also found that in the heat of combat, they could fight
as potential battlefield killers. A host of factors could induce men
to fight and try to kill, whether it was military authority, survival,
adrenaline, anger, vengeance, or coolness under fire. Even among
soldiers reluctant or ambivalent toward killing, many found that
they could fight just as purposefully and potentially lethally as
their more sanguine comrades. Furthermore, the nature of Civil
War combat potentially masked and shielded soldiers from the certainty of knowing that they personally had killed. A soldier's duty
seemed to be to kill the enemy, and many of the men in blue and
gray tried to perform this duty to the best of their ability.

In combat, the Civil War infantryman primarily fought as a
musketeer (a rather antiquated European term) or a rifleman.
That is to say, he primarily fought—and tried to kill—the enemy by
shooting his weapon, whether it was a smoothbore musket, rifle
musket, or rifle. The average infantryman on both sides carried a
single-shot muzzleloader. To load and fire such a weapon required
the following procedure: take a paper cartridge from the cartridge

box, bite open the cartridge with one's teeth, pour the powder down the barrel, insert the ball or bullet in the barrel, draw a steel ramrod from its groove underneath the stock, use the ramrod to push the charge to the bottom of the barrel, withdraw the rammer, return it to its groove, bring the gun hammer to half cock, prime with a percussion cap, pull the hammer to full cock, aim, and fire. In theory, a well-trained soldier could load and fire three shots per minute under this system.

Civil War soldiers primarily fought using linear tactics, engaging the enemy in a "line of battle," two ranks of men standing elbow to elbow. While historians debate the efficacy of linear tactics in the face of changing technology during the Civil War, this system did maximize a unit's firepower against the enemy. S. L. A. Marshall, though he scarcely would have advocated a return to fighting in line of battle, likely found much to envy in the efficiency and control such tactics provided. In making his controversial claim that only a fraction of combat GIs in World War II fired their weapons in action, Marshall used that claim to argue that the US military needed "more and better fire." Combat units, he suggested, could maximize firepower (i.e., the number of men firing effectively) through better training and by officers exercising greater fire control over their troops in battle. A military textbook from 1921 defines fire control as "the ability to open fire, stop fire, change the range and objective, and to resume fire." If nothing else, Civil War tactics provided commanders with a markedly firm grip on fire control. Enlisted men exercised little individual initiative but instead followed their superiors' orders when it came to movement and firing. An Ohio veteran reckoned that in most armies of the day, "a soldier in the ranks was a portion of a great machine, and was not supposed to think or use human instinct; on the contrary, to obey orders and look out for himself as a secondary matter, was all that was required of the common soldier." Responsibility for directing their troops' musketry fell to officers, maneuvering battle lines to the best advantage for firing on the enemy, much like the captain of an old man-of-war steering his ship to bring his broadsides to bear. Officers controlled not only when their men fired but also how they fired—whether it was in a single crashing volley, firing by rank, firing by file (creating a rippling fire down the line), or allowing the men to fire at will.[1]

Civil War tactics not only allowed commanders to exercise fire control but also maximized the chances that enlisted men would fire their weapons at—and potentially kill—enemy soldiers. This system provided two factors that Dave Grossman identifies as encouraging men to kill in battle: the demands of authority and group absolution. Officers represented powerful authority figures when it came to fostering combative behavior—so much so that enlisted men primarily relied on their express commands when it came to firing their weapons. Effective officers supervised their soldiers' musketry in battle. The duties of company officers and sergeants included posting immediately behind the firing line, steadying the men, providing them extra ammunition, watching for misfiring weapons, and potentially even correcting soldiers who inadvertently or deliberately were not shooting to kill. Fighting as part of a line of battle also encouraged killing in the form of group absolution. Like authority figures, the presence of numerous comrades reinforced and legitimized the act of firing on the enemy. Strong senses of camaraderie and cohesion especially characterized Civil War units, which were usually raised from the same locality, and thus a strong desire not to let their comrades down animated men to faithfully fulfill their military duties. Furthermore, fighting as part of long lines of fellow soldiers loading and firing created a sense of anonymity in shooting, making it difficult to tell whose bullet did any actual killing. Together, these factors helped encourage Civil War soldiers to behave combatively and to overcome any hesitancy to fire on the enemy, and they potentially shielded them from any guilt they might feel from killing in battle.

To be able to fight according to the tactics of the day, the citizen-soldiers of the Civil War first had to be trained in those tactics. While Union and Confederate soldiers' military training did encourage them to heed officers' commands, it largely did not prepare them for the reality of shooting to kill in combat. Many units, especially early in the war, went into battle without ever having fired their issue weapons with live ammunition. For some recruits, this meant going into battle without ever having shot a firearm. This oversight persisted in some subsequent battles when newly raised regiments entered the fight alongside veteran troops. At the Battle of South Mountain, the green 9th New Hampshire received "for the first time . . . orders to load," one of its soldiers wrote. "Some have never before loaded a gun, few have ever loaded with a ball cartridge, and many must be shown the whole process."[2]

The men of the 34th Illinois were among those fortunate enough to be introduced to the use of their muskets before having to fire them in battle, and the introduction proved to be a memorable one. In November 1861, their officers formed them up in line of battle to experience loading and firing as they would in action. First they fired a regimental volley, with the discharge of "nearly a thousand muskets" leaving the Illinoisans "dazed and half blinded with the noise and smoke of our performance," Sergeant Lyman S. Widney remembered in his memoirs. "The order was then given to load and fire at will, when there was a crackling of musketry along the line, which, joined to the exciting exercise of loading and firing, completely jumbled our ideas into chaos." Even so, it was a fraction of the excitement and chaos they would experience when there was an enemy firing back at them.[3]

Clearly many commanders, thanks to time constraints or their own misjudgments, failed to instill adequately in their troops some of the basic skills they would need to fight a battle. Moreover, Civil War armies lacked a systematic program of target practice for new recruits, such as the US military would implement in the twentieth century. Nevertheless, it would be wrong to assume that target practice was nonexistent among Federal and Confederate forces. Once it became clear that the war would not be a short conflict, and as armies found themselves in lulls of inactivity between campaigns, officers found time to improve their soldiers' proficiency with their weapons. The system lacked precision and thoroughness, as the decision to provide target practice was usually at the discretion of regimental and company commanders, yet a number of soldiers documented such training. "The reg't practicing at targets," a Floridian in the Army of Tennessee noted in his diary in the spring of 1862. On the eve of the Overland Campaign, Tar Heel soldier Louis Leon described his brigade's corps of sharpshooters "target practising," shooting offhand (standing and without a rest) at 500 yards, an incredibly challenging task for a shooter. "Some very good shooting was done," Leon wrote approvingly in his diary. His next entry proudly recorded scoring a bull's-eye himself.[4]

Like their Confederate counterparts, Union forces at times found opportunities for practicing marksmanship. "We practice now at target-firing," wrote a soldier-correspondent from the 12th New York State Militia, stationed at Harpers Ferry, adding, "we can boast some very good shots, too." A Wisconsin soldier in the Iron Brigade recorded in a January 1864 diary, "Practiced with my gun at the mark this AM." Some men found impromptu means to improve their marksmanship. Soldiers on picket duty carried loaded weapons and after their relief were expected to safely unload their weapons. The most expedient method was to simply shoot off the round; otherwise a soldier would have to use a tool attached to a ramrod to draw the bullet from the barrel. Usually Civil War armies forbade soldiers from discharging weapons in camp because a shot signaled an alarm on the picket line. "I have loaded several times on Picket," wrote Simon Bolivar Hulbert of the 100th New York, "but never have been ordered to fire it off & it is contrary to the rules of the camp to fire a gun any where near the Camp." Some commanders, however, made allowances that permitted pickets to clear their muskets by firing them. Private Hulbert took advantage of the opportunity to better his shooting when the rules were relaxed for his unit. "Get back to camp, unload our guns by firing at a target," he recorded in one diary entry. "I made a very good shot this morning."[5]

Some soldiers, Bolivar Hulbert among them, took a personal interest in improving their shooting skills. "I suppose that you would like to know how I get along learning to be a marksman," the New Yorker wrote in a May 1862 letter to one of his brothers. "I have never fired my gun yet," he admitted, explaining that pickets were not (yet) allowed to fire their muskets off duty. "Shoot at target, 5 shots, but I did not make a good shot myself," Hulbert recorded months later in his December 2, 1862, diary entry. Three days later, he eagerly shared his progress in another letter to his brother: "Time passes very pleasantly here now. It is drill, Dress Parade & target shooting all the time. I have not got to be a great marksman yet, [b]ut am improving every time that we go out to shoot." For Hulbert and his comrades, weapons training had become a more regular feature of camp life: "Two days in the week we go out & fire five rounds a piece, then we go on Picket once a week & when we return from picket we have to discharge our guns."[6]

Historians have made much about the poor shooting skills many Civil War soldiers displayed early in the war but have neglected to consider their ability to advance their skills as veterans in the course of their service as citizen-soldiers. Some men found practical benefits to improving their marksmanship. "Having made some good shots in our Regimental target practice," Almeron Stillwell of the 5th Wisconsin recorded in his diary, "I am now, with a picked man from Each Company, provided with a Sharps Rifle and permitted temporarily to join the Sharpshooters." The 1859 Sharps rifle was an accurate breechloading weapon, one especially prized by Union sharpshooters. Similarly, Illinois sergeant Lyman Widney described how his entire brigade engaged in an epic target firing session, with the two best shots from each company recruited into a special sharpshooter battalion. Confederate forces seem to have been even more active in evaluating their troops' marksmanship in order to identify the ablest sharpshooters (as opposed to Union forces' penchant for forming sharpshooter regiments straight from civilian recruits). Like Private Stillwell and his comrades, the best Confederate marksmen were rewarded with prized weapons, such as highly accurate British muzzleloaders run through the blockade.[7]

Although some Civil War soldiers found opportunities to improve their marksmanship, their training was still not best suited to preparing them for the task of killing in battle, according to modern authorities in warrior science. Military and law enforcement experts emphasize the need for realistic training to condition trainees for the conditions they will experience in combat scenarios. Specifically, conditioning a recruit to kill calls for realistic targets in order to acclimate a shooter to firing at a fellow human being when the time comes. S. L. A. Marshall's findings from World War II, Korea, and Vietnam showed substantial increases over time in the percentage of combat infantrymen "engaging the enemy" with their weapons. This change coincided with changes the military had made in the targets used on the firing range. Targets transformed from the traditional bull's-eye of World War II to simple silhouettes resembling a man's head and shoulders to actual illustrations of human targets. Today's military and law enforcement training continues the trend in terms of ultrarealism, including "photo realistic" targets and video simulations.[8]

Realism was far removed from Civil War target shooting. If soldiers fortunate enough to be accorded target practice used any kind of formal target, the mark they typically fired at was the ubiquitous bull's-eye. The US Army's Ordnance Department tested the accuracy of small arms by firing at a plain white square divided into quarters by crosshairs. Such target choices emphasized the precision of one's marksmanship over any semblance of realism. A number of cases can be found in which Civil War soldiers used human-looking targets, perhaps most notably the occasions when sharpshooter Hiram Berdan used a crudely drawn effigy labeled "Jeff Davis" as a target. Examples like Berdan's, however, reflected facetiousness and making a political statement rather than a serious attempt at combat conditioning. The British army of the era, on the other hand, used as a long-range musketry target a life-size line drawing of an artillery team in action. Even in this case, however, the rationale seems to have been the need for a practical target, both for visual purposes (used at ranges of 600 yards and beyond) and assessing the theoretical effectiveness of the shots fired, rather than realistic conditioning for killing. Compared to modern standards in military training, the Civil War soldiers' training underserved them in preparation for shooting to kill.[9]

One of the critical factors that shaped Civil War soldiers' experience of combat and killing was visibility on the battlefield. Not being able to clearly see the enemy or the effect of his shots against the enemy potentially divorced the soldier from the knowledge of whether his fire took lives in battle. Evidence from twentieth-century conflicts suggests that fighting men such as artillery crews, bomber crews, and sailors experience less resistance to killing than do combat infantrymen, ostensibly because "most of them don't have to kill anybody directly," Dave Grossman observes. Physical distance from the target emotionally distances the warrior from the reality of killing.[10] On the basis of the nature of Civil War combat, a Union or Confederate soldier could find it harder to see the enemy or know whether he hit anyone than would a modern soldier firing a weapon using smokeless powder, especially in short-range combat such as in urban or jungle warfare. Civil War small arms and artillery exclusively used black powder, which produces clouds of white, sulfurous smoke when burned. Black powder weaponry created a literal fog of war that could severely limit visibility on the battlefield.

Enlisted men's accounts testify to poor visibility and the uncertainty of the Civil War battlefield. "Soldiers do not take aim after the first shot because the smoke is so thick," explained Bolivar Hulbert, "but they only bring the gun to the Shoulder & and then pull." North Carolina soldier Preston Ledford concurred, explaining, "Instead of selecting a certain soldier in the enemy's line to shoot at, a soldier merely leveled his gun and fired at the line of battle of the enemy, dimly seen through the smoke and dust, then loaded his gun with another cartridge and repeated." Remembering his first battle as a seventeen-year-old private, Virginia veteran Alexander Hunter wrote in his memoirs how "we couldn't see a thing, but away we fired as fast as we could load, blazing away in every direction."[11]

Seeing at whom to shoot became still more difficult when confronting an enemy dug in behind substantial cover. Union soldiers at the Battle of Fredericksburg understood this all too well, gamely trying to return the fire of Confederate troops fighting behind the stone wall along Marye's Heights. "We cannot now see distinctly any rebels to fire at, as they seem to seek the shelter of their works," Sergeant Edward Simonton of the 20th Maine wrote, "but we can see puffs of smoke all along their line, and hear the storm of musketry and shot and shell over our heads, and we know the Johnnies are there, so we blaze away at the puffs of smoke and the earthworks on the hill-side opposite."[12]

A handful of soldiers left behind invaluable detailed accounts in which they described their mind-sets amid a Civil War firefight. Perhaps not surprisingly, documents discussing choosing one's targets in battle tend to come from soldiers who demonstrated a positive or pragmatic attitude toward killing in combat. Weeks after the Battle of Antietam, the sisters of Iron Brigade soldier William R. Ray asked him in a letter whether he "took aim at any particular Rebbel" in battle. Historians can only ponder how many civilian family members wondered about this aspect of soldiers' wartime experience, or how many directly queried them about the subject of killing. More letters from Civil War soldiers have been preserved for posterity than letters sent to them, partly because letters could more easily be preserved by family members on the home front than by soldiers on campaign. Ray's let-ter from his sisters, Phebe and Cordelia (which referred to his own published letters), should be considered a valuable document in its own right. Just as valuably, their brother, William, answered them candidly in his reply. "I took aim at one several times but they always fell before I could fire," he wrote of the recent battle. "Some times when I would get a good aim at one rebel there would be another rebel come up before him so I could not hit the one I aimed at." Ray admitted that the enemy "fell so fast" that he could not tell whether he had hit any, "but I know I tryed as hard as I could to kill some of them." Ralph Rea of the 7th Michigan used much the same language when writing to a family member of his active participation in battle. "It was a hard fight I ashure you," the Wolverine infantryman wrote a cousin days after the clash at Gettysburg. "In two days I shot somewhere about one hundred rounds[;] you better believe I took good aim."[13]

Other soldiers shot to kill in battle but could still feel ambivalent having slain one of the enemy. Frank Potts, an Irish-born soldier in the 1st Vir-ginia, first saw the elephant at Blackburn's Ford, a skirmish fought days before First Manassas. There he witnessed one of his messmates die from a Yankee bullet, an experience the adopted Virginian recorded in his diary as "bringing . . . home to me" the deadly nature of combat. "I fired twice at random, into the woods," Potts wrote, "and then growing cool, I loaded deliberately, and waited, with my piece at 'a ready' for a sure shot." His chance came when he spied a blue-coated soldier moving forward, his own weapon at the ready. Potts vividly recounted what happened next: "I came to aim, steadied my piece, and aiming at his breast, I fired—I saw him no more, God have mercy on him—the distance was about 70 yds and I could not miss him." Certain that he had hit his mark, Potts could not help but feel both pity for his foe and a sobering sense that he had killed. In his diary, Potts quickly rationalized the killing as part of his duty as a Confederate soldier, that he had been right and his enemy in the wrong: "Well, I was fighting for my home, and he had no business there." Potts thus identified himself as one of many Confederates motivated to defend their land from men they saw as invaders and aggressors. One might also infer that seeing a close comrade shot down in front of him might also have helped motivate Potts to fire with lethal intent in battle. Potts's detailed account of killing in battle marks him as a soldier who recorded mixed feelings about taking life yet also cited personal and ideological motivations to justify killing the enemy.[14]

Some soldiers borrowed the hunting expression "buck fever" to describe the hurried nervousness and excitability affecting a soldier trying to decide where to aim in the heat of battle. Henry Dwight, a lieutenant in the 20th Ohio, concurred with William Ray that when it came to trading shots with the enemy, a soldier had to think fast. During an incredibly close-range fire-fight at the Battle of Raymond, the Ohioan noticed a Confederate officer on the enemy battle line, perhaps only thirty feet away, calmly fill and light his pipe. With his pipe lit, the enemy officer took his revolver, secured to his wrist by a cord, and began "popping away at us as leisurely as if he had been shooting rats." Dwight marveled that the man, making such a conspicuous target at such close range, was not hit. Like William Ray, he spoke of the frenzied nature of trying to pick a human target and sticking with him amid the chaos of combat. "The fact is when you start to draw a bead on any chap in such a fight, you have to make up your mind mighty quick whom you'll shoot," Dwight wrote after the war. "There are so many on the other side that look as if they were just getting a bead on you that it takes a lot of nerve to stick to the one that you first wanted to attend to. You generally feel like trying to kind of distribute your bullets so as to take in all who ought to be hit. So a good many get off who are near enough to be knocked over the first time."[15]

"Target attractiveness" is one key factor that influences a combatant's willingness to fire and how he directs his shots. Dave Grossman explains that "a soldier is more likely to kill the [target] that represents the greatest gain to him and the greatest loss to the enemy." For a great majority of soldiers throughout history, the most attractive target has been an enemy who presents an immediate threat of killing him. Lieutenant Dwight alluded to this when he refers to soldier's difficulty in fixating on one target when it seemed that so many other enemies "look as if they were just getting a bead on you." In a stand-up firefight, many Civil War soldiers sought to shoot down opponents who seemed poised to fire at them. Confederate memoirist Sam Watkins espoused such a mind-set, explaining, "I always shot at privates. It was they that did the shooting and killing, and if I could kill or wound a private, why, my chances were so much the better."[16]

While Sam Watkins scrupulously directed his aim at enemy enlisted men, for other soldiers, enemy officers represented especially high-value targets. Sharpshooters traditionally focused on officers; by picking off enemy leaders, they could disrupt command and control on the opposing side for a sound tactical advantage. In addition to the Civil War's best marksmen, some ordinary infantrymen did their best to kill officers. "I shot 4 times at an officer on a horse, but did not fetch him, so I gave up and went to firing into the crowd which were much nearer," Massachusetts infantryman Roland Bowen wrote after Antietam. In changing his aim, Bowen came closer to Sam Watkin's rationale for targeting enlisted men instead of officers, as the latter expressed in *Co. Aytch:* "I always looked upon officers as harmless personages. . . . If I shot at an officer, it was at long range, but when we got down to close quarters I always tried to kill those that were trying to kill me."[17]

At the Battle of Ezra Church, Sergeant Edwin W. Smith of the 54th Ohio tried even harder than Private Bowen to shoot a Confederate officer and experienced even greater frustration. During the fighting, he spied a man on a white horse rallying the Rebels. "Singling him out I took deliberate aim," Smith wrote. "I won't say, like Washington's Indian, that I fired 17 times; but I did fire until I got disgusted." The Ohioan hailed one of his comrades, and together they dashed forward to a tree, behind which they then took turns shooting at the prominent figure: "One would fire and the other watch the result. Then we would both try together. It was no go; like Banquo's ghost he would not down."[18]

Anything that made a man visually conspicuous could draw enemy fire. While carrying the colors was considered a post of honor in the Civil War, it was also among the most dangerous. Battle flags made of brightly colored silk or cotton, sometimes more than six feet square, were intended to be easily identifiable above the smoke of battle, yet this visibility also made their bearers prime targets. The colors were posted in the center of a regiment, allowing soldiers on either end to align themselves accordingly. As men fell in battle, the battle line would shrink inward as the soldiers closed up their files, rallying ever closer to the battle flags. Numerous soldiers directed their fire at this center point. Describing the fire his 5th New Hampshire poured into the Confederates in Antietam's Bloody Lane, Colonel Edward Cross wrote triumphantly, "We shot down the rebel color bearers as fast as they could get up, killed their officers, broke their ranks and piled them in heaps among the tall corn." An Indiana private, also at Bloody Lane, remembered how "we did our best to kill them all before they could reach their ditch, but they came in splendid alignment, their colors fell as fast as they were raised and each time they fell, there was a man to seize them but he couldn't more than wave them once until down he would go."[19]

Just wearing colors beyond the typical blue, gray, or butternut could single a man out. The 16th New York proudly wore "white straw hats" they had been given during the hot summer months on the Virginia peninsula in 1862—that is, until after they wore them in battle. At Gaines Mill, the regiment suffered 40 percent casualties, including a disproportionate number of wounds to the head and upper body, according to the survivors. Many of the New Yorkers believed that the Rebels had aimed for their distinctive hats, though some men also reckoned this had caused some of the shots to fly too high. Whatever the case, most of the regiment left off wearing their conspicuous headgear thereafter. After fighting at Raymond, Osborn Old-royd, another 20th Ohio soldier, recorded in his diary, "In front of us was a reb in a red shirt, when one of our boys, raising his gun, remarked, *'see me bring that red shirt down,'* while another cried out, *'hold on, that is my man.'* Both fired, and the red shirt fell—it may be riddled by more than those two shots." As Oldroyd concluded, "A red shirt is, of course, rather too conspic-uous on a battle field."[20]

Other garb that some men deemed rather too conspicuous were the gaudy Zouave uniforms, based on those worn by French colonial troops in North Africa, often featuring bright trim and baggy red trousers. Zouave regiments wore their bold uniforms with pride, but some men reckoned the exotic attire made them better targets. In a letter written after 1st Manassas, the battle that saw perhaps the motliest assemblage of uniforms of the en-tire war, a Virginia artilleryman described "the Zouaves whose conspicuous red pantaloons made an admirable mark for our men and which you may well suppose we didn't fail to avail ourselves of." The chaplain of the 1st Delaware supposed that at Antietam the Zouave uniforms worn by one of the companies in his regiment "attracted the especial attention of the en-emy, for they suffered, in numbers, more heavily than other companies."[21]

The experience of combat brought about extraordinary physical and emotional effects on Civil War soldiers, effects both tangible and intangible, that carried them through battle and enabled them to fight—and some-times kill. With their adrenaline surging, combatants experienced extremes of energy and excitement. Rufus Dawes remembered the "great hysterical excitement, eagerness to go forward, and a recklessness of life" on display in the bloody fight for the Cornfield at Antietam. Leading the 6th Wiscon-sin, Dawes noted, "The soldier who is shooting is furious in his energy. . . . The men are loading and firing with demoniacal fury and shouting and laughing hysterically."[22]

"War gives to men strange turns of nature when battle becomes nature's subject of thought," observed an Ohio officer. The extraordinary mania that possessed many soldiers transformed them into enthusiastic partici-pants in combat. "I . . . loaded & fired my gun until I had blisters on my fingers as big as 10 cent peaces from Ramming down the loads & my gun was so hot I could not touch the barrel with my hands. . . . I never wanted to load & shoot so fast in all my life before," Private David Smith of the 12th New Jersey wrote his wife after Gettysburg. "Our blood was hot, we fought for home, and against an invading foe and we could not give up at all," William Bevens of the 1st Arkansas wrote of the furious fighting at Chickamauga.[23]

The soldiers themselves often found it difficult to put into words to explain to the uninitiated exactly how it felt to be in combat. "One who has never been in battle cannot begin to imagine the feeling that possesses you," Virginia veteran Samuel Buck noted in his memoirs. "I wish I could describe the feelings that possess us at such a time," New York soldier Seymour Dexter wrote to a friend. "With me, and I think the experience of nearly all, the fear which one feels before the engagement begins is entirely gone and a recklessness takes on and thus it is that men will give cheer after cheer while advancing directly up to the cannons' mouth with their comrades falling thick and fast about them."[24]

Numerous soldiers concurred that the excitement and urgency of battle seemed to banish their fears. Shortly after First Manassas, one Confederate wrote at length describing the incredible transformation combatants underwent:

> What a metamorphosis! With your first shot you become a new man. Personal safety is your least concern. Fear has no existence in your bosom. Hesitation gives way to an uncontrollable desire to rush into the thickest of the fight. The dead and dying around you, if they receive a passing thought, only serve to stimulate you to revenge. . . . Such is the spirit which carries the soldier through the field of battle.

Wilbur F. Crummer, a Union veteran of the Western Theater, described with similar eloquence the dramatic change from intense fear to battle mania. After their baptism by fire at Fort Donelson, his comrades in the 45th Illinois eagerly discussed with one another how they had felt before and during battle. One Prairie Stater suggested that "the greatest strain was waiting in line of battle"; listening to the oncoming roar of battle, "I felt as though my heart was in my mouth, and there came a desire to run for a place of safety." Once his regiment joined the storm of battle, all those feelings were swept away: "I forgot where my heart was and had no desire to run; fear had been displaced by a savage instinct to inflict injury on the enemy." Crummer supposed that "battle affects men in different ways," but he and his fellows concluded that this "description of the feeling is about right." If the Illinoisans' experiences were typical, then a great many Civil War soldiers experienced during the frenzy of combat a willingness to injury—and even kill—the enemy.[25]

Many soldiers indeed experienced tremendous anxiety in the immediate anticipation of battle but found catharsis in firing their first shots at the enemy. Military historian Paddy Griffith explains that firing functioned as "a positive act" for Civil War soldiers that provided "a physical release for their emotions." After firing his "first shot in an open, stand-up battle" during the fight for Corinth, Samuel Byers of the 5th Iowa recalled, "I was burning up with excitement, too excited to be scared." At Chancellorsville, Rice C. Bull discovered that once he and his comrades from the 123rd New York opened fire, "the nervousness and fear we had when we began the fight passed away and a feeling of fearlessness and rage took its place." Describing how at Fredericksburg he and his fellow Mainers had blazed away at the Rebels' "puffs of smoke," Edward Simonton observed, "This opportunity to fire at something in the enemy's direction has the effect to give the soldier confidence in himself, even if his own fire does no material execution."[26]

Not all Civil War soldiers fought in a state of hyperactivity. Others experienced a kind of steely calm in the heat of battle. Having fought three bloody battles in as many weeks, Hugh Perkins of the 7th Wisconsin wrote to a friend shortly afterward, "I have had over one hundred good fair shots at the gray back and I have got so that I can shoot just as cool and deliberate at them as I can at a prairie chicken. . . . It has got so that it does not excite me any more to be in action than to be in a corn field hoeing, or digging potatoes." Washington Ives of the 4th Florida observed in a letter to his father, "I did not feel any different under fire than I did doing any other kind of work and I took 20 deliberate shots picking my man every time and one time saw the man fall but the others I could not see on account of my smoke." One of Ives's comrades even praised him as being able to "load and shoot the fastest and as cooly as any man that he ever saw."[27]

Union veteran Frank Holsinger described a similar steadiness when he recounted his own experience of battle in a postwar address called "How Does One Feel under Fire?" "The mind being engaged by a thousand circumstances, fear has been dissipated, and a sense of relief has taken its place," he noted. "I think I can truthfully say I was most comfortable under a most galling fire." Rather than being unnerved by the sight of comrades falling around him, Holsinger focused instead on fighting back: "The desire to get in your best licks is all you care for." Yet he also testified to experience exhilaration in combat, particularly when the fight seemed to go in the Federals' favor. As Holsinger recounted, "You yell, you swing your cap, you load and fire as long as the battle goes your way. . . . It is the supreme minute to you; you are in ecstasies."[28]

Still other Civil War soldiers experienced little or no exhilaration in combat—those men in the Federal and Confederate ranks who held strong reservations or opposition to killing in battle. Sergeant John G. Marsh of the 29th Ohio found that the nature of battle only temporarily overcame his pity for his slain Southern countrymen and his compunction against killing. "Poor fellows, I can't help pitying them if they are Rebels, for they have no doubt been deceived," he wrote his father after the First Battle of Kernstown. "In the excitement of battle I could aim at them when only forty or fifty yards away from me, as cooly as I ever did at a squirrel. But now it seems very much like murder." Marsh wrote on, describing the sight of the Confederate fallen and passionately decrying what he saw as the dehumanizing nature of taking life in war: "They would throw up their hands and fall almost every time we would get a fair shot at them, and we would laugh at their motions and make jest of their misfortune. I don't nor can't imagine now how we could do it. The fact is, in battle, man becomes a sinner and delights in the work of death. And if his best friend falls at his side he heeds it not, but presses on eager to engage in the wholesale murder."[29] For Sergeant Marsh, the excitement and urgency of battle only sustained him as long as battle lasted, leaving him to contemplate the human cost afterward.

For William L. Nugent, a lieutenant in the 28th Mississippi Cavalry, no thrill of battle could overcome his sadness at the lives taken. "You have frequently heard of the wild excitement of battle. I experience no such feelings," he wrote his wife, Nellie. "There is a sense of depression continually working away at my heart, caused by a knowledge of the great suffering in store for large numbers of my fellow men, that is entirely antagonistic to any other emotions." Though Nugent allowed that he shared in the pleasure of a victory won and a foe defeated, he insisted, "Still I cannot be happy as some men are in a fight," believing that "the whole machinery of war is indefensible on moral grounds."[30]

The cost of battle also fired many Civil War soldiers with the desire to kill the enemy. Numerous accounts describe how the sight of comrades being killed and wounded around them provoked them to exact lethal revenge from the foe. "The feeling that was uppermost in my mind was a desire to kill as many rebels as I could. The loss of comrades maddened me," Oliver Norton of the 83rd Pennsylvania wrote to his siblings after the Battle of Gaines Mill. "You say it seems hard to have so many killed," John Brobst wrote his sweetheart during the Atlanta Campaign. "So it does, but we have the pleasure of knowing that we can and will revenge our brother soldiers." During the same campaign, fellow Wisconsinite Chauncey Cooke described to his parents the sight of his companions on the firing line "crying like children . . . and cursing the rebels for killing their comrades."[31]

Avenging the deaths of their comrades motivated Confederates to kill as well. At Shiloh, William Bevens went to the aid of a fallen comrade. Temporarily attached to the Infirmary Corps, soldiers tasked with assisting the surgeons in providing basic medical care, Bevens tried to make his friend as comfortable as possible, only to realize that the man had been killed. The loss inspired the Arkansan to set aside his medical duties and return to a combat role. "I thought I would get revenge for my comrade," Bevens recalled in his memoirs, "so I levelled beside a tree, took good aim at a Yankee, and fired." The Confederate veteran did not record, if he knew, the result of his shot.[32]

Civil War companies and regiments were close-knit units, often recruited from the same city, hometown, or county. As such, their ranks often contained not only friends and neighbors but also family members—cousins, brothers, fathers, and sons. The killing or wounding of family members could especially incite soldiers to seek revenge in battle. Having seen his brother, George, killed in the charge up Missionary Ridge, Iowa soldier John Rath wrote that his "feelings . . . can easier be imagined than described." The intensity of such feelings extended to female family members as well, even if they could not fight as soldiers. Mary Callaway feared for the safety of her only brother fighting in Virginia, the family having received no news from him since his regiment's latest battle. "I feel all the time that I could fight bravely if I only knew how, and if they do kill my brother, think I will find out how," she wrote to her cousin, Joshua, an officer in the Army of Tennessee. "It seems to me revenge can-not be a sin in this war."[33]

In addition to the killing or wounding of comrades, physical harm to themselves at the hands of the enemy could also fuel soldiers' desire for revenge. Wounded at Pine Knob, 33rd New Jersey adjutant Stephen Pierson received from the regimental surgeon a generous drink of whiskey, which he had never consumed before. The combination of the liquor and his outrage at having been hit put Pierson in a bellicose mood: "I was *fighting mad*, and they tell me my one desire was to get out and kill the fellow who had shot me, and they had to detail a man to keep me from going out to do it." At the Battle of Cedar Mountain, a newspaper correspondent encountered an Ohio soldier who had had two fingers from his left hand shot off. After the reporter bandaged the maimed hand as best he could, the soldier told him, "Stranger, I wish you would just load up my shooting-iron for me; I want to have a little satisfaction out of them cusses for spiling my fore paw." The reported obliged him by reloading his weapon, after which the Buckeye "started back for the top of the hill at a double-quick, in quest of satisfaction."[34]

Setbacks less dire than deadly harm to themselves and their comrades could also provoke threats to seek revenge against the enemy. At times Civil War soldiers used vengeful rhetoric with varying degrees of seriousness or humor in times of frustration and annoyance. Yanks and Rebs regarded receiving their mail as a necessity almost as important as food, and few setbacks perturbed them as much as interference with the mail. When news arrived that the Confederates had intercepted their mail, an Ohio lieutenant wrote, "The boys would vow to take dire vengeance by putting extra bullets into their muskets the first time they had a chance." The misery of soldiering in the worst kinds of terrain and weather could also bring out a vengeful streak. Recounting a miserable night march on muddy roads and in driving rain, a captain from Georgia noted, "I thought on this march that I could ring the necks from every Yankee in existence if only I had a chance." After slogging their way through a South Carolina swamp in February 1865, cold and wet soldiers of the 10th Illinois swore that "they would show no quarters to any Rebs that might come in contact with them or fall at their mercy this night." If any soldier seemed deadly serious over a grievance with the enemy, it was Wisconsin soldier John Brobst, who wrote to his sweetheart, Mary, with palpable outrage over how the Confederates had captured his cherished photograph of her. "Lord, but I should to kill the one that has that picture if they have it yet," the aggrieved Badger told her in one letter. "I could kill him with a good heart and clear conscience."[35]

Personal revenge motivated some men to kill in battle, but not all. Sergeant Lyman Widney noted that at Ezra Church some of his comrades in the 34th Illinois took great satisfaction in having littered the field with Rebel bodies after bloodily repulsing a Confederate assault, remembering how the roles had been reversed at Kennesaw Mountain. Widney did not share their gratification. "In truth it is poor satisfaction to see hundreds of brave fellows stretched upon the bloody field, even if they do wear they gray," he insisted. Widney believed soldiers should be motivated by a noble cause and that wartime animosity should not preclude a sense of humanity for the foe: "We are not fighting for revenge that we should withhold sympathy for the wounded or respect and sorrow for the dead."[36]

In contrast to the soldiers who expressed positive or matter-of-fact attitudes toward killing, still others reacted with ambivalence or regret. In some cases this reflected their personal conviction against taking human life. Informing his father that "I fired my first shot at the enemy" at the Battle of Front Royal, Henry E. Handerson of the 9th Louisiana added, "I can, however, safely state that, if my shooting has not improved upon my first shot, my conscience is free of every stain of blood." Others rejected the propriety of killing the enemy when they grew disenchanted with their nation's cause. Richard Robert Crowe of the 32nd Wisconsin believed he had enlisted to fight for his country, but by summer 1864 he had grown frustrated with the war's progress and had cynically concluded that the fighting only profited vainglorious generals, scheming politicians, and radical abolitionists. "I used to think it was all for the country, and wanted a chance to kill something, but I find it is mostly a money making, avaricious, nigger-worshipping matter; only benefitting the ambition of a few, and causing needless suffering and misery all over the North," Crowe declared to his mother, "and now I would not of my own free will, fire a shot, or march forty rods for all the schemers, or abolitionists from Washington City to the 'Daily Life' office."[37]

Some Union and Confederate soldiers described with remarkable similarity an uncertainty of whether their shots fired in battle had done any harm and their hopes that they had not. Louisiana infantryman Thomas Benton Reed recalled how he took "three cracks" at a group of running Yankees "as thick as you ever saw blackbirds fly" during the first day's fighting at Gettysburg. "I don't know whether I killed one or not," Reed wrote in his memoirs, "but I hope I did not." Despite his efforts to improve his marksmanship, Bolivar Hulbert of New York felt ambivalent over the prospects of the shots he fired in battle killing someone. "I fired where I saw the gun flash of the enemy. Dont know whether [I] done good execution or not," he wrote his sister in late 1863. "I dont know as I care about knowing. I shall feel better if I do not know probably."[38]

Two different soldiers, one Confederate and one Federal, took comfort in the uncertainty of whether their shots killed, even as they admitted to themselves that their marksmanship skills made it likely that in fact they had. During the Battle of Resaca, Kentucky cavalryman John Will Dyer traded shots with a Union opponent. "Did you hit him?" Dyer asked himself in his postwar reminiscences. "Well, I am glad to say I don't know, but I had a good aim at short range and the Springfield rifle that I used had brought squirrels out of the highest trees for me and never missed a hog, running or standing, under 200 yards." Fighting in the very same battle, Union soldier Chauncey Cooke wrote his parents, "I emptied my cartridge box many times during the day as did the others. I saw men often drop after shooting, but didn't know that it was my bullet that did the work and really hope it was not," adding, "but you know that I am a good shot."[39]

At least three significant elements stand out from the accounts in the previous two paragraphs. First and most apparent, all four soldiers suggested or affirmed that they preferred not knowing whether they personally killed any of the enemy. Nor did their sentiments necessarily reflect only postwar attitudes of reconciliation between North and South. Confederate veterans Reed and Dyer expressed their reservations about killing in postwar reminiscences, yet Federals Hulbert and Cooke voiced the very same feelings in wartime letters to their families.

Second, conditions on the battlefield prevented each of them from positively knowing that their shots had struck any of the enemy. Although circumstantial evidence, such as seeing enemies fall after they fired or knowledge of their shooting skills, suggested that some of their shots may in fact have done "good execution," each of the last four men cited stressed that they did not positively know that they had killed.

Third, and perhaps most significant, each of these soldiers seems to have done his best to fire effectively at the enemy, despite preferring not to know if his shots had killed anyone. It would hardly be remarkable if a soldier who harbored reservations about killing intentionally misdirected his shots, yet the four ambivalent soldiers cited here stated or implied that they in effect were doing their best to fire effectively during battle. John Will Dyer described his encounter as "a duel with a Yankee" and noted how one of his opponent's bullets wounded him in the hip, throwing off his own aim. Chauncey Cooke and his comrades each fired over a hundred rounds in one desperate battle, and like Dyer he suggested that amid the desperate fighting, his skill with a rifle trumped his misgivings over taking lives. Together, such accounts suggest that many Civil War soldiers, even those who preferred not to know if they personally killed, could fight as effective battlefield killers in the danger and excitement of combat. Union soldier Hamlin Alexander Coe encapsulated this conflict between a soldier's feelings and his actions in combat when he wrote, "Now I am afraid I should shoot if I could see a Rebel."[40]

Other soldiers held even stronger compunctions against killing and as a result tried to direct their shots so as not to hit anyone. At Gettysburg, Corporal Henry Meyer of the 148th Pennsylvania noticed a young soldier behind him "sitting flat on the ground and discharging his piece in the air at an angle of forty-five degrees, as fast as he could load." When Meyer asked why he was shooting in the air, "To scare 'em" was the answer he received. "He was a pious young man," the Pennsylvanian explained, "and the true reason why he did not shoot at the enemy direct, was because of his conscientious scruples on the subject."[41]

Val Giles of the Texas Brigade recorded similar behavior at Chickamauga, observing one of his comrades "shooting straight up in the air and praying as lustily as ever one of Cromwell's Roundheads prayed." A lieutenant in the company tried to correct his aim, but the soldier ignored him. Next his captain "threatened to cut him down with his sword if he didn't shoot at the enemy, for the woods in front were full of them." The wayward shooter defiantly retorted, "You can kill me if you want to, but I am not going to appear before my God with the blood of my fellow man on my soul." The soldier's refusal to kill did not diminish his physical courage, Giles observed admiringly, recalling how the man "never flinched, but stood squarely up, exposed to every volley of the enemy's fire."[42]

These incidents at Gettysburg and Chickamauga reveal the challenge a soldier who refused to try to kill posed in a Civil War army. In a firefight, company officers were responsible for steadying their men and directing their fire, and in both instances, it stood out as irregular. In the latter case, two officers stepped in to try to adjust the soldier's shooting. In some cases, officers and file closers threatened to shoot or cut down men who ran from the firing line, and notably among the Texans, Giles's company commander made the same threat to the soldier who refused to shoot to kill. Given how many Civil War soldiers described how they themselves tried to fire effectively in battle, whether they did so aggressively, dutifully, or reluctantly, many enlisted men may also have resented a comrade who deliberately wasted his salvos. In battle, the lethality of a battle line's musketry could often prove the difference between victory and defeat—even between life and death. During the fierce fighting at Chickamauga, the Texans clearly felt hard-pressed, with the woods to their front filled with Yankees, so it is little wonder that the company officers would exhort their men to make every shot count.

My research for this study has turned up few examples of soldiers describing their comrades deliberately wasting their shots; I was unable to find a soldier who explicitly admitted that in the heat of battle he deliberately tried not to kill. The fact that such actions might have carried a strong stigma, since a soldier who tried to fight nonlethally was ostensibly doing less than his duty, may account for the scarcity of such accounts. On the other hand, the lack of evidence may well indicate that Civil War soldiers who in combat tried to shoot without killing represented a distinct minority.

Other soldiers shot to kill in combat despite feeling that such killing was tragic. Confederates at Fredericksburg had an easy time shooting down waves of Union attackers, but Private David E. Holt of the 16th Mississippi found it a sad duty. "I never enjoyed the sport of shooting at men," he explained. "There was no spirit of murder in my heart." Nevertheless, the necessity of driving back the "invading Yankee infantry" inspired Holt to fight as effectively as he could: "I pigeon-holed my sentiments and shot for keeps." One wonders if the Mississippian as a reluctant killer felt like an outlier among his comrades. Unlike Holt, did the majority of his fellow soldiers revel in "the sport of shooting at men"? Whatever the case, Holt's account suggests that some Civil War soldiers could commit themselves to the work of killing in battle—"shooting for keeps"—even if they took no joy in the work.[43]

Grossman suggests in *On Killing* that more Civil War soldiers tried to avoid killing than they themselves admitted on the basis of two key sources of evidence. First, he looks to the evidence provided by the 27,574 muskets the US Army recovered from the Gettysburg battlefield. Among these weapons, the Ordnance Department found that about 12,000 (approximately 43.5 percent) had improperly been loaded with more than one charge of powder and ball. Furthermore, 6,000 of those weapons (approximately 22 percent of the total) contained three to ten rounds. Civil War historians traditionally attributed these improperly loaded weapons to lack of training and nervousness among soldiers. Presumably the men wielding these muskets had either forgotten to prime their weapons or failed to notice that they were misfiring, and thus they had rammed round after round down the barrel instead of successfully discharging them. Grossman, however, insists, "The obvious conclusion is that most soldiers were *not* trying to kill the enemy." Because commissioned and noncommissioned officers tried to monitor soldiers' aim in the line of battle (as Giles's Chickamauga account illustrates), Grossman reasons, "If a man truly was not able or willing to fire, the only way he could disguise his lack of participation was to load his weapon . . . bring it to his shoulder, and then *not actually fire,* possibly even mimicking the recoil of his weapon when someone nearby fired." If true, then ostensibly Civil War soldiers were declining to fully participate in combat in ways comparable to S. L. A. Marshall's 75 to 85 percent of World War II GIs who supposedly would not fire their weapons in battle.[44]

Second, Grossman cites the apparently slow rate of killing on Civil War battlefields as further proof that large numbers of Union and Confederate soldiers avoided killing in battle. He accurately corrects popular misconceptions that at the bloody Battle of Cold Harbor, Union attackers suffered between 7,000 and 13,000 casualties in the first eight minutes of fighting. While Confederate firepower did manage to thwart many of the assaults within those first minutes, in point of fact Union forces suffered 7,000 casualties during the course of eight hours of fighting on June 3, 1864, not eight minutes. Because it took so much longer to inflict these casualties than popularly supposed, Grossman believes this reflects a widespread reluctance to kill among Civil War soldiers and other fighting men through the ages:

> The simple fact appears to be that, like S. L. A. Marshall's riflemen of World War II, the vast majority of rifle- and musket-armed soldiers of previous wars were consistent and persistent in their psychological inability to kill their fellow human beings. Their weapons were technologically capable, and they were physically quite able to kill, but at the decisive moment each soldier found that, in his heart, he could not bring himself to kill the man standing before him.[45]

But do these conclusions in *On Killing*, a book whose primary research derives mainly from twentieth-century soldiers, actually reflect the attitudes of Union and Confederate soldiers toward killing?

The suggestion that soldiers loaded and reloaded their muskets without firing in order to disguise their lack of participation does not convincingly explain what Grossman calls the "dilemma of the discarded weapons." This hardly would have been the most practical way of abstaining from killing in battle. Granted, it would be foolish to assume that all men under the extraordinary stress of combat always behave rationally, but this particular explanation strains credibility. If a soldier loaded more than one round in his muzzleloading weapon, the ramrod would stick out higher and higher as charges of bullets and powder stacked up inside the barrel, potentially alerting a watchful officer to the problem. Furthermore, if the soldier emerged from the fighting unscathed, he would have to remedy the problem of his improperly loaded weapon before the next weapons inspection, either by laboriously extracting the bullets from the gun bore or exchanging his weapon for an empty one from the battlefield. True, this latter option would help account for the high number of misloaded weapons on Civil War battlefields, yet in a chaotic, fluid battle like Gettysburg, this was not necessarily a luxury on which the soldier could rely. If a soldier did want to disguise the fact that he was not shooting to kill, it would have been far easier for him to load his musket with only powder (as participants in today's reenactments and living history events do), discard the bullet, prime, and actually fire the blank charge. This, or deliberately firing live rounds over the heads of the enemy, as some killing-averse soldiers did, would have been a much more practical and convincing subterfuge than ramming down extra rounds and only mimicking the act of firing.

Conventional explanations account more convincingly for the multiplicity of discarded weapons with multiple rounds in the barrel. A nervous or insufficiently trained soldier could quite plausibly forget to prime his weapon with a percussion cap and thus continue to cram more and more rounds down his barrel without successfully firing. Modern warrior science tells us that the stress of combat and exhaustion can impair physical coordination, so that a Civil War combatant, even if satisfactorily trained, could experience a breakdown in his ability to load and fire. Once an individual's heart rate reaches 115 beats per minute, fine motor skills (necessary for handling a small percussion cap) begin to diminish. At 145 beats per minute and beyond, complex motor skills deteriorate, which could impair other physical motions in the loading process.[46] Moreover, while the percussion weapons of the Civil War were far less susceptible to misfire than the flintlocks of previous generations, the buildup of fouling from burned black powder could still interfere with firing. If the weapon clogged somewhere in the vent between the gun's breech and the cone where a percussion cap fit, a soldier might cap his musket and still fail to discharge his round. If the soldier could not tell that his weapon failed to fire amid the smoke and noise of his comrades firing around him, then he could unintentionally continue to load multiple rounds down the barrel.

What about the argument that casualties accrued slowly during Civil War battles because many of the combatants were trying *not* to kill? Soldiers themselves knew of the vast gap between the great many shots fired and the relatively few men hit by them. It took a man's weight in lead to kill in battle, so a saying among the blue and gray went. Chauncey Cooke imagined an even higher ratio, assuring his mother "that it takes ten ton of iron and lead to kill one soldier." Nevertheless, Civil War soldiers could be impressed by the lethality of their own firepower, sometimes even exaggerating the results. When his regiment poured a deadly volley into a mounted charge by Rebel cavalry at Pleasant Hill, one Illinois soldier wrote, "I will guarantee not 50 got back to their friends alive." Numerous accounts describe particularly effective and deadly volleys, both on the delivering and receiving ends. Such accounts suggest that numerous Civil War soldiers believed that a great many men on the battlefield were both trying to kill and succeeding.[47]

The notion that many Civil War combatants, perhaps even a majority, were doing their best not to kill one another would likely have surprised many of the soldiers themselves, especially at fiercely contested battles such as Gettysburg. Val Giles did not recall a reluctance to kill among the men engaged in the epic three-day clash. Instead, "there seemed to be a viciousness in the very air we breathed." Remembering the bitter contest for Little Round Top, he wrote:

Our spiritual advisers, chaplains of regiments, were in the rear, caring for the wounded and dying soldiers. With seven devils to each man, it was no place for a preacher, anyhow. A little red paint and a few eagle feathers were all that was necessary to make that crowd on both sides into the most veritable savages on earth. White-winged peace didn't roost at Little Round Top that night! There was not a man there that cared a snap for the golden rule, or that could have remembered one line of the Lord's Prayer. Both sides were whipped, and all were furious about it.[48]

From Giles's description, the Union and Confederate soldiers vying for Little Round Top seem less like reluctant killers and more like novelist Michael Shaara's "killer angels."

One of the strongest apparent sources of evidence for Civil War soldiers avoiding killing is their well-documented penchant for firing too high. Numerous times musket fire sailed harmlessly over soldiers' heads. Some units recorded surviving enemy volleys that were aimed too high. Observers on battlefields found tree trunks and branches well above a man's height shredded by bullets.[49] Officers tried strenuously to correct the soldiers' aim; in battle, men in authority from noncommissioned officers to generals repeatedly exhorted the men, "Aim low!" For soldiers reluctant or refusing to take human lives, firing over the enemies' heads was a relatively simple way to avoid killing. Moreover, accounts such as those from Henry Meyer and Val Giles confirm that some soldiers on both sides intentionally aimed high for this very reason.

Unwillingness to kill is one documented reason for soldiers overshooting in the Civil War, but it is not the only reason. Several additional reasons also account for why soldiers, including those who were ostensibly trying to use their weapons effectively against the enemy, sometimes fired too high in battle. The nature of Civil War ballistics contributed to overshooting. Most rifle muskets were sighted for a minimum 100 yards' range. Theoretically a rifle musket with accurately set sights (and without raising the rear sight) would shoot to point of aim at 100 yards. As with any other projectile, the rifle ball would have to travel upward in an arc to counteract the pull of gravity in order to hit point of aim. Many Civil War firefights took place within 100 yards, so this parabola could potentially create a safe zone in which a bullet from a rifle musket fired at shoulder level could pass harmlessly over the target. Officers tried to compensate for this effect by urging their men to aim low—not at shoulder height but at the beltline or knees of the enemy.

Various kinds of human error also account for soldiers unintentionally shooting over the heads of the enemy. Several factors made it a natural tendency for Civil War soldiers to aim too high. For an individual trying to shoot to kill, the head and torso make effective, high-value points of aim. Modern pistol training for military, law enforcement, and self-defense typically emphasizes aiming for center of mass on the torso for the dual purposes of increasing the chances of hitting and incapacitating a human target. This, however, applies to handguns sighted in for close-range firing, not to rifle muskets sighted in for 100 yards or more. In order to compensate at close range for his weapon's high point of aim, a Civil War soldier would have to heed his officers' instructions to aim low, somewhat below center of mass. If he ignored those instructions and instead intuitively aimed at an enemy's head or upper torso, and if he did so at a range closer than 100 yards, then he might well overshoot his human target.

Excitement and nervousness could also offset a soldier's aim. The closer the range and the more desperate the circumstances, the more important volume of fire became over accuracy. "All stood together to shoot and be shot," a Michigan officer wrote of the bloody fighting at Antietam. "The one that could load and fire the fastest did the rebs the most damage." A musket-armed soldier in a stand-up firefight could afford to simply point his weapon at the enemy and fire rather than take precise aim—that is, so long as he pointed it reasonably well at the enemy. A regular army lieutenant at First Manassas complained, "Our men fired badly; they were excited, and some of the recruits fired at the stars."[50] The same physical breakdown in coordination and concentration that could cause a soldier to improperly load his weapon could also impair his ability to aim effectively. A Civil War soldier armed with a muzzleloader loaded his weapon with the barrel pointed upward, and thus he always had to bring the muzzle downward to bear on a target at his own level. Overshooting could be as simple a matter as failing to lower the barrel sufficiently before firing—a motion requiring only a fraction more time and effort, but one that could make all the difference between a lethal or a harmless shot.

A soldier desperately trying to load and fire as fast as possible could in his haste easily waste his shot by firing his weapon while it was still aimed upward or at shoulder level rather than aiming for the beltline or lower. Sometimes this occurred among soldiers fighting behind cover, opting to fire hastily over their defenses instead of exposing their upper bodies a fraction longer by taking careful aim. Pickett's Charge survivor Frank Nelson, a lieutenant in the 56th Virginia, believed that this was why so many of his comrades managed to close with the defenders on Cemetery Ridge: "If the

[Union] infantry behind the stone wall had fired properly not a single Confederate would have reached it. To take aim a man had to lift his head above that structure which meant almost sure death."[51]

When it came to Civil War soldiers' attitudes toward shooting and killing, their choices amounted to more than either shooting to kill or deliberately firing so as not to kill. One of Dave Grossman's most substantial contributions to our understanding of the psychology of Civil War combat is to suggest a third option: posturing. In Grossman's usage, posturing refers to aggressive behavior that seeks to intimidate the enemy but falls short of possible life-and-death combat—behavior that we see extensively among both humans and members of the animal kingdom. The use of gunpowder weapons, he suggests, granted soldiers "superior *posturing* ability" because their noise and muzzle flashes could help intimidate an approaching foe. For the soldier on the firing line, posturing could mean firing in the general direction of the enemy rather than taking deliberate aim. In this sense, the act of firing could reflect soldiers' desire simply to drive away the enemy rather than kill.[52]

Numerous cases of Civil War soldiers' conduct in battle seem to reflect Grossman's concept of posturing. Perhaps the most apparent examples occurred in the fighting at Spotsylvania and Franklin, battles in which Union and Confederate soldiers found themselves shooting at one another from the opposite sides of the same wall of earthworks. Because of the intense volume of fire and the uncomfortably close proximity to the enemy, many infantrymen simply pointed their weapons up and over the works, firing blindly overhead rather than exposing themselves by aiming. In such cases, soldiers' obvious intent was to keep the enemy at bay with volume of fire over accuracy. Other instances reflect the notion of posturing behavior in battle. At Gettysburg, with his 71st Pennsylvania blazing away at the oncoming assault by Pickett's Division, Colonel Richard Penn Smith took up a musket and fired several rounds at the attackers. Smith's rationale for taking a hand in the firing reads like a textbook definition of posturing in combat: "I fancied that if I could at least, Chinese-like, scare [them] with noise, and I might, by accident, hit a gray-coat." From the colonel's account, it is unclear what exactly he meant by shooting a Confederate "by accident." Did Smith mean he was genuinely not trying to kill anyone, or (perhaps more likely) was he speaking deprecatingly of his chances of hitting anyone in the smoke and confusion at Gettysburg's "Bloody Angle"?[53]

Repeating rifles offered soldiers still greater posturing ability than single-shot weapons. Weapons with multishot magazines meant a soldier could send bullets downrange faster and more recklessly than if he was armed with a rifle or musket capable only of being loaded and fired one shot at a time. Modern military and law enforcement tactics take advantage of this rapid fire capability, including laying down covering fire intended to suppress an opponent through sheer volume of shots fired. Conversely, in modern parlance, a shooter who empties his magazine too quickly and indiscriminately is said to be engaging in "spray and pray." In dire situations, repeater-armed soldiers often fired as fast as they could work the levers of their advanced weapons. John M. King of the Lightning Brigade, a force of mounted infantry armed with seven-shot Spencer rifles, described a desperate skirmish in Alabama between his own 92nd Illinois and "a whole brigade of rebel cavalry." The Prairie Staters "peppered away" at the enemy, King remembered. "The only thing we thought of was how much we could shoot. Co. F came to our side and pumped with all their might and Co. I from every tree, stump, or brush did its very best. It was not a volley but a continued roll from our repeating Spencers."[54]

In contrast to the men who took solace in the uncertainty of whether their shots hit anyone, other soldiers after a battle actually sought out the bodies of enemies whom they believed they had killed. For some of these men, this reflected a desire to confirm that they had successfully killed. For others, taking a man's life represented a strange new reality, and curiosity drove them to put a face to the enemy they had slain. After Second Manassas, Marion Hill Fitzpatrick of the 45th Georgia proudly wrote to his wife, "I went to where I fired last and three of the devils were lying there." For good measure, Fitzpatrick claimed "a good yankee zinc canteen," which he happily found was nearly full. At Antietam, O. T. Hanks of the Texas Brigade spied a Union soldier sheltered behind some fence rails about thirty yards away. "I had a good gun and drew directly at his breast," the Texan recounted. "I thought to myself, 'If we whip [I] am going to see if I killed you.'" Hanks's comrades often said they never knew for sure if their shots had killed, and Hanks wanted to be sure. Just then, however, a bullet clipped him under the left arm, exiting under the shoulder, requiring the Texan to head to the rear for a field hospital.[55]

Among Union soldiers, some men described similar searches to find the men they had shot, like hunters tracking down their kills. During the assault on the Confederate fort at Arkansas Post, John S. B. Matson, a corporal in the 120th Ohio, managed to pick off one of the defenders. "I loaded and looked, and saw a curl of smoke and as he raised to fire, I fired and there was no smoke coming from that place," he recorded in a letter. Matson felt no remorse over the kill, matter-of-factly writing, "If my ball killed I have no regrets, for I never took more deliberate aim at a woodpecker." After the fort's capture, the Buckeye corporal "had the curiosity to go in where I saw the smoke curl, and found a Reb shot in the forehead. He had a bad wound, but didn't look as though it hurt him much." Like Fitzpatrick, Matson also took a valuable trophy from his kill. Appropriately enough for a man of Matson's marksmanship skills, he collected the fallen Rebel's weapon: "He had dropped a very nice Enfield rifle, which I captured and have yet."[56]

At the Battle of Piedmont in the Shenandoah Valley, a soldier in the 34th Massachusetts, like Matson, managed to bring down a Confederate and subsequently find the body, but this Bay Stater felt more mixed emotions than did his counterpart from Ohio. During the fighting, he spotted a Rebel kneeling and shooting behind a large pine tree less than a hundred yards away. Seeing the man taking aim, the soldier turned to his captain "and told him that I'd just bet I could spoil his aim for him. He was just bringing his gun to his shoulder in our direction; the captain said he didn't believe I could hit him. I took good aim and fired. The Johnny fell over backwards." Union forces subsequently drove the Confederates from the field, and in the advance, the Bay Stater came across that man he had killed: "As we passed the big pine tree, I saw my Reb lying there with a bullet through his head. I felt sorry for the poor fellow and to ease my conscience as much as possible, and went to work and did all in my power to relive the sufferings of the poor fellows who laid wounded around among the trees." The soldier's chagrin contrasted with the enthusiasm and belligerence he had shown earlier in the fight. He described the battle as "just the prettiest fighting you ever saw," and, before his lethal shot, had targeted another enemy soldier, "a great six foot Reb behind a tree." He had stealthily approached the Rebel and "had just got the best bead on him you ever saw" when his quarry spotted him and quickly surrendered to another nearby Federal. On that occasion, the Bay Stater had "felt quite disappointed to be cheated out of my shot for I was sure of him." Later, having successfully killed another Confederate, seeing the dead man up close apparently cooled his ardor, and he sought instead to aid the enemy wounded.[57]

One of the key factors that influenced how bearable Civil War soldiers found killing in combat was their physical proximity to the enemy. Grossman theorizes that soldiers experience progressively less resistance to killing the greater their physical distance from the enemy and the easier the actual means of killing. In such instances, physical distance from the enemy makes it harder to discern the lethal effect of their weapons, thus psychologically distancing them from the reality of killing. For most Civil War soldiers, the most agreeable kind of combat they could experience was fighting behind stout defenses with the enemy approaching them in the open like so many targets in a shooting gallery. Although Federals and Confederates found combat more bearable the further they were able to keep the enemy away, their accounts suggest that it was the threat to their own lives that stressed them far more than the certainty that they were killing the enemy. Captain Samuel T. Foster described the ease which his fellow Texans defended a portion of Missionary Ridge from Union attackers, writing, "Now we give them fits. See how they do fall, like leaves in the fall of the year. . . . *Oh this is fun to lie here and shoot them down and we not get hurt.*"[58]

Contrast Captain Foster's carefree account with the ordeal of Sam Watkins and his comrades in the 1st Tennessee defending the slopes of Kennesaw Mountain. Watkins's regiment found itself holding the Dead Angle, a portion of the Confederate line that became a focal point for Federal assaults. The Tennesseans desperately fought off determined Union attackers. "It seemed impossible to check the onslaught," Watkins remembered. As with Foster's Texans, there was no doubt among Watkins and his comrades that they were killing the enemy: "I have heard men say that if they ever killed a Yankee during the war they were not aware of it. I am satisfied that on this memorable day, every man in our regiment killed from one score to four score, yea, five score men. . . . All that was necessary was to load and shoot."[59]

Watkins described the defense of the Dead Angle as desperate, and therefore stressful, not because his regiment killed so many Yankees but because they had to fight so frantically just to survive and because, unlike Foster's men, they found themselves in considerable danger from the Union onslaught. According to Watkins, "There was not a single man in the company who was not wounded, or had holes shot through his hat and clothing." The Confederate memoirist recounted his own life-or-death encounter on the Kennesaw line in breathless detail: "I had just discharged the contents of my gun into the bosoms of two men, one right behind the other, killing them both, and was reloading, when a Yankee rushed upon me, having me at a disadvantage, and said, 'You have killed my two brothers, and now I have got you.' Everything I had ever done flashed through my mind. I heard the roar, and felt the flash of fire." Sam Watkins was not hit. Instead, he saw William A. Hughes, his dearest friend in the regiment, grab the muzzle and pull it toward himself, receiving a mortal wound in the act of saving his comrade's life. "Reader, he died for me," Watkins wrote feelingly. "In saving my life, he lost his own." What burned into Sam Watkins's memory on Kennesaw Mountain was not the sight of Union soldiers killed by the shots he fired. It was the terror of staring down the barrel of a vengeful Yankee's rifle, and the shock of seeing his brother-in-arms take a bullet meant for him.[60]

Physical distance was not the only factor that made killing easier on a Civil War battlefield. Some men found that a retreating enemy also offered an inviting target. For a soldier, an enemy who had turned his back, like a distant enemy, was easy to kill partly because he represented a low-risk target, one who was less able to fight back. Other psychological factors also explain why retreating soldiers offered easy kills. Grossman observes, "It is when the bayonet charge has forced one side's soldiers to turn their backs and flee that the killing truly begins, and at some visceral level the soldier intuitively understands this and is very, very frightened when he has to turn his back to the enemy." This is hardly a recent military insight, he points out. Carl von Clausewitz and Ardant du Picq "both expound at length" how in battles throughout history the greatest casualties tended to be inflicted during the victors' pursuit of a broken enemy. Two probable factors contribute to this proclivity to kill a fleeing enemy. The first Grossman identifies as the "chase instinct," evidenced among all predatory animals that literally close in for the kill in pursuit of fleeing prey. Second, because both physical and emotional distance from the target make killing easier, Grossman explains that a human target whose back is turned is dehumanized in the eyes of a human assailant: "The eyes are the window of the soul, and if one does not have to look into the eyes when killing, it is much easier to deny the humanity of the victim."[61]

Soldiers' accounts confirm that some Federals and Confederates did indeed find a fleeing enemy to be easy prey. At Antietam, the Iron Brigade's 7th Wisconsin managed to come up behind a brigade of Louisianans and began firing killing volleys into their ranks. Hugh Perkins described how he and his fellow Badgers continued to mercilessly gun down the Rebels, even once they began running for their lives: "Then we had fun picking them off. We might have taken them all prisoners, but we wasn't in for that. We killed every one of them; even a wounded man could not be seen creeping off without being plugged by a minie. They refused to surrender to us, but they had to our minie balls." At the Battle of Franklin, Confederate soldiers had a chance to kill a retreating enemy on an even grander scale. Two Union brigades had been foolishly positioned forward of the main Union defenses, and two Confederate corps slammed into this salient, sending the defenders stampeding back to their comrades. Veteran Confederate troops, realizing they now had a golden opportunity to cross the deadly ground behind a human shield of Yankee refugees, shouted to one another, "Go into the works with them!" Captain Joseph Boyce of Cockrell's Missouri Brigade described how "we crossed the enemy's advance line of rifle pits, raised the glorious old yell, and rushed upon the main works a frantic, maddened body with overpowering impulse to reach the enemy and kill, murder, destroy." Kill the enemy they did, recorded Samuel Foster of Texas, "yelling like fury and shooting at them at the same time."[62]

The behavior of officers offers another example of Civil War soldiers' willingness to kill. Theoretically, a commissioned officer's place when his unit was trading volleys with the enemy was behind the firing line overseeing his men, yet a number of officers, either out of sheer excitement or in desperate situations, took up weapons and joined their men in firing at the enemy. This behavior suggests a departure from the example of officers in most European armies of the day. In an age of professionalized armies, officers began exercising more command and control and in turn taking less combative roles. Historian John Keegan tells of a British officer in the defense of the Hougoumont at Waterloo who held his sergeant's musket while the latter helped reinforce one of the gates. When a French grenadier began climbing over the gate, the officer handed back the musket to the sergeant, who in turn shot the grenadier.[63]

Civil War officers seemed to have shown less reluctance to fight like common soldiers than their European counterparts. Samuel Buck told of a close-range fight in which he, then a lieutenant in the 13th Virginia, "picked up a gun *as was my custom* and shot at an officer only a few yards from me who fell killed or wounded, back into the works." Later, during a skirmish in the 1864 Shenandoah Valley Campaign, he borrowed a rifle and engaged a Union sharpshooter in a long-range duel. At Antietam, Captain James Cooper Nisbet of the 21st Georgia picked up a rifle from a fallen soldier and fired the remaining rounds in his cartridge box. Nisbet noted that this marked "the only time I fired a rifle at anyone during the war, except at Kennesaw Mountain." Normally in a close-quarters fight, he explained, he relied on his Colt Navy revolver. Captain Eugene Blackford of the 5th Alabama carried his own Sharps carbine into battle and even "bagged a man or two occasionally," even though he admitted that "my time could have been bettered employed in caring for my men, and making them shoot." When William Pitt Chambers was promoted to ordnance sergeant in the 46th Mississippi, he remained an enlisted man, but the position meant not going into battle with his company. Chambers successfully petitioned to be returned to his old duties, and thus, "I gave up my sword and resumed a gun, feeling much better equipped for killing Yankees."[64]

A number of Union officers demonstrated the same proclivity for stepping into the battle line and fighting with a musket like their men. During one battle in the Peninsula Campaign, the 44th New York found itself hard pressed by a Confederate attack. Lieutenant Colonel James C. Rice, commanding the regiment, reported, "Most of the officers during the engagement used the muskets of the dead and wounded with great effect, which added great courage to the men." During the Union attacks at Fredericksburg, the untried 7th Rhode Island went to ground in a swale in the face of Confederate fire. To steady his men, Colonel Zenas Bliss took up a musket, stood up amid the bullets zipping all around, and traded shots with the Rebels, actions for which he received the Medal of Honor years later. During the morning phase of the Battle of Cedar Creek, Union soldiers once again found themselves on the defensive, this time trying to stem a gray and butternut tide pouring out of a dense fog. As soldiers from two Union corps desperately loaded and fired, a "great many line and staff officers took muskets, and lay down in the ranks of the men, while all mounted officers used their holster revolvers," noted the 116th Ohio's regimental history. Among those officers, Captain Daniel C. Knowlton of the nearby 114th New York "was instantly killed in the foremost in the fight, loading and fighting among his men."[65]

Civil War soldiers experienced changes over the course of their military services that inured them to killing in battle. Multiple accounts describe how many Federals and Confederates became desensitized to the sight of dead and wounded bodies on the battlefield, the very products of killing in combat. Veterans who looked back over their service understood that they had changed over time through their exposure to death and killing. Lyman Widney recalled in his memoirs how he and his comrades, trudging through the mud, came across the remains of a Rebel soldier. Men ahead of them had obviously used the body as a stepping stone, "but our party was not yet sufficiently hardened to so use it." Later, Widney lamented how individual deaths came to lose a sense of import: "Alas, that human life is held so cheap that we scarcely make note of its loss unless the victims are numbered by the hundreds." Other veterans found a kind of black humor in their nonchalance toward body counts. Marching toward the escalating battle around Gettysburg, members of Berdan's Sharpshooters encountered Pennsylvania citizens fleeing the fighting, including a distraught woman who informed them that "they are fighting terribly up there. There's two men killed in our back pasture." To her surprise, the remark drew hoots of laughter from the seasoned veterans. "Two men killed would not fit the bill for terrible fighting," Sergeant Wyman White wrote, "and the woman's answer was a byword among the boys to the end of the war."[66]

A number of soldiers described their exposure to killing and death in terms of desensitization. "I have had my feelings awfully hardened since my eighteenth birthday," nineteen-year-old Eugene Kingman from Maine wrote his father. "I can look on now and see a man killed and not stir me a bit." The process of hardening began early in the men's service as soldiers. In a letter to his brother back home in Georgia, First Sergeant A. Campbell McPherson told how the rout of Union forces at First Manassas had left the victorious Confederates with the task of burying the Yankee dead and tending to their wounded. "Such scenes were at first sickening," he wrote, "but they were so numerous that we soon got 'used to it.'" John Casler, a veteran of the Stonewall Brigade, concluded that "war has a demoralizing effect upon the soldier," as he "becomes familiar with scenes of death and carnage, and what at first shocks him greatly he afterwards comes to look upon as a matter of course." Notably, Casler uses the term "demoralizing" not in the modern sense of detracting from the soldier's morale but rather, in an older sense, from his morals. Specifically, he referred to the practice among some soldiers of looting the bodies of enemy dead, explaining, "It was difficult for a soldier to figure out why a gold watch or money in the pocket of a dead soldier, who had been trying to kill him all day, did not belong to the man who found it as much as it did to anyone else."[67]

A host of factors—duty, comradeship, self-defense, adrenaline—sustained Civil War soldiers during the heat of battle. Once battle ceased and the guns fell silent, however, they were confronted with the end results of combat—the reality of killing, death, and carnage on the battlefield. It was in their reactions to the aftermath of battle that many combatants expressed, quite understandably, their most negative attitudes toward death, killing, and war. "O it is a dredful si[gh]t to he[a]r the moaning of the wounded and to see the men shot down all around you," Pressley Boyd wrote his father in South Carolina, even though during battle itself "a man has no time to think nor look at outhers." Confederate artillery officer S. H. Dent, having witnessed the hanging of "sixteen Yankee bushwhackers," lamented, "This is certainly the most horrible war the world has ever seen."[68]

Other Confederates like Dent found themselves able to pity the Union dead, even Yankees they themselves had helped kill. At Fredericksburg, General James Longstreet surveyed the killing ground before his position on Marye's Heights and declared that even if the entire Army of the Potomac attacked, "I will kill them all before they reach my line." No Union soldier did reach his line. Instead they piled up in mounds of dead and dying men, moving Longstreet to describe the terrible spectacle as "one of the most distressing I ever witnessed." Viewing the same slaughter, his commander, Robert E. Lee, famously professed, "It is well this is so terrible!

We should grow too fond of it!" Similar sentiments could also be found among the rank and file of Lee's army at the same battle. "As I witnessed one line swept away by one fearful blast from Kershaw's men behind the stone wall," wrote Virginia private Alexander Hunter, "I forgot they were enemies and only remembered that they were men, and it is hard to see in cold blood brave men die." Lieutenant Charles S. Powell of the 24th North Carolina likewise observed, "They were brave men and it looked like a pity to kill them."[69]

Union soldiers similarly lamented the destruction of human life. "It is awful to see this fine country the scene of such terrible slaughter," a New York soldier wrote his sister the day after Antietam, the war's deadliest one-day battle. "I wish this war was over," Pennsylvania soldier John Gould wrote his father in the midst of the bloody Overland Campaign, "For the sights a fellow sees and what he has to go through is enough to sicken any-one of a soldiers life." The men who wore the blue could likewise empa-thize with their fallen enemies in gray. Early in his service, Lyman Widney found himself unnerved by the sight of the Confederate dead at night. "It was not the time or the place to find consolation in the belief that I was in the right and they in the wrong," the Illinois veteran recalled. "A multitude of the dead, if given voice, would denounce me as an invader of their land, accessory to their death."[70]

A number of soldiers specifically mourned that theirs was a civil war that saw Americans slaying fellow Americans. "Three years ago we was the most prosperous nation on the globe all nations looked up to us," Wis-consin soldier Michael Cunningham wrote his wife in 1863, "and now we are fighting and killing one another as fast as we can and the other Nations laugh at us for doing it." Contemplating "the horrors of war," Hamlin Coe recorded in his diary, "Will God forgive men for such work is a question I often ask myself, but I receive a silent reply and utter my own prayers for the safety of my poor soul and my country." As his regiment went into action at Fredericksburg, the attentions of Private Benjamin Borton of the 24th New Jersey also ranged heavenward: "O, I thought, why this shedding of blood? Why should brother take his brother's life?" The twenty-year-old soldier "instinctively cast a look upward to see if I could not behold a winged messenger of peace," but none appeared, and the battle raged on.[71]

Some soldiers recorded more ambivalent attitudes toward the enemy dead. After his capture at Jonesboro, Orphan Brigade soldier Johnny Green saw the scores of Union wounded at their own field hospitals and "could not help feeling sorrow as well as satisfaction when I beheld the work we had made for the surgeons." Alexander Thain of the 96th Illinois recorded similar mixed feelings when he surveyed the killing ground at Franklin, site of a terrible bloodletting for his foes in the Army of Tennessee. "The battlefield . . . was truely a sad and at the same time a glorious sight," he wrote in January 1865. "It was sad to see so many graves for although they were rebels still they were men," Thain explained, adding, "but it was glorious to see the evidences of so great a victory."[72]

Though many Civil War soldiers lamented the human destruction of the battles they fought, a number of them stated or implied that it was primarily the men from their own side for whom they mourned, and less so those of the enemy. When Illinois veteran James Sexton addressed his brother Union officers regarding the Battle of Franklin, he declared the deaths of "hosts of brave souls" to be "a bitter wrong, a monstrous injustice," but Sexton spoke specifically of those given "a scanty burial by rebel hands," not the Rebels themselves. Likewise, the "butchery" at Franklin haunted Confederate memoirist Sam Watkins, who wished "to God I could tear the page from these memoirs and from my own memory." As with Sexton, however, when Watkins mourned the "brave and gallant heroes" who fell, he spoke only of those from his own side.[73]

The loss of their comrades in battle could prompt both Federals and Confederates to, as Abraham Lincoln phrased it, "take increased devotion to that cause for which they gave the last full measure of devotion." Some soldiers, however, voiced their devotion to fallen comrades in terms harsher and more vindictive than had Lincoln in his address at Gettysburg. John Brobst, who in a later letter described "the pleasure of knowing that we can and will revenge our brother soldiers," explained to his sweetheart, "It is not in times of action that chills the blood, but after the action when you see your comrades with arms and legs shot off and mangled in all forms." After his first experience of battle at First Manassas, Captain Matthew T. Nunnally of the 11th Georgia recorded, "Here it was I heard the groans of the wounded and dying; it was here I deeply felt the horrors of this terrible war, it was here I resolved that I should fight them as long as I could raise an arm." Almost a year later, after the bloody Confederate defeat at Malvern Hill, the suffering of his comrades elicited the same feelings. Nunnally wrote his sister, "If you could have but heard the groans of the wounded and dying that night you would have sworn eternal vengeance against the whole Yankee tribe."[74]

Still other soldiers extended their animosity even to the enemy dead, to foes who had paid with their lives. An outraged Confederate soldier-correspondent wrote that the Yankees had left an inscription on a part of the Antietam battlefield reading, "There lie the bodies of sixty Rebels. The way of the transgressor is hard." Challenging this judgment with charges of Union depredations in Virginia, the same soldier wrote of the Union dead, "Like thieves they came and like dogs they are buried, their epitaphs shall not be written nor marked their graves, for their deeds have proven them unfit for place in Heaven or on earth." Confederate rhetoric against Northern invasion and subjugation could more than match Yankee spite. "Ah, my silent friends! You came down here to invade our homes and teach us how to wear the chains of subordination and reverence a violated constitution," wrote Virginia artilleryman George Neese, contemplating the newly buried Union dead at Cedar Mountain. "In the name of Dixie, we bid you welcome to your dreamless couch under the sod that drank your blood, and may God have mercy on your poor souls and forgive you for all the depredations that you have committed since you crossed the Potomac." For such men, killing the enemy did not erase the antagonism between themselves and the other side but rather represented divine judgment for the iniquity of their cause and conduct as enemies of the Union or the Confederacy.[75]

Battle not only tested a Civil War soldier's ability to stand enemy fire but also whether he could return that fire in hopes of killing the enemy. Most Federals and Confederates who experienced battle passed this test. While their training may have inadequately readied them to kill, many found that when it came time to see the elephant, they could indeed shoot to kill. Multiple factors in battle could prompt soldiers to fight in a potentially lethal fashion, including military discipline, survival, excitement, anger, and desire for revenge. Soldiers' accounts reveal a spectrum of attitudes, from enthusiastic and purposeful killers to reluctant killers to those who deliberately avoided killing, suggesting that only the most militant opponents of killing took drastic measures in combat to avoid taking lives. Many men who felt ambivalent about killing nonetheless found themselves fighting in such a way that they surmised that some of their shots may have found a human mark, yet those with such misgivings often could take comfort in the smoke of battle and the crash of volleys that made it impossible to ever truly know if they had killed. Whether they fired accurately or not, most Civil War soldiers fought as duty commanded, doing their best to kill the enemy.

# 3

## Good Execution

### The Language of Killing

Understanding the experience of killing in the Civil War relies primarily on the accounts that Union and Confederate soldiers left to posterity in letters, diaries, and memoirs. Reconstructing those experiences does not depend solely on how soldiers described their feelings and impressions, however. Students of the Civil War can consider not only what Federals and Confederates had to say about killing in combat but also how they said it. In addition to their actual commentary regarding killing, the terminology and turns of phrase that soldiers used speak volumes about their attitudes toward taking life in war. The variety of word choices and expressions found in soldiers' writings constitute the language of killing in the Civil War.

At its most basic level, the language of killing offered word choices and phrases that could substitute for the inescapably blunt term "kill." This was more than simply a case of seeking variety in language. Substitutes for the verb "kill" distanced the writer or speaker from the harsh reality of taking human life in war. Various terms and turns of phrase obscured that reality, sometimes recasting killing in battle using professional military phraseology, sometimes by making light of the deaths of enemy soldiers. This kind of coded language could offer Civil War soldiers a way to protect them from any guilt or anxiety they might feel in regard to killing in combat. By choosing less direct ways of referring to killing, Union and Confederate fighting men potentially could ignore or overcome the negative ramifications of taking other men's lives.

At the same time, we should not assume that all Civil War soldiers used coded language as a defensive means of protecting their consciences and psyches. Combatants reconciled to or untroubled by killing in battle did not necessarily need to downplay the reality of killing for their own benefit. Instead, the language of killing offered them an active means of framing how they wanted others to perceive their accounts of battle. By describing killing in battle in indirect, clinical, or lighthearted terms, they signaled to their audience in what light they should view the killing described to them.

Civil War soldiers' accounts offer a colorful and varied vocabulary for describing battle with the enemy. Describing his regiment's role in the Battle of Chantilly, a soldier in the 40th New York reported, "We fought for three-quarters of an hour, the enemy 'peppering' us and we 'salting' them." This "peppering" and "salting" was truly of a deadly nature, for, as the soldier-correspondent noted, his regiment suffered over 50 percent casualties in the fight. Perry Mayo wrote his parents of a skirmish in Tennessee in which he and his comrades in the 2nd Michigan awaited a Rebel attack while concealed in tall weeds. Once the enemy "came in range of our rifles . . . we rose up and just *'gave em fits,'*" creatively describing both the Michiganders' volley and its effect downrange. On the receiving end of enemy fire, Illinois infantryman William Wiley wrote how in one engagement "the rebels rattled it to us pretty lively."[1]

Some soldiers applied slang and euphemisms both to the shots they fired at the enemy and the shots fired back at them, suggesting a workmanlike, matter-of-fact attitude toward the business of war. Sergeant Horatio Staples of the 2nd Maine offered a thoroughly colloquial and entertaining account of seeing the elephant at First Bull Run. His regiment had just crested Henry House Hill when they came in view of an enemy battle line behind a rail fence:

> The instant we made our appearance . . . they gave us a hearty "how'd doo" in the shape of a volley of musketry slap in our faces. To this very day I confidently believe the rascals did it on purpose. We gave them five hundred of the same kind of pills. 'Twas the first time we had shot and been shot at in earnest. It was our first gunpowder christening—a species of battle confirmation so to speak.

As Staples tried to recollect his feelings at that moment, it seemed to him that there had not been any time to feel fear, explaining, "There were guns to be fired, and guns to load and fire again; there was a nasty line of grizzly gray scoundrels on the other side of that fence to practice real shooting on." Staples's postwar account speaks for those Civil War soldiers who during and after the war accepted and affirmed killing in combat, even to the extent that they could make light of it after the fact.[2]

Many expressions dealt specifically with killing individual soldiers, some of them still familiar in modern speech. "Bite the dust" seems to have been an already well-established idiom by the time of the Civil War, and one popular with soldiers in blue and gray. After first meeting the Yankees in battle at Seven Pines, Lewis Branscomb wrote his sister back in Alabama, "I think I made some of the red mouths bite the dust, or mud rather, for we were in mud and water all the time." Private Joseph L. Cornet of the 28th Pennsylvania remembered how during an interlude in the Battle of Antietam his comrades had boasted of "how many rebels had been made to bite the dust." A Yankee or Rebel might speak of "wiping out" the enemy. To "rub out" someone might sound more like the parlance of a twentieth-century gangster than a Civil War soldier, but its use in American English has been documented as early as 1848. Other nineteenth-century euphemisms for killing changed slightly over the years to become expressions we recognize today. To "blow down" someone became "blow away"; to "bump" someone morphed into "bump off" in the 1920s.[3]

A less familiar expression to modern audiences was saying someone had gone to his "long home" as a euphemism for death. A number of reference works cite the phrase as referring specifically to a coffin or a grave, but the phrasing seems flexible enough to allow a dual meaning of the subject in question having entered eternity. Like "bite the dust," going to one's "long home" could be used in a passive sense referring to someone having died rather than having killed them, and in this sense the expression seems to have been common in the nineteenth century. Still, it too found its way into the soldiers' language of killing. Confederate Tar Heel Louis Leon, taken prisoner at the Wilderness, recorded in his diary that his brother, Morris, was subsequently captured at Spotsylvania, noting that "before he surrendered he sent two of the enemy to their long home with his bayonet." The next month at the Battle of Piedmont in the Shenandoah, a soldier in the 34th Massachusetts described how his regiment "delivered a volley that sent many a poor Reb to his long home."[4]

Civil War soldiers came up with a number of inventive circumlocutions to describe shooting and killing the enemy. During the Battle of Wauhatchie, fought at the foot of Lookout Mountain, H. Howard Sturgis of the 44th Alabama spotted a Yankee and a Rebel grappling with one another, each trying to take the other prisoner. A Confederate lieutenant intervened, with the result that "the deadlock was broken with a bullet." Shuddering at the memory of the fight, Sturgis further wrote, "I saw a man roll down the mountain side, started by a ball from my gun when only a few feet distant from its muzzle." The regimental historians of the 103rd Illinois wrote how during their regiment's assault up Tunnel Hill, a Confederate sergeant attempted to capture one of their men. Another Illinoisan, Isaac Harn, "gave the big Sergt. the contents of his gun, bringing him to the ground."[5]

Eugene Kingman of the 12th Maine spoke of "knocking over" enemy soldiers in letters home to his family. During the Siege of Port Hudson, he used the euphemism twice during his correspondence. On June 1, 1863, he wrote, "Tell Charley [his brother] that I think I knocked over one Secesh in good shape and shall do the same by another if I get a good chance." That same month, on the 29th, he wrote directly to Charley that "to all appearances I knocked over another Reb if not two." Kingman used a different euphemism in another letter to Charley written two months later, telling his younger brother, "I can say by my Enfield what you, I hope may never have to say by yours, that it has spit fire at the enemy more than once and I hope with beneficial effect in at least *two* cases."[6]

Soldiers even more belligerent than Kingman when it came to killing used slang and euphemisms, further illustrating that soldiers' vernacular did not always reflect guilt or avoidance. William Bellamy of the 18th North Carolina described a heated "picket skirmish or *duel*" along the Chickahominy in 1862 in which "I . . . did my best to drop a dirty villain on a grey or white horse, who rashly & boldly rode out in the open field & apparently requested us to do him the honor of introducing to his ears the report of our muskets." Bellamy waxed both poetic and anatomical in recounting what happened next: "We made him acquainted with powder & lead, introducing not only to his ears the sound of our guns, but *into* his left side some where in some of the (Thoracic viscera) a piece of lead carefully molded & and of a conical shape—*who* killed him *no one knows*—I say I did, and every other man in the squad ditto—so let it remain, enveloped in mystery."[7]

One way soldiers' vernacular colloquialized killing was to emphasize one element of an enemy's presence on the battlefield that had been eliminated, instead of more directly saying an enemy soldier's life had been ended. A number of combatants spoke of killing the enemy in terms of ending the threat he posed to oneself or one's comrades, thus emphasizing the "him or me" nature of self-defense. According to Captain Silas S. Canfield, regimental historian of the 21st Ohio, "He'll never kill any more Yanks" was a typical expression to hear on the firing line from a man who had hit his mark. In his June 29 letter describing "knocking over" a Confederate soldier, Eugene Kingman explained, "I fired at him several times and the last time he threw up his hands and went over, pretty badly hurt anyhow and I think he has fired his last bullet." Other accounts opted to focus on ending more prosaic elements of an enemy's existence. Confederate infantryman Thomas Benton Reed engaged in a sharpshooting duel during the Overland Campaign, firing several shots at his Yankee adversary's muzzle flashes and smoke until he finally "stopped his noise."[8]

Captain Charles I. Wickersham of the 8th Pennsylvania Cavalry authored one of the most memorable circumlocutions of a deadly battlefield encounter. During the Battle of Chancellorsville, the Pennsylvanians accidentally rode into a column of Confederate infantry and found themselves having to cut their way out with their sabers. One of the regiment's officers had his horse's bridle seized by a Rebel officer, who aimed a revolver and demanded the rider's surrender. "The reply," Wickersham wryly noted, "was what is known in the sabre exercise as 'left cut against infantry.'" As a result of the encounter, he explained, "The rebel officer did not respond to roll call the next morning." Who was the Pennsylvania cavalry officer who used his saber so effectively? Wickersham's account appeared in a published edition of papers read before a gathering of the Military Order of the Loyal Legion of the United States, a fraternal organization of former Union officers. The editors of the volume noted that the officer in question had been the author himself, Charles I. Wickersham.[9]

How do we explain Captain Wickersham's anonymous and roundabout account of killing (or at least grievously wounding) a Confederate officer? Does his account reflect a positive, negative, or ambivalent attitude toward killing? In the rest of his presentation, "Personal Recollections of the Cavalry at Chancellorsville," Wickersham did not shy away from talking about himself directly. On the contrary, he spoke in considerable detail regarding his personal actions and command decisions during the battle. So why describe the violent encounter with the Confederate officer so circumspectly? Why only tell his audience that the story involved "one of our officers," rather than identifying himself? It seems unlikely that Wickersham felt troubled by the incident, considering that he derived a bit of sardonic humor from it. He described his saber cut as his "reply" and as a technique straight out of the cavalry manual, a detail his brother officers likely appreciated. Then he coyly concluded the account by stating that his assailant "did not respond to roll call the next morning." Wickersham may have hid his involvement not out of regret but modesty. Considering that his address already detailed his role in the battle, he could have chosen not to identify himself so as not to appear too self-important. Civil War veterans were no strangers to their peers boasting of and exaggerating their accomplishments, particularly when it came to their generals. Perhaps Wickersham felt the tale was simply too good not to tell, so he attributed it to an anonymous officer lest he appear too self-aggrandizing. Trying to understand the subtext of accounts such as Charles Wickersham's ultimately requires a deal of speculation and interpretation.[10]

Small arms accounted for most casualties in Civil War combat—more than the big guns of the artillery and far more than edged weapons such as bayonets and sabers (Captain Wickersham's exploits notwithstanding). Not surprisingly, such weapons attracted their share of killing-related vernacular. Some soldiers euphemistically referred to fighting the enemy in terms of working their weapons. Silas Canfield wrote that soldiers in the 21st Ohio, confident in their aim and the accuracy of their weapons, could be heard saying things like, "This gun never deceives me" and "I know right where she carries." During the Battle of Williamsburg, Sergeant Salem Dutcher of the 7th Virginia threw down his powder-fouled weapon, snatched up another out of a fallen soldier's hands, and "set her to talking."[11]

The ammunition used to inflict death and wounds attracted its own unique vocabulary. A Civil War soldier's cartridge box typically could hold forty paper-wrapped cartridges containing powder and ball. In soldiers' parlance, this complement grimly became known as "forty dead men." In a similar fashion, a Wisconsin soldier-correspondent expressed his desire "to send a few messengers of death into the hearts of those who have made all this trouble." While some men emphasized the deadly nature of their ammunition, others used slang that sardonically made light of that purpose. One of the most common nicknames for bullets and balls was "pills," preceded by various modifiers to indicate either who was doing the shooting or who was on the receiving end. Wisconsin volunteer John Brobst insisted that he and his comrades dreaded Camp Randall (where their regiment had been mustered and trained) "worse than we do old Jeff Davis' pills that his men send at us." Sergeant J. T. Boggs described how at Shiloh the 3rd Iowa waited until the Confederates came "within twenty rods of us when we gave them a full dose of Northern Pills, which took good effect on the gray devils." Other soldiers labeled bullets according to their intended targets. One New York soldier-correspondent remarked how he composed his letter to the *Sunday Mercury* "writing on a cartridge-box containing fifty rounds of Secesh pills, which, I have no doubt, will shortly be used in curing the rebels from using their legs so freely."[12]

Several phrases appear so frequently in soldiers' accounts of combat as to merit special attention. These three expressions—"good execution," "deliberate aim," and "murderous fire"—constitute a triumvirate of reoccurring Civil War terminology. Together, these phrases made up a significant and revealing portion of Federal and Confederate combatants' language of killing.

Civil War accounts abound with descriptions of soldiers and their weapons doing "execution" in battle. Almost invariably this referred to firepower that took a deadly toll, killing and wounding many of the enemy. Referring to shooting down the enemy in such a clinical and dispassionate manner as doing "execution" might seem primarily characteristic of officers' battle reports and memoirs, men supposedly more detached from the actual practice of killing. The specific phrase "good execution" appears approximately 200 times in the *Official Records of the Union and Confederate Armies*. In his postwar reminiscences, Rufus Dawes described how at the Battle of Brawner's Farm the men of the 7th Wisconsin had merged with his own 6th Wisconsin, noting, "Our united fire did great execution." Yet the official-sounding expression was not used exclusively by officers, for the rank and file used it as well. "All seem anxious to go & I dare say will do some execution should they meet Lincoln's abolition cohorts," Mississippi infantryman Robert A. Moore recorded in his diary in 1861. Soldiers often described deadly firepower as doing "good" or "much" execution among those on the receiving end. The expression acquired a variety of other descriptors, all denoting effective killing in battle. Accounts from the war's opening battles and skirmishes in 1861 include such variations as "fearful execution," "splendid execution," and "most telling execution." During the Peninsula Campaign, Private John Edgar Thompson of the 28th Georgia wrote his father that by the Yankees' "own accounts, our regiment did terrible execution."[13]

All this talk of execution begs the question of what meaning the word was meant to convey. Most significantly, by referring to the killing of the enemy as execution, did Civil War soldiers mean to suggest that they were executioners? Was this a play on words, another example of the grim humor Federals and Confederates often found in war? The answers appears to be no. Generally speaking, officers and enlisted did not intend "execution" to suggest capital punishment. Contextually, their accounts give little evidence to suggest they were using the word rhetorically to suggest a double meaning. Instead, they usually used the word in a straightforward, nonironic manner. In Civil War usage, "execution" could refer to an act of capital punishment, but it was not the only meaning. More simply, it could mean executing, or carrying out, any given action. Contemporary dictionaries described *execution* foremost as an "act of executing" and "performance, the act of completing." The difference in the possible meanings was the same as that between *executor*, "one who executes," and *executioner,* "one who executes (i.e., puts to death) someone." In a prosaic sense, a general's plan might be well executed, or a regiment might perfectly execute a particular drill maneuver. In a more deadly sense, well-aimed musketry or artillery might inflict great execution on the enemy.[14]

Rather than suggesting that killing in battle was akin to an execution, Civil War soldiers' use of the word suggests the businesslike attitude that many men on both sides adopted toward warfare. The word choice implied that the purpose of shooting at the enemy was to kill the enemy, and thus the suggestion that shooting that killed many of the enemy constituted "good execution" of the soldier's trade. To be sure, the expression downplayed the harsh reality of taking human life, and as with other kinds of colloquial language relating to combat, soldiers troubled by that reality may indeed have found comfort in obliqueness. Alternatively, by speaking of killing the enemy as good execution, a soldier could also reflect a soldier's dispassionate, pragmatic conclusion that killing the enemy was his goal in battle. Tellingly, many users of the word "execution" attached to it such superlatives as "good," "great," and "splendid," indicating their satisfaction that their musketry or artillery had exacted a sizable toll from the enemy, as it was intended to do. Even the use of more ambiguous descriptors such as "terrible" does not necessarily reflect a negative attitude toward killing. Traditionally, "terrible" has carried with it a variety of connotations, depending on the context. Contemporary dictionaries offered such synonyms as "dreadful," "formidable," and "frightful." Longmuir's combined Anglo-American dictionary defined *terrible* itself as meaning "adapted to excite awe, dread, fear, &c." Moreover, a soldier could deem the human carnage of the battlefield dreadful and frightful yet still feel impressed and even pleased with the formidable effect of his side's weaponry against the enemy. In describing the "terrible execution" his unit wrought in battle, Private Thompson from Georgia also proudly noted that Union prisoners credited them as a regiment of sharpshooters, so deadly had they practiced the soldier's craft.[15]

If a soldier wanted to do good execution with his weapon, he might do well to take "deliberate aim," another almost ubiquitous phrase in Civil War accounts. The phrase's meaning was fairly straightforward; deliberate aim was aim taken slowly, carefully, and purposefully. It contrasted with the hurried, almost unaimed fire to which so many soldiers resorted in the haste and poor visibility of battle. This rushed form of aiming in which the shooter simply raises his weapon and fires in the general direction of the target as quickly as possible is known in modern parlance as snap firing or snap shooting. Still other soldiers found opportunities in battle to take more careful aim. A soldier aiming deliberately would typically single out a specific individual as a target, carefully align him in his sights, and squeeze off the most accurate shot he could make. Private Washington Bryan Crumpton of the 37th Mississippi described how at Peachtree Creek he and his comrades managed to disable a Union battery and drive away a general and his staff with careful marksmanship. "We all loaded, elevated our sights, dropped behind a log and took deliberate aim," he wrote. "In a moment we saw them scampering away." References to "deliberate aim" appeared not just in print but could also be heard in the heat of battle. Officer's duties included making sure their troops took as accurate aim as possible in order to maximize the deadly effect of their firepower. Conrad Wise Chapman, a Rebel in the Orphan Brigade, recalled how at Shiloh, "an officer cautioned us to aim low and take deliberate aim."[16]

To say he had taken deliberate aim usually indicated that a soldier had done his best to kill the enemy. Fighting in the West Woods at Antietam, Sergeant William H. Andrews of the 1st Georgia spotted a Union soldier defiantly waving the Stars and Stripes. Andrews decided "that it would be honor enough for one day if I could cause it to strike the ground; and placing my rifle to my shoulder I took deliberate aim at the color bearer's breast; but as I pressed my trigger my gun snapped." His rifle having mis-fired, Andrews was unable to drop his man, though a charge by his regiment did force the Federals opposing them to retreat.[17] Civil War soldiers used the phrase "deliberate aim" similarly to how in modern parlance we might speak of "shooting to kill." The two phrases should not be thought of as entirely identical because the first describes the precision of the shooter's aim while the second speaks of his intent. Moreover, "deliberate aim" should not necessarily be taken as a euphemism, even if it sounds less blunt, considering that the soldiers themselves using the phrase do not seem to have thought of it as prevaricating or sugarcoating. Rather, men like Sergeant Andrews left little doubt that they were indeed shooting to kill when they took deliberate aim in battle.

One of the most enigmatic elements of the language of killing concerned the word "murder" and its derivatives. Various appearances of "murder" in soldiers' accounts of battle had the potential to call into question whether one could truly differentiate between legitimate and illegitimate killing in war, yet in the majority of appearances soldiers did not appear to be critiquing the idea of killing in war.

One of the most commonly appearing variations was "murderous fire." Much like "good execution," the phrase also described shooting that managed to hit numerous human targets. Often Civil War soldiers invoked the phrase when they were on the receiving end of deadly firepower. Storming Marye's Heights at Fredericksburg, Captain John H. Donovan of the Irish Brigade recorded being "greeted by a murderous fire of grape and canister and Minnie balls." Captain Isaac Cusac likewise described how his 21st Ohio launched a counterattack at Chickamauga, only to be "met by a murderous fire which killed and wounded many of our men." The phrase also worked when one's own side was doing the shooting. Private John K. Duke of the 53rd Ohio described how his regiment repulsed a charge by a brigade of Floridians outside Dallas, Georgia, the Rebels hitting a concave portion of the line where they found themselves hit by Union fire to their front and on both flanks. "Our murderous fire, while we had them in this death-trap, was that of precision," the veteran Buckeye infantryman wrote. "Our aim was deadly. It seemed as though nothing short of utter annihilation could stop them." Another Ohioan, Lieutenant Edmund E. Nutt, recounted how at Atlanta the 20th Ohio loosed deadly enfilade fire into the flank of a Confederate attack: "We poured into their flank a murderous volley. . . . We sprang over our works and gave them a volley which laid many low, and scattered the others to cover."[18]

Contextually, it appears that most soldiers who described volleys and salvos as "murderous" did not use the word in an accusatory sense, as if to condemn killing in battle as murder per se. Rather, they seem to have used the term as essentially synonymous with "deadly." In the following account from the Atlanta Campaign, Sergeant John H. Ferguson of the 10th Illinois used the latter word in a similarly neutral tone, much akin to the previously cited examples: "When they got within 30 or 40 yards, our infantry poored a deadly fiar into there ranks." Contemporary dictionaries confirm that "murderous" did not exclusively mean unlawful or immoral killing. Worcester's 1860 American dictionary defined the word alternatively as "guilty of murder" or simply "bloody." Longmuir's 1864 Anglo-American dictionary associated the word with the crime of murder but also offered the synonyms "bloody, sanguinary, cruel, savage."[19]

Some soldiers did specifically refer to killing in battle as murder, yet in many of these cases the word's use suggests rampant slaughter or lopsided casualty counts rather than a moral condemnation of killing in war. Civil War combatants often spoke of murder to describe battles in which well-fortified defenders cut down attackers with relative ease and in great numbers, and in which the attackers stood little chance of success or even striking back at the defenders. Watching in reserve while his fellow Confederates mowed down charging Yankees at Fredericksburg, Val Giles of Texas wrote of the slaughter below Marye's Heights as "splendid murder" and "as grand a battle-scene as mortal man ever witnessed." At Ezra Church outside Atlanta, the roles were reversed. Major James A. Connolly wrote home to his wife in Illinois describing the grievous casualties the Rebels had suffered—how they had attacked Sherman's forces with "senseless desperation," only to be gunned down by Union defenders. "Why it was a perfect murder," Connolly remarked. Similar to references to murder, soldiers also used words like "butchery" to describe copious slaughter on the battlefield. "Ye Gods!" marveled a Confederate defender at Fredericksburg at the sight of Federal attackers melting away under infantry and artillery fire. "It is no longer a battle; it is butchery!" On the receiving end of Rebel firepower during the Overland Campaign, John Gould of the 90th Pennsylvania wrote his mother, "The fighting here is terrible, in fact regular butchering."[20]

Civil War soldiers often described slaughter on the battlefield as murder or butchery, but when it came to assigning blame for such bloodshed, many of them blamed their own officers rather than the enemy troops doing the actual killing. For soldiers who accepted killing as part of the business of war, it was only natural that the enemy would try to kill them, just as they would try to kill the enemy. They could, however, heap blame on their own officers whom they believed guilty of throwing them into battle recklessly or foolishly. At Antietam, the men of the 16th Connecticut marched into their first battle, only to be cut apart by "a perfect storm of shell and grape" and "a regular hail of musket balls," according to Private Walter Smith. The nineteen-year-old infantryman did not know whom to fault by name but felt certain that the responsibility belonged to one of his own commanders. "Where the blame lies for ordering us there, I do not know," Smith wrote the day after the battle, "but I do know that was criminal carelessness some where, as we stood no chance at all, and it was nothing but murder to place us there." For Smith, the slaughter constituted murder for twofold reasons. Not only had the 16th suffered significant casualties (emerging from the battle "very badly cut up"), the regiment had also been placed in a position with "no chance" of success against the deadly Rebel artillery and musketry.[21]

Just as bloody frontal assaults especially attracted labels such as "murder" and "butchery," Civil War soldiers often laid the blame for the deaths in those attacks on the generals who ordered them. After their defeat at Fredericksburg, Union soldiers felt especially bitterly toward Ambrose Burnside, who had launched charge after charge against Marye's Heights, each one bloodily repulsed. "I am willing to go almost anywhere and endure anything," Major Francis E. Pierce of the 108th New York wrote in the wake of Burnside's debacle, "but deliver me from ever being marched into such useless wholesale murder ever as that was." Among Confederate generals, John Bell Hood received more than his share of condemnation for presiding over bloody attacks against dug-in Yankees, especially at Atlanta and Franklin. After describing the sanguinary repulse of the Army of Tennessee at Ezra Church as "perfect murder," Federal officer James Connolly blamed the enemy commander for the bloodshed: "We slaughter them by the thousands, but Hood continues to hurl his broken, bleeding battalions against our immovable lines, with all the fury of a maniac." Some Confederates under Hood's command condemned their general in even harsher terms. Writing in his diary, Captain Samuel T. Foster of Granbury's Texas Brigade insisted that Hood "had near 10,000 men murdered around Atlanta" just to prove "that he was a greater man than Genl Johnston" and darkly predicted that "the wails and cries of widows and orphans made at Franklin . . . will heat up the fires of the bottomless pit to burn the soul of Gen J B Hood for Murdering their husbands and fathers." Hood's attacks at Franklin, Foster declared, "can't be called anything else but cold blooded Murder."[22]

To be sure, some Civil War soldiers did suggest that killing the enemy, even in battle, could constitute murder. In the successful assault on Missionary Ridge, Jacob H. Allspaugh of the 31st Ohio and other Union soldiers managed to not only breach the Rebel defenses but also outflank and attack some of the enemy defenders from the rear. "One heroic young Southerner," the Buckeye recounted, escaped capture by dashing across the front of the ad hoc Union battle line, even as Union bullets whistled about him. Allspaugh did not join his comrades in trying (and failing) to kill the fleeing Confederate, explaining that he "never believed in downright murder, so held [my] fire, taking for granted that some other wrathful Yankee would do the murderous work." The Ohio infantryman may have refused to shoot a lone man running for his life, but he did not object to using his weapon against a higher-value target. Moments later, Allspaugh felt "rewarded" that he had not emptied his rifle when he spotted a Confederate artillery team galloping away from the fray. Allspaugh and several other Federals fired, hitting the leading two horses and bringing the entire limber team—horses, men, and gun—to a crashing halt.[23]

Some of the Civil War's most famous utterances include examples of likening wartime killing to murder. Three such examples—all authored by generals—used remarkably similar language to suggest a particular battle or action had been not war but murder. Confederate general Daniel Harvey Hill remembered how soldiers of the Army of Northern Virginia had bravely advanced up the slopes of Malvern Hill into the face of massed

Union artillery, only to be cut down and hurled back by deadly canister fire. "It was not war—it was murder," Hill wrote. Evander Law, another of Lee's generals, offered a similar recollection of the slaughter at Cold Harbor, where well-fortified Confederates had mowed down charging Federal infantry. The sight reminded Law of similar Yankee bloodbaths in front of the railroad cut at Second Manassas and below Marye's Heights at Fredericksburg, "but I had seen nothing like this," he insisted. "It was not war; it was murder." William T. Sherman provides the final example, in an account from his memoirs of his army's encounter with Rebel land mines (then known as torpedoes) outside Savannah. Sherman rode up on a group of men attending to a young staff officer who had fallen victim to one such weapon. The officer's horse had triggered a buried eight-inch shell, the blast of which had killed the horse and maimed one of the young man's legs so badly that it would require amputation. "This was not war, but murder," Sherman pronounced, "and it made me very angry."[24]

As with many other soldiers' statements, the three generals' "not war but murder" statements ostensibly stop short of condemning conventional wartime killing. For Confederate generals Hill and Law, describing bloodily repulsed assaults, the "murder" label seems to denote the scale of slaughter and disproportionate losses rather than the censuring the killing itself. Both D. H. Hill and Evander Law stressed the staggering number of casualties in the face of insurmountable defensive firepower. Immediately before affixing the "murder" label to the Battle of Malvern Hill, Hill emphasized the distance the Confederate assault had to cross and the scale of Union ordnance facing them. Although neither account offers any explicit condemnation, if they imply any blame, it reflects more negatively on the decisions to attack than on the soldiers who repulsed the attacks. Rather than resenting the fearsome killing power of Union gunners, D. H. Hill unreservedly paid tribute to them in his retrospective on Malvern Hill, declaring that the battle "proved . . . that the Confederate infantry and Federal artillery, side by side on the same field, need fear no foe on earth."[25] Of the three selected statements, only William Sherman's definitively uses "murder" to denote and condemn a form of illegitimate killing, and in this instance he specifically applied it to the use of explosive mines—relatively unconventional weapons for their time, which killed indiscriminately and outside the scope of regular combat. Coming from Sherman, a practitioner of "hard war" and a professional soldier well versed in the rules of nineteenth-century warfare, the implication is that one could (and should) distinguish between militarily legitimate and illegitimate kinds of killing.

Civil War soldiers conveyed their attitudes toward killing in combat not just in the feelings and reactions they described but also in the words and phrases they chose. A host of terms and turns of phrase gave Federals and Confederates alternatives to the bluntness and brusqueness of "kill." These expressions allowed them to define the taking of life in their own terms, whether they sought to distance and shield themselves from the reality of killing or chose to frame combat for their audience as they already saw it, be it in positive, neutral, or businesslike fashion. Their phraseology could denote lamentable slaughter or wry satisfaction in slaying the foe; it could differentiate between legitimate and illegitimate forms of killing on the battlefield. Their words reflect a significant portion of fighting men who could tolerate, affirm, and even celebrate fighting and killing. Whether they wrote of sending the enemy to his long home, making him bite the dust, or doing good execution with deliberate aim and murderous fire, Yankees' and Rebels' varied and creative vocabularies composed the Civil War's rich language of killing.

# 4

## With Bayonet and Clubbed Musket
### Killing in Hand-to-Hand Combat

Fighting hand to hand was one of the most extreme forms of killing that Civil War soldiers could experience. Close-quarters melees were quite literally exceptional incidents, occurring relatively rarely in Civil War combat. Union and Confederate soldiers could be rightly grateful that such fighting proved so uncommon. Although many of their commanders touted the efficacy of the bayonet, soldiers' training often did little to prepare them adequately for the challenge of wielding the weapon. Moreover, hand-to-hand combat represented perhaps the most dangerous, terrifying, and psychologically taxing form of fighting that Federals and Confederates, or warriors from any age, could experience. Men from North and South seemingly resisted no other form of fighting as strongly as they did the prospect of trying to kill one another face-to-face on a brutally personal level. To bring Yankees and Rebels to physical blows with one another generally required considerable bravery and resolution, as well as specific battlefield conditions. For soldiers who experienced this kind of fighting, regardless of whether they emerged physically unscathed, the encounter was certain to leave its mark.

Some remarks about terminology seem useful here. Hand-to-hand combat might be reasonably construed as referring only to fighting in which the combatants actually come in direct physical contact one another. However, loaded weapons could be and were fired in melee encounters, and Civil War soldiers demonstrated a strong preference in combat to shooting over striking an opponent. For the purposes of this chapter, hand-to-hand combat refers to any fighting in which the opponents encounter one another within physical reach, regardless of whether it involved firing or the use of edged weapons, blunt objects, or other instruments. In addition, this chapter uses such terms as "hand to hand," "close quarters," and "melee" as essentially synonymous, except when making deliberate distinctions.

Many Northerners and Southerners went to war assuming that hand-to-hand combat would play a larger role in the fighting than it actually did. Partially this assumption reflected how the media of the day portrayed warfare. Captain John De Forest from Connecticut recalled how he went into action at a skirmish in Louisiana with both sword and revolver drawn in expectation of close-quarters fighting, "not yet having learned that bayonet fighting occurs mostly in newspapers and other works of fiction." Sensationalized hand-to-hand fighting figured prominently in wartime lithographs and woodcuts, especially among illustrations that relied more on the artist's imagination than on firsthand experience. Such depictions made for good copy; an image of Federals and Confederates locked in a furious melee offered greater drama than soldiers firing at a distant, unseen enemy. These scenes also symbolically tapped into both artists' and consumers' assumptions about war itself. With Americans at war with one another, civilians and citizen-soldiers new to war imagined the opposing sides fighting against one another physically as well as figuratively, picturing battle like something out of an ancient or medieval tableau instead of the more distant nature of nineteenth-century combat.

Soldiers' accounts reveal the extent to which the moral and psychological power of hand-to-hand combat infused their imaginations. A number of Federals and Confederates invoked melee fighting in their wartime rhetoric. In a published poem called "Who Wouldn't Be a Fire Zouave," a New York sergeant boasted, "With bayonets bright we'll win the fight / Or perish hand in hand." Writing after First Manassas, adopted Louisianan Henry Handerson suggested in a letter to his father that the Yankees had possessed better long-range weapons at the battle, yet reasoned, "Perhaps the comparative inefficiency of our weapons contributes, however, to the efficacy of our troops, as it necessitates a conflict at close quarters, and a spirited charge,—the forte of southern soldiers,—often decides the fate of an action." One Pennsylvanian invoked the bayonet to express his seething hatred for Stonewall Jackson after "the dirty rebel" had humiliated Union forces in the Shenandoah Valley. "I would like him to be tied to a tree, then, I would like to charge bayonets on him," Henry Snyder wrote his sister. "I don't think I would leave much of him till I got done."[1]

Civil War volunteers' assumptions that hand-to-hand combat would play a major role in the fighting were reflected in the craze for sidearms early in the war. One of the most common and most easily obtainable extra weapons was a large knife, variously described as a belt knife, fighting knife, or butcher knife. Many of these knives featured blades eight to twelve inches long; some were even longer and might be better classified as short swords. Thomas Benton Reed, an Alabama native in a Louisiana regiment, brought with him "a butcher-knife about two feet long and weighing about one and a half pounds," boasting that he "was going to chop Yankees into sausage-meat." Quite a few followed the design of the quintessentially American Bowie knife, with its distinctive clipped point. Civil War knives ranged in quality from finely crafted blades to crude affairs hammered out by local blacksmiths out of old files, a popular form of knife making throughout American frontier history. Orlando T. Hanks and his fellow Texans carried the latter kind: "Some were about twelve inches long, one and one-half inches wide. Others were 16 or 18 inches long and about 3 inches wide. Every fellow ground and polished his own knife; some nice jobs, others not; all owing to the taste of the person. Nevertheless, they answered the purpose." Because Hanks and his comrades mustered with a hodgepodge of muskets and rifles, some of which were not designed to be fitted with bayonets, their company opted for knives in lieu of proper bayonets. An ingenious workman specially modified both the Texans' gun muzzles and their knife handles so that the butcher blades could be affixed to the weapons, achieving a degree of military regularity.[2]

While some Civil War soldiers brought fighting knives to war out of a sense of necessity, many also brought them enthusiastically, hoping for a chance to use them on the enemy. Numerous volunteers, especially in early war photographs, posed proudly displaying their fearsome blades, some managing to look quite intimidating in the portraits. Confederates celebrated reports from their victory at Manassas of how Wheat's Tigers, a rowdy Zouave unit recruited from New Orleans's street toughs and dockworkers, had wildly charged the New York Fire Zouaves with their butcher knives bared. Eagerly awaiting his own knife being made for him at home in Arkansas, Private Alexander Spence enthusiastically wrote, "Knifes are the things in close quarters with the Yankees. The Tiger Rifles from La tried theirs at Manassas on 'Ellsworths Pet Lambs.'"[3]

Man for man, Confederates were more likely than their Union counterparts to equip themselves with fighting knives, and more likely to keep them throughout the war. Belt knives, especially blades such as the Bowie knife and the "Arkansas toothpick," were much more a part of Southern than Northern culture. In a society in which disputes and questions of honor could result in duels or brawls, a fighting knife made for a practical weapon. Unlike a pistol, an edged weapon did not need to be reloaded; nor was it prone to malfunction. Among some well-to-do Southerners, a Bowie knife served as both a practical weapon and a fashion accessory, much as the sword had been for generations of European nobility. Nineteenth-century media in the North often invoked the Bowie knife in print and illustration as a partisan symbol of Southern violence, barbarity, and aggression.

Nevertheless, soldiers from the North were hardly strangers to knives as weapons, particularly volunteers from the Old Northwest, who, like their countrymen from the Deep South, were less removed from the frontier than Easterners. Period artifacts and accounts testify that some Union soldiers also went to war sporting belt knives. Sergeant Lyman Widney wrote that before being issued their muskets, he and his comrades outfitted themselves with "butcher knives," which in camp they "use[d] to carve food, but they are evidently intended to carve the enemy, in default of any better weapon." In October 1861, they were traveling by rail through Kentucky when their train suddenly stopped in the middle of the night at the news of an imminent Rebel attack. Preparing to meet the threat, the Illinoisans gamely drew their motley collection of revolvers and knives, one of Widney's comrades asking, "Well, do they expect us to put down the rebellion with butcher knives?" To the partial relief of the men, orders arrived for twenty men from each company to draw muskets and ammunition from the baggage car. The 200 newly armed Federals formed a line of battle to meet the expected attack, "while the revolver corps and the butcher knife brigade were held in reserve for close quarters," Widney wryly noted. Fortunately for the Illinoisans (and any Rebels that might have tried to tangle with them), no attack materialized, and within days the 34th finally received their muskets.[4]

On occasion, Union soldiers could even get the better of their knife-wielding Confederate foes. At Second Manassas, the 2nd New Hampshire gained a foothold in the railroad embankment held by Stonewall Jackson's men, fighting hand to hand with the Rebel defenders. After an accidental collision with one fleeing Confederate, a New Hampshire sergeant "yanked from the Johnny's belt a ferocious looking 'Yankee killer,' fashioned from a huge flat file—such as many of that regiment seemed to carry for side arms—and swung it aloft for the finishing blow." Seeing "the glint of vengeful steel," the helpless Rebel cried out, "Oh, for God's sake—*don't!*" The sergeant checked his blow, tucked the knife into his own belt, and made the "Johnny" his prisoner. The 2nd New Hampshire's regimental historian recounted the episode as proof that "in this wild turmoil of murder there were not wanting instances of man's humanity to man."[5]

Civil War soldiers exhibited a similar early war passion for acquiring revolvers and pistols. As with knives, numerous volunteers posed for their photographs with pistols in hand or tucked into their belts, sometimes with multiple weapons on display. Collectors debate whether some of these weapons were photographers' props added as a touch of bravado, but the accounts of the soldiers testify that at least some guns were the soldiers' own, whether privately purchased or received as gifts. Like most handguns today, those of the Civil War era were primarily useful at short range, suggesting that the soldiers who privately purchased them, like those carrying fighting knives, intended them as backup weapons for personal defense in close-quarters situations. Revolvers turned out to be highly practical weapons for mounted troops, but even in such cases, the weapons' effective range of about twenty-five yards limited their usefulness to short-range work.[6]

The revolvers and pistols that Civil War soldiers carried can be informally characterized into two types, belt guns and pocket guns, according to their size and how they were intended to be worn or carried. A third variety, horse pistols, were so heavy and bulky that they were best suited to being carried in saddle holsters. By the 1860s, horse pistols had largely been phased out in favor of lighter models. Civil War buyers had a host of handguns from which to choose, with variables in makers, designs, quality, and price. During the preceding decades, Samuel Colt had perfected the revolver and revolutionized the arms industry by turning out his famed six-shooters on the assembly line on a grand scale. Colt's patent on his "revolving gun" expired in 1857, opening the market to Remington, Smith & Wesson, and a host of other competitors just in time for a bonanza in firearms demand.

Civil War soldiers, especially the hard-marching infantrymen, quickly learned to lighten their loads, and often the knives and pistols that many volunteers had taken with them to war were the first items that they sent home, sold, or simply tossed aside. Marcus Toney and many of his comrades in Company B of the 1st Tennessee initially wore "a six-shooter Colt's revolver buckled around them, and on the other side was a large Damascus blade (made at a blacksmith's shop)." During a march under "a sweltering August sun" in 1861, Toney tired of the extra weight and decided to divest himself of the extra weapons: "I tried to give my six-shooter away, but could not find any one to accept it, and over in the bushes I threw it. I then unbuckled my Damascus blade, made an offer of that, but was likewise refused, and it was thrown into the bushes."[7]

Not all infantrymen who carried pistols early in their service decided to toss the weapons aside. Some enlisted men not only carried personal sidearms throughout the war but also found themselves in situations in which they successfully saved themselves from death or capture. While they were stationed in Colliersville, Tennessee, Theodore Upson and his friends in the 100th Indiana developed a friendly acquaintance with a local planter and his wife who claimed to be loyal Unionists. The husband, Bud Raymond, invited one of Upson's comrades to his plantation to hunt wild turkeys. As Upson told the story, Raymond hosted the Indiana soldier at his home and early the next morning led him to a swamp for his hunt. Raymond went on ahead, ostensibly to call in the turkeys. Instead of turkeys, two Rebel cavalrymen came galloping out of the brush. The Indianan quickly leveled his rifle and shot one of the Confederates out of the saddle. Drawing a pistol from his breast pocket, he fired a shot that felled the second trooper from his horse. Upson's comrade then "whirled about" to see Raymond running toward him, revolver in hand. The Hoosier fired again, wounding the planter in the arm. Once the soldier's comrades, alerted by the shooting, reached him, they found him leading the wounded Raymond as his prisoner. According to Upson's telling, his comrade's weapon was evidently some model of pocket revolver, small enough to be practical for an infantryman to carry. During the unexpected encounter, the well-armed Hoosier used his weapon as coolly and effectively as any Western gunfighter.[8]

Sidearms aside, the Civil War infantryman's intended weapon for close-quarters combat was a steel bayonet fixed to the muzzle of his firearm. Two different styles of bayonets were used among soldiers of both sides. The most common was the socket (or spike) bayonet designed for muskets and rifle muskets, the base of which fitted around the muzzle and could be locked around the front sight or bayonet lug. Socket bayonets typically featured blades shaped like a three-sided spike, seventeen or eighteen inches long, and tapering to a sharp point. Less common but perhaps more fearsome looking was the sword bayonet, so called because its blade actually resembled a short sword, complete with both a point and edged blade. Sword bayonets were longer than socket bayonets—the US model of sword bayonet featured a blade over twenty-one inches long—primarily to provide extra reach to shorter models of rifles. Unlike socket bayonets, sword bayonets fitted onto the sides of gun muzzles, usually clipping to a special mount. Both varieties allowed a soldier to load and fire his weapon even with the bayonet fixed, although it made loading and aiming somewhat more cumbersome. The bayonet-tipped musket of the eighteenth and nineteenth centuries effectively turned two soldiers from the seventeenth century, the musketeer and the pikeman, into one deadlier warrior, armed with both the gun's firepower and a deadly stabbing weapon.

Because hand-to-hand combat occurred relatively rarely during the Civil War, popular lore has derided the usefulness of the bayonet, treating it as a throwback to wars past by the 1860s. Academic and popular histories often emphasize how Civil War soldiers frequently found their bayonets more useful as camp tools than as lethal weapons. True, Federals and Confederates did find numerous ad hoc uses for their bayonets, including as entrenching tools, cooking utensils, and even candlesticks. These factors do not establish the bayonet's supposed uselessness. Even in purely physical terms, a fixed bayonet rendered the Civil War soldier a formidable warrior. Its addition gave a musket or rifle the potential to be used as a thrusting weapon with considerable reach, suitable for fighting both offensively and defensively. For a defending soldier, the fixed bayonet gave him a backup weapon if he was attacked in the process of reloading or if he had run out of ammunition entirely. On the defensive, the bayonet also offered effective protection against mounted cavalry charges. The traditional tactic to defend against cavalry was to form infantry into hollow squares two or more ranks deep, the soldiers facing outward with bayonet-tipped muskets. Horses would almost never charge against such a bristling hedgehog defense but instead would instinctively shy away. Even infantry in line formation could ward off a cavalry charge by presenting their bayonets to any horsemen foolish enough to charge straight at a well-formed battle line.

Much of the misunderstanding over the bayonet's role in nineteenth-century warfare stems from failing to appreciate its psychological value. As military historian Brent Nosworthy explains, the bayonet as a psychological weapon surpassed its effectiveness "as a means of physical destruction." Writer and Union veteran Ambrose Bierce went further, declaring, "The bayonet is a useless weapon for slaughter; its purpose is a moral one." Much of that moral purpose was to undermine enemy morale. Just as a bristling line of defenders armed with fixed bayonets could deter a cavalry charge, a disciplined force of attackers tipped with sharp, glistening steel was calculated to unnerve any enemy in its path. During the Revolutionary War, British forces achieved many of their battlefield victories with bayonet charges. On numerous occasions, Patriot forces melted away in the face of the redcoats' steel, often because American forces lacked the discipline and effective musketry (and sometimes bayonets of their own) to effectively repulse a bayonet charge. Civil War generals appreciated this psychological effect, which helps explain why they adhered so loyally to a kind of "cult of the bayonet" throughout the war. To better understand this, Nosworthy urges students of Civil War combat to distinguish between bayonet charges and actual bayonet fights. A bayonet charge did not have to result in actual hand-to-hand fighting to succeed; a charge in which the defenders fled from the approach of the attackers' bayonets was as much a success as one that drove off the defenders after a bayonet fight.[9]

The order to fix bayonets could produce an opposite psychological affect among the attackers themselves, steeling them for the task of an assault and potentially of killing. Private Henry T. Childs of Tennessee noted the sobering effect of hearing the command "Fix bayonets," explaining, "Every old soldier knows what that means. It means that somebody is going to get hurt." Describing his regiment's successful counterattack down the slope of Little Round Top, Joshua Chamberlain claimed that his order of "Bayonets!" was all that was needed to send the men of the 20th Maine charging forward: "The word was enough. It ran like fire along the line, from man to man, and rose into a shout, with which they sprang forward upon the enemy, now not thirty yards away." The experience of a bayonet charge itself could similarly electrify the attackers. At Shiloh, Henry Stanley, a Welsh-born private in the 6th Arkansas, described how in the course of a charge "our men raised a yell, thousands responded to it, and burst into the wildest yelling it has even been my lot to hear. It drove all sanity and order from us," a wave of voices that "accelerated our pace, and filled us with a noble rage." Stanley waxed poetic in describing the exhilaration of the charge that he had felt: "Then I knew what the Berserker passion was! It deluged us with rapture, and transfigured each Southerner into an exulting victor. At such a moment, nothing could have halted us."[10]

Most bayonet charges resulted in either the repulse of the attackers or the retreat of the defenders, with an actual bayonet fight between the two sides coming in a distant third. By and large, Civil War historians have correctly gauged that it was relatively rare for Yanks and Rebs to engage one another in hand-to-hand fighting. A number of reasons seem to account for this. For decades, historians supposed that the increased range of rifle muskets and rifled artillery made it increasingly difficult to overcome defensive firepower and physically close with the enemy. This theory posits that Civil War weaponry made obsolete the linear tactics of the eighteenth and early nineteenth centuries and marked a growing dominance of defensive firepower over the tactical offensive, an ascendency that reached its apogee with the stalemated trench warfare of World War I. More recent scholarship, notably that of Paddy Griffith and Earl Hess, has challenged the supposed decisiveness of rifled weaponry in the Civil War. This new school contends that Civil War armies did not successfully take full advantage of rifle weaponry's superior range and accuracy and that consequently linear tactics were not as ill suited to Civil War combat as commonly supposed.[11]

Military historians caution us against assuming that hand-to-hand combat was less common in the American Civil War than it had been in previous wars in the Western world dominated by smoothbore weaponry. "Those who study warfare during the eighteenth century and the Napoleonic Wars," Nosworthy observes, "know that . . . personal combat, at least on open ground, was equally rare during the pre–Civil War era." A bayonet charge might have enjoyed great chances of success in previous wars, but even among earlier generations of both American and European soldiers, charges more often ended with the attackers or the defenders retreating without an actual bayonet fight.[12] According to this, it seems that the psychology of combat and killing, addressed later in this chapter, explains the rarity of hand-to-hand combat as much as the effectiveness of firepower.

Civil War soldiers themselves testified to the rarity of hand-to-hand fighting. Heros von Borcke, a Prussian nobleman who served as chief of staff to J. E. B. Stuart, averred that "as far as my experience goes, recalling all the battles in which I have borne a part, bayonet-fights rarely if ever occur, and exist only in the imagination." Confederate memoirist William A. Fletcher insisted that "the first and last time I ever saw blood from the stick of a bayonet" occurred in camp when a soldier accidentally nicked an officer in the cheek with one. "We hear a great deal about hand-to-hand fighting," Ohio lieutenant Henry Dwight wrote *Harper's Monthly* in 1864. "Gallant though it would be, and extremely pleasant to the sensation newspapers to have it to record, yet . . . it is of very rare occurrence."[13]

Actual instances of hand-to-hand fighting stood out so strongly in fighting men's minds in part because such combat was rare and extraordinary. Soldiers and veterans often underscored their accounts of close-quarters combat with reminders of its exceptionality, particularly the survivors of notoriously desperate battles such as that fought at Franklin, Tennessee. "You read about hand-to-hand fighting, which does not come very often," explained James K. Merrifield of the 88th Illinois. "[Franklin] was the only time I ever saw the bayonet and musket butts used," wrote a soldier in the 73rd Illinois, "and, let me tell you, both were used freely there." W. M. Crook of the 13th Tennessee fought in all the Army of Tennessee's battles "from Shiloh to Bentonville, but Franklin was by far the closest quarters that I was ever in."[14]

Civil War soldiers were fortunate that they experienced hand-to-hand combat so rarely, in part because their training did so little to prepare them for it. If many Union and Confederate infantrymen were inadequately trained in the basics of loading and firing their muskets, then their training left them even more unprepared for the less likely prospect of crossing bayonets with the foe. The omission of bayonet training for many (though not all) Civil War soldiers did not come from a lack of available techniques. In European military circles, fighting with a fixed bayonet was considered the "fourth form of fencing," after the foil, saber, and épée. Bayonet fencing came with its own varieties of thrusts, parries, and ripostes, and included techniques for facing opponents both on foot and mounted. A number of manuals were available to Civil War officers. Among Union forces, the most prominent manual had been prepared by General George B. McClellan, which he translated from a French manual and presented to the US Army in 1852 as a captain in the Corps of Engineers. Confederate officers could avail themselves of McClellan's manual or choose a homegrown alternative such as "Carey's Bayonet Exercise and Skirmisher's Drill" (also inspired by the French), intended "for the use of the volunteers of the State of Virginia and the South."[15]

Civil War officers did not so much lack available techniques for training their men in hand-to-hand combat as they lacked the time and resources to turn their men into proficient bayonet fencers. French fencing instructor Antonin Gomard, whose manual on the bayonet George McClellan translated, described three forms of instruction: lessons with the plastron (a padded jacket); mutual lessons, in which pupils were paired off to spar with one another; and figurative lessons, "in which the scholar has no antagonist, and in which the direction of the thrusts and parries must be taken with reference to his own person." Gomard described lessons using the plastron and other protective equipment and engaging the trainee (or "scholar") with the instructor as "the best method of instruction." As with other forms of training for physical combat, this naturally would provide soldiers with the most realistic (and reasonably safe) experience of squaring off with an actual opponent. Gomard realized, however, that the expense and availability of instructors and equipment did not make such lessons practical for all soldiers, but he assured readers that "the figurative lesson will fully enable the soldier to provide for his personal defence."[16]

Monsieur Gomard guessed rightly when it came to the limits of personalized and protected instruction; providing instructors and fencing equipment to Union and Confederate armies proved wholly impractical, if it was considered at all. True, some resources were available. Gomard's manual suggested creating fencing bayonets by sawing off the blades and replacing them with lengths of whalebone, tipped with a leather or rubber button. A feature in an 1862 issue of *Scientific American*, insisting that "skillful handling of the bayonet . . . is one of the most important arts for the soldier to learn," highlighted "Ernst's Bayonet Guard." The invention included the means to secure the bayonet scabbard onto the blade and to enlarge the scabbard's tip to accommodate a ball of India rubber that would render practice thrusts harmless.[17] The magazine's enthusiasm aside, actual use of such bayonet guards was few and far between. Officers who attempted to school their men in bayonet drill usually opted for figurative lessons, the simplest and safest option, in which soldiers conducted the maneuvers without a partner. Typically for such instruction, soldiers deployed in skirmish order and in multiple, well-spaced ranks, thus giving each man plenty of room all around for him to maneuver his bayonet safely and to allow his trainers to evaluate his technique.

In this figurative form of instruction, soldiers essentially fought empty air as they conducted their thrusts, parries, and ripostes. Such a drill was not unlike practicing loading a musket without powder, ball, or caps—itself not an uncommon occurrence. Just as a solder was unlikely to become accomplished at loading or marksmanship without live firing, this form of bayonet training may have had little usefulness. In theory it would at least teach the soldier useful techniques with the bayonet and create a muscle memory that would kick in if he found himself in actual close-quarters combat, yet such practice was still far removed from actually sparring with an opponent, much less actually crossing blades in battle. Just as human-looking targets on the firing range seem to increase soldiers' likelihood of shooting to kill in battle, realistic targets for bayonet drill might have better prepared Civil War soldiers for the prospect of stabbing and hitting fellow human beings with bayonet-tipped muskets. In fact, one of the reasons many militaries retained bayonet training into the twentieth century and beyond, when bayonet fighting has become even rarer than in the American Civil War, has been "to instill aggressiveness and fighting spirit," to better foster a readiness to kill. Yet actually striking a target, realistic or otherwise, was largely absent from the bayonet manuals of the day and from soldiers' actual training.[18]

Discerning how many Civil War soldiers trained in bayonet drill and how much training they received proves a difficult task, though it seems it occurred less often than other forms of drill. For reasons of tactical practicality, officers found it more imperative to focus on the ability of their men to maneuver in formation and to load and fire their muskets successfully. As with musketry training, neither side imposed a standardized form of instruction, instead largely leaving such decisions to the discretion of individual commanders. Some of the colorful Zouave regiments, especially those organized before or early in the war, tried to excel in bayonet drill, aspiring to the specialized tactics of the elite French colonial troops whose uniforms they adopted. Zouave units raised later in the war, however, tended to be more mainstream in their training and only really reflected the Zouave tradition in their colorful uniforms. Anecdotal evidence suggests that bayonet drill may have been more common among Union than Confederate forces, especially in the eastern theater, where the Army of the Potomac took shape under the tutelage of George McClellan himself.

Anecdotal evidence from Civil War soldiers also suggests that many experienced bayonet drill more as a military curiosity than a form of rigorous instruction. In April 1864, Eugene Kingman of the 12th Maine wrote his father several times regarding his regiment's progress "in the French bayonet exercise," which he described as "pleasant drill" at which they were "getting along pretty well." This training occurred some two and a half years after the regiment was organized in 1861, during what was essentially their downtime while stationed in New Orleans. The Mainers did not see battle again until the summer after they shipped out to Virginia. One gets the sense that the officers may have introduced bayonet exercise among the troops as much to keep them busy as to improve their fighting skills. A survey among Wisconsin soldiers serving in various theaters turns up a number of men who recorded conducting bayonet drill but usually referring to it on an equally casual basis. In April 1863, a soldier from the 29th Wisconsin mentioned that they had begun "drilling in the 'Bayonet Exercise' three hours each day," a fairly rigorous routine. Stationed in Helena, Arkansas, the 29th, like Kingman and his comrades, conducted their exercises during a lull in garrison duty, and the Badgers would see even less action than the 12th Maine. Several months later, while still training at Camp Randall in Madison, a Badger in the 30th Wisconsin matter-of-factly recorded in his diary, "We had a company drill in the forenoon and a company drill in the afternoon."[19]

Some soldiers might have done better to abstain from bayonet exercise altogether, at least on an informal basis. Early in his service, Private Ogden Greenough of the 30th Illinois received a "slight wound" while practicing bayonet exercise with one of his comrades. As Greenough explained to his mother, what he called a "slight" wound occurred when his sparring partner's bayonet "entered my wrist exacting in the joint striking the bone and glancing out at the side of the wrist," a wound that "spread open showing the bones and tendons plainly." Greenough did not specify whether his injury occurred in an authorized "mutual lesson" in bayonet exercise or merely as a result of two young soldiers recklessly fooling around with their weapons.[20]

Soldiers who did train in bayonet drill offered mixed reviews as to its usefulness. Some felt the training bolstered their confidence in being able to meet the enemy face-to-face. Sergeant Lucius B. Swift, a New Yorker in the Army of the Potomac, believed that the men of his regiment "had no reason to shrink" from such fighting, "for we had been carefully drilled in bayonet exercise."[21] Others saw training with the bayonet not just as a military curiosity but openly lampooned it, considering it a laughable and impractical import from the Old World. In his fictionalized memoir *Corporal Si Klegg and His "Pard,"* Army of the Cumberland veteran Wilbur F. Hinman wrote,

> Some companies with ambitious officers spent a great deal of time and perspiration in learning the picturesque "bayonet-drill." This drill was a Frenchy affair—with its "parry" in "prime," "se-conde," "tierce" and "high quarte"; its "guard," "lunge," and "blow with the butt," its "advance," "retreat," and "leap to the rear, kneel and over the head, parry"—that kept the men jumping around like so many animated frogs. It was a sort of gilt-edged drill and, like a ring in a Fiji Islander's nose, much more ornamental than useful. Companies that had become proficient in this manual, used to give impressive exhibitions on Sundays and idle days, before admiring crowds of soldiers whose military education was defective in this respect. Perhaps they fight on these scientific principles in France, but in "our war" nobody ever heard any of these commands given in battle. An officer who attempted to put the drill into actual practice would have been sent to the rear and clothed in a strait-jacket. The fancy drill was as useless as a blanket to a Hottentot.[22]

The exact nature of the pervasiveness and usefulness of bayonet training among Civil War soldiers remains open to speculation.

While some soldiers found training with the bayonet in camp a laughable exercise, many men who actually experienced coming to physical blows with the enemy found it a terrible ordeal indeed. One of the salient reasons why seems to be because hand-to-hand fighting confronts combatants with killing on an intensely personal level. The study of men's behavior in battle suggests it is one of the most psychologically taxing forms of combat a warrior can experience. Close-range killing, writes Dave Grossman, "results in a situation with enormous potential for psychological trauma."[23] In such fighting, gone are the uncertainty and anonymity that physical distance provides. Fighting hand to hand brings combatants face-to-face with one another; it is truly up close and personal. The soldier who successfully kills in close-quarters combat might witness his enemy's death at a graphically intimate level. It is not a matter of shooting at a distance and seeing the target fall. Pulling a trigger allows powder and ball to do the physical work of killing, whereas stabbing, slashing, or clubbing requires the combatant to interact bodily with the foe. A soldier may witness the physical carnage he manages to wreak on the body of a fellow human being. He may encounter blood and other bodily materials, maybe even become covered in some of it himself. He may see the results in his opponent's face, perhaps the features distorted in a rictus of pain or the sight of the life going out of him.

As in other kinds of fighting, hand-to-hand combat confronts the soldier not only with the potential fear of killing but also the fear of being killed. Another reason making close-quarters fighting such a fearsome prospect is the degree to which it endangers his own life. Throughout history, one of the great advantages of the firearm as a weapon is its role as an equalizer; a well-placed bullet can negate all manner of advantages an enemy might possess, such as greater size, superior arms and armor, or a lifetime of training. Conversely, to physically battle an opponent requires hazarding one's own life in a contest of strength, reaction time, skill, and even chance. Face-to-face confrontations leave soldiers vulnerable to being psychologically intimidated by the enemy and his weapons. As one professional soldier from the twentieth century put it, "The thought of cold steel sliding into your guts is more horrific and real than the thought of a bullet doing the same—perhaps because you can see the steel coming."[24] In the case of Civil War soldiers, numerous Federals and Confederates received little or no training in physical combat, and even those schooled in the bayonet exercises of the day may have been inadequately prepared for the prospect of an actual physical encounter. It was for a host of reasons both timely and timeless that Yankees and Rebels might have dreaded the prospect of hand-to-hand encounters with one another.

The psychological nature of hand-to-hand combat might not only have affected Civil War soldiers' experience of such fighting and their willingness to engage in it but also how they fought in such situations. Multiple histories assert that Civil War soldiers preferred to fight by bashing or clubbing with their musket butts rather than stabbing with a fixed bayonet. For instance, Grossman suggests, "Numerous accounts of American Civil War battles indicate . . . resistance to use of the bayonet on the part of the vast majority of soldiers on both sides." Conversely, my research for this book did not uncover an example of Union or Confederate soldiers explicitly stating that they found fighting with clubbed muskets preferable or more bearable to bayonet fighting (though admittedly this is a different distinction than that made in Grossman's statement). The two best leads so far do offer corroborating evidence for this tendency, however. First, in a report after an action during the Chattanooga Campaign, an Army of the Cumberland surgeon noted finding only blunt force wounds—no bayonet wounds—among the casualties from a melee fight: "In such an action as this, if anywhere, we would look for bayonet wounds. Here was a charge—a hand-to-hand contest literally; some of the contusions were given by clubbed muskets. Not a bayonet wound is recorded. I looked for them, but neither saw nor heard of any. There was none." Second, in his memoirs, William T. Sherman authoritatively affirmed this tendency for clubbing over bayoneting: "Rarely did the opposing lines in compact order come into actual contact, but when, as at Peachtree Creek and Atlanta, the lines did become commingled, the men fought individually in every possible style, more frequently with the musket clubbed than with the bayonet, and in some instances the men clinched like wrestlers, and went to the ground together."[25]

Dave Grossman observes that some authors have supposed "that a specific characteristic of this brother-against-brother civil war must have been the cause of the soldier's reluctance to bayonet his enemy," but he rightly refutes this notion. In fact, evidence from similar conflicts in the horse-and-musket era of warfare suggests other fighting men instinctively relied on the musket butt over the bayonet; it was hardly a phenomenon unique to Union and Confederate troops. Moreover, the tendency even predates the use of musket and bayonet, applying to age-old weapons such as the sword. For instance, the legions of ancient Rome relied on a short sword, the *gladius hispaniensis,* as their primary infantry weapon, intended primarily for stabbing and thrusting. Ancient sources suggest that one of obstacles that the Romans' training sought to overcome was recruits' tendency to hack with the blade instead of stabbing. A propensity among warriors to swing or hack with hand weapons rather than to stab ostensibly can be traced from antiquity to the Civil War and beyond.[26]

From a purely technical standpoint, opting to club with a musket rather than stab with a fixed bayonet seems to forfeit unwisely the considerable advantages of the latter weapon. Physically, the fixed bayonet represents a more efficient weapon than the "clubbed" musket for several reasons. In terms of speed, a practiced soldier could deliver multiple pistonlike thrusts with a bayonet in the same time it would take for an opponent to wind up and swing his musket like a baseball bat. In terms of physical space, a soldier with a bayonet-tipped musket needed only room enough to thrust and retract the weapon, whereas a soldier trying to swing his clubbed musket might more likely find himself hampered by the press of men in a melee. In terms of wounds inflicted, blows from a musket butt could certainly kill or incapacitate an enemy on the receiving end, but the extent of such wounds would rely significantly on the physical strength with which they were delivered. The same could be said of bayonet thrusts, but throughout military history, stab wounds, especially to the torso, have proved notoriously efficient killers, requiring only a few inches of depth to be fatal.

If the fixed bayonet could theoretically surpass the clubbed musket as a hand-to-hand weapon, then why did so many soldiers apparently prefer to fight with musket butts over bayonets? The most frequently cited and potentially most decisive explanation is that human beings experience strong psychological resistance toward stabbing one another. "It is far easier to deliver a slashing or hacking blow than a piercing blow," Grossman observes. "To pierce is to penetrate, while to slash is to sidestep or deny the objective of piercing into the enemy's essence." One of Grossman's interviewees describes killing with a bayonet as a kind of "intimate brutality." Among the advantages of clubbing an enemy instead of stabbing him is that the soldier can simply bash his opponent out of the way. The victor in such an encounter is not overtly confronted with the damage he has caused. In contrast, the soldier who stabs his enemy undergoes the sensation of plunging cold steel into human flesh. Aside from the practical consideration of needing to quickly extricate his blade and not have it become trapped, the soldier faces the terrible prospect of having his foe transfixed at the opposite end of his blade—an intimate brutality.[27]

In addition to a psychological taboo against stabbing a human being, several secondary factors may also help account for the apparent preference for clubbed muskets over bayonets. As noted, many Union and Confederate soldiers received little or no training in bayonet exercise—training that might otherwise have increased their confidence in the use of the bayonet and counteracted any innate tendency to club instead of stab. In the absence of such training, Yankees and Rebels reverted to what came naturally. For nineteenth-century America's citizen-soldiers, there was probably not much intuitive about lunging and stabbing with a spearlike weapon such as a fixed bayonet, except perhaps pitchforking hay. Wielding a musket like a club, on the other hand, mirrored motions from everyday life such as swinging an ax or maul. Nor was a clubbed musket a shabby weapon in its own right. Before the introduction of the bayonet and improvements in the smoothbore musket's reliability, it was standard practice for the musketeer of the seventeenth century to reverse his musket for close-quarters fighting. The sturdy, metal-bound butts of eighteenth- and nineteenth-century muskets helped make them ad hoc clubs, and bayonet manuals of the day included strikes with the musket butt. The bayonet's considerable advantages over the clubbed musket aside, in terms of physical reach, they were nearly equal. According to calculations with Civil War weapons, a musket held by the muzzle and one held in a standard combat stance with fixed bayonet can each reach about forty-five inches from the furthest extended hand. Thrusting the musket one-handed or with both hands grasping the neck of the stock provides a sixty-inch reach, but these were specialized maneuvers intended for use against enemy cavalry.

Given the foreboding and dangerous nature of hand-to-combat, what circumstances were necessary for Union and Confederate soldiers to come to physical blows? Most documented instances of melee fighting in the Civil War shared in common several physical and psychological factors. Two battles that saw some of the fiercest and most extraordinary hand-to-hand fighting—Spotsylvania and Franklin—aptly illustrate these factors in action. One battle was fought in the East and one in the West. One pitted Union attackers against Confederate defenders and the other reversed the roles. In the early morning hours of May 12, 1864, just north of Spotsylvania Courthouse, Virginia, a powerful Union assault column smashed into a projecting portion of works in the center of the Confederate line known as the Mule Shoe. About twenty-two hours of close-quarters fighting followed as the two opposing forces shot, clubbed, and stabbed at one another on alternating sides of the earthworks in the rain, mud, and blood. Later that year, on the afternoon of November 30, outside Franklin, Tennessee, a Confederate charge overwhelmed a forward line of Federals and successfully followed them into the center of the main Union line. Similarly vicious fighting broke out for control of the breach that lasted for hours and into the night before exhaustion set in on both sides.

The presence of fortifications and other kinds of protective physical features could help make physical clashes between enemy forces possible. If hand-to-hand combat itself occurred relatively rarely in nineteenth-century warfare, then it was especially rare in the open field. For instance, military historians tell us that during eighteenth-century warfare, "the only instance in which infantry on both sides engaged in wholesale bayonet fighting on open terrain" occurred at the Battle of Moys (September 5, 1757).[28] Recall that most bayonet charges ended either with the attackers retreating or going to ground, or with the defenders retreating or surrendering. The stronger the fortification or other kind of protection behind which a defender fought, the better he was able to stand and hold his position. In physical terms, cover provided him protection against enemy bullets or bayonets, enabling him to better survive the onslaught by a superior number of attackers. The protection afforded by cover could likewise bolster the defender's confidence in being able to defend successfully his position. Psychologically, it also gave him something tangible to hold and protect, essentially making a soldier standing behind an earthwork or stone wall king of his castle, writ small. At both Spotsylvania and Franklin, the Confederate and Union defenders (respectively) benefited from the protection of stout, well-made defenses of earth and logs.

Cover could work to the advantage of the attacker in the prelude to hand-to-hand fighting as well. Physical protection in front of enemy defenses could allow more attackers to survive a bayonet charge, providing strong enough numbers potentially to bring about an actual bayonet fight. Attackers who made it all the way to the opposite side of a defended earthwork or wall would enjoy similar protection to that enjoyed by the defenders. In general, fortifications and other kinds of cover could allow more opposing combatants to come within closer range of one another because physical protection negated firepower, increasing the chances the one or both sides would hazard a hand-to-hand fight. During the Overland and Atlanta Campaigns, the opposing armies increasingly relied on field fortifications, with the result that the troops could confront one another over shorter distances. Such conditions could increase the chances of close-quarters fighting taking place. "Many of the enemy reached our line; some got across it," wrote Richard Tuthill, a Michigan artillery officer who survived the fierce Confederate counterattacks outside Atlanta. "Many were bayonetted, many killed with clubbed muskets; hand-to-hand conflicts were frequent."[29] Other kinds of broken terrain, such as woods or boulder-strewn ground, could bring enemy forces within point-blank or even striking range of one another, as could buildings, as demonstrated by the house-to-house fighting that took place in Fredericksburg on December 11, 1862.

Other human factors usually needed to be in place in order for hand-to-hand fighting to break out. Typically, each side needed a degree of numerical strength, a critical mass of men, to engage in a melee. If too few attackers or defenders remained, often discretion proved to be the better part of valor, and one side or the other would retreat rather than fight. Perhaps even more important was that one or both sides possessed the will to take the fight to close quarters. Often this took the form of a kind of impetus, a physical and moral momentum to close with the enemy. At Spotsylvania, the Army of the Potomac stormed the Mule Shoe with some 20,000 men in a "heavy column" multiple regiments deep, a great human battering ram in Federal blue that "rolled forward like an irresistible wave into the enemy's works." At Franklin, the Army of Tennessee also hurled about 20,000 men at the defenders. When the assault overwhelmed two brigades of Federals unwisely deployed in front of the main Union line, the Confederates sensed a golden opportunity to cross the killing ground on the heels of the fleeing defenders. With shouts of "Go into the works with them!" the victorious Rebels surged forward, punching a hole in the center of the Union army. In both battles, fresh defenders in reserve raced into the breach to contest the breakthrough. Spotsylvania and Franklin featured strong attacking forces successfully gaining a lodgment in enemy defenses, then met by timely counterattacks by enemy reserves, thus pitting two sizable and highly motivated forces that clashed in brutal hand-to-hand fighting.[30]

Although the close-quarters fighting at Spotsylvania and Franklin lasted for hours, Union and Confederate soldiers only spent a fraction of that time fighting in immediate physical contact with one another. For the troops to have engaged in continuous melee fighting for that duration would have proved physically and emotionally impossible. Instead, the combatants spent much of that time fighting across the works, as the participants described it, with each force occupying the opposite sides of the defenders' earthworks, separated by only a few feet or yards of earth and logs. After the initial impact of the attacking and counterattacking forces, the Federals and Confederates hunkered down on either side of the fortifications, after which most of the literal hand-to-hand fighting would be isolated to sorties by individuals or small groups of men. Much of this "across the works" form of close-quarters fighting consisted of shooting. A few especially daring men would mount the works and, handed loaded muskets by their comrades, would fire down into the enemy at point-blank range until they themselves were shot. Most of the firing involved soldiers raising their weapons just enough to fire over the parapet or underneath the head logs without exposing the rest of their bodies to enemy fire. Obviously this meant firing virtually blindly at the nearby foe. This behavior offers one of the clearest examples of Grossman's formulation of shooting at the enemy as "posturing." Presumably some of these combatants did in fact hope that their blindly fired rounds would hit the enemy. However, rather than actually expose themselves to the enemy's own fire at brutally close range, soldiers prioritized volume of fire over accuracy, firing vaguely at the enemy rather than directly into his ranks. Short of climbing over the works and renewing the fight with bayonets and clubbed muskets, keeping up a blistering wall of flame and lead offered the best means of resistance and self-preservation. Short of deliberately killing the enemy, many desperate soldiers on each side hoped that through sheer firepower, they could drive away the enemy, or at least keep him at bay.

Fighting across the works presents a snapshot into the psychology of killing and combat in the Civil War. To the dispassionate observer, it may seem perverse that opposing lines of soldiers should spend hours on end huddled against opposite sides of earth and log walls, firing blindly at one another, yet under those extraordinary circumstances, it offered the surest and most bearable means of survival. Doubtless many soldiers would gladly have torn themselves away from such terrible fighting if they could have, but for each side at these bloody battles, this would mean retreating across the open ground behind them and exposing themselves to enemy fire. Instead, they clung desperately to their own side of the works for protection. To go over the top meant plunging yourself into a mass of enemy soldiers ready to shoot, stab, and club you to death. In addition to the danger to your own life, it also meant subjecting yourself to the terrible prospect of your having to shoot, stab, or club someone face-to-face. Without the physical and moral impetus that fresh troops provide, how could either side renew an assault with any hope of success? In addition to the desperate bravery required to hurl oneself over the top, how amid the noise, smoke, and encroaching darkness could leaders in the thick of the fighting at Spotsylvania and Franklin hope to persuade and coordinate enough men to surge forward in order to carry the day? With no easy answers to such questions, ordinary soldiers rejected the alternatives of a hazardous retreat or renewing the horrors of direct hand-to-hand fighting. Instead, they reverted back to their primary combat role and the task for which their training had best prepared them: loading and firing their weapons as quickly as possible.

In addition to bitter fighting across the works, some of the Civil War's fiercest hand-to-hand fighting swirled around the contests for the capture and defense of regimental battle flags. The protection of the colors was a post of high honor and trust within a regiment. The duty of bearing the colors fell to sergeants, protected by a color guard of usually eight corporals, under orders to use their muskets and bayonets only in the immediate defense of the colors. To lose one's colors to the enemy was one of the greatest disgraces a regiment could endure. In turn, to capture an enemy's banner in battle was one of the greatest triumphs, representing one of the highest-prized trophies of victory. The practice of carrying large, colorful banners represents one of the starkest differences between warfare in the Civil War and the modern age. Consequently, Civil War soldiers' willingness to kill and risk being killed for the defense or capture of these flags stands out to some modern observers as one of the hardest elements of the conflict to fathom. Understanding the deadly struggles for these banners on the battlefield requires understanding Federal and Confederate soldiers' deep emotional investment in the flags they carried. "The flag almost transcended the definition of symbol," observes historian Brian Pohanka, explaining that to the fighting men of the Civil War, the "flag was intrinsic to all that they themselves stood for, as a soldier and as a human being, in that it was almost a living thing itself."[31]

The devotion of the blue and gray to their banners sprang from multiple deeply personal sources. Most obviously, the flags they bore into battle signified their national and political identities. "The sentiment of the old soldier for the flag of his regiment can not be described. . . . It is to him the glory and majesty of his country. It is the emblem of his native land," declared an Illinois veteran.[32] For Union soldiers, the Stars and Stripes represented the Union that many of them expressly fought to preserve. Per President Lincoln's order, the United States flag retained all its stars regardless of Rebel state governments' efforts to tear themselves from the Union. Conversely, the various incarnations of the Rebel battle flag signified Confederate soldiers' fight to establish an independent Southern nation.

Regimental battle flags also symbolized the pride and honor of the regiments whose names they bore. Veteran regiments often added battle honors to their flags, painting on the names of actions in which they had fought. Even before such honors could be applied, a bullet-scarred banner offered mute testimony to the storm of battle that the regiment had endured. For the soldiers, their battle flags also represented the home they had left behind. Regiments often first received their colors in formal presentations as part of special ceremonies in their home communities before departing for war. Many times the flags had been commissioned and purchased at considerable expense by local ladies. These delegations of women featured prominently in flag presentations, usually making speeches with strong appeals to the soldiers' bravery and manhood, bespeaking an "implied covenant between soldier and community," notes one historian. In Ottawa, Illinois, a woman presenting a homemade company flag told the recipients, "Our hands have made it, yours must defend it, and if needed for the purpose, the choicest blood in your veins, we doubt not will freely pour out. . . . See to it that this flag is never insulted with impunity." A New Orleans woman presented to a local company "colors woven by our feeble but reliant hands," a flag that the ladies hoped would "not only inspire you with the brave and patriotic ambition of a soldier aspiring to his own and his country's honor and glory, but also . . . be a sign that cherished ones appeal to you to save them from a fanatical and heartless foe." Though decorously spoken, the subtext of these appeals was often not far removed from the message of ancient Spartan mothers presenting shields to their sons, instructing them to only return from war "with it or upon it."[33]

The tremendous symbolic and sentimental value attached to battle flags ensured that many Civil War soldiers would pour out not only their own blood but also that of the enemy for control of these banners on the battlefield. In the confused to-and-fro fighting in the Wheatfield at Gettysburg, Confederate soldiers managed to shoot down the bearer of the 4th Michigan's regimental colors and seize the flag. Seeing this, Colonel Harrison Jeffords of the 4th Michigan dashed forward and felled the flag's captor, either with his sword or revolver. Jeffords reclaimed the colors, only to be bayoneted in the chest by another Confederate. A party of Michiganders rushed in and managed to recover both their colonel and the flag. Harrison Jeffords died of his wound the next day, the highest ranking officer of the war known to have been killed by a bayonet, having fought and died in the defense of the colors.[34]

Confederate soldiers displayed the same willingness to fight and if necessary kill in defense of the colors. At the Battle of Gaines Mill, staff officer John Cheves Haskell found himself in a desperate struggle for both the colors and his life. Riding up to a wavering regiment in Law's Brigade, the South Carolinian grabbed their battle flag and led a new charge against the enemy. Haskell's horse was shot dead as it leaped over the Union earthworks, falling to the ground and pinning one of Haskell's legs beneath its weight. As Haskell remembered, "A Captain, I think of a New York regiment, ran up to me and grabbing the flagstaff called out to me, 'You damned little rebel, surrender.'" Instead, Haskell jerked back on the staff with one hand and struck out with his sword in the other. The captain in turn pulled back and, drawing his revolver, began firing. For the next few moments, the two officers grappled, each with one hand grasping the flagstaff and the other trying to fight with his weapon. During the struggle, Haskell managed to free his leg and stand up, by which point more Confederates were pouring over the works, prompting the Union captain and many of his men to flee. Not content to let his assailant escape, Haskell pursued and with his sword "cut down on him with both hands, expecting to split him, as we used to read of in novels." The blow only knocked the Federal to his knees, however, and he managed to turn and raise his pistol. Immediately, Haskell countered: "I never doubted but that he was about to shoot again and ran him through." The captain died minutes later, but not before his vanquisher promised to send home his personal effects.[35]

Accounts of vicious battles for control of the flags stand out prominently in the histories penned by Civil War veterans. At the Battle of Cedar Creek, men of the 8th Vermont and the other regiments in their brigade received orders to make a nearly suicidal counterattack in order to delay the Confederate assault that had already routed the Union left wing. Plunging into the face of the Rebel onslaught, the Vermonters found themselves assailed on three sides. As the regimental historian recounted:

> Suddenly a mass of rebels confronted the flags, and with hoarse shouts demanded their surrender. Defiant shouts went back. "Never!" "Never!" And then, amid tremendous excitement, commenced one of the most desperate and ugly hand-to-hand conflicts over the flags that has ever been recorded. Men seemed more like demons than human beings, as they struck fiercely at each other with clubbed muskets and bayonets.

Likewise, Captain S. E. Howard of the 8th Vermont wrote, "Men fought hand to hand; skulls were crushed with clubbed muskets; bayonets dripped with blood. Men actually clenched and rolled upon the ground in the desperate frenzy of the contest for the flags. . . . The men realized that they were in a terrible mess and fought like tigers." At least three men died carrying the colors, and amid the murderous melee, every man in the color guard was either killed or received a wound. Ultimately, with the Rebel tide threatening to encircle them, the Vermonters had to break for the rear. The regiment had lost three-quarters of the men who had made the counterattack as casualties, but the regimental colors that they had defended so ferociously remained firmly in their possession. As the regimental history proudly noted, amid "that vortex of hell men did not forget the colors."[36]

Just as some of the most desperate firefights prompted company and regimental officers to join in the shooting, the maelstrom of hand-to-hand combat often swept officers into the action alongside their men. A well-armed Civil War officer might go into battle with a sword and revolver, which theoretically equipped him for both shooting and physical combat, yet his intended role in battle was not so much to fight as it was to command. His weapons were sidearms largely intended for defense of his person in extreme circumstances. An infantry officer's sword indicated his rank; on the battlefield, the blade served more often as a flashy pointer than a weapon. Nevertheless, under desperate circumstances, some officers did use their swords to shed enemy blood. One such instance occurred during the chaotic Union retreat through the streets of Gettysburg on the battle's first day. Captain Friedrich von Fritsch of the 68th New York encountered a bayonet-wielding Confederate who seized his horse's bridle and demanded, "Surrender! Get Down, you damned Yank!" Shouting back, "*You* be damned," the German-born officer swept down his sword, severing the Rebel's outstretched hand, and made good his escape.[37]

The Battle of Franklin especially saw officers plunged into the thick of the fighting. Defending a shoulder of the breach in the Union defenses, Captain James Sexton and his brother officers blazed away with their pistols at the Confederates threatening to overwhelm their left flank. "Every officer was busy with his revolver," Sexton wrote. "I discharged my own weapon nine times and the most distant man I shot at was not more than twenty feet away." Colonel Emerson Opdycke, leading his brigade in the counterattack that sealed the breach, emptied his revolver into the Rebel ranks, then reversed the weapon and began clubbing away at his foes. One of Opdycke's regimental commanders, Major Arthur MacArthur of the 24th Wisconsin, spurred his mount at a Confederate color-bearer, only to have his horse shot out from under him. Struggling forward on foot, he took a bullet to the shoulder; then a nearby Confederate major put a pistol ball in his chest. MacArthur managed to run the officer through with his sword before receiving another pistol ball in the knee as the two collapsed on the ground.[38]

In theory, no military arm was more expected to rely on and excel at hand-to-hand combat than the cavalry. On European battlefields, great formations of mounted swordsmen and lancers put fear into the hearts of soldiers on foot. The saber was ostensibly the Civil War cavalryman's primary weapon. This curved, single-edged sword "was the cavalry arm par excellence, and to add to its glamor, it even had a French name, the *arme blanche*," notes one historian.[39] A number of factors limited the impact of hard-charging, cut-and-slash cavalrymen on the Civil War battlefield. Although, like bayonet fighting, it would be a rarity in clashes between Yankees and Rebels, mounted hand-to-hand fighting made exceptional but dramatic appearances in Civil War combat.

Americans had been slow to re-create the killing power of the cavalry charge. Nineteenth-century America's woods and broken terrain made traditional saber charges less practical than they had been on Europe's open fields. Until 1855, the US Army had not even included regiments of cavalry per se. Before that year, the republic's horse soldiers were mostly limited to regiments of dragoons and mounted riflemen, mounted troops whose primary function was to ride to battle and then fight dismounted. In fact, advances in firearms technology seemed to suggest that this was the most effective use of Civil War cavalry in battle. The prevalence of rifle muskets among infantrymen increased the prospects of bloodily repulsing a cavalry charge, while the emergence of breechloading and even repeating carbines made the cavalry trooper a more effective dismounted fighter than ever before.[40]

The fully armed Civil War cavalryman was a formidable warrior, armed (ideally) with a saber, carbine, and six-shot revolver. Despite the handicaps to successful mounted tactics, cavalry training privileged the saber. As with bayonet treatises, saber manuals included a host of cuts and parries against both mounted and dismounted opponents that a trooper was expected to learn. The cavalry seems to have trained their recruits more rigorously with their close-quarters weapon than the infantry. Many troopers, perhaps aspiring to the romantic ideal of the bold cavalier, expressed more enthusiasm for saber drill than the average infantryman did for bayonet drill. "Our first saber drill was something to be remembered," Sergeant Thomas Crofts wrote in his regimental history of the 3rd Ohio Cavalry. "Methinks that could the hosts of rebeldom have seen the way in which we cut great gashes in the atmosphere they would have realized that their cause was hopeless, and would have at once given up the conflict."[41]

When it came to mounted combat between opposing bodies of cavalry, Civil War soldiers debated among themselves whether the saber or revolver was the better melee weapon. Generally speaking, Union cavalry tended to favor the saber as their close-quarters killing tool, while their Confederate opponents usually relied on revolvers. Confederate partisan leader John S. Mosby noted how he "dragged [a saber] through the first year of the war," but complained that the weapon proved useful only for spitting meat over a fire. Instead, Mosby's rangers and other mounted guerrillas armed themselves with two, four, or more revolvers each, using their personal arsenals of six-shooters with deadly effect in hit-and-run attacks on Union troops. An article in *Scientific American* echoed the Rebels' preference for the revolver, citing a European military expert who declared, "Let the horse be ever so swift, the sabre ever so sharp, or the rider ever so bold, the conical ball is too much for him."[42]

Confederates seemed to have had the stronger argument that the six-gun was mightier than the sword, yet the saber had its defenders, and not without good reason. Sergeant Crofts observed that although his regiment increasingly relied on dismounted tactics during the war and that they often found sabers an encumbrance, he dutifully noted that "there is no disputing that in a hand to hand conflict it is a very effective weapon, is always loaded and never misses fire." In a cavalry melee, a revolver was only effective so long as it had loaded chambers. Reloading a Civil War percussion revolver was a time-consuming process, which is why troopers who especially relied on them tried to carry as many as possible. The saber could in fact prove the decisive weapon in a mounted melee. A New York cavalry captain insisted that he "never remembered an instant in which the saber charge, resolutely pushed, did not fail to drive the pistols." Confederate cavalry suffered for lack of sabers in the 1864 Shenandoah Valley Campaign, particularly at the Battle of Toms Brook, where the saber-charging Union cavalry so thoroughly routed Confederate troopers that the battle was dubbed the "Woodstock Races."[43]

What role did the psychology of combat and killing play in the revolver versus saber debate? British military observer Arthur Fremantle dismissed the clashes he witnessed between Union and Confederate horsemen as "miserable affairs" and criticized both sides for failing to charge home with the saber: "They approach one another with considerable boldness, until they get to within about forty yards, and then, at the very moment when a dash is necessary, and the sword alone should be used, they hesitate, halt, and commence a desultory fire with carbines and revolvers." This behavior may have reflected hesitancy on the troopers' parts to commit themselves to a charge and thus plunge themselves into the dangers of melee combat. Indeed, the reliance on firearms described by Fremantle parallels Civil War infantrymen's preference for shooting over bayonet fighting.[44]

The psychology of killing does not necessarily explain why Union horsemen tended to favor the saber and Confederates the revolver. At least one historian suggests that the deciding psychological factor at play may have been cavalrymen's concern for their mounts, noting, "The generally poor condition of Civil War mounts favored the revolver over the saber in close combat." Just as the momentum of fresh troops could change the course of a bayonet fight, the shock effect of a well-formed saber charge could decide the winner of a cavalry melee, yet the frenzy of such fighting exposed not only the rider to mortal harm but also his horse. Confederate cavalry recruits usually had to bring their own mounts, which meant that they benefited from healthy, familiar horses in which they had great confidence, but it also made them warier of hazarding them in combat. If a Confederate cavalryman's horse died, he was expected to provide his own remount, or he could find himself relegated to the infantry. In contrast, Union troopers typically received army-issue horses and could expect a government remount. Neither side's cavalry could afford to be profligate with the lives of its horses, yet a Union cavalryman faced less dire consequences if his mount was harmed in combat, and thus he could afford to fight more aggressively in close-quarters mounted combat.[45]

Whichever weapon they favored, Civil War cavalrymen could be lethal opponents in close combat. During the Battle of Chancellorsville, the 8th

Pennsylvania Cavalry encountered Confederate infantry on a narrow forest road and spurred into an impromptu saber charge that slammed into the enemy. "Not a shot was fired by our regiment, the sabre being the only weapon used," Captain Charles I. Wickersham recounted, "and with it the regiment literally cut its way through the dense ranks of the enemy, who pressed us so closely that many of our horses were wounded by their bayonets." When a Confederate officer, revolver in one hand, seized the bridle of Wickersham's horse and ordered the Pennsylvanian to surrender, Wickersham's response came straight out of the cavalry drill book. "The reply was what is known in the saber exercise as 'left cut against infantry,'" Wickersham sardonically observed. "The rebel officer did not respond to roll call the next morning."[46]

The month after Chancellorsville saw mounted combat on full display at the Battle of Brandy Station, the largest clash of cavalry not only in the Civil War but in all of North America. A major in the 1st New Jersey Cavalry remembered it as "the most spirited and hardest fought cavalry fight ever known in this country." A trooper in the 12th Virginia Cavalry described the swirling, chaotic melee between Union and Confederate horsemen: "It was then warm work, hand to hand, shooting and cutting each other in desperate fury, all mixed through one another, killing, wounding, and taking prisoners promiscuously." A Georgia cavalryman described an encounter in which the two sides' typical preferences for saber or revolver were reversed, proudly writing of how "we dashed upon the infuriated Hessians [i.e., Federals] with drawn sabres (while they used the pistol chiefly) with such impetuosity that led the Yanks to believe that the rebs intended to wound their feelings; there was weeping and wailing and cracking of Yankee skulls."[47]

In contrast to the cavalry, of the three main military branches, soldiers in the artillery were the least suited or equipped for hand-to-hand combat. Heavy artillery regiments were trained and equipped as both artillery and infantry, in part so that they could better garrison and defend fortified posts. Most Civil War armies, however, primarily employed "light" or "field" artillery whose crewmen were less formidably armed. The US Army issued sabers and swords to artillerymen, but these were rarely carried in the field, especially by crews working their guns. Historians debate the extent to which Civil War artillerymen carried revolvers, either of military issue or private purchase. Some evidence suggests that only sergeants and the outriders on limbers and caissons were permitted to carry revolvers—weapons largely intended to shoot wounded horses, putting the beasts out of their misery and stopping the violent thrashing that could injure other horses in the team. Gunners in the field carried few or no sidearms because their combat role was for each crew to work together loading and firing a cannon. As Major Joseph Roberts affirmed in his *Handbook of Artillery*, "An artilleryman must never forget that his gun is his proper arm; here lies his strength; that his post of honor and his duty."[48]

Ideally, artillerymen were to avoid close-quarters contact with the enemy. Serving their guns usually in the rear of the line of battle, soldiers in the artillery typically suffered light casualties in action. Although Civil War artillery possessed considerable defensive firepower, tactical doctrine for both sides prudently called for infantry or cavalry support to ward off enemy attacks. Nevertheless, during a number of hard-fought battles, enemy infantry and cavalry did manage to storm artillery positions and get in among the guns and their crews. Sometimes these encounters ended in the capture of the cannons, other times in the attackers' repulse. Despite being ill-equipped to fight hand to hand with better-armed infantry and cavalry, in many of these instances the crews literally stuck to their guns and bravely fought to defend themselves. Like gunners in many other Western armies, Civil War artillerymen took pride in their guns and deemed it a great dishonor to lose any to capture; many of them could thus be counted on to protect them fiercely. "Men, whenever the enemy takes a gun from my battery, look for my dead body in front of it," famed Confederate artillery commander Willy Pegram told his gunners. "Dearer to the cannonier than life itself, it is said, is the gun he serves," a Pennsylvania regimental history said admiringly of the Union gunners at Gettysburg. "Death on the soil of our native State, rather than lose our guns."[49]

In desperate situations in which attackers got in among the guns, artilleryman lacking conventional sidearms turned to the tools of their trade. The use of two items predominate hand-to-hand accounts from the artillery: the large wooden ramrods used to swab and load gun tubes, and handspikes, stout wooden poles about the size of a baseball bat (though much thicker) that were used to leverage a cannon around by the trail. Gunners turned to both tools as clubs when hard-pressed. At Brandy Station, a standard-bearer in Stuart's Horse Artillery recalled how "a regiment of Yankees charged our Battery, and after giving them canister until they got too close, and we could not work our guns, we received them with sabers, pistols, hand-spikes, and sponge-staffs." Like his Confederate counterpart, Union veteran Augustus Buell recorded how Union gunners at Cedar Creek fought with a similar mix of formal and informal weapons. Confederates stormed the Sixth Corps batteries atop Cemetery Hill, and "in a second they were amongst us, amid smoke, fog, wreck, yells, clash and confusion which no pen can depict and no pencil portray," Buell wrote in his memoir *The Cannoneer*. "It was now man to man, hand to hand, with bayonet and musket butt on their side and revolvers, rammer heads, and handspikes on ours!" Some resilient gunners turned to other tools at hand. At Franklin, Private Jacob Steinbaugh of Ohio threw an ax to kill a "daring rebel" climbing into his battery, then "disabled another with a pick," actions for which his section commander singled out Steinbaugh in his after-action report.[50]

Regardless of the branch in which they served, to numerous soldiers the carnage, viciousness, and terror of hand-to-hand combat seemed much like hell on earth. Numerous survivors thus turned to infernal imagery to describe it. Combatants on both sides characterized men as fighting like "demons." A Louisiana soldier suggested, "In every great battle of the war there was a hell-spot," a part of the battlefield over which the two sides would grapple in furious close combat because control of it could decide the course of the battle. At Spotsylvania's Bloody Angle, the mud, blood, and grime combined to make it hard to tell the two sides apart. "No Mardi Gras Carnival ever devised such a diabolical looking set of devils as we were," remembered a Mississippi infantryman. "It was no imitation affair of red paint and burnt cork, but genuine human gore and gun powder smoke that came from the guns belching death at close range." A Confederate veteran of Franklin wrote that it was "as if the devil had full possession of the earth." The devil's domain could not even compare with the horror of Franklin, insisted an Illinois officer: "The contending elements of hell turned loose would seem almost as a Methodist love-feast compared to the pandemonium that reigned there for the space of ten or twenty minutes."[51]

Hand-to-hand combat in the Civil War was exceptional in more than one sense. That it occurred relatively rarely made it the exception to the norm in Federals' and Confederates' experience of battle. Moreover, such combat represented one of the most extreme forms of killing that soldiers could encounter. Although commanders believed in the bayonet's psychological power and deadliness, they failed to train most of their soldiers in preparation for the harsh reality of actual fighting with the weapon. Many soldiers recoiled from the prospect of melee combat, especially because such fighting threatened them with gruesome and fearsome ways of killing and being killed. Under the right conditions, including having enough impetus and numerical strength and in contested struggles for battle flags, Union and Confederate troops could overcome those fears and plunge themselves into bitter close combat. Whether they killed with bayonets, clubbed muskets, swords, revolvers, knives, or tools, such battles between citizen-soldiers of the blue and gray were terrible to behold.

# 5

## Hunters of Men
### Sharpshooters and Killing

Often the nature of Civil War combat left soldiers firing hastily or blindly, perhaps leveling their weapons at a distant battle line or firing at the enemy's muzzle flashes through clouds of powder smoke. In the words of a twentieth-century military adage, bullets fired so uncertainly did not so much have a victim's name on them but were instead addressed "to whom it may concern." In contrast, the Civil War's surest and deadliest shots, those especially expected to take "deliberate aim" and do "good execution" in battle, could be far more certain of killing the man in their sights. Such soldiers carried the name "sharpshooter."[1]

No individual soldier on the Civil War battlefield knew the business of killing as well as the sharpshooter. Because of this, both scholarly and popular opinion has tended to assume that such a man was an aberrant figure in Union and Confederate ranks, one detested by civil society and by the majority of his comrades. Closer inspection, however, throws these assumptions into doubt. Although the United States had not maintained officially designated sharpshooters as part of the small peacetime army, both Union and Confederate forces moved relatively early in the war to raise units of skilled marksmen, a decision that generally met not only with approval from civilians but keen interest as well. Sharpshooters' deadly effectiveness with the rifle made their presence felt in combat, a lethality that, it is true, some soldiers denounced as purposeless murder. Though many Federals and Confederates learned to fear sharpshooters' deadly aim, many took a pragmatic view, appreciating the achievements of their own marksmen and attempting to match the skills of the enemy's own crack shots.

Most sharpshooters did not consider themselves merciless killing machines but rather held to their own standards of what constituted fair play in war. The Civil War sharpshooter may have been more purposeful and relatively more at peace with the reality of killing in combat than the average soldier, yet what separated him the most from the rank and file was the skill with which he could shoot to kill.

The Civil War sharpshooter resembled the warrior better known today as the sniper, although by the 1860s his craft had not reached the level of sophistication it would achieve in the twentieth and twenty-first centuries. The sharpshooter was a marksman, one literally capable of sharp shooting—accurate and precise. A combination of skill, training, and equipment made him so, and this in varying degrees. "Sharpshooter" did not constitute a precise military designation but instead varied; sharpshooters included troops specially organized and used as marksmen as well as ordinary soldiers who informally elected to try their shooting skills against the enemy. Sharpshooters turned up in battles and sieges anywhere especially accurate shooting was needed, bringing down ordinary soldiers and skirmishers, picking off officers and gun crews, or countering enemy marksmen.[2]

Americans North and South could enthusiastically employ sharpshooters in their civil war in part because they shared a military heritage that celebrated the marksman on the battlefield. Since the Revolutionary War, the image of frontier riflemen had enjoyed a cherished place in the young nation's mythology. "Impress upon your soldiery that the Revolution of '76 was won by the Tennessee rifle," the adjutant general of that state wrote to a militia colonel, "and that we fight in defense of our homes and all that we hold dear." In his official history of the Army of Northern Virginia's sharpshooters, Major William S. Dunlop proudly compared his unit to Revolutionary War hero Daniel Morgan and his "Scotch-Irish riflemen." Americans had similarly lionized the frontier riflemen of the War of 1812, particularly those who fought alongside Andrew Jackson at the Battle of New Orleans. Jackson's presidential campaign song literally sang the praises of "The Hunters of Kentucky" and popularized the most enduring name for the American long rifle: the Kentucky rifle. Union sharpshooter Harrison DeLong likened his own comrades to these celebrated marksmen as they became as expert with their own weapons "as the famous riflemen of Kentucky."[3]

By the time of the Civil War, sharpshooting represented a legitimate, accepted element of military science in the Western world. For over fifty years, European nations had incorporated specially organized units of trained marksmen and sharpshooters into their armies. Much of the impetus came when these nations found themselves engaged in irregular warfare among civilian and native populations, requiring troops who could fight effectively in open order rather in the formal ranks of the line of battle. The French and Indian War especially impressed on Britain, France, and their respective colonists the value of imitating the loose form of forest warfare at which the various Indian tribes of the eastern woodlands excelled. Civil War soldiers harkened back to this aspect of the American military tradition when they described skirmish and sharpshooter tactics as fighting "Indian style." Rifle and light infantry units in European armies often took their names from their own language's word for "hunter"—*Jäger* (German), *chasseur* (French), *caçadores* (Portuguese), *cazadores* (Spanish)—though the British and Americans more prosaically dubbed their sharpshooters "riflemen." These troops relied on such hunting skills as marksmanship, stalking, and concealment, and not coincidentally, many drew their recruits from huntsmen, gamekeepers, and poachers. Unofficially, the "hunter" appellation also signified that on the battlefield, the sharpshooter's role was to be a hunter of men.[4]

On a national level, both United States and Confederate forces officially sanctioned and encouraged the formation of sharpshooter units. Only weeks after the firing on Fort Sumter, noted marksman and inventor Hiram Berdan began corresponding with Northern governors for authority to recruit in their states in hopes of assembling a regiment of the North's best shots. By June, Berdan received authority from General in Chief Winfield Scott to form what would be designated the 1st Regiment, United States Sharpshooters. A second regiment quickly followed, and together, the 1st and 2nd US Sharpshooters, known collectively as Berdan's Sharpshooters, became the most famous of the Civil War's elite marksmen. Berdan clothed his men in dark green uniforms as a step toward camouflage, a standard choice among European rifle regiments, but among Civil War soldiers, they were practically the only sharpshooters so distinctively uniformed. Although some Confederate volunteers began organizing themselves as self-styled companies and regiments of riflemen and sharpshooters at the outset of the war, the Confederate States government acted more slowly than the United States in officially incorporating such units. In April 1862, the Confederate Congress authorized the War Department to organize and equip a sharpshooter battalion for each infantry brigade, taking qualified volunteers from soldiers already enlisted.[5]

Because they were recruited nationwide and in the early rush to arms, Berdan's Sharpshooters came into being with great enthusiasm and fanfare. The positive public attention they received strongly suggests that Victorian America had few qualms in principle when it came to the deliberate use of sharpshooters in war. Berdan recruited companies from New Hampshire, Vermont, New York, Pennsylvania, Michigan, Wisconsin, and Minnesota, organizing shooting examinations in these states to find qualified marksmen. Recruits were required to bring their own rifles for qualification, ranging from common hunting rifles to heavy-barreled target rifles made especially for competition, and they were allowed to use any shooting stance they chose. To make Berdan's cut, they had to be able to put ten consecutive shots into a ten-inch target at 200 yards. These much-publicized examinations were as much social events as they were military procedures, drawing large crowds of spectators, just as a civilian shooting match might. In October 1861, *Harper's Weekly* carried a front-page illustration of a similar event, a public marksmanship exhibition by Berdan and a New Hampshire company of enlistees. The illustration featured a number of vignettes from the day of newly recruited sharpshooters loading their rifles, firing, and checking their targets, complete with crowds of well-dressed male and female onlookers. There could be little doubt the shooting exhibition was a respectable event, especially since *Harper's* proudly noted that the "New Hampshire marksmen are all men of excellent moral character, more than ordinary intelligence, and of good social position."[6]

Berdan's Sharpshooters enjoyed the endorsement of no less a personage than Abraham Lincoln, who admired their marksmanship but also winked at the deadly nature of purpose. The president visited the sharpshooters' camp outside Washington during one of their shooting exhibitions in fall 1861, even trying his hand at one of the heavy target rifles. "Abraham Lincoln handled the rifle like a veteran marksman, in a highly successful manner, to the great delight of the many soldiers and civilians surrounding," Captain Charles A. Stevens of the 1st USSS wrote approvingly in the regimental history. Berdan and his men had been firing at canvas targets with life-size Rebel soldiers sketched onto them, and the last target brought before him had "Jeff Davis" written overhead. The sharpshooters' commander had previously shown off his skill using facsimile targets of the Confederate president, but now he "remarked that I did not think it was exactly the thing to fire at Jeff Davis in the presence of the President of the United States." Lincoln, apparently unperturbed at the prospect of an effigy of Davis as a target, "laughed heartily," telling Berdan, "Oh Colonel, if you make a good shot it will serve him right." Berdan took his shot, drilling the right eye of the Davis target, to the great amusement of Lincoln and those assembled.[7]

High-ranking officers in both armies also endorsed the use of sharpshooters. During the 1862 Siege of Yorktown, Union general Fitz John Porter noted a particular Confederate officer overseeing part of the Rebel defenses. Porter dispatched a staff officer to Berdan's men, attached to his division, with instructions that he wanted the enemy officer "killed or driven off." A shot from a Vermont rifleman killed the Confederate, supposedly at a range of 1,400 yards. It seems the Sharpshooters' abilities pleased Porter in no small measure, for Colonel Berdan received an appreciative letter from division headquarters, informing him that the general was "glad to learn, from the admission of the enemy themselves, that they begin to fear your sharpshooters. Your men have caused a number of rebels to bite the dust. The Commanding General is glad to find your corps are proving themselves so efficient." Captain Stevens reported that General Alexander Hays harbored a prejudice against the Sharpshooters when they were attached to his brigade in 1864, but not because he objected to the deadly nature of their duty. Rather, Hays suspected the green-coated marksmen's abilities were overrated, that "the Sharpshooters were pets, and not particularly expert with the rifle." Eager to dash Hays's skepticism, the 1st Regiment's commander selected ten reliable men and staged a shooting exhibition at brigade headquarters. The Sharpshooters' prowess so pleased Hays that he ordered a pair of rifle-green trousers from the regimental quartermaster for himself. Hays was wearing the green pants when he was killed in the Battle of the Wilderness, "dying a Sharpshooter at heart and in sentiment."[8]

Perhaps no Civil War general promoted sharpshooting as energetically and systematically as Patrick Cleburne of the Confederate Army of Tennessee. Born in Ireland, Cleburne served three years as an enlisted man in the British army before immigrating to the United States. During the nineteenth century, Britain's army enjoyed great success not only in employing elite units of riflemen but also introducing advanced marksmanship training throughout the army once the rifle musket became the standard weapon for the common infantryman. Within his own division—perhaps the finest in the Army of Tennessee—Cleburne organized "an elite corps" of sharpshooters, one that reported directly to his headquarters. Initial recruits came from marksmen throughout the division nominated by their company officers, and from among these the best shots were selected. Cleburne's picked force received specialized training, particularly in range estimation in a variety of terrain types. Cleburne also worked diligently to provide his sharpshooters with the best available weapons, including several dozen British-made Whitworth and Kerr rifles successfully run through the blockade. These were among the most accurate muzzleloading rifles of the day, highly coveted by Confederate sharpshooters, and Cleburne's men received "more than was given any other division," as one staff officer proudly noted.[9]

Sharpshooters' letters and reminiscences reveal how they understood their combat roles as well as the appeal to joining such units. An officer recruiting for Hiram Berdan informed Wyman White of New Hampshire "that the Sharpshooters would not have any picket duty to do, would never have to fight in the line of battle," and they would be armed with advanced Sharps breechloading rifles. "He made it appear," Wyman wrote, "that all they would have to do would be to pick off Rebel officers and other troublesome Rebels," though in fact Wyman and his comrades in the 2nd USSS would find themselves in more than their share of fierce firefights. Luke Emerson Bicknell of Massachusetts' Andrews Sharpshooters similarly recorded, "The work of the company was to be picking off officers and artillerists in battle, or s[ie]ge, and from the unweildy character of our guns [heavy-barreled target rifles] we were to be free from duty in line of battle and, also, from the same reason were to go scott free from drill and guard duty." A Confederate sharpshooter writing home to his sister paralleled closely the advantages White and Bicknell described. Belonging to the "corps of sharpshooters" excused him from guard duty, and, as he noted proudly, "We are formed for the purpose of going in advance in the time of battle to shoot officers. We are to be armed with the best guns." Georgia sharpshooter W. R. Montgomery described his unit's skirmish tactics in more detail, deployed to "clear the way" in front of their brigade. "We Sharp Shooters are in front all the time from 100 to 500 yards of the Yankies," he wrote to an aunt. "We keep up a prettie heavy fire all the time, take a shot whenever a Yankie shows his head."[10]

These Union and Confederate recruits offered almost verbatim descriptions of the attractions to enlisting as a sharpshooter. Excusing elite specialty troops such as sharpshooters from guard duty was a common privilege in eighteenth- and nineteenth-century armies, as was sparing them from manual labor on fatigue duty. White discovered he and his comrades were not exempted from picket duty, however, as sharpshooters' marksmanship and adeptness at operating in open order made it natural to place them at the outskirts of their army on the picket lines. "As it was the province of the sharp shooter to shoot some body," Lieutenant Colonel William Ripley of the 1st USSS explained candidly, "it was necessary that he should be placed where there was some one to shoot." Sharpshooters also cited the prime weapons promised to them. A soldier naturally wants the best weapon his government can provide, and many Civil War soldiers brought with them a discerning eye toward their armament, but the experienced hunters and target shooters who flocked to be sharpshooters were especially enticed. The specialized Sharps rifles promised to Berdan's recruits were an especially strong inducement—so much so that when it seemed the weapons would not come and they would be forced to accept inferior rifles, Berdan's strong-willed recruits almost mutinied. The special weapons that they did eventually receive reflected additional incentive for enlisting as a sharp-shooter: the appeal of belonging to an elite unit.[11]

Clearly factors apart from an eagerness or willingness to kill, such as the privileges and pride of belonging to a select unit, could draw men to sharp-shooting, yet other incentives did relate directly or indirectly to killing. Captain Clifford Shore, a British sniper in World War II, observed, "Sniping . . . is the personal individual killing of a man in cold blood," yet the desire to kill was not what made a good sniper, he insisted:

> I often heard it said that a sniper should be filled with a deadly hatred of the Hun, or enemy. But I found that the men who had a seething hatred in their hearts for all things German . . . were not the type to make good rifle killers. The man I wanted was of cold precision, the peace-time hunter who had no hatred for his quarry but just a great interest in the stalk and in the kill. . . . The tree hunter is never a butcher; he does not desire to kill for killing's sake, but there is something elemental in the stalk and slaying which swamps every other feeling and makes the heart and brain exultant, and filled with action-elation.

Numerous Civil War soldiers who likened skirmishing and sharpshooting to hunting anticipated Shore's assessment, particularly William Ripley, who eloquently described the "peculiar fascination" such service held for his men. "Sharp shooting is the squirrel hunting of war; it is wonderful to see how self-forgetful the marksman grows—to see with what sportsmanlike eyes he seeks out the grander game, and with what coolness and accuracy he brings it down," wrote the Vermont rifleman. "At the moment he grows utterly indifferent to human life or human suffering, and seems intent only on cruelty and destruction; to make a good shot and hit his man, brings for the time being a feeling of intense satisfaction." While Ripley's sharp-shooter seems to want to wreak "cruelty and destruction," he notably precedes that statement with the clarification that in the moment he has not grown desirous of human suffering but rather indifferent to it.[12]

Armies throughout the centuries have done well to recruit hunters because they possess the necessary skills for sharpshooting and sniping not only through training but also by temperament. Like a hunter of game, the battlefield's hunter of men functioned as a self-reliant, goal-oriented killer.

Sharpshooters' writings consistently list the killing of enemy officers as one of their key duties. This, along with silencing gun crews and targeting opposing skirmishers and sharpshooters, squares with what Grossman describes as "target attractiveness" and "the payoff of killing," affirming that soldiers are especially willing to eliminate enemy commanders and those operating dangerous weapons. A man who prized his marksmanship and woodcraft might understandably be drawn to a service where such skills would be more appreciated and could be put to better use, over the alternative of the chaotic, imprecise killing of the line of battle. Accounts from Wyman White and other sharpshooters illustrate that not having to fight shoulder to shoulder with the rank and file offered an incentive as well. Just as modern audiences have difficulty understanding the reasons for the orderly, stand-up mode of fighting that nineteenth-century tactics entailed, so too did many Americans in the 1860s decide such fighting was not for them. "Indian-style" fighting gave the soldier more control over self-protection, as well as granting him more independence from the control imposed by his superiors. As one historian notes, the skirmish line, unlike the firing line, "depended on the temperament of individuals rather than on the machine-like obedience required of soldiers in massed formations."[13]

Sharpshooters' relative comfort level with killing in combat can be inferred from the jocularity they used when speaking of their kills. Sharpshooters' accounts display a penchant for describing dispatching the enemy with wry or euphemistic turns of phrase. At Cold Harbor, marksmen from the 15th South Carolina sallied out of their entrenchments to target a Union sharpshooter perched high in a tree. A well-timed volley knocked the Federal from his aerie, sending him tumbling as he flailed helplessly at the branches. The Carolinians returned to their lines, content that "one Yankee, at least, had been given a long ride in midair." Supporting a Confederate attack at Petersburg, Major Dunlop described how his marksmen "with merciless accuracy were peeling the topknots from every Federal head that peered above their rifle pits." Union marksmen spoke of their exploits in the same spirit. One of Berdan's Sharpshooters wrote home, "I fired five shots and am well satisfied that I have finished the career of two Rebels." Another wrote an uncle how one of the officers used a heavy target rifle on a Rebel sharpshooter and thus "gave him the order to lie down with a Union bullet thro' his head." Sergeant White of the Sharpshooters' 2nd Regiment recounted how at Petersburg he and his comrades encountered an erratic shooter they concluded was a civilian "that came out to get a chance to shoot a few yanks." For the amateur marksman, White mused, the "experiment was a fatal one." A Sharpshooter's bullet pitched him backward, arms in the air, a lesson that it "did not make much [sense] swapping shots with Yankee sharpshooters."[14]

If these turns of phrase can be deemed euphemistic, then it raises the question why sharpshooters would substitute "good speech" as part of the language of killing. Could such phrasing be considered distancing language needed to disassociate soldiers from guilt or trauma from having killed? Certainly not every sharpshooter relished every kill. During the fighting around Petersburg, Tennessee sharpshooter Henry Manson suddenly encountered a Union soldier less than forty paces away. The Federal fired a shot that missed; Manson fired a shot that did not, accompanied by "a prayer for the soul of the bravest Yankee I ever saw." At the same time, however, other accounts reflect genuine satisfaction at a well-aimed shot and the killing of a dangerous adversary. In the incident Wyman White described with the armed Confederate civilian, White's comrade, Private Nathan Morse, noticed the man would bob his head above the trench several times before taking a shot, so Morse trained his rifle on the spot and tried to anticipate his appearances. With perfect timing, he fired the shot that felled the man, prompting Sergeant White to marvel appreciatively, "Comrade Morse was a genius." In contrast to Manson's encounter, White unambiguously seems to have appreciated Morse's kill. Still, it is possible that a given sharpshooter could be pleased by an enemy's death and yet wish on some level to distance himself from the impact of the killing. At a certain point, only speculation is possible when soldiers provided limited information as to their personal feelings regarding complex personal episodes.[15]

Civil War sharpshooters also reflected their acceptance of killing in their readiness to claim credit for high-profile kills, a trait they shared with their forbearers from the Revolutionary War and the War of 1812. On May 9, 1864, during the Battle of Spotsylvania, Major General John Sedgwick became the war's most famous victim of a sharpshooter's bullet. The beloved and much-respected Sixth Corps commander gently admonished his men for ducking as Confederate rounds buzzed unsettlingly close. Like other veterans throughout the age of gunpowder, "Uncle John" reminded his men that if they could hear the bullet, it meant it had already safely passed by. Seeking to encourage his soldiers, Sedgwick insisted that the troublesome Rebel marksmen "couldn't hit an elephant at this distance," shortly before a bullet struck him under his left eye, killing him instantly. Georgia sharpshooter Berry Benson wrote that fellow marksman Ben Powell of the 12th South Carolina reported having shot a Union officer the same day as Sedgwick's death, and Major Dunlop's history credited Powell and his Whitworth rifle with the death of the "gallant and distinguished soldier." Powel described hitting a mounted officer, whereas Sedgwick was definitely on foot at the time of his death, so either the details of Powell's shot were confused in the retelling, or Powell and his comrades were mistaken in concluding that he had killed Sedgwick. Sedgwick's killer may in fact have been killed by Union forces shortly after the fatal shot. William Dunlop and other Confederate veterans clearly wanted to credit "the man behind the gun" in the famous episode whose name "has never before been mentioned," but the Confederate sharpshooter's name may well be lost to history.[16]

The fight for Fort Donelson, one of the war's first major battles, illustrated the tactical benefits of sharpshooters as well as the only semiformal nature of their employment. The wooded ridges surrounding the Confederate defenses proved a natural haven for the sharpshooting mode of war, and scores of Confederate defenders deployed into the woods to snipe at approaching Union forces. This move not only maximized the defensive potential of the terrain but also served to harass and keep at bay Federals seeking to reconnoiter and encircle the fort. "Sharpshooters of the enemy kept up their firing all through the day," wrote an Illinois soldier, "and every now and then one of our good people would get one of their bullets and fall." Union accounts from the battle almost invariably refer to these Rebel marksmen as "sharpshooters," though few if any units in the Confederate garrison seemed to have been officially armed, trained, or designated as such. Throughout the Civil War, combatants referred generically to soldiers fighting in such fashion as sharpshooters, regardless of whether they were fighting in that capacity formally or informally. Of course, sharpshooters ideally opted for concealment and tried to keep a healthy distance between themselves and the enemy, so naturally most soldiers never got a clear view of them. For most Civil War soldiers, what marked a man as a sharpshooter was not so much what headquarters called him, or how well armed or trained he was, but how he was fighting—outside the line of battle and trying to fire as accurately, and lethally, as possible.[17]

Rebel sharpshooters proved a formidable foe at Fort Donelson, particularly one wily marksman noted by numerous Union participants and dubbed "Old Red Shirt" for his distinctive manner of dress. Approaching the fort, wrote Charles F. Hubert of the 50th Illinois, "we got a glimpse of Red Shirt. . . . His situation was behind a large stump in our front, and just outside the Rebel works. He was a remarkably good shot." According to Hubert, a number of officers in the regiment experienced "narrow escapes" after coming in his sights, including the colonel and the chaplain. Others were less fortunate. The regiment's adjutant saw a sergeant "borne to the rear with a great hole under his left cheek bone, perhaps from the gun of Old Red Shirt." To confront Old Red Shirt and his comrades, Ulysses Grant's army could bring to bear a specially prepared regiment of marksmen, Birge's Western Sharpshooters (subsequently designated the 66th Illinois). Armed with civilian hunting and target rifles, some with telescopic sights, these riflemen from the Old Northwest wore squirrel tails in their hats as tokens of their marksmanship. Hubert and his comrades appreciated the Western Sharpshooters and their "long range guns," which proved "quite a help to us, as they kept the enemy . . . behind their works."[18]

Union soldiers' reactions to Confederate marksmen at Fort Donelson offer a telling look at Civil War soldiers' attitudes toward sharpshooters, especially at what for many was their first experience of combat. Many of the common soldiers in Grant's army did not simply content themselves with letting the Western Sharpshooters face off with their enemy counterparts, nor do they seem to have expressed anything resembling moral outrage that their Rebel foes were trying especially hard to shoot them down. Instead, their initial reaction seems to have been to fight fire with fire—to fight sharpshooters with sharpshooters. A South Carolina infantryman at the Siege of Petersburg aptly summed up this pragmatic sensibility, matter-of-factly writing that Union sharpshooters "have kild a great many of our men. We pay them back in the same kind of corn."[19]

The Union response at Fort Donelson illustrates the Civil War soldier's ability to take to sharpshooting readily and enthusiastically. "Skirmish fighting was a new thing to us then," wrote Charles Hubert, "and very many of us would beg permission of the officers to go to the front." One of the regimental officers borrowed a rifle from Birge's men "to get a shot or two." Another of Hubert's comrades, fighting alongside the Western Sharpshooters, dubbed himself "a volunteer sharpshooter." Beset by enemy marksmen, Henry Uptmore and his comrades in the 11th Illinois "received permission to fire upon them also, and even I fired a few shots at them." Fred Mensendike, also of the 50th Illinois, was especially keen to bring down Old Red Shirt and may well have played a part in the Confederate marksman's demise: "I looked and saw Red Shirt aim and fire, and a soldier to my right fell dead. . . . I was determined to shoot Old Red, if I could, and in a short time he appeared, and I, with many others, fired, saw him throw up his arms and fall back." For men of both sides, the skirmish lines around Fort Donelson proved a deadly site.[20]

The year after the fight for Fort Donelson, the Siege of Vicksburg demonstrated perhaps the most widespread evidence of both the often ad hoc nature of Civil War sharpshooting and the willingness of common soldiers to try their hand at it. Ulysses Grant's army essentially lacked any specially trained or designated sharpshooter units, so instead Grant deployed ordinary infantry units to the trenches en masse, generously supplied them with ammunition, and encouraged them to blaze away at the Rebels day in and day out. Sheer volume of fire, helped by some talented marksmen in the ranks, managed to pin down Confederate defenders along much of the siege lines. William Reid, an eager amateur sharpshooter from Illinois, wrote how his comrades "enjoyed themselves by shooting at the rebels in and around the forts, some half mile away." Some men fancied sharpshooting so much that they pursued it on their own time, as one Iowa soldier recorded: "Many of the men consider the sharp shooting fun & and many when not otherwise engaged will take their pockets full of ammunition & go to [the] skirmish line." With plentiful ammunition, enthusiastic riflemen could hone their target shooting. "If this siege is to last a month, there will be a whole army of trained sharpshooters," Buckeye soldier Osborn Oldroyd boasted, "for the practice we are getting is making us skilled marksmen."[21]

Not all soldiers shared in the enthusiasm for sharpshooting. To Edward Potter of the 29th Wisconsin, "this going out once or twice a day to shoot at human beings like ourselves seems strong business to me yet the boys all like better to shoot at a man than to shot at the loop holes of the Fort." Potter's account not only places him among those Civil War soldiers who felt ambivalent about killing in combat but also illustrates that he perceived he was in the minority in that regard. Most of his comrades seemed to enjoy sharpshooting against the enemy. Moreover, Potter indicates that it was possible to engage in sharpshooting in such a way as merely to keep the defenders' heads down, but most of Potter's comrades evidently preferred shooting to kill over simply providing suppressing fire.[22]

Perhaps the most dangerous service for Civil War sharpshooters came about when they faced off against their own kind, engaging in what modern military science calls countersniper tactics. When Union and Confederate soldiers opposed their enemy counterparts, they took on the roles of both hunter and hunted. Marksmen in gray, blue, and green quickly acquired a healthy respect for enemy sharpshooters. J. Smith Brown of the 1st USSS wrote that when the regiment joined the Siege of Yorktown "we discovered the rebels had Sharp Shooters also, and I will give them the credit of having as good shots as I ever saw, and some better than I want to see again." Swiss-born Rudolph Aschmann, a captain in the same regiment, allowed that at the Siege of Petersburg, "concealed enemy sharpshooters did not fail to aim with good accuracy at all who showed their heads above the earthworks, but we were too experienced in this kind of warfare to get the worst of that contest." A Mississippi sharpshooter in Lee's army described one particular advance against Union marksmen as "a more trying ordeal then any event of the campaign thus far," in which he imagined "that each Federal sharpshooter had selected his Confederate; that his rifle was pressed against his shoulder; and that he was taking aim and had begun pressing the trigger gently."[23]

Long-range duels between sharpshooters could be bitter contests indeed. William Dunlop wrote of one such encounter in which the "Federal sharpshooters . . . displayed an animus of vindictive spirit, which the boys in gray were not slow to reciprocate." Soldiers on both sides resorted to the time-honored ruse of lifting a hat just above a trench as a decoy to draw an enemy sharpshooter's fire, thereby allowing one's own marksmen to aim for the telltale puff of smoke. John West, a sharpshooter in the 4th Georgia, described how he and his comrades worked in pairs, one raising a hat on a ramrod and another waiting with rifle ready, so that "when the Yankee showed his head to shoot at the hat the other would put a bullet through his head." During the Petersburg Siege, James Ragin of Berdan's Sharpshooters encountered a Confederate counterpart whose skill almost fatally matched his own. Taking aim at one another, the two marksmen fired simultaneously it seemed, the Rebel's bullet clipping Ragin's scalp. No more shots came from the Confederate's position; presumably Ragin had killed the man who so nearly killed him.[24]

Sharpshooters were often as keen as other soldiers to avenge the death of a fallen comrade, and a sharpshooter who managed to kill one enemy marksman might not live long enough to tell the tale. William Ripley described a drawn-out duel at Yorktown between a New Hampshire private and "a particularly obnoxious and skillful" Confederate marksman. The two traded several shots with one another, drawing the attention of men from both sides. Finally the Federal was killed by a shot to the forehead as he began aiming his own rifle, prompting cheers from the Confederate lines. The cheers were soon cut short, however, as one of the officers took up the dead man's weapon, a heavy target rifle with a telescopic sight. Taking aim, the sharpshooter officer "soon saw the triumphant rebel, made bold by his success, raise himself into view; it was a fatal exposure and he fell apparently dead."[25]

Sergeant White had harsh words for one enemy sharpshooter he encountered. During the Overland Campaign, he encountered a former schoolmate, a sergeant in a Massachusetts regiment. The fellow sergeant had lost three pickets killed by a Confederate marksmen and "was very anxious that I should try and silence the wicked rebel Sharpshooter." Approaching the shooter, White experienced two close calls, once as a Confederate fired on him as he dashed for cover and another that whistled past his head as he peered around a large tree. Having spotted his adversary, White loosed half a dozen rounds as fast as he could work the action of his Sharps. White never knew if any of his shots had hit the enemy marksman, though it did silence the Confederate sharpshooting on that front. In later years, White's friend told "the story of my silencing his murderous rebel quite often to our native townspeople, which is not offensive to me for if I should tell it to them they might think I was boasting."[26]

Did Wyman White mean it as a condemnation when he described his Confederate sharpshooter as "wicked" and "murderous"? If so, how did he rationalize such sentiments if White celebrated the sharpshooting prowess of himself and his comrades? Did he only deem Confederates sniping at Federals to be wicked? White's reaction might be because the Rebel marksman came close to killing both his friend and himself. Still another clue may lie in the fact that the enemy sharpshooter was targeting Union pickets. Soldiers on both sides widely abhorred the shooting of pickets as unnecessary and illegitimate, a subject explored more thoroughly in the following chapter. Civil War sharpshooters often operated on the picket lines, yet many of their kills—especially outside of fixed sieges—were enemy troops actively fighting or performing some other aggressive function, not unsuspecting victims like pickets. Sergeant White recorded an episode at Petersburg in which the opposing lines traded coffee and tobacco by tossing the goods across the lines. When the Confederates' parcel of tobacco landed just out of reach for the Union troops, they promised not to shoot if the Yankees left cover to fetch it, but they warned them of a sharpshooter lurking in an old chimney who would "surely shoot you if he has a chance." So some sharpshooters clearly would make few or no exceptions when it came to killing. However, White's account does not make it expressly clear whether he believed shooting pickets to be fair play or not. Furthermore, if White did not mean to denounce the shooter but only used words like "wicked" and "murderous" as a rhetorical flourish, then such theorizing becomes moot. Once again, when soldiers' accounts raise as many questions as answers for modern readers, only speculation remains.[27]

The deadly, personal nature of sharpshooting did provoke disgust and dismay among some observers, both civilians and soldiers. Civilian artist Winslow Homer created an iconic image, first in an engraving for *Harper's Weekly* and later as a painting, of a Union sharpshooter perched in a tree taking aim with a scoped target rifle. During a visit with Berdan's Sharpshooters in the trenches around Yorktown, he had an opportunity to watch Confederate soldiers through the scope of one such weapon. The ability to view an unsuspecting victim through the scope's magnification shocked

Homer: "[As] I was not a soldier—but a camp follower and artist, the above impression struck me as being near murder as anything I could think of in connection with the army & and I always had a horror of that branch of the army." During the Siege of Port Hudson, Captain John De Forest of Connecticut noted how his men and the Rebels daily "shot at each other . . . from morning to night." De Forest vehemently deprecated the practice as "a lazy, monotonous, sickening, murderous, unnatural, uncivilized mode of being. . . . Some of the officers tried sharp-shooting as an amusement, but I could never bring myself to what seemed like taking human life in pure gayety."[28]

Two of the most passionate (and most often cited) denunciations of sharpshooters in Civil War accounts come from two artillerymen, one Confederate and one Union. "Sharpshooting, at best . . . is a fearful thing," wrote Major Robert Stiles. "The regular sharpshooter often seemed to me little better than a human tiger lying in wait for blood. His rifle is frequently trained and made fast bearing upon a particular spot,—for example, where the head of a gunner must of necessity appear when sighting his piece,— and the instant that object appears and, as it were, 'darkens the hole,' crash goes a bullet through his brain." Private Frank Wilkeson of the 4th US Artillery remembered fervidly, "I hated sharpshooters, both Confederate and Union, in those days, and I was always glad to see them killed." The young gunner doubted that picking off a few men here and there could influence the course of the war; nor he did he approve of what he saw as their skulking, predatory tactics:

> As a campaign cannot be decided by killing a few hundred enlisted men—killing them most unfairly and when they were of necessity exposed,—it did seem as though the sharpshooting pests should have been suppressed. Our sharpshooters were as bad as the Confederates, and neither of them were of any account as far as decisive results were obtained. They could sneak around trees or lurk behind stumps, or cower in wells or in cellars, and from the safety of their lairs murder a few men. Put the sharpshooters in battle-line and they were no better, no more effective, than the infantry of the line, and they were not half as decent.

Wilkeson went on to describe what he saw as one of the most indecent behaviors among sharpshooters, explaining, "There was an unwritten code of honor among the infantry that forbade the shooting of men while attending to the imperative calls of nature, and these sharpshooting brutes were constantly violating that rule."[29]

Many historians have taken such accounts as reflecting the majority of Civil War soldiers' attitudes toward sharpshooters. One art historian's essay on Homer's painting, *The Army of the Potomac—A Sharp-Shooter on Picket Duty*, suggests, "For many foot soldiers, as reflected in their journals and diaries, sharpshooting was an unceremonious and vicious tactic that amounted to nothing more than murder." In his excellent study *The Union Soldier in Battle*, Earl Hess notes, "Although some soldiers took to sharpshooting with diligence, even fulfillment, most detested the role of the sniper." On closer examination, scholars seem to have based such conclusions not on a wide survey of soldier accounts but on repeated reliance on the same few sources, especially Stiles and Wilkeson. A number of histories only specifically cite one or both of these memoirs when interpreting attitudes toward sharpshooters and thus conclude that antipathy toward these soldiers was the norm. Bruce Catton, in his Pulitzer Prize–winning *A Stillness at Appomattox*, paraphrases Wilkeson's belief that sharpshooting could not contribute to the outcome of a campaign and attributes this view to soldiers at large, before quoting the rest of the artilleryman's denunciation of sharpshooters. Like Catton, a popular history of elite American troops cites Wilkeson's hatred of Union and Confederate sharpshooters and appreciation of their deaths, concluding that he "probably spoke for a majority of men on both sides."[30]

Some scholars have even taken apparently neutral accounts and have interpreted them as denouncing sharpshooters. The essayist on Homer's painting *Sharp-Shooter* takes a statement from Private Alfred Ballard at Yorktown—"On each of our posts was stationed one of Berdan's sharp shooters, who were always on the look out for game, and woe to the rebel who put himself in their way"—and suggests the account "revealed negative feelings." However, at face value, Bellard's account is morally neutral, offering neither a positive nor negative judgment.[31]

It is perhaps more than mere coincidence that two of the most vehement denunciations of sharpshooters came from two artillerymen. Perhaps no branch of service in the Civil War was as vulnerable to skilled marksmanship as the crew of a field gun. "Artillerymen could stand anything better than they could stand sharpshooting," Confederate marksman John West wrote, for they "could pick off the gunners so easily." Under ideal conditions, a Civil War cannon had a crew of nine to maneuver it around the battlefield and to load and fire it. A stationary cannon with its handful of crewman performing their duties about the gun made a choice target for marksmen, skilled or unskilled. The team of six horses that drew the limber to which a cannon attached for transportation, and that during battle was parked just six yards behind the gun, also made tempting targets.

Before the widespread introduction of the rifle musket to the battlefield, artillery could deploy within several hundred yards of enemy infantry, safely beyond the range of smoothbore musketry. The rifle evened the playing field, giving the foot soldier the additional range to lethally engage artillery. A few well-placed shots could quickly thin an artillery crew or drop the limber horses in their tracks, potentially stranding the gun. Ironically, while Private Wilkeson argued that sharpshooting could do little to influence the outcome of a campaign, on a tactical level, his own branch of service could most easily be checked by skilled marksmen. Rifle fire could silence an artillery battery by killing or wounding crewmen and horses, thus causing them to seek cover, stranding them on a battlefield, or simply causing them to retreat to a safer distance. Disproportionately, a few sharpshooters could dethrone artillery, the reputed "king of the battlefield." Silencing or impeding the enemy's artillery represented a considerable tactical advantage, one that might be likened in twentieth-century combat to knocking out enemy machine gun nests. Targeting enemy artillery might alter the course of a battle, and it represented a major reason why astute generals such as Patrick Cleburne used sharpshooters as eagerly as they did.[32]

Psychological factors might also account for the hatred expressed by soldiers such as Stiles and Wilkeson toward sharpshooters. When it came to awareness of and identification with the reality of personally killing in combat, the two service branches operated at different extremes of the experience of battle. Sharpshooters unmistakably targeted and killed individuals in action, whereas the average artilleryman could be far more removed physically and emotionally by the reality of taking lives than any other combat soldier in the Civil War. Artillery ideally operated to the rear in support of the line of battle. Firing at long range, it would be hard to discern the actual physical results of their work upon the enemy. Granted, artillerymen were not entirely divorced from the deadly capabilities of their cannon. Gunners might well see the results of their firepower, especially in the aftermath of a battle and if enemy troops had come within range of antipersonnel ammunition. In the midst of Pickett's Charge, Union artillerymen who fired deadly blasts of canister point-blank into the attacking Confederates reported seeing bloody mist over their gun smoke. Moreover, if attacking infantry got in among the guns, many artillerymen could be counted on to fight bitterly to defend their guns from capture.

Nevertheless, typical artillery service distanced crewmen from the reality of killing. Operating an artillery piece was a team effort, requiring different men to assist in loading, aiming, and firing the gun, effectively diffusing responsibility for whatever the results downrange. Evidence from twentieth- and twenty-first-century combat suggests that artillerymen, bomber crews, and sailors, despite facing very real danger in war, experience fewer "psychiatric casualties" and less resistance to killing than combat infantry. All these fighting men operate crew-served weapons and typically engage the enemy at great distances, and Grossman and others attribute the lesser combat burden they seem to bear to their physical and emotional separation from the awareness of killing. An artilleryman, more so than any other Civil War soldier in a combat, could deny or ignore the potential reality (if he was so inclined) that he was killing fellow human beings. For those reasons, one can easily imagine why an artilleryman, distanced from the reality of killing and particularly vulnerable himself to sharpshooting, could despise a soldier whose function in battle was to fix a fellow man in his sights and pull the trigger.

We should not assume, however, that all artillerists felt like helpless victims of sharpshooters or that they could not be effective killers themselves. Some veterans became proficient enough in the science and art of gunnery that they might be likened to sharpshooters in their own right, only operating weapons of far greater caliber. At Spotsylvania, Union gunners in the Sixth Corps managed to exact a measure of revenge after they lost John Sedgwick to Confederate sharpshooters. An infantry patrol directed the crew of a rifled cannon to a tree in which some of the Rebels were perched. "The first shot cut the tree off about 40 feet from the ground & down came Mr. sharp shooter head first," one Federal wrote approvingly. "That ended the sharp shooting at this time."[33]

Sergeant Frank Elliot of the 1st New York Light Artillery recorded a similar episode of skilled gunnery during the Atlanta Campaign when his two-gun section came under fire from Confederate marksmen in a cotton gin. With comrades falling dead and wounded around him, Elliot ordered a gunner aiming one of the pieces, "You must shoot lower and hit that fellow or he will kill the whole of us." For Elliot, the situation clearly amounted to a case of kill or be killed. As the Rebels continued to score hits and his own artillery salvos continued to miss, Elliot decided the erring gunner had "lost his head" and so put him to work loading while Elliot himself took over sighting the cannon. As the sergeant recounted,

In my two years' previous service as gunner I had fired or aimed a 10-pounder Parrott for more than 1,500 rounds, and with the old gun could have hit a man's face every time at that short range. This gun was a brass 12-pounder Napoleon, and I had not studied the ranges; consequently my first shot was three feet too high and passed through the roof. My second shot was as much too low. . . . My next aim was correct, and as I gave the finishing turn to the [elevating] screw the fellow shot again and knocked the muzzle sight of the piece. I gave the order to fire. The shot seemed to burst against the building. . . . For an instant the atmosphere in that vicinity was filled with smoke, splinters, clapboards and building materials. There was a hole in the end of the gin that a mule and cart could have gone through. Some 20 long-legged rebels who were inside concluded that was a good place to make tracks from, and they started for the woods with much cheering from our side, emphasized by a few shots from the infantry boys.

With good aim and greater firepower, Frank Elliot proved some artillerymen could best sharpshooters at their own game.[34]

A possible indicator that Civil War soldiers did not despise the practice of sharpshooting as thoroughly as supposed is a general lack of atrocities committed against sharpshooters. In many twentieth-century conflicts, particularly World War II, many frontline troops operated on an unwritten principle that snipers were not to be taken prisoner but killed outright. Certainly talk of showing no quarter to sharpshooters was bandied about in the Civil War. Union prisoners told the Kentuckians of the Orphan Brigade that they "would kill a captured man if he was found with a Kerr rifle," a British muzzleloader highly prized by Confederate sharpshooters. As late as 1864, a newspaper in the besieged city of Petersburg, reporting the capture of several men from the 2nd USSS, editorialized that "in our estimation they are nothing but murderers creeping up & shooting men in cold blood & should receive the fate of murderers. No quarter should be shown them by any Confederate soldier." Nevertheless, sharpshooters themselves testified that such talk was overblown. The official history of Berdan's Sharpshooters recounts how at Gettysburg a detail from the 1st Regiment rushed the boulders of Devil's Den and captured a party of Confederate sharpshooters. The prisoners "were much alarmed at being caught, because as sharpshooters they expected no quarter, and begged lustily for their lives . . . until they learned that their captors were Berdan Sharpshooters, when a sudden change came over their dejected spirit to one of undisguised happiness," reported Captain Stevens. "That old idea that sharpshooters would be strung up, was discarded by our men after the Peninsula campaign." Typically, when Civil War soldiers managed to kill a sharpshooter, it was not by capturing and summarily executing him but by beating him at his own game—at long range with a well-aimed bullet.[35]

Some soldiers did express animus toward sharpshooters, but with notably less vitriol than Stiles and Wilkeson. Naturally, soldiers could be expected to feel hostile to an individual trying to kill them, especially when a sharpshooter managed to gun down one of their comrades. When Captain Lewis Buzzell of the 13th New Hampshire was killed in a Virginia skirmish, shot through the heart by a hidden marksman, "his death f[ell] upon the Regiment like a cold-blooded murder committed in their midst, and not as a stroke of war," wrote the regimental historian. Other soldiers condemned specific kinds of conduct by sharpshooters, such as Wilkeson's reference to firing on men trying to answer a call of nature. One Confederate soldier-correspondent wrote that in the aftermath of the Battle of the Crater, Union wounded trapped between the lines could be heard "begging piteously for water and praying to be cared for." A number of Confederates sought to go to their aid but could not, ironically because "they were in full range of the enemy's sharpshooters, who had not ceased their firing, even under such appalling circumstances as we have described."[36]

Positive accounts from other soldiers about sharpshooters challenge the assumption that they were pariahs within their own armies. Men who believed in the necessity of killing the enemy tended to respect their lethal marksmanship. "There are great anecdotes told of our sharpshooters killing [Rebel] gunners inside the batteries," a New York infantryman wrote during the Siege of Yorktown. Assisting a storming party at Vicksburg, Illinois officer John Edmiston reported that his company "experienced no loss as the rebels were unable to fire on us without exposing themselves to the fire of the sharpshooters occupying the trenches." On the opposing side, the Orphan Brigade's Johnny Green also appreciated sharpshooters' ability to keep enemy artillery at bay, describing the Kerr rifles wielded by his fellow Kentuckians as "a great terror" to Yankee gunners. He also noted the dangers of sharpshooting duty. The Orphans had just thirteen of the treasured Kerr rifles, and among the men entrusted with the weapons, several were killed and all wounded at least once. Despite the hazards, Green recorded, "whenever needed there were numerous volunteers." Whether it was pride of place, independence, or better opportunities to kill Yankees that attracted them the Kentuckian did not say, yet among Johnny Green's comrades there was no shortage of volunteers willing to try their hands at the deadly craft of sharpshooting.[37]

In contrast to the men who deplored sharpshooting, other soldiers ungrudgingly admired the skill of even enemy marksmen, much like the Berdan Sharpshooter who gave the Confederates "the credit of having as good shots as I ever saw, and some better than I want to see again." Some of his Rebel foes returned the compliment. "The Yankees had some splendid marksmen," J. D. Bethune of the 2nd Georgia wrote during the Peninsula Campaign. Alabama veteran John Mason remembered the "nip and tuck" fighting with the "Burdine sharp shooters" at Petersburg, appraising them as "good marksmen better than any we had." William Fletcher of Texas, himself an aggressive skirmisher and sharpshooter, warned his comrades that not all the Yanks were the "poor woodsmen and marksmen" he had been led to believe. Some, he had learned for himself, possessed "the cunningness of wild turkeys." According to one especially impressed Confederate veteran, "Some of those Yankee sharpshooters were marvelous. . . . The best shooters were in the Union army. Most of them came from the west, and many of them had been scouts in the Indian country. They rarely missed a man at a distance of a mile."[38]

While some soldiers despised the sharpshooter's craft as barbaric and inhumane, most sharpshooters, not surprisingly, did not view their role in such a brutal light. Despite being more inured to the taking of individual lives than the average soldier, many sharpshooters professed their own clear standards as to what constituted legitimate warfare and what they deemed beyond the pale. Captain Rudolph Aschmann of the 1st USSS could accept with resignation the deaths of comrades in battle, including at the hands of enemy marksmen, but he loathed the guerrillas "who haunted the army's flanks" and "committed treacherous murders out of ambush." While both guerrilla warfare and ambush had legitimate places under the rules of war, Aschmann described in his memoirs irregular partisans who probably operated without the sanction of the Confederacy and without uniforms, men who Aschmann testified killed and robbed both military and civilian personnel from the Union army. Opposing Captain Aschmann and his Army of the Potomac comrades, Major Dunlop of the Army of Northern Virginia condemned the Union attempt to breach the Confederate lines at Petersburg by exploding a mine packed with 8,000 pounds of gunpowder as a "fiendish plot."[39]

Many Civil War sharpshooters also held firm ideas about legitimate conduct on the battlefield. Wyman White of Berdan's Sharpshooters described a skirmish in which he and his comrades netted five prisoners. As the surrendering Rebels approached White's men, a nervous new recruit who was also "a little deaf" fired on them. White reproved the recruit "that the men were prisoners and it was a wicked thing to fire on men who had surrendered," then reassured the frightened foes they were not going to be "murdered." White described the recruit as "green enough to fire on unarmed men," suggesting that veteran troops would have better presence of mind to distinguish men giving themselves up from armed combatants.

Although not expressly stated, White may also have been implying that veterans who had faced the enemy in battle and gained a rough respect for fellow fighting men might be more generous in extending mercy to the other side, given the opportunity.[40]

Sharpshooters' writings offer multiple accounts of deadly marksmen staying their hands in the interest of mercy or fair play. Sharpshooters seemed to possess the same proclivity for fraternization and unofficial truces as other combat troops. Captain Aschmann recounted a peaceful period during the Siege of Petersburg during which the opposing pickets settled into an understanding that they would not fire on one another. When an errant shot was fired from Confederate lines, the Federals, "indignant at this breach of the peace," prepared to return fire. Before the aggrieved Yankees could retaliate, however, the Rebels made a decisive gesture as a means of an apology. Forcing the offending shooter out of the trench, carrying a heavy beam, his comrades forced him "to parade back and forth" between the lines for the next two hours, to the sound of appreciative Union applause.[41]

Lieutenant Colonel Ripley wrote feelingly of the humane side of his men, noting after his description of the "intense satisfaction" successful sharpshooting could produce, "Few, however, care to recall afterwards the look at the dying enemy, and there are none that would not risk as much to aid the wounded victim of their skill as they did to inflict the wound." Waxing philosophical, Ripley observed, "War is brutalizing, but the heat of the actual conflict passed, soldiers are humane and merciful, even to their foes." Sergeant White recounted an extraordinary act of forbearance on the part of his comrades. After capturing a handful of enemy pickets at Kelly's Ford, the Sharpshooters noticed one Confederate soldier across the river who neither turned himself in nor tried to run away but instead settled in behind a stump. Although White believed they could hit the Confederate, he and his comrades began peppering the stump with their shots, a technique they used a number of times to induce reluctant Rebels to give themselves up. When the lone soldier showed no reaction, a Sharpshooter lieutenant elected to investigate, stripping off most of his clothes and then swimming the river with a rifle. The Confederate appeared to be both mentally and physically impaired, and the lieutenant safely brought the unfortunate man back across the river into Union lines.[42]

There were limits to sharpshooters' willingness to kill, even when it came to enemies that might seem fair game. For some men, killing seemed easier in the heat of battle, such as fighting on the skirmish line or dueling with an enemy marksman, in contrast to sniping at an unthreatening enemy. William White, who excelled both as a skirmisher and a sniper, described himself in one sharp firefight as "doing my best sending bullets" into the oncoming Confederates. For others, however, a reluctance to take human life crept in when bullets were not flying. Theodore Upson of the 100th Indiana fancied himself a good shot with his privately purchased Henry repeating rifle, and at the Battle of Bentonville he was encouraged to try his marksmanship against a Confederate gun crew limbering up their small cannon with a team of mules. Upson at first took aim to shoot one of the mounted artillerymen, "which I could easily have done as his whole body showed plainly above the mule," but then Upson's conscience pricked at him: "Just as I was going to fire something seemed to say to me: 'Don't kill the man; kill the mule,' so I dropped my rifle a little and shot the off mule just behind the fore leg." Upson had spared the rider but had still crippled the team, enabling his comrades to successfully capture the gun.[43]

Confederate cavalryman J. W. Minnich described an encounter in which he helped a Whitworth-armed marksman draw a bead on a distant Union horseman scouting their lines. Just as the sharpshooter fired, the Federal happened to spur his horse forward a step, causing the well-aimed bullet to only nick the horse's rump. "By golly! I missed him, and I was sure I'd get him," Minnich's comrade remarked, adding, "Well, his time had not come to die today, and I am not sorry he got away. It looked too much like murder. He was a brave fellow, and I hope he'll get through all right." A diligent soldier in combat, Minnich nevertheless found himself sharing the sharpshooter's relief: "To tell the truth, I felt a bit like that myself, although in those days I felt it my duty to do the enemy as much damage as I could, and never failed to try when the opportunity presented."[44]

Civil War sharpshooters stood out as the deadliest individual warriors on the Civil War battlefield, a reality that brought them both hatred and acclaim. Some soldiers and civilians despised them for their ability to kill unexpectedly from afar, yet this abhorrence was hardly universal. Many in both military and civilian circles recognized theirs as a legitimate part to play on the battlefield. While some despised the sharpshooter, others celebrated and tried to emulate his skills. Men volunteered their marksmanship skills on formal and informal bases for a variety of reasons, including the benefits of belonging to an elite unit, the excitement and independence that skirmishing and sniping offered, and a desire to exercise their shooting skills and kill the enemy in the best way they knew how. The sharpshooter's role was the common soldier's duty writ large. His job was to kill the enemy, and his skill with the rifle meant he could kill well.

Americans were killing one another in the streets of Baltimore only days after the firing on Fort Sumter. On April 19, 1861, a secessionist mob armed with bricks, clubs, guns, and other weapons attacked the men of the 6th Massachusetts as they tried to pass through the city en route to Washington, DC. The regiment in turn fired into the mob. Four soldiers and twelve civilians died in the clash. (Library of Congress)

Americans North and South found rival heroes in the violent deaths of Elmer
Ellsworth and James Jackson on May 24, 1861. Having hauled down a large
Confederate flag from the Marshall House hotel in Alexandria, Virginia,
Ellsworth was descending a flight of stairs when hotel owner Jackson killed him
with a shotgun. Corporal Francis Brownell then shot and bayoneted to death
his commander's killer. Unionists mourned Ellsworth as a martyr and hailed
Brownell as his avenger, while Confederates celebrated Jackson as a patriot who
fought and died in defending his home and cause. (Library of Congress)

A sanguinary envelope commemorates Ellsworth's death and Brownell's act of retribution. (Liljenquist Family Collection of Civil War Photographs, Library of Congress)

The nature of battle in the Civil War contributed to soldiers' ability to potentially kill in combat. Linear tactics provided commanders effective fire control. For soldiers in the ranks, firing on command and in large formations, as well the poor visibility on the battlefield, could mitigate potential feelings of responsibility or guilt regarding killing. (Anne S. K. Brown Military Collection, Brown University Library)

Civil War combat often came down to desperate firefights. In this postwar illustration of the Battle of Chickamauga, a Confederate battle line loads and fires amid heavily wooded terrain. (*Battles and Leaders of the Civil War,* HathiTrust)

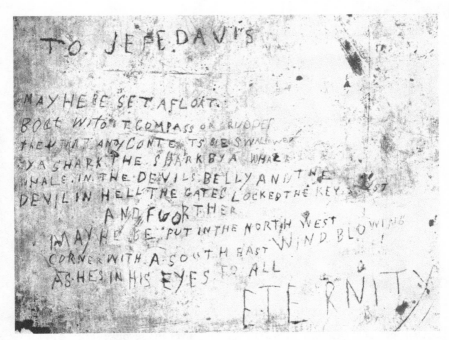

Rival presidents Abraham Lincoln and Jefferson Davis were targets of violent rhetoric by enemy soldiers. Union prisoners held in the Winchester, Virginia, courthouse carved into the walls this curse on the Confederate president. (Courtesy Shenandoah Valley Battlefields Foundation)

Many newly enlisted soldiers posed for photographers brandishing an impressive array of personal weapons, such as the Bowie knives and revolvers carried by brothers Daniel, John, and Pleasant Chitwood of the 23rd Georgia (*bottom*). (Courtesy Georgia Archives, Vanishing Georgia Collection, gor517.) In some cases, such weapons were photographers' props, as was likely the case with this unidentified Federal (*top*). (Liljenquist Family Collection of Civil War Photographs, Library of Congress.) Other soldiers brought such weapons when they marched off to war, indicating that some men anticipated needing them in close-quarter combat.

Hand-to-hand combat proved relatively rare in the Civil War. Even when Union and Confederate soldiers came within striking distance, they often preferred to load and fire rather than engage in melee combat. At fights such as the Mule Shoe at Spotsylvania, the combatants fought one another from opposite sides of the same breastwork. (*Battles and Leaders of the Civil War,* HathiTrust)

Battles over control of flags produced some of the war's fiercest hand-to-hand fighting. Soldiers' zeal to defend or capture regimental banners could overcome their instinctive aversion to close-quarter combat. At Cedar Creek, the 8th Vermont fought such a battle; the regimental history recounted, "Men seemed more like demons than human beings, as they struck fiercely at each other with clubbed muskets and bayonets." The Vermonters suffered 75 percent casualties in the battle but saved their colors. (*History of the Eighth Regiment Vermont Volunteers, 1861–1865,* HathiTrust)

A Confederate sharpshooter perched in a tree takes deadly aim in this postwar illustration. While such a pose may seem characteristic of sharpshooters, most often Union and Confederate marksmen plied their trade on the skirmish line or in siege lines. (Wikimedia Commons)

Sharpshooters were among the deadliest killers on Civil War battlefields. Civilian artist Winslow Homer, who painted this iconic depiction of a Union marksman, averred, "I always had a horror of that branch of the army." While some soldiers expressed contempt for sharpshooters, many others admired them and aspired to be marksmen themselves. (Wikimedia Commons)

Not only did Civil War armies recruit sharpshooters but also the civilian world generally celebrated these proficient warriors. This *Harper's Weekly* cover from October 1861 shows respectable ladies and gentlemen admiring the shooting skills of New Hampshire sharpshooters, described in the accompanying article as "all men of excellent moral character, more than ordinary intelligence, and of good social position." (Courtesy Amon Carter Museum of American Art)

Black soldiers were among the war's most passionately motivated combatants. The striking regimental color of the 22nd United States Colored Troops, painted by black artist David Bustill Bowser, suggests the willingness of such soldiers to slay enemies who would keep their people enslaved. (Library of Congress)

Vicious fighting and postbattle atrocities often characterized clashes between Confederates and black Federals. No incident was more notorious than the massacre of black soldiers and Southern Unionists at Fort Pillow, Tennessee. Many black regiments afterward went into battle with cries of "Remember Fort Pillow!" (Wikimedia Commons)

In contrast to trying to kill one another on the battlefield, Civil War soldiers frequently fraternized with the enemy during lulls in the fighting. Artist-correspondent Edwin Forbes depicted a typical scene in his sketch "Pickets Trading Between the Lines." Numerous contemporary accounts commented on the friendly relations between enemy combatants but also observed that most soldiers quickly switched back to the business of fighting when the time came. (Library of Congress)

# 6

## Murder and Mercy
### The Extremes of Killing

Whether they did their fighting in the line of battle, in skirmish order, or in the clash of steel, Civil War soldiers' behavior in combat
was not always as simple as the question to kill or not to kill. Societies at war and their militaries legitimize and even encourage their
fighting men to kill the enemy's fighting men, but soldiers' actions
in battle do not always fall within the scope of sanctioned killing.
Sometimes they exceed the limits of legitimized killing and kill
under circumstances deemed contrary to the laws of war. Other
times they stop short of this standard and deliberately choose not
to kill an enemy they could otherwise lawfully kill. This chapter
examines the various ways Union and Confederate soldiers experienced these extremes of combat.

The idea of extremes of killing and not killing may best be understood if we picture conduct in battle as a continuum. Imagine all the circumstances and scenarios in which a soldier could
lawfully be called upon to kill as the center portion of the continuum. Extending along one portion of this scale would be
the various kinds of unlawful killing a soldier could commit.
These are the acts we deem atrocities—or, put more simply, acts
of murder. Conversely, sliding along the scale in the opposite
direction are in-stances in which soldiers purposefully held back
from the chance to kill the enemy. These instances in which
soldiers declined to kill were acts of forbearance or mercy.
These contrasting behaviors illustrate the extreme responses of
Civil War soldiers to the nature of killing in combat, but they also
reveal the limits both of soldiers' savagery and restraint.

During the opening months of the Civil War, rumors ran rampant in both North and South claiming that the enemy was committing various kinds of atrocities on the battlefield. In one sense, these reflected typical fears and propagandizing on the part of any society at war. However, such atrocity rumors also effectively demonstrated how sectional hatred and rivalry had made Americans capable of thinking the worst of their fellow countrymen. Decades of bitter political battles and demonization gave credence to tales of battlefield outrages. Stories of cruel enemies who took no prisoners and showed no mercy circulated. In the wake of the Union disaster at First Bull Run, a New York soldier wrote the *Sunday Mercury,* claiming, "The rebels were seen cutting the throats of the wounded and bayonetting them to death." Confederates harbored similar fears regarding their Yankee opponents. Months after Bull Run at the Battle of Belmont, in which troops under Ulysses Grant overran a Rebel camp, an Illinois colonel remarked how the enemy wounded "implored our men not to murder them, being evidently under the belief of the false and wicked impression so industriously sought to be made by many of the leaders of this cursed rebellion that we were barbarians and savages, but instead of murdering them some of our men ministered to their wants and conveyed them to places of safety."[1]

One of the more curious fears of enemy barbarism concerned rumors of poisoned bullets. The origin of these stories seems as least partially attributable to Confederate soldiers finding Union ammunition containing bullets designed by Philadelphia inventor Elijah D. Williams. These Williams bullets featured a detachable zinc base designed to improve windage and to help clean powder fouling from the barrel. Rebel soldiers who found these curiosities presumed they were designed as a poisonous projectile. Ironically, one reason that Confederates found so many of these rounds is that many Union soldiers, fearing that the strange bullets would actually damage their rifle barrels, tossed them away rather than use them.[2]

Most atrocity rumors died slow deaths simply because little evidence arose to substantiate them. For many soldiers, prolonged service and the experience of a battle or campaign dispelled the most outlandish claims. As the latter half of this chapter demonstrates, Federals and Confederates could often behave magnanimously in victory toward a captured enemy. Furthermore, the practice of fraternizing and trading with the enemy underscored the humanity of the other side and often revealed to Rebels and Yankees how much they had in common.

Civil War soldiers did not, however, behave entirely blamelessly in battle. The furor and stress of combat could lead men into transgressing the rules of war. Some soldiers committed acts of unlawful killing dubbed "surrender executions" by historians. In such cases, a soldier tries to give himself up but is summarily killed by the enemy instead of being taken prisoner. Military history is replete with accounts of such killings, usually carried out according to an unspoken rule among men in battle that an enemy who resists too long deserves no quarter, especially in cases where they have just seen the enemy kill one of their comrades. Soldiers committing surrender executions believe that an opponent who only moments before was doing his best to kill them deserved to be killed himself. The laws of war under which Union and Confederate soldiers operated (and under which modern US forces operate today) forbid such killings; an enemy soldier is entitled to quarter as soon as he offers his surrender, regardless of his previous actions.

Nevertheless, the impulse to carry out surrender executions existed among Civil War soldiers. One Tennessee soldier wrote after the war of a Yankee who was lucky to escape such a fate. Amid the rout of two Federal brigades at the Battle of Franklin, W. M. Crook was reloading his musket when he saw ten feet from him a Union officer shoot down one of his comrades, then throw up his hands when another Rebel pointed a musket at him. Crook recalled, "A Southern lieutenant, not seeing the captain shoot our man, and thinking his man ought not to shoot an enemy with his hands up, knocked the gun down, and pointed the federal captain to the rear." Crook's account implies that he felt the captain deserved to be killed at that moment; perhaps he also believed the Confederate lieutenant would have agreed had he seen the entire episode. Soldiers trying to surrender were not always so fortunate. A Michigan soldier described a bloody encounter between Confederate infantry and Union cavalry: "Two [Rebels] . . . fired on a squad of our cavalry killing one man. They then threw down their arms and offered to surrender, but the cavalrymen refused to make prisoners of any such men. They cut one fine enough for mince pies. The other was brought in minus one ear and part of his scalp." Although surrender executions violated the letter of the law, more than a few Civil War soldiers believed that an enemy who killed one moment and then asked for quarter the next deserved no mercy.[3]

One of the most common scenarios in which Confederates indulged in nonbattlefield killing and execution of Federal soldiers occurred when they encountered Union foraging parties. The specter of Union forces as invading hordes and their depredations of the Southern countryside—real and imagined—powerfully kindled Confederate wrath, almost as much as did the introduction of black US soldiers. For some soldiers in butternut or gray, the immediate threat of Northern invasion of the South equaled or trumped the Confederacy's political ideology of slavery and Southern rights as a reason for armed resistance. As one captured Rebel soldier pithily told his Yankee captors, "I'm fighting because you're down here."[4] This real threat to hearth and home made some Confederates especially eager to kill Yankees whom they caught in the act of despoiling their beloved South, both in actual combat and in cold blood.

Two Union forays into the South in fall 1864 especially drew vengeful Rebels like angry hornets: Sheridan's destruction of the Lower Shenandoah Valley—still remembered as "the Burning"—and Sherman's March to the Sea. Less well remembered than the latter, the former predated it by about a month and consisted of a smaller but more concentrated targeting than the march through Georgia and the Carolinas. Both Sheridan and Sherman conducted their campaigns with similar goals in mind. Grant ordered Sheridan to render the fertile Shenandoah Valley "a barren waste," while Sherman famously declared on the eve of his march to "make Georgia howl." Union armies in both campaigns not only captured or destroyed crops and war matériel but also sent the Confederacy a powerful political message by bringing the war directly to the home front. Like the English *chevauchées* through France in the Hundred Years' War, the Burning and the March signaled to Southern civilians that the Rebel government in Richmond was all but helpless to stop Federal forces marching at will through their territory. The political, social, and material implications of such campaigns account in part for fierce Confederate attacks on Union soldiers at the forefront of the destruction.

The killing of Union foragers sometimes took place in a gray area of morality. Operating miles from their own armies in hostile country, Federal foraging parties often encountered bands of Confederate cavalry and partisans, resulting in sharp skirmishes. In such cases, killing by both sides was just as legitimate as in any other battle, large or small. Often Union foragers managed to repulse their attackers, especially when nearby parties rode to the sound of the guns to assist their comrades. In other cases, Yankees searching for food or plunder were routed or surprised by their opponents and when captured found themselves at the mercy of vengeful Rebels. During Sherman's March through Georgia and the Carolinas, the best remembered and most mythologized execution of Union hard war policy against the Confederate home front, Union soldiers commonly found the bodies of their comrades executed by Confederates, with signs reading "Death to All Foragers" hung about their heads. Often it was clear that such men had been summarily executed after capture, or at least that their bodies were mutilated after they were killed. John Hill Ferguson of the 10th Illinois recorded in his diary that four foragers from his regiment were found with their throats cut. Men of the 33rd Massachusetts found ten of their comrades hanging from trees, complete with "Death to All Foragers" placards.[5]

In some instances, Rebels compounded their violations of the rules of war by wearing captured Union uniforms to waylay their foes. The 34th Illinois suffered its two final casualties of the war mere days before Joseph Johnston opened surrender talks with Sherman. Two Southerners rode up to Lieutenant Edward B. Harner and Private George W. Barr wearing blue Federal overcoats and claiming to belong to an Ohio unit. The two disguised Rebels struck up a conversation with the Illinoisans, then suddenly pulled their pistols and fired. Lieutenant Harner fell dead, shot through the heart, while Private Barr managed to escape into a nearby swamp only slightly wounded.[6]

The killing and murder of Yankee foragers offered outraged Confederate soldiers and irregulars an immediate chance to avenge themselves on their invading foes, as well as executing acts of terror calculated to discourage foragers and to intimidate and demoralize other Union soldiers. Some of these atrocities were committed by lawless bands of Southern guerrillas not beholden to Confederate authority. Still others, however, came at the hands of actual Confederate soldiers, such as troopers under the commands of Joseph Wheeler and Wade Hampton, both of whom tried to harry the men during Sherman's March, as well as the mounted rangers of John S. Mosby who plagued Sheridan's army in the Shenandoah Valley. Some of these cavalrymen publicized their role in eliminating foragers. The *Galveston Weekly News* printed the letter of a trooper from Terry's Texas Rangers fighting in Georgia. Writing to his parents, the Texas horseman recounted how he and his comrades "found 3 Yanks driving off a lady's cows. We soon scattered their brains and moved on."[7]

At times Confederates who captured Union foragers took the lives of their victims with calculated cruelty. The firing of barns especially characterized the Burning in the Shenandoah Valley; Sheridan claimed his army put over 2,000 to the torch. Shadowing them were Confederate cavalry eager for a chance to deal "out vengeance with a vengeful hand," remembered a veteran of the Stonewall Brigade. "Whenever they caught a party burning," wrote John Casler, "they would take no prisoners, but shoot them down; and often threw them in the fire alive when they caught them burning their own homes." Sherman's men could expect similar treatment if captured. On April 16, 1865, Rebel horseman intercepted three foragers from the 68th Ohio near Durham Station, North Carolina, close to where Johnston would surrender his army to Sherman only eleven days later. The

Rebels disarmed the trio and instructed them to run, then shot down the fleeing Yankees. Only Corporal Joshua Dicus survived, despite a grievous wound through the body, the bullet having exited his chest. Left for dead by his foes, he managed to crawl to a nearby farmhouse, where Union forces subsequently found him. Dicus recovered from his wound, a survivor of Rebel retribution for foraging.[8]

If considered dispassionately and in historical perspective, the phenomenon of "death to foragers" atrocities stands out as grossly disproportionate acts of violence by Confederates, the message itself ridiculously so. The signs attached to dead Union soldiers belied the supposedly unconscionable nature of the "crime." Rather than label their victims with a more damning epithet, such as "thieves" or "vandals," the sign makers almost invariably condemned the Union dead simply as "foragers," as if foraging were some sort of egregious war crime. In fact, living off the land in enemy territory and destroying contraband were legitimate, age-old military policies. Robert E. Lee allowed his Army of Northern Virginia to forage aggressively during his 1862 and 1863 invasions of the North. Moreover, some civilians in the path of Union armies complained that Confederate cavalry harrying the enemy behaved in a more unruly manner and filched as much food as the Yankees. Contrary to Lost Cause mythmaking, both Sheridan and Sherman pursued limited policies of destruction, particularly in regard to civilians. Both generals prohibited burning private dwellings, except in militarily sanctioned acts of retaliation, and took measures to ensure that families were not left entirely without food.[9]

Southern civilians themselves offered telling evidence of the limited nature of the Federals' hard war policy. The typical response to the approach of Union forces was for the men of a Southern family to drive their livestock into the woods to hide them and to leave the women and children at home to meet the invaders, because occupied homes were more likely to be respected than abandoned ones. That women and children could safely be left in the path of an enemy army speaks volumes about Southerners' confidence in Union armies' civilized conduct.[10]

A written exchange between Generals William Sherman and Wade Hampton offers a revealing look at competing Union and Confederate perceptions toward Federal troops' treatment of Southern civilians. In February 1865, after the discovery of twenty-one foragers with their throats cut, Sherman wrote the Confederate cavalryman to challenge the slayings. Although Sherman suggested that he could "hardly think these murders are committed with your knowledge," he informed Hampton that his army would execute a like number of Rebel prisoners and would continue to do so as long as the murder of foragers persisted. "Of course you cannot question my right to 'forage on the country,'" Sherman insisted. "It is a war right as old as history." It was not the first time Sherman had instructed an opponent on justifiable military conduct. The previous summer he had rebutted a protest from John Bell Hood over the Union shelling of Atlanta, in which Hood tried to lecture him on the supposed unlawful nature of the bombardment. Sherman pointed out that the city's status as "a 'fortified town' with magazines, arsenals, foundries, and public stores" made it a legitimate military target, tersely adding, "See the books." Replying to Sherman, Hampton insisted that the only foragers he had authorized his men to kill had been those caught burning civilian homes, an offense "justly execrated by every civilized nation." Hampton claimed to recognize the right of Sherman's army to forage but countered, "But there is a right older, even, than this, and one more inalienable—the right that every man has to defend his home and to protect those who are dependent on him; and from my heart I wish that every old man and boy in my country who can fire a gun would shoot down, as he would a wild beast, the men who are desolating their land, burning their homes, and insulting their women."[11]

Actually, Hampton overplayed his hand, making exaggerated claims of supposed "offenses against humanity and the rules of war." Desolate the land they may have, but as for burning homes, Sherman's army as a rule only burned dwellings that had been used by the Rebels for military purposes or that were abandoned. Needless to say, they certainly fired no homes with the occupants inside. Hampton elaborated on the alleged "insults" to Southern women, using a euphemism that could imply unwelcome sexual advances or even rape. "The Indian . . . with all his barbarity . . . always respected the persons of his female captives," Hampton wrote. "Your soldiers, more savage than the Indian, insult those whose natural protectors are absent." In this claim, Hampton spoke too generously of Indian captors and unjustly of Sherman's men. Instances of rape were exceedingly rare during the march through Georgia and the Carolinas; historians can reliably document only two or three possible cases.[12]

Hampton's letter also recycled Hood's complaint from Atlanta, insisting he had unlawfully fired on Columbia. Because the city had been actively defended by Confederate troops at the time, Sherman's refutation of Hood applies to Columbia as well. Hampton also charged Sherman with the subsequent fires that swept the city, insisting that he had deliberately "laid the whole city in ashes." Most historians agree that the fires in Columbia started when retreating Confederates put the torch to stores of cotton in the city. The resulting fires might have been exacerbated by liberated Union prisoners and freed slaves, as well as some lawless, drunken soldiers from Sherman's army. In point of fact, Union soldiers still under orders tried to save the city, fighting the fires and helping evacuate civilians and their belongings.[13]

Wade Hampton's reply to Sherman reflected a pervasive pattern of behavior among Confederate soldiers and civilians, one that persists in popular memory of the Civil War. Like Sherman's nemesis in the Carolinas, they made exaggerated, distorted, and sometimes false accusations of Yankee atrocities and cruelty. While certainly not all Union soldiers conducted themselves blamelessly, even their most destructive campaigns, such as the Burning and the March, were largely justifiable under the rules of war in their conduct. Confederates saw Union "invaders" execute destructive measures, understandably painful and sometimes regrettable, and rashly declared them war crimes. Of course, Confederate ideology held that the Confederate States were a new sovereign nation, and thus its citizens could spin any aggression by Federal armies into an unlawful act. As a result, they demonized all US soldiers as guilty of crimes committed by only a few. Belief in such charges created an impression of moral legitimacy for men who killed surrendering Federals. If a Rebel soldier believed only half of the supposed outrages attributed to the enemy, then he was primed to commit atrocities himself.

Despite the popular narrative that casts the American Civil War as a total war, a number of historians persuasively argue for its limited nature. The relative restraint of Union destructiveness highlights Confederates' disproportionate retribution toward foragers. A far more proportional example of civilian violence against brutal conquerors would be the various European resistance movements to German occupation during World War II. Given the remarkable scarcity of authentic crimes against Southern civilians, the wanton killing of Union foragers somewhat resembles the infamous Commando Order from the same conflict, by which Adolf Hitler criminally authorized the summary execution of uniformed Allied raiders without trial.[14]

The legitimacy of Union war policy toward the Confederate home front need not diminish the quite understandable anguish and anger on the part of Confederate soldiers and civilians who witnessed the desolation of their homes and destruction of valuable property at the hands of Union invaders. Confederate staff officer Henry Kyd Douglas captured such feelings in his recollection of the Burning:

I try to restrain my bitterness at the recollection of the dreadful scenes I witnessed. I rode down the Valley with the advance after

Sheridan's retreating cavalry beneath great columns of smoke which almost shut out the sun by day, and in the red glare of bonfires, which, all across that Valley, poured out flames and sparks heavenward and crackled mockingly in the night air; and I saw mothers and maidens tearing their hair and shrieking to Heaven in their fright and despair, and little children, voiceless and tearless in their pitiable terror.[15]

Douglas insisted that it was "an insult to civilization and to God to pretend that the Laws of War justify such warfare," but in that claim he was mistaken. Painful as if proved to the South, the destructive hard hand of war sanctioned by Union commanders in the latter half of the conflict fell within the bounds of legitimate warfare. Actual crimes against civilians, in contravention of Union policy, were few and far between. Moreover, from the Union's perspective, it represented a more humane course of action because it served to shorten the conflict by weakening the Rebel states' ability to wage war, instead of limiting it to soldiers killing one another on the battlefield. Understandable as their outrage was, the reprisals carried out by some Southern fighting men were unjustifiable. Unlike the destruction of crops, livestock, and matériel, it was the murder of captured Union foragers that violated the rules of war.

Unlike the embattled South, the North experienced only limited Confederate raids and forays into its territory. As a result, Union soldiers at large did not experience the same level of outrage toward an invading foe that Confederates felt toward marauding and plundering Yankees. However, considering Union soldiers' antipathy toward Northern opponents of the war—derisively dubbed "Copperheads"—offers a compelling analogue for Confederates' hostility toward invaders and foragers. At first glance, the two subjects seem markedly different. Most notably, they differed in the reality of lethally acting out on the intense hatred felt toward their enemies. Fighting on Southern soil, Confederates had the opportunity to kill and execute Union foragers, and did so on multiple occasions. In contrast, Union soldiers in fighting regiments could not confront Copperheads unless they were furloughed home, and when they did have the means, most confrontations amounted only to isolated riots and brawls. Nevertheless, the Copperhead threat stirred up emotions among Federals similar to Confederates' reaction to Northern invaders. Both sets of enemies in their own way represented threats to the home front. Although Confederate soldiers had greater opportunity to take revenge on foragers than Union soldiers on Copperheads, fighting men on each side felt largely helpless and unable to fight back against these respective threats. Soldiers had their own battles to fight at the front instead of tending to enemies at home. Moreover, Union and Confederate fighting men tended to despise their home-front enemies as cowardly and inferior foes. Although Union foragers were soldiers themselves, many Confederates perceived them to be making war on Southern women and children. Similarly, Union soldiers who nursed a hatred for Copperheads considered them cowards who hurt the war effort from the safety of home instead of hazarding their lives in combat. Many Yanks and Rebs could respect one another as fellow fighting men who braved the dangers and hardships of a soldier's life, but they harbored a special kind of loathing for men they believed chose a craven, dishonorable way of "fighting."

Northern opponents of the war and Confederate sympathizers—Copperheads to their enemies, "Peace Democrats" to those more charitably or neutrally inclined—varied in the positions and tactics they adopted. These ranged from principled political opposition to the Lincoln administration's policies and advocating compromise with the rebellious states to actively plotting against the US war effort, including aiding and abetting Union deserters. Many Union soldiers, especially Republicans and opponents of slavery, tended to lump all such opposition together, denouncing them collectively as a treasonous fifth column trying to undermine the republic at home in the North. The pejorative "Copperhead" cast Peace Democrats as dishonorable, clandestine foes, expressly likening them to a venomous snake infamous for striking without warning. Union soldiers especially opposed to the Copperheads waged a rhetorical war against them, denouncing them in public resolutions drafted by their units and in letters home to family, friends, and Republican newspapers. A soldier-correspondent writing to the *Philadelphia Inquirer* insisted, "We have a viler enemy in our rear than in our front . . . more cowardly and dastardly cruel," a "suicidal crew who would stab us in the back." Similarly, another Pennsylvanian, Lieutenant Colonel George Fisher McFarland, described the Copperheads as "those of the North who would strengthen the arm of the rebellion; openly talk and write treason, and, assassin-like, stab those who are fighting for them!" Wisconsinite Chauncey Cooke echoed the sentiment that antiwar Northerners were a boon to the Confederacy, writing his father, "They are more dangerous than rebels at the front because the South is made to believe they have lots of friends in the North."[16]

For some Union soldiers, anti-Copperhead rhetoric amounted to more than a war of words. Many of their letters, both public and private, included implicit and explicit threats of violence. Prominent antiwar leaders such as Clement Vallandigham, the ex-congressman from Ohio who had been arrested by Federal authorities and deported to the Confederacy, were special targets of vitriol. Sergeant Henry Hayward of the 28th Pennsylvania believed that "if such men as Vallandigham should come here and talk the way he does in Congress the soldiers would kill him." Specific incidents of antiwar unrest also provoked soldiers' wrath, such as on March 28, 1864, when a Copperhead mob in Charleston, Illinois, attacked Federal troops on furlough, killing six soldiers. "My blood boyls at the thought of it," Sergeant Ferguson of the 10th Illinois fumed in his diary. "How I wish I had been there with our company armed and equipped." When it came to the "hell doomed Copperheads," Ferguson declared, "I would say hang or shoot them down as quick as caut."[17]

A number of soldiers insisted they would more gladly kill their enemies at home than the Confederates who had the courage to meet them face-to-face. "An *honest* Secessionist is not one-tenth part as *Mean* as a sneaking Copperhead," opined George Tillotson of the 89th New York. "I would bayonet such men sooner than rebels in the open field," the 2nd Michigan's Perry Mayo declared. Die-hard Republican Simon Bolivar Hulbert extended his hatred to fellow Union soldiers he witnessed "skedadleing," assuming them all to be disloyal members of the opposition party: "If I should see one of those Democrats running before ordered to retreat, I will shoot them sooner than I would a Rebel."[18]

Some of this harsh talk may have been idle threats voiced by soldiers angered by political opponents whom they believed were treasonously undermining the cause for which they and their comrades risked their lives. Still, many of these same soldiers explicitly expressed a desire to return to their homes and mete out the same lethal treatment to Copperheads that they gave Rebels on the battlefield. "We will save our country first by crushing the Rebellion in our front, and then turn our attention to the cowboys at home," one Pennsylvanian vowed. "It makes the boys mad to read about copperheads at home," Chancey Cooke wrote his parents. "They had better lay low if we ever get back home." Fellow Wisconsinite John Brobst voiced his hostility to Confederate sympathizers even more vehemently, writing to his sweetheart, "May the copperheads fear us for we are going to clean them out as soon as we get home." In a subsequent letter, Brobst expressed his mortal hatred for enemies on the home front even more forcefully and graphically: "I could shoot one of them copperheads with a good heart as I could shoot a wolf. I would shoot my father if he was one, but thank God he is not one of the miserablest of all God's creatures, a copperhead, a northern traitor."[19]

Not all threats were to individual Copperhead leaders or their followers.

Some Federal volunteers warned of radical consequences when their state legislatures acted detrimentally to the Union war effort. Perhaps the most widespread and drastic example was what historian Mark Neely terms the "near-revolt of the Illinois line." During the 1862 midterm elections, Northern Democrats scored substantial gains, including winning control of the Illinois legislature in Springfield. In 1863, the Democrat majority began drafting antiwar measures, including legislation that would deny Republican governor Richard Yates control of the state militia. Resenting the defeat of pro-Union rule and fearing a plot to recall Prairie State soldiers from the front, thousands of Illinois volunteers responded vociferously. Nearly sixty Illinois regiments drafted resolutions condemning the legislators' action, many of them direly threatening to "return and crush out Treason" if so ordered by Lincoln or Yates.[20]

Violent anti-Copperhead rhetoric suggests a disturbing undercurrent in the attitudes of Union soldiers: threats of behavior beyond the rules of war, not unlike Confederates' summary execution of Union foragers. Here were citizen-soldiers of a republic, one which expressly rendered the military subordinate to civil authority, openly speaking of marching home and using martial force—even lethal force—to compel loyalty and punish dissent. Such rhetoric, notes one historian, suggests that many of these soldiers "believed that they possessed the right to dictate governmental policy to the civilian population, maintaining that they wielded authority to regulate or repress any dissent on the home front." These men "hinted at legitimating violence toward a treasonous population, which makes the Civil War unique in American military history," observes the same scholar. "In no other case has the American military collectively voiced such an angry and malevolent response aimed at quelling antiwar dissent on the home front."[21] That response also suggests the intense fervor of many Union soldiers' political ideology, one that could motivate them to kill fellow Americans on the battlefield and even contemplate doing so within their own states and communities.

Nonetheless, a number of factors potentially mitigate just how dire or troubling Union soldiers' violent rhetoric seems. Most significantly, most Federal troops never acted out on their physical threats. There was no bloody purge of antiwar Northerners when the men marched home on furlough or at war's end. The most action Sergeant Hayward's 28th Pennsylvania took against Copperheads was to throw army-issue salt pork at railroad workers (whom they had been informed were staunch Democrats) as they rode the rails through Ohio. Furthermore, not every fervent Union soldier envisioned suppressing innocent political dissenters. Rather, many genuinely believed that Confederate sympathizers were contemplating actual armed rebellion at home. Lieutenant Colonel McFarland had just such an emergency in mind when he publicly wrote, "If these 'Copperheads' have the courage enough to inaugurate rebellion in the North, they will find a mighty army of patriots ready to crush them to the earth." Many soldiers also saw their rhetoric as just that—rhetoric—a means of expressing their will to the home front. Their anti-Copperhead letters and resolutions offered them the opportunity to bolster Union morale at home, reassure civilians of their soldiers' continued devotion to the cause, and urge them to vote for candidates who would resolutely prosecute the war, especially in the case of soldiers whose state legislatures barred them from voting in the field.[22]

Ultimately, Union soldiers' threats to violently suppress the North's antiwar movement was never fully put to the test, as their worst fears of home-front rebellion and widespread pro-Confederate subterfuge never manifested on a large scale. In part this was because the Lincoln administration and Union military district commanders in the North dealt harshly with individuals and institutions suspected of disloyalty. In addition, successive Union victories in the autumn of 1864 and Lincoln's reelection decisively took the wind from the Copperheads' sails, with the result that antiwar Northerners increasingly retreated from the national stage as a pro-Union, antislavery triumph for the republic grew increasingly certain. As such, Lincoln's soldiers never had to prove whether they would make good on their threats of political violence, and how far they would have gone emerges as yet another "what if" question of Civil War history. What their anti-Copperhead rhetoric does reveal is that perceived threats to the American nation and outrage over a vocal civilian opposition to the cause for which they were risking their lives prompted many citizen-soldiers in Federal blue to contemplate and publicly declare their willingness to bring their new-found military might back home to suppress political dissent. If pushed too far, they threatened, they would turn the bullets and bayonets they bore against uniformed Rebels and use them against dissenters and suspected traitors, fellow civilians whom they viewed as "a viler enemy in our rear."

Both Confederates slaughtering Union foragers and Federals threatening to exterminate Copperheads reflected the strain of the war's duration. In each case, this held true for both sides of the issue. The North's hard war policy represented a departure from the conciliatory posture toward the Rebel states from early in the war. When a limited war failed to bring the rebellion to heel, Lincoln and his generals took off the gloves, adopting such policies as emancipation of slaves and harrowing the Confederate home front. Many Union soldiers, having chafed under early conciliatory measures, enthusiastically led the way in ushering in a harsher way of war that they believed would end it that much sooner. Confederates, for their part, had waxed propagandistically from the war's start in casting Union forces as plundering vandals, but now the pivot toward hard war in 1864 seemed to turn their rhetoric into reality. Moreover, this change in war policy coincided with successful Union campaigns that sliced their way into the Confederate heartland. Sensing the tide of war going against them and seeing the hated Yankees despoil their homeland, Confederates familiar with killing Northerners in battle now resorted, in some cases, to killing foragers and barn burners in ways exceeding the rules of war.

Likewise, the Copperhead question also reflected the strains of the war dragging on. Antiwar Northerners grew frustrated with the war's mounting cost to the nation and the failure to achieve victory, just as did their more bellicose countrymen, but the former also railed against the antislavery measures increasingly favored by the administration and the threats to civil liberties at home. When Peace Democrats agitated and legislated to end the war on less than victorious terms, soldiers who demanded total victory and total loyalty struck back. These fervent Federals declared their willingness to march home and use the weapons they had deployed against Rebel soldiers to suppress any attempt to compromise the cause for which they fought. Just as certain Confederate soldiers and irregulars acted on the desire to exact terrible revenge on Yankee invaders, so did the Yankee soldiers themselves openly contemplate exceeding the rules of war by taking the killing from the battlefield to an embattled home front.

On occasion, acts of unjustifiable killing—real and imagined—prompted Union and Confederate forces to authorize executions of prisoners in retaliation. This was killing detached from the kind that characterized a contested battlefield. Commanders chiefly used retaliatory executions (and threats thereof) to deter future unlawful killings by the other side, as well as vicariously exacting retribution for the offense itself. This was essentially the nuclear option of military justice—brutally straightforward in the manner of an eye for an eye. Executions ordered by generals fell to regimental officers and enlisted men to actually carry out. For soldiers on both sides, taking part in a firing squad or a hanging often constituted the most disagreeable and disturbing duty that military authority called them to perform. For these men, carrying out an execution sorely tested the extremes of killing they could tolerate.

Both the Burning in the Shenandoah Valley and the March to the Sea resulted in retaliatory executions between the armies. Among the Confederate forces that harried Sheridan's campaign was the 43rd Battalion, Virginia Cavalry, better known as Mosby's Rangers. Mosby's men counted among the Confederacy's ablest and most formidable partisans, but at Front Royal, they ran into trouble. On September 23, 1864, a party of mounted rangers attacked a Union wagon train, not realizing it was backed up by Union cavalry. The troopers scattered the rangers, managing to capture seven of the partisans. Because of their past conduct, Ulysses Grant had issued orders stating, "Where any of Mosby's men are caught hang them without trial." The seven unfortunate prisoners (in separate locales and instances) were summarily shot or hanged. When news reached John Mosby, he was told that General George Armstrong Custer had ordered their deaths. In fact, there is little direct evidence to suggest that Custer played any role in the executions. Nevertheless, Mosby was convinced that Custer was responsible, and he resolved to exact retribution from Custer's division.[23]

In the ensuing weeks, Mosby sent most of the Union soldiers his men captured south to Richmond, but he kept behind those he believed belonged to Custer. On November 6, Mosby's men assembled twenty-seven prisoners in Rectortown and made them take part in a death lottery. A hat with twenty-seven slips of paper was passed down the line of prisoners (which included infantrymen and artillerymen who could not have belonged to Custer). Those that drew one of seven numbered slips were slated to die. Mosby's men were deadly opponents in battle, but they botched these executions. After leading the unlucky men to a different site closer to Federal lines—accidentally allowing one Federal to escape along the way—the rangers began hanging the remaining prisoners one at a time. Using nooses made of bed cord and thrown over a tree limb, a ranger on horseback hauled back the rope to hoist his prisoner off the ground. Uneasy about operating so close to Union forces, the partisans decided this method was taking too long. "This hanging is too damned slow work," noted one of the Union survivors. The Confederates decided to shoot the last three prisoners. Perhaps the shooters were nervous, or perhaps they were unnerved by having to kill unarmed men, but none managed to kill his man. Two of the Union troopers were badly wounded and left for dead, while another made good his escape on foot when the revolver pointed at his head misfired.[24]

Only three of the seven condemned men had died, but Mosby was satisfied that justice had been served. Had it been revenge that he sought, he later insisted, he could have executed more prisoners to make up the difference. Mosby sent a letter to Sheridan, informing him that he had exacted retribution for the Front Royal hangings, as well as informing the general that any Union soldiers captured in the future by Mosby's men would be treated as prisoners of war, "unless some new act of barbarity shall compel me to adopt a policy repulsive to humanity." There were no further executions between Mosby's Rangers and Sheridan's army.[25]

Union soldiers on Sherman's March were called on to conduct similar retaliatory executions for the murder of their foragers. Not long after the discovery outside Columbia of twenty-one foragers with slit throats, soldiers from the 30th Illinois discovered one of their own who had been captured and murdered by the Rebels, his head "pounded to pieces with a pine club." General Frank Blair, their corps commander, ordered a Confederate prisoner to be shot in retaliation. The execution proved one of the most trying executions Union soldiers conducted. Major William C. Rhodes, commanding the 30th Illinois, was ordered to oversee the execution; only when threatened with losing his regiment did he accept the duty. Like Mosby's prisoners, captured Confederates were made to draw lots from a hat. The unfortunate prisoner was forty-five years of age—old for a Civil War soldier. Rhodes assembled a firing squad of twelve men. Of the twelve muskets readied for the task, only six were loaded with powder and ball; the other six were loaded with blank charges of powder. This was a traditional practice in firing squads, one that hid the identity of the men actually doing the killing. A shooter would almost certainly know from the telltale recoil of a loaded musket if he had fired a live round, but the practice would still grant members of the squad anonymity among those watching the execution.[26]

The condemned man spoke his last words in front of the firing squad, his circumstances tugging at their heartstrings. "I was forced into the army, never was in a battle, never wished the yankees any harm," he said calmly, going on to mention his "large family, all girls who live about 40 miles from here," and noting, "I have been a local Methodist minister." For a Confederate soldier, he could have hardly been a more sympathetic or unoffending figure to the dozen men ordered to end his life. Moreover, he faced his death bravely. Standing in front of a tree, he accepted a blindfold but declined to be bound. He agreed to give the signal to fire himself, holding out a handkerchief that he would drop when he was ready. Major Rhodes ordered his men to aim true and thus spare the condemned Confederate a prolonged death. The handkerchief fell. Twelve muskets fired. Six bullets found their mark. "As the smoke floated away among the tall pines our boys looked with sadness upon the bleeding corpse of a brave old man who met death unflinchingly and heroically for the crime of another man," a Wisconsin soldier at the scene remembered. "If the old man had bounded away into the forest we'd never have run a step to catch him." Like Mosby's retribution, the execution proved brutally effective, if only partially; the 30th Illinois lost no more foragers.[27]

Few soldiers were ordered to be part of firing squads, but many in the course of their service witnessed executions firsthand. More often than not the condemned man was a soldier from the observers' own side rather than an enemy offender. Military executions were public affairs, formally witnessed by the men of the prisoner's own regiment or brigade in formation. Such assemblies served two purposes. First, offenses such as desertion essentially represented crimes against one's comrades, and thus troops were drawn up to witness the punishment for such an affront. Second, officers intended the sight as a deterrent, sending a clear message as to what fate other soldiers could expect if they too transgressed.

Soldiers could find executions troubling even when the condemned had committed serious capital crimes. Lieutenant S. H. Dent from Alabama expressed unease over the prospect of witnessing two men shot the following day, one for killing his own sergeant and the other for striking a captain. "I am very much afraid we will be marched off to witness the execution. I do not wish to see it," he wrote to his wife. "Men grow callous enough at best in the army and I do not wish to witness any more such sights than are absolutely necessary." Dent found the nature of killing on the battlefield far more tolerable than on the parade ground: "There is great difference between shooting down men (enemies) (at least to one's feelings) when the blood is warm and we are excited to the highest pitch & witnessing the shooting of one of our own men." Dent expressed those thoughts in November 1861, before he had ever heard a shot fired in anger. Still, veterans of two or three years of war recorded similar reactions. Thomas Barron, another Alabamian, wrote his sister of the sorrowful sight of two men executed for desertion in April 1864. Like Dent, seeing two men's lives ended so coldly troubled him: "This is dreadful to bring out a man in good health an[d] in a moment plung[e] his soul into ever lasting perdition."[28]

Yet another Alabamian left his own harrowing account of witnessing the execution of three men from his own regiment. John Mason recounted that one soldier "went nearly crazy when he heard that he had to take part in the shooting," going among his comrades offering $100 to any man who would take his place, until his captain finally excused him. Mason himself had his own misgivings about his part to play in the execution. With his company tasked with loading the firing squad's weapons, Mason debated whether to load a bullet but ultimately concluded "that the more balls the quicker the poor fellows would be put out of their misery." A great many of his comrades must have shared his abhorrence at having to gun down their own men, for "a great many balls" plunged into the ground in front of the condemned or cut into tree limbs overhead. John Mason even admitted that had he been assigned to the firing party, he too likely would have deliberately missed. Despite their reluctance, enough of the Alabamians aimed true to kill the condemned men with merciful quickness.[29]

The subject of military executions offers a suitable point to transition from extreme acts of killing to acts by which soldiers stopped short of killing. Firing squads represented an extreme not because they were unlawful but because they departed from the soldier's norm of killing in battle. Additionally, soldiers' discomfort and sensitivity with regard to executions greatly tested the limits of their tolerance for killing.

The following discussion examines acts of forbearance in which Civil War soldiers declined to kill, sometimes not even treating soldiers from the opposing side as enemies at war. Despite political and social animosity and the natural hostility between enemy soldiers, Americans wearing the blue and gray had ample reason to identify with one another. As rivals in a civil war, they shared considerable common ground in terms of culture and language. Federals and Confederates enjoyed equal claim to a proud national identity and heritage, one that Abraham Lincoln tried to appeal to in his first inaugural address, hoping that sectionalism would not "break our bonds of affection" and "mystic chords of memory." Fighting men from North and South also shared a foundation in biblical Christianity, one that sanctioned killing in just wars but also esteemed mercy and loving one's enemies.

One manner in which Civil War soldiers exercised mercy and forbearance in battle was in the taking of prisoners. Of course, taking prisoners hardly constituted a rejection of their duty as soldiers. Military law in fact specified instances in which enemy soldiers had to be shown quarter. Nevertheless, the frenzy of combat and the animosity of war ensured that the merciful treatment of enemies trying to surrender could never be taken for granted, as previously discussed transgressions demonstrate. Such factors make acts of mercy by Civil War soldiers all the more remarkable. Furthermore, sometimes in the heat of battle combatants found themselves in situations in which they did not accept the surrender of the enemy but in fact compelled their surrender—cases in which it would have been just as easy (and legitimate) to kill the enemy as it was to offer him quarter. Many Union and Confederate soldiers demonstrated a tremendous capacity and willingness for taking prisoners, even amid the chaos of combat.

One of the war's most famous and dramatic episodes of taking prisoners under dangerous circumstances took place during the first day's fighting at

Gettysburg. In the fighting north of the town, a brigade of Mississippians and North Carolinians occupied an unfinished railroad cut that offered a ready-made trench from which to pour enfilade fire into the nearby Union battle line. Apprehending the threat this posed, Lieutenant Colonel Rufus Dawes of the Iron Brigade's 6th Wisconsin led his own regiment and the nearby 95th New York and 14th Brooklyn in a desperate charge against the railroad cut. The three regiments suffered heavily in the attack, but once they closed with the enemy, the first Wisconsinites and New Yorkers to reach the cut began to take their toll on the defenders with bullets, bayonets, and musket butts. Confederates now found themselves trapped in the deep cut with no easy means of escape as Union attackers loomed over them. Rufus Dawes recounted that his men, now poised over the cornered Rebels, began calling out to them, "Throw down your muskets! Down with your muskets!" Meanwhile, the regiment's adjutant lined up a score of men with leveled weapons as a further means of persuasion, allowing Dawes to successfully demand the surrender of the closest regimental commander among the Confederates. The "general cry" that called on the Rebels to surrender had first come from the Union enlisted men themselves, Dawes wrote, and in his memoir he warmly praised the quick thinking and humanitarian instincts of his men: "The coolness, self-possession, and discipline which held back our men from pouring in a general volley saved a hundred lives of the enemy, and as my mind goes back to the fearful excitement of the moment, I marvel at it."[30]

Confederate soldiers experienced their own share of moments of fearful excitement in which they too spared the lives of Union opponents under desperate circumstances. At Chickamauga, men of the 54th Virginia experienced a standoff perhaps even more nerve-wracking than did the Union soldiers astride Gettysburg's railroad cut. The Virginians were approaching an abandoned Union battery when their officers suddenly ordered them to about-face in reaction to a Union unit that emerged to their rear. Colonel Robert C. Trigg, their brigade commander, boldly rode toward the Yankees and in his "stentorian voice" shouted, "Stack your arms and lie down, or I'll cut you all to pieces!" The Union soldiers dropped to the ground but kept their muskets leveled. Trigg advanced his brigade, wheeling round one of his regiments to flank the Union line. The Virginians "steadily advanced," Private James M. Weiser wrote, "guns loaded, bayonets fixed, finger on trigger, and thumb ready to cock gun in a fraction of a second." The Confederates closed to within perhaps twenty feet of the Federals without a shot being fired, until suddenly one of Weiser's comrades accidentally discharged his musket. "Instantly came the deadliest, most menacing sound

I have ever heard, the click of cocking locks of both lines, while the boys in blue jumped up and, with guns at shoulder and fingers pressing triggers, awaited the command to fire," Weiser remembered. At any moment, it seemed, one or both sides might trigger a deadly, point-blank volley. As at Gettysburg's railroad cut, the enlisted men took the initiative, with the Rebels urging the Yanks, "Surrender, boys, we've got you." As Weiser recounted, "Our opponents finally began lowering their guns, which we took and threw behind us." With the tense standoff at last defused, hostility quickly gave way to camaraderie: "Then at once we became friends and began a frenzied trading of tobacco for coffee, and forming friendships which lasted for long years after the war and resulted in a number of visits between former foes in Ohio and Virginia."[31]

These standoffs experienced at Gettysburg and Chickamauga rival the tensest "shoot/no-shoot" scenario that a warrior or law enforcement officer might encounter today. Both situations could easily have ended quite differently with far more bloodshed, yet in both situations Union and Confederate captors alike displayed what Rufus Dawes heralded as "coolness, self-possession, and discipline." A number of factors may well account for the forbearance and presence of mind these Wisconsinites and Virginians exercised. If any of the soldiers involved harbored serious reservations over killing, they would have been especially loath to kill under these circumstances. In both the Gettysburg and Chickamauga scenarios, the combatants encountered one another within mere feet of one another, able to look their adversaries in the eye, one of the circumstances in which soldiers can find it the hardest to kill. No small amount of self-preservation may have come into play as well. In both cases, continuing or commencing killing would likely have meant that one's opponents would have tried their best to kill as well. For the 54th Virginia especially, with two battle lines facing off with loaded weapons, opening fire could easily have triggered a return Union volley and caused mutual destruction. Furthermore, a genuine humanitarian impulse seems to have factored in during both encounters, even as Wisconsinites and Virginians girded themselves to do their worst if their opponents did not submit. Both Dawes and Weiser underscored how the common soldiers in their regiments took a lead role in offering their foes a chance to surrender safely, and Weiser further highlighted how quickly captors and captives befriended one another once the Yanks capitulated. For Civil War soldiers from the Old Dominion to the Badger State, a complex set of influences contributed to their ability to spare one another's lives even under the most dangerous circumstances.

Some evidence suggests that veteran soldiers were more apt than untried troops to take prisoners. Men who had endured the ordeal of combat, it seems, were more likely to empathize with enemy soldiers as fellow fighting men, making them readier to show mercy to foes who found themselves in terrible circumstances. At the Battle of Franklin, charging Confederates found themselves ensnared in an abatis, an obstruction in front of the Union defenses consisting of a row of felled trees with their tangled branches facing the enemy. Attackers in front of the 175th Ohio "hollered to the boys to cease firing—they would surrender." However, the 175th, a new regiment in their first battle, refused and continued to fire away into the helpless Rebels. "So much the better," Private Isaac Miller of the 93rd Ohio wrote approvingly. "All they kill we won't have to fight or feed anymore." Miller specifically attributed the Ohioans' refusal to spare the Rebels to the 175th being a new regiment. Ostensibly, most of his fellow veterans would likely have taken pity on the trapped attackers, appreciating that they could do the rebellion about as much damage if they made prisoners of the Rebels as they could shooting them down.[32]

An act of mercy taking prisoners might be, but soldiers often voiced offers of quarter as angry, and usually profane, demands to surrender. In the early stages of the Battle of Cedar Creek, with the Army of West Virginia surprised and routed, Rutherford B. Hayes found himself having to make an ignominious retreat—ignominious especially for a future president of the United States. Having had his horse shot out from under him, the dazed division commander had to make a hobbling flight with angry Confederates hot on his heels, demanding his surrender. "I cannot repeat their language even in the privacy of the family," Hayes wryly recalled in a postwar address to his fellow veterans. "The names they called me reflected disrespect on my parentage."[33]

The taking of prisoners was not only an act of mercy but also an act by which the soldier potentially risked his own life. Trying to force an enemy's surrender in the middle of combat could be almost as hazardous as trying to surrender. Just as a surrendering combatant had to convince a hostile enemy soldier to offer him quarter instead of killing him, so did a soldier trying to offer quarter have to pause in his fighting and lower his guard in order to do so, leaving him vulnerable. Demanding the enemy's surrender in the middle of a close-quarters battle was a high-risk, high-reward proposition. If the enemy did surrender, it could end the fighting at hand immediately in the captor's favor. However, in those cases when the enemy refused a surrender demand in the middle of a heated clash, the other side often expressed their defiance with a bullet. At the Battle of Jonesboro, with Union attackers sweeping over Confederate lines, a "great big Yank" jumped atop the works held by the 9th Kentucky, demanding, "Surrender, you dam rebels." "The H———l you say," snapped back one of Johnny Green's comrades as he shot the man dead. At the Battle of Franklin, the roles were reversed; this time, Confederates from the Army of Tennessee breached the Union lines. Suddenly, "a rebel colonel mounted our breastworks, and in language not choice, but profanely expressive, demanded our immediate surrender," remembered Captain James Sexton. An Illinois soldier answered by jabbing his loaded musket in the colonel's belly and grimly uttering "I guess not" as he pulled the trigger. The blast "actually let daylight through the victim" and toppled him into the ditch.[34]

Some soldiers would go to great lengths to avoid capture, including outright deceiving enemies willing to offer quarter. During the Battle of Glendale, Private Enos Bloom of the Pennsylvania Bucktails found himself separated from his regiment. Fighting "a little on my own hook," Bloom fired away at the Rebels from behind a tree and made several "bite the dust," as he proudly recounted in a letter home to his father. When two Confederates approached, Bloom shot one with his musket. The survivor, rather than trying to shoot or attack the Pennsylvanian, instead demanded that he drop his weapon. Bloom rammed home another cartridge, and as the Confederate approached, somehow managed to continue loading even as he assured his would-be captor that he surrendered: "I told him not to shoot, I would give up; and as he was coming up I put a cap on my gun and still held at the hip; when I let the rammer fall to the ground he was no more than five steps from me. I did not sight the gun, but pulled the trigger. He jumped about two feet high and hollowed 'My God I'm shot' and fell to the ground dead." With more Confederates on the way, Bloom beat a hasty retreat, living to fight another day. While Bloom matter-of-factly described his deception in his letter, many Civil War soldiers, even some from his own side, would have condemned his conduct as treacherous. Having shot a man from whom he had asked for quarter, it is doubtful any nearby Rebels would have offered any mercy. Had Bloom tried to give himself up a second time, he likely would have been a victim of a surrender execution.[35]

Prisoners could prove dangerous to their captors even away from the field of battle. Like today's soldiers, Civil War soldiers understood it as a duty of prisoners of war to attempt escape. Moreover, the breakdown of the prisoner exchange system late in the war and the deadly conditions inside prisoner of war camps gave Union and Confederate soldiers ample motive to resist captivity. A number of soldiers stood ready, even as prisoners, to kill in order to make their escape. When seventeen-year-old Georgia cavalryman Alfred Gibbons was captured in the fighting outside Atlanta, his

Union captors failed to find the revolver he carried. As one of the men led him to the rear, Gibbons considered using it on his captor: "I was certainly tempted to shoot him, but as the Federal line was between me and the Confederates I did not think I could get away." Instead, Gibbons disposed of the revolver and was marched into captivity. Bill Nicholson, a former Texas Ranger fighting in a regiment raised in his native Mississippi, was able to succeed where Gibbons failed. During the Battle of Peachtree Creek, Nicholson became separated from his comrades, who gave him up for lost. To their surprise, "Old Bill" limped into camp that night, telling of how Yankees had fired on him and chased him. His pursuers had not counted on the former ranger's skill with his trusty six-shooter. "They undertook to run me down," Nicholson told his comrades, "and I got five of them with my revolver." Such stories testify to how life-threatening trying to take an enemy combatant alive could be.[36]

Acts of mercy in combat also occurred when soldiers stayed their hands and declined to kill individual enemy soldiers. For a variety of reasons and circumstances, soldiers in battle on occasion decided to spare an enemy when killing him seemed shameful or unnecessary. Extraordinary displays of courage convinced some combatants to spare an enemy they deemed "too brave" to kill. Captain James H. Franklin of the 4th Alabama described a costly Union assault at Cold Harbor in which a Federal color-bearer continued marching forward alone, not realizing that his comrades had retreated, gone to ground, or been shot down. Confederates facing the lone attacker ceased firing and began waving for him to turn back, shouting, "Go back! Go back! We don't want to kill you! Go back!" Realizing his predicament but refusing to retreat ignominiously, the color-bearer halted, furled his flag, touched his cap in salute to his gallant foes, smartly faced about, and marched back from whence he came. Thrilled by the Yankee's courage and spirit, the Alabamians tossed their hats in the air and "yelled in admiration until his retiring figure was lost in the deep recesses of the far-away lines." Half a year later, the Battle of Franklin found the roles of attacker and defender reversed from those at Cold Harbor. Brigadier General John Adams led his Mississippians across the Tennessee fields toward the Union works, riding tall in the saddle. Moved by the general's bravery, the colonel of the 65th Illinois urged his men to spare such a brave man. At first the Illinoisans held their fire, but when the color guard perceived that Adams was riding straight for their banners, they loosed a volley that killed the gallant general and his mount.[37]

Some soldiers took a dim view of sparing an enemy deemed too brave to kill. During the 1862 Valley Campaign, one of Stonewall Jackson's colonels reported to him how three Union cavalrymen had been killed in a desperate charge against his regiment. The colonel regretted not having stopped his men from shooting down a handful of brave men "who had gotten into a desperate situation." Jackson, a general more ruthless than romantic in his philosophy toward war, would have none of it: "No, colonel. Shoot them all. I don't want them to be brave."[38]

In some instances, soldiers spared or tried to spare nonthreatening enemies who simply found themselves in the wrong place at the wrong time. In the fighting around Atlanta, a Michigan artilleryman recounted how a Confederate artillery captain, wearing a fine uniform and mounted on a fine horse, accidentally rode into Union lines. Many of the Federals had doffed their uniform coats in the Georgia heat and in their shirtsleeves were hard to distinguish from Confederates. "A thousand rifles, in the hands of men who could hit a squirrel's eye at twice the distance this enemy was from them, were pointed at his breast; a thousand fingers were touching the triggers,—the slightest movement of one would have caused the instant death of the poor fellow," wrote Lieutenant Richard S. Tuthill. "But no finger pressed upon the trigger, no shot was fired. It would have been too much like murder." Sensing his predicament, the rider asked what unit this was. Tuthill feared the Confederate would try to ride away and realized such an attempt would be suicidal. "For God's sake," he called out to the Rebel officer, "ride over these works or in an instant you will be a dead man!" The captain graciously gave himself up, making a small bow and replying, "All right, gentlemen! It's my mistake; I surrender." Inside Union lines, the captain gave Tuthill his spurs and a decorative dagger, presumably as a gift for helping save his life.[39]

Almost a year earlier at Chickamauga, a Union officer who found himself in a similar situation proved far less fortunate. Like the Confederate captain at Atlanta, the Union major in question made a bold appearance, wearing "full uniform" and "mounted on a splendid bay horse." He spurred forward with one arm raised in warning, as if he had taken the approaching Confederates for his own men. "Some one cried out, 'Don't shoot!' but it was too late," wrote Val Giles, a sergeant in the famed Texas Brigade. "Two or three muskets went off, then a whole volley." Horse and rider "plunged forward," falling into a dry streambed. By the time the Texans reached them, both were dead.[40]

Civil War soldiers also acted mercifully toward one another on the battlefield by arranging battlefield truces, normally to recover the dead and wounded between the lines. Sometimes senior officers agreed to formal truces between the armies, such as during the aftermaths of Antietam and

Cold Harbor. On other occasions, however, semiformal or informal truces occurred at the initiative of regimental officers and enlisted men themselves. Often these took place when Union and Confederate troops found themselves in fixed positions in close proximity to one another, as in a siege or after a failed assault.

A number of such truces occurred during the fighting on Kennesaw Mountain, where Sherman's men, having unsuccessfully stormed the well-fortified and well-defended heights, dug in under enemy fire to secure what ground they had gained rather than continuing to retreat under the defenders' guns. In the no-man's-land between the opposing lines, the bodies of hundreds of dead and wounded Union soldiers lay strewn on the ground. In front of the Confederate line held by Arkansans from Cleburne's Division, powder embers among the dry leaves caught fire, creating a blaze that threatened to engulf the trapped Federal casualties. "Boys, this is butchery," declared an Arkansas colonel resolved to spare his enemies from the flames. Climbing atop the defenses and waving a white handkerchief, he called out to the men of both sides, "Cease firing and help get out those men." Both Confederate and Union soldiers quickly complied. "Our men, scaling the head logs as though for a counter charge," Private William T. Barnes wrote, "were soon mixed with the Yankees, carrying out the dead and wounded Feds with those who, a few minutes previous, were trying to 'down our shanties.' Together, the Rebs and Yanks soon had the fire beat out and the dead and wounded removed to the Federal side."[41]

In addition to formal and informal battlefield truces between units, Civil War soldiers also treated their enemies with compassion on an individual basis. General Joseph Kershaw recounted what is likely the most famous one-man act of mercy from the Civil War. At the Battle of Fredericksburg, Union causalities littered the ground in front of the Confederates' position on Marye's Heights. As Kershaw told it, Richard R. Kirkland, a sergeant in the 2nd South Carolina, sought him out. Moved by the pitiful cries of the Union wounded along their front, Kirkland asked his brigade commander's permission to go over the stone wall to bring water to them. Kershaw at first tried to dissuade him, warning the sergeant that the Union soldiers who had gone to ground below their position might well shoot him as soon as he exposed himself. Kirkland was willing to accept the risk, and Kershaw relented, remarking that "the sentiment which actuates you is so noble that I will not refuse your request, trusting that God may protect you." The general would not, however, permit Kirkland to show a white handkerchief, perhaps thinking it would be taken as a sign for a formal truce and fearing he lacked the authority to authorize one.[42]

After gathering canteens from among his comrades, Kirkland climbed out of the sunken road to go to the aid of his fallen enemies. At first Union troops fired on him, thinking he had ventured out to plunder the dead and wounded, but then ceased once they realized his mission of mercy. For the next hour and a half, Kirkland made his way among the Union wounded, giving water to desperately thirsty men and doing his best to make them comfortable as they lay on the cold, hard ground. In his postwar account, Kershaw extolled the sergeant's actions in the warmest terms, calling him a "ministering angel" who exemplified "Christ-like mercy." Richard Kirkland entered Civil War lore as "the Angel of Marye's Heights." Some historians have questioned the tale's veracity, pointing out that the story did not emerge until Kershaw's account in 1880. No contemporary accounts from Fredericksburg corroborate the story, and Kirkland himself, mortally wounded months later at Chickamauga, left no evidence. Regardless of its authenticity, the story of the Angel of Marye's Heights is clearly a story that both Civil War veterans and later generations of Americans wanted to believe. Perhaps no other action by a Civil War soldier has been so often retold and reproduced, including a larger-than-life bronze statue on the battlefield itself. The story of Kirkland's merciful actions has become a cherished symbol of the shared humanity between the blue and the gray, and of their brotherhood as soldiers and Americans.[43]

For some soldiers, hostility toward the enemy ended as soon as the shooting stopped, especially in the case of any enemy who had been rendered hors de combat. A number of men even came to the aid of opponents whom they themselves had shot. Perry Mayo from Michigan wrote his parents of a successful attack in which "I shot my first man that I am sure of," having hit a Rebel soldier in the ankle. Mayo sought out the man and offered him water from his own canteen, but the Confederate's was already full. Evidently the man bore Mayo no grudge, good-naturedly telling him that he had made a "d——d good line shot but a little too low for comfort." Lieutenant James O. Churchill of the 11th Illinois managed to enjoy a similarly amicable moment with a Confederate opponent at Fort Donelson, despite lying painfully wounded with a broken hip and thigh. Having been put out of action by a close encounter with an enemy cavalryman, Churchill hailed a Rebel trooper he spotted and asked to see what sort of weapon he carried. The cavalryman handed him his Colt revolving rifle, an uncommon weapon with which the men of his regiment were quite proud to be armed. Agreeably, Churchill "replied that I was satisfied with their efficiency and was a sample of it."[44]

Acts of mercy on the battlefield were matched by acts of respect and friendship off the battlefield. One arena in which hostilities broke down was on the picket line. Almost all Civil War soldiers stood sentry as pickets (on foot) or vedettes (mounted), usually on a regular basis. Picket duty rotated among companies or regiments along a front. Networks of picket lines guarded an army's perimeter, looking outward to detect enemy attacks and infiltration and inward to stop attempts at desertion. Enemy pickets might find themselves within sight or earshot of one another even outside of battle, such as during the prelude or aftermath of actual fighting, or when opposing armies were separated by obstacles such as a river. Such circumstances sometimes tempted pickets, especially nervous recruits, to fire at each other. Experienced troops found it far more expedient to adopt a live-and-let-live policy. Thomas Bigbie, a Confederate soldier in the army besieging Union forces in Chattanooga, wrote home that "wee stand picket in hunderd yds of the yank but we have quit shootin at each other." Thomas Galwey, an Irishman in an Ohio regiment serving in the East, described pickets as "unwilling to harass or be harassed unless an advance, retreat, or some decided movement is attempted by the other side." Yet even among veterans, a handful still proved aggressive enough to flout this policy and take a shot on the picket line if a prime target presented himself. "Came on picket this morning, was put on post at the ford," Virginia soldier Newt Bosworth matter-of-factly wrote in his diary one day in January 1864, "and shot a Yankee off his horse from nearly 700 yards away with an Enfield rifle."[45]

"Soldiers rejected picket [duty] as a proper sphere of combat," observes one historian. Some described picket firing as "mere wantonness," "wanton cruelty," and "a miserable and useless kind of murder." Some modern observers have assumed from this that by declining to shoot at one another on the picket line, Civil War soldiers thereby evaded or compromised a duty to kill the enemy. In fact, such behavior conformed to military regulations. No less an authority than US general August Kautz declared, "The practice of pickets firing upon those of the enemy is barbarous; and retaliation is scarcely a sufficient excuse for doing it." Kautz authored in 1864 *Customs of Service for Non-Commissioned Officers and Soldiers*, a handbook reflecting standard operating procedures in Civil War armies. Military regulations only authorized pickets to fire their weapons in defense of their immediate persons, to warn of an approaching enemy attack, or to stop deserters. Proscribing reckless picket firing served a practical as well as moral purpose. A gunshot on the picket line sounded an alarm to the rest of the pickets and potentially to the main body in the rear. If pickets fired whenever an enemy soldier came in their sights, it would render such an alarm system meaningless and produce chaos and confusion along the army's front, particularly at night.[46] A quiet picket line was a happy picket line, and the peace and security of the army easily trumped the minuscule benefit of haphazardly killing or wounding an enemy soldier trying to perform the same duty. Humanitarian and pragmatic impulses prompted Civil War soldiers not to fire on enemy pickets, but such behavior corresponded with the wishes of the military establishment rather than defied them.

The acts of pickets declining to fire on one another and soldiers arranging impromptu truces with the opposing side made possible the most famous cases of nonhostility between Civil War soldiers: Federals and Confederates fraternizing with one another. In these instances, rather than simply not shooting at one another, opposing soldiers met and traded. Rather than working out of necessity to recover the dead and wounded, soldiers from North and South who had no more pressing concerns sought out one another out of curiosity. These friendly meetings and exchanges appear prominently in our literature, art, and films about the Civil War, just as they figure prominently in the letters, diaries, and memoirs of the soldiers themselves.

The chance to trade for curiosities and luxuries provided a key incentive for fraternization. Soldiers, often hungry for reading material and other diversions, enjoyed swapping newspapers with one another. Journalists North and South wrote cavalierly both in terms of their rhetoric and the military information (or misinformation) they would divulge, and Federals and Confederates found enjoyment in what the other side printed about them. A soldier in Lee's army wrote home of the "friendly chats and interchanges of papers, tobacco and coffee" between the rival armies. Coffee and tobacco proved especially prized commodities for trade. Yanks enjoyed a steady supply of coffee and Rebs an abundance of tobacco—goods that the common soldiers of the opposing sides found harder to come by. Thus, supply and demand created a natural commerce between enemy lines—a textbook case of the mutual benefits of trade.

While refraining from picket firing accorded with military regulations, fraternizing and trading with the enemy most certainly did not. Usually this called for avoiding the prying eyes of officers, and the seclusion of picket duty often helped make this possible. During the Siege of Chattanooga, Private Robert A. Jarman of Mississippi noted that the pickets of each side not only traded such staples as newspapers, coffee, and tobacco, but "I have seen some swap hats and shoes, and talk for half an hour at a time, but this was only when no officer was present on either side." Even some officers, especially junior-level company officers, indulged in such behavior. Lieutenant Robert M. Collins from Texas, also at Chattanooga, recounted how "when no big officers on either side was near, we would sometimes get up a temporary armistice, lay down our arms and meet on half way grounds and have a nice friendly chat, swapping our flat tobacco for Lincoln coffee, our little 8 × 10 newspaper, 'The Chattanooga Rebel,' for their big blanket-sheet dailies, such as the New York Herald, Tribune, Cincinnati Times and Louisville Journal."[47]

Even some "big officers" made allowances for fraternizing between the two sides. During the Petersburg Campaign, after some Confederate generals offered furloughs to men who could bring in Union prisoners, two young officers concocted a plan to capture a Yankee using a trade as a trap. One of the pair showed himself over the siege lines waving a newspaper as if inviting a trade, with his accomplice hiding nearby. One Union soldier, "a burly Irishman," took the bait and approached. When his quarry came close enough, the first officer tried to wrestle the Irishman back into Confederate lines but found it no easy task. Only when the second officer produced a pistol did the big Yankee come along quietly. However, when the officers appeared before their superior, George E. Pickett, the general was less than impressed with their ruse de guerre. Because the prisoner had been captured unarmed and under the false pretext of a truce, Pickett ordered the Irish Yankee returned to his own lines. No prisoner, no furlough.[48]

Some commanders did take a hard line on fraternization, and not without good reason. Friendly relations between opposing armies could especially aggravate the problem of desertion. All a soldier wishing to abscond from the army had to do was to meet the opposite side between the lines and continue on into enemy lines. Desertion especially plagued the Confederacy in the war's final year, as trench warfare ground down its armies and invading Union armies menaced soldiers' homes. Union soldiers understood how fraternizing offered their opponents a temptation to desert, and they eagerly sought to entice hungry and disaffected Rebels into their lines. Dug in around Kennesaw Mountain, Sergeant Ferguson of the 10th Illinois recorded in his diary how a Confederate who came into their lines to share a cup of coffee mentioned he would be willing to stay for a clean shirt. Ferguson's comrades quickly produced a fresh shirt, thereby costing the Confederacy another soldier to desertion. Later that summer, outside Atlanta, several men from Ferguson's regiment tried to parley with the Rebels, holding up newspapers as a signal they wanted to trade. "A Rebel liewtennant stood up on the works and told them to go away and stay away or they would be fired on," recorded the Illinois sergeant, "for it was strictly against their orders to hold conversations with the enemy." Ferguson heard a rumor that Confederates had tried to desert en masse—"a whole brigade of Rebs started to come into our lines"—but their own army began blasting them with artillery to turn them back. Union artillery had apparently responded with counterbattery fire, allowing some 200 Rebels to safely escape. Regardless of the accuracy of Ferguson's tale, it suggested that some officers recognized the security risk that fraternizing with the enemy posed and the drastic lengths they would go to combat it.[49]

In addition to facilitating desertion, rampant friendliness between opposing soldiers raised the question of whether troops who fraternized with the enemy would be willing to kill the enemy when duty called. Whereas Civil War commanders seem to have largely couched their objections to fraternization in terms of concerns over discipline and security, generals from World War I spoke more directly and severely of the necessity that their men be able to kill. In early December 1914, British corps commander Sir Horace Smith-Dorrien warned, "Experience of this and of every other war proves undoubtedly that troops in trenches in close proximity to the enemy slide very easily, if permitted to do so, into a 'live and let live' theory of life." Because "such an attitude . . . destroys the offensive spirit in all ranks," the general insisted, "friendly intercourse with the enemy, unofficial armistices (e.g., 'we won't fire if you don't' etc.) and the exchange of tobacco and other comforts, however tempting and amusing they may be, are absolutely prohibited." The general's fears seem to have come to fruition weeks later in the form of the Christmas Truce, a phenomenon along various sectors of the Western Front in which thousands of British and German soldiers ceased hostilities on Christmas Day, some venturing out into no-man's-land to socialize with one another. In the truce's aftermath, many British and German officers adopted harsh measures to ensure such a breakdown in the "offensive spirit" never occurred again. "Any attempt at fraternization with the enemy . . . such as occurred last year at Christmas and New Year at several points on the Western Front, is strictly forbidden; this crime will be considered as high treason," read a German order. "General HQ have issued instructions . . . that fire will be opened on every man who leaves the trench and moves in the direction of the enemy without orders."[50]

World War I generals' fears and drastic countermeasures amplify the question of whether fraternization inhibited Civil War soldiers' willingness to fight and kill. The very word "fraternize," derived from the Latin root *frater,* "brother," literally means "to turn people into brothers." How decisively did this affect Americans fighting against one another in a civil war said to pit brother against brother? To be sure, some Union and Confederate soldiers reported feeling less willing to fight after impromptu truces and meetings with the enemy. "It seems too bad that we have to fight men that we like. Now these southern soldiers seem just like our own boys, only they are on the other side," Chauncey Cooke, a sensitive soul, wrote his parents. "They talk about their people at home, their mothers and fathers and their sweethearts just as we do among ourselves." William Pitt Chambers, a Mississippian in Vicksburg's garrison, described a truce begun in order to bury Union dead, after which "we, the common soldiers of both armies, met on halfway ground and had a friendly chat." Chambers reported seeing not one but two pairs of brothers, each from the opposing armies, reunited during the truce. "After such a meeting it was with seeming reluctance that the firing was resumed," he wrote, "and even the next day it seemed less vicious than before."[51]

One of the most unusual yet most heartwarming truces between the blue and gray occurred during the standoff around Chattanooga in autumn 1863. Chauncey C. Baker of the 1st Wisconsin Heavy Artillery described how one day a little girl, possibly a toddler, came wandering into their picket line. Delighted by their unexpected visitor, "we surrendered to her without the firing of a gun," Baker charmingly wrote. The appearance of an innocent child temporarily swept away the reality of the war and reminded the fathers in the ranks of their own children far away. Union soldiers lovingly doted on the little girl, presenting her with gifts of sugar and presents of handkerchiefs and ribbons. When one Federal asked the child to whom she belonged, she answered, "Uncle Jim," pointing toward Confederate lines. Presently a Union soldier waved a white handkerchief tied to a ramrod to arrange the necessary truce.

One last gift was made before sending the girl home. The adorable visitor had even charmed Baker's comrade, Bob Chambers, "one of the biggest devils in our company." Chambers gave the child a bag of coffee for her Uncle Jim, saying, "I'll bet he hasn't had a good cup of coffee since the war began." Another Wisconsin soldier carried the girl beyond Union lines to meet a group of Confederates, which included her grateful uncle. Jim explained that the girl's father had been killed at Chickamauga and her mother had died shortly afterward, and that he would soon be taking her back to his own home. He hoped that the battle that was brewing would be over and done with by the time he returned to the army, "for damned if I feel like shooting at you fellows after this," adding with smile "at least, for some time to come." No doubt he spoke for many of the men on both sides that had experienced this touching episode of sweetness and goodwill.[52]

Establishing a personal relationship with soldiers from the other side through truces and fraternization convinced some Yanks and Rebs that the enemy was not really so terrible, and that they were not really so different. Some men even wistfully suggested that perhaps the conflict could be resolved peacefully if it could be left up to the common soldiers who did the actual fighting—a sentiment one can find throughout military history, both in soldiers' accounts and in popular depictions of men at war. In a letter home, James K. Newton of the 14th Wisconsin described a truce between the two sides during the Vicksburg Siege, quite possibly the same truce in which William Pitt Chambers had participated. Between the lines, he and his comrades had enjoyed a "long talk" with the besieged Rebels. "They agreed with us perfectly on one thing," Newton wrote his parents. "If the settlement of this war was left to the Enlisted men of both sides we would soon go home."[53]

Such sentiments, however, were hardly universal among Civil War soldiers, even for those who enjoyed friendly contact with the enemy. One of Newton's fellow Badger Staters, George W. Gore of the 1st Wisconsin, recounted for his hometown paper a friendly encounter between his captain and a Rebel major during a truce between the lines. After each had good-naturedly joked that the other was fighting for the wrong side and had debated the prospects of conquering the Confederacy, the two officers "agreed it was really a pity that such good fellows should be fighting against each other, but supposed it was their destiny." The captain and the major parted "amidst the warmest adieus and leave taking of the friendliest description," yet no one involved seemed to think the amiable meeting had sapped their will to fight. Gore concluded that "the next time they meet it will most likely be on the battlefield, and their salutations will be with the edge of the sword and the point of the bayonet." Another Federal, Private J. A. Dernten, directly addressed the notion that "some had prophesied that if two hostile armies should ever meet in battle array, they would drop their weapons and rush into each other's arms," sadly concluding that in fact battlefields told "a terribly different story."[54] Some Federals and Confederates imagined that the problems between North and South could be peaceably worked out if only left to ordinary men like themselves. Yet for other soldiers, especially among the great many who enlisted and fought out of deep and sincere commitment to their respective causes, the stakes involved were so momentous and the enemy so fundamentally wrong that the conflict could only be resolved with fighting and killing.

Numerous Civil War soldiers who witnessed or took part in truces and fraternizing marveled in their personal accounts at the incongruity of previously deadly enemies socializing with one another on the friendliest and most brotherly terms. During the Siege of Vicksburg, Union and Confederate soldiers peppered one another with sharpshooter fire but by mutual understanding held their fire at night, using the time instead to fraternize and arrange truces. Ohio soldier Joseph Bowker found it "strange that men, who an hour before were doing their utmost to kill each other, should, when darkness sets in, freely converse with each other and sometimes even meet half way and trade tobacco for hard bread." After an all-day truce at Kennesaw Mountain, a Confederate staff officer wrote, "The troops of both armies were sitting on top of the respective breastworks talking with each other, where, if they had dared to show their heads twenty-four hours ago it would have been shot off." At a subsequent truce, a major from Ohio marveled at the sight of Union and Confederate soldiers shaking hands, drinking, and talking "as though they never had tried to kill each other."[55]

Civil War veterans and subsequent generations of Americans celebrated stories of Union and Confederate soldiers putting aside their deadly work to enjoy fellowship with another, a trend that continues as strongly as ever today. Yet this sentiment masks the other side of the story—that in almost all cases after official and unofficial truces, Civil War soldiers returned to the business of trying to kill each other. "Amazing though it was to participants, and remarkable as it is to their descendants," writes historian Bell I. Wiley, "Yanks and Rebs who met between the lines to swap coffee for tobacco, and who lingered to talk sympathetically over common problems, could in the space of a few minutes go after one another with demoniac yells and awful destructiveness." William Wiley of the 77th Illinois observed a Vicksburg truce in which "details [from] the Union and rebel armies mingled together in a friendly way, shook hands and talked of their experiences and complimented each other on their fighting qualities and in a little while they were back in their respective positions trying their best to kill one another again." Sergeant Hamlin Alexander Coe from Michigan recorded in his diary a truce in which "the pickets from both armies are having as good a time as a lot of schoolboys just let loose from school," then added, "I presume tonight they will be shooting at each other." Colonel William Ripley recounted an interlude in the relentless fighting of the Overland Campaign in which Union and Confederate soldiers engaged in the perennial swapping of coffee and tobacco, "a curious scene [that] illustrated one phase of war." The following day, he observed, "the truce being over, hostilities were resumed and the men who had so lately fraternized together were again seeking opportunity to destroy each another." Both parties to the truce, the crack shots of Berdan's Sharpshooters and the veterans of the Army of Northern Virginia, knew well the business of trying to destroy the enemy.[56]

Many Civil War soldiers' behavior toward the enemy alternated between deadly antagonism and peaceful coexistence, depending on the demands of war and the conditions in which they found themselves. An exchange of messages between rival pickets near Bermuda Hundred, Virginia, exemplified the shifting, circumstantial nature of interactions between Yanks and Rebs. Soldiers of the 48th New York received a note from a Rebel picket, signing himself only as "Sugar," who wrote, "I am your friend on the picketline, but your foe in battle." One of the New Yorkers, replying as "Salt," wrote back, "All right. I am your friend everywhere but in battle."[57]

As the war dragged on, the peacefulness of the picket line began to erode. This proved particularly true when it came to siege operations and trench warfare as Union forces sought to capture such key Confederate cities as Vicksburg, Atlanta, and Petersburg. Armies facing off against one another from trenches were less interested than troops in the field in coexisting peacefully with one another during the interludes between actual battles. Pickets operated at the perimeters of armies, but in siege warfare, the perimeter facing the enemy was an active combat zone in its own right. Confederate defenders sought to keep Union encroachments at bay, while Union besiegers needed to suppress defensive firepower. Civil War armies on both sides endeavored to wear down one another's troop strength as attrition became the name of the game. In some situations pickets were still required to refrain from needlessly firing, but in siege operations the line between pickets and skirmishers became increasingly blurred. Just as Civil War soldiers often could not know with certainty whether those shooting at them were officially organized sharpshooters or ordinary infantrymen, in the trenches they could easily confuse pickets with enemy forces on orders to fire at them.

One of the most remarkable aspects of Civil War soldiers' attitudes toward killing was their seemingly effortless ability to transition between shooting at and fraternizing with one another. Some men described fighting in the trenches in sporting terms, with socializing with the enemy providing a diverting change of pace. Orson Young of the 96th Illinois wrote his parents from outside Atlanta about how the opposing sides traded shots with one another "for amusement" at 200 yards' distance from their respective rifle pits. "When we would be tired of shooting at one another," he explained, "we would stop and talk to each other a while to vary the amusement." Nor were Westerners the only men in Sherman's army to adopt a sporting attitude toward combat. "Our boys . . . enjoy the excitements of the picket line as well as they ever did squirrel shooting at home," observed Major Lewis D. Warner of the 154th New York. "Occasionally the pickets, which are generally within hailing distance, will suspend their fire, and hold a short discourse with each other, generally of the blackguard order, and winding up with 'Take care, rebels, or Yank,' when bang goes the musket, and the conference is at an end, and each looks out for his own head."[58]

Still other soldiers wrote lightheartedly of this casual sort of combat. Louis Leon of the 1st North Carolina, fighting in Virginia, wrote in one diary entry, "We are shooting at the Yankees to-day for fun." In a pitched battle soldiers might fight one another in a spirit of hatred or revenge, but according to some men a lack of hard feelings toward the enemy helped explain the flexible shifting between shooting and socializing. "You must not think up there that we fought down here because we are mad," John Brobst wrote his sweetheart, Mary, back in Wisconsin. In fact, he explained, "we fight for fun, or rather because we can't help ourselves." Brobst counted himself with those who felt that if "they would let the soldiers settle this thing it would not be long before we would be on terms of peace."[59]

John Brobst's letters to Mary reflected the complicated nature of some Civil War soldiers' attitudes toward fighting and the enemy. During the Atlanta Campaign, he happily described fraternizing with nearby Rebels, sitting down to impromptu dinner with them, even picking blackberries together. Brobst was among those Union soldiers who claimed he would rather kill a Confederate sympathizer at home than a Confederate soldier at the front. Yet at other times the hotheaded Brobst expressed thoughts toward the Rebels that were more hostile than fraternal. In a subsequent letter to Mary about the Battle of Jonesboro, he described with satisfaction how "we killed more of the rebs than they do of us," thus managing to "revenge our brother soldiers." In the same battle Brobst's baggage was captured, including his photograph of Mary. The loss clearly rankled him, writing in still another letter of his wish to kill the Rebel who had looted the picture. Civil War soldiers could express themselves both eloquently and forcefully, yet critically reading accounts such as Brobst's in their entirety reveals the often complex and enigmatic—sometimes even contradictory—nature of their attitudes toward the war they found themselves fighting.[60]

This behavior begs the question, why were Civil War soldiers able to switch back and forth between fighting and fraternizing so easily? A number of factors help account for this pattern. As previously noted, Yanks and Rebs shared so much common ground—culture, religion, national heritage, language—that fraternizing came quite naturally. On the other hand, the citizen-soldier of the American Civil War stands out as among the most strongly motivated fighting men in American history. A host of factors— political ideology, religious faith, expectations of family and neighbors, loyalty to one's comrades—maintained the Civil War soldier's motivation to continue the struggle. A Union or Confederate soldier might soften his attitudes toward the enemy, finding him a source of curiosity, diversion, or trade. He might rationalize such thoughts, telling himself that not every man who wore the opposing uniform was foully evil, that an enemy soldier might simply be a deluded pawn, depending on his allegiance, of the "Black Republicans" or the "Slave Power." For most Federals and Confederates, empathy for the enemy did not preclude still believing one's cause just and victory paramount. Pacifists may ask, "Suppose they gave a war, and nobody came?" yet the majority of Civil War soldiers believed so strongly in their respective causes that they would not countenance calling off the war simply because they discovered the men on the other side were much like themselves.

Alternating between friendliness and hostility toward the enemy also reflected Civil War soldiers' attitudes toward fighting itself. Like the soldiers of Shakespeare's *Henry V,* they were "but warriors for the working-day." When the enemy threatened or when their officers ordered them into battle, fight they would. When the fighting ebbed and no enemy threatened, however, often they were more than happy to leave the enemy alone if he would leave them alone. The pace of the campaigns beginning in 1864 upset this balance. Before the war's bloodiest year, the armies generally had fought a campaign climaxing in one major battle, and had then drawn back to refit and recuperate until the next campaign. The Union drives on Richmond and Atlanta changed that tempo. Grant and Sherman drove their armies on, fighting battle after battle, targeting those cities and the Rebel armies defending them. As a result, Union and Confederate soldiers experienced weeks of almost continuous fighting, not unlike that experienced by soldiers during the campaigns of World War II. Trench warfare exacerbated the problem by putting the armies in sustained close contact with one another under hostile circumstances. This threatened the peacefulness of the picket line, because picket lines were now also battle lines and thus legitimate spheres of combat. Soldiers sought relief from relentless campaigning and sharpshooting; they thus found it beneficial to adopt a live-and-let-live attitude, even if temporarily. At times in the trenches they renewed the picket cease-fires and truces from earlier in the war. Men like Orson Young found conversing with the enemy a fun diversion from the digging, watching, and shooting of trench warfare, yet they also believed enough in winning the war that the shooting could be a source of fun as well.

Even as Civil War soldiers veered into extremes of killing and not killing, other factors came into play that tempered those extremes. Some men wantonly killed their enemies on and off the battlefield, yet such transgressors remained a minority. On occasion their commanders authorized the execution of prisoners in reprisal, yet actually carrying out such orders pushed soldiers' tolerance for killing to the limit. Zealous Union soldiers threatened to violently subjugate political dissenters at home, but by and large no actual violence followed their violent rhetoric. At the opposite extreme, many Federals and Confederates fraternized with the enemy on and off the battlefield, yet most men who fraternized did not afterward rebel against or reject the notion of fighting. Soldiers might stop trying to shoot one another for truces, to talk, and to trade, but they almost always reverted back to shooting at each other afterward. Men on both sides might go to selfless extremes to take the enemy prisoner rather than slaughter him, yet often they remained poised to kill in cases in which the enemy refused quarter. The limits of the extremes suggest that most Civil War soldiers operated in a middle ground when it came to their attitudes toward the enemy and killing him. Yanks and Rebs could hate one another and could respect one another; a great many of them must not have felt entirely one way or the other about the man on the opposite side but instead a complex mixture of the two. Circumstances and temperament influenced whether Federals and Confederates saw the other side as a friend or foe—just how good a friend, and how terrible a foe.

The common soldier of the Civil War did not merely face a question of killing or not killing. Rather, the conflict resulted in fighting men from the North and South engaging in a continuum of behavior in combat. Besides killing or trying to kill under normal combat circumstances, a soldier might be tempted to indulge in one extreme or another by killing in a fashion that violated the rules of war, or by staying his hand and sparing the enemy. At opposite ends of the killing spectrum were acts of murder and acts of mercy. On the murderous side were atrocities such as killing prisoners and murdering foragers, as well as the specter of political violence against civilians and civil government. On the merciful side could be found the taking of prisoners, battlefield truces, caring for the enemy dead and wounded, and unabashed fraternizing with the enemy. Just as Civil War soldiers experienced a wide gamut of personal attitudes toward killing in combat, so too could they act on those feelings along a whole spectrum of lethal and nonlethal behaviors.

# 7

## Killing in Black and White
### Race, Combat, and Hate

The problem of slavery lay at the heart of the Civil War. Abraham Lincoln, whose 1860 election had sparked the first wave of secession, knew better than anyone "that slavery is the root of the rebellion," as he affirmed to a delegation of Christian Chicagoans. Likewise, he told a deputation of Northern freemen, "But for your race among us there could not be war." It was only fitting, then, in fighting a rebellion motivated and sustained by the institution of slavery that the United States allow men of that enslaved race to share in the fight. Lincoln's Emancipation Proclamation, by freeing slaves in the rebellious portions of the South and by welcoming Americans of African descent into the US military, changed the nature of the Civil War. Nationally, it shifted the war from a limited conflict to preserve the Union status quo antebellum to a more expansive war, one in which the United States would attack the institution of slavery as a means of preserving the Union. For tens of thousands of black men, whether born free or enslaved, it offered them an opportunity to fight personally for themselves and for their people, as well as to prove their valor and worth on the battlefield. That opportunity would also pit black Federals and white Confederates in some of the bloodiest, bitterest, and most savage combat of the Civil War.[1]

The service of black troops in the Civil War represents one of the proudest chapters in both US military and African American history, yet it is also haunted by some of the war's grimmest moments. Soldiers who were separated by the color of both their uniforms and their skin became some of the conflict's fiercest and most merciless enemies. For Confederates, armed black men on the battle-field represented a host of calamities. Their presence affronted their honor as Southern whites, threatened the social order of their society, and conjured up their wildest imaginations' visions of an apocalyptic race war. For black Federals, Confederates represented the society whose social order degraded their race by binding their lives, abusing their bodies, and tearing asunder their families. The conflict between white Union and Confederate soldiers could be tempered by forbearance and mercy, but clashes between Confederates and black Federals resulted in some of the most blatant, unrestrained killing of the war. Racial attitudes and Confederate policy combined to discourage Rebel soldiers from showing mercy toward wounded or surrendering black soldiers, and black troops responded likewise—in spirit and sometimes in deed. As a result of this cycle of brutality and retaliation, battles between white and black soldiers soon became combat in which quarter was neither asked nor given.

In order to appreciate how race influenced killing in the Civil War, it is important to understand the roles that violence and the power over life and death played in the institution of slavery. American chattel slavery was made possible by the Atlantic slave trade, in which Europeans, Middle Easterners, and Africans themselves colluded to capture black Africans and sell them into bondage. Slave traders brutally packed enslaved men, women, and children into slave ships for the tortuous voyage to the New World known as the Middle Passage. Compared to those taken to Central and South America, slaves stood a better chance of long-term survival in North America, where a self-perpetuating slave population was achieved much sooner. Nevertheless, nearly every aspect of the lives of American slaves was subject to control. Masters and overseers decided the food that slaves received, the clothing they wore, the quarters in which they lived, and the severity of their workload. Slavery violated black family life by regulating matches between men and women, splitting up families by selling off children and spouses, and subjecting slaves to sexual exploitation.[2]

Slave codes legitimized the use of physical force to discipline and punish slaves. Masters, overseers, and professional slave breakers often meted out punishments; in some cases, local peace officers could perform these "services" for slaveholders. No tool of violence was more associated with American slavery than the lash. "We will . . . prove by a cloud of witnesses," Theodore Dwight Weld wrote in *American Slavery as It Is*, "that the slaves are whipped with such inhuman severity, as to lacerate and mangle their flesh in the most shocking manner, leaving permanent scars and ridges." Slave owners themselves testified to the marks the whip left on their human property, describing their scars to identify escaped slaves in runaway notices. Southern newspapers commonly carried such descriptions as:

- "Much marked with the whip."
- "His back is *very badly scarred.*"
- "Very much scarred about the neck and ears by whipping."
- "His back shows *lasting impressions of the whip,* and leaves no doubt of his being A SLAVE."

Other slave punishments included branding, mutilations, and beatings. In one particularly chilling notice, an owner wrote of his runaway, a mother of two, "a few days before she went off, *I burnt her with a hot iron,* on the left side of her face, *I tried to make the letter M."* In the heat of the moment, an irate master might seize on any handy implement to strike at a slave. Abolitionist John Brown never forgot a moment from his adolescence during the War of 1812 when he witnessed a landlord beat a slave boy Brown's own age with a fire shovel.[3]

Unlike the Roman pater familias, the American slaveholder did not possess complete power over the life or death of his slave, at least in theory. The law did not give masters the power to willfully execute their slaves, but, granting the necessity of physical punishment, it generally sided with the owner, in deference to the very real possibility of a slave dying as the result of punishment. A 1669 Virginia law exempted masters from prosecution in cases in which a slave "by the extremity of the correction should chance to die," which was based on the presumption that murderous intent could not "induce any man to destroy his own estate." After the Revolution, the same spirit that prompted Northern states to abolish or phase out slavery induced some Southern states to pass laws promoting more humane treatment of slaves, including laws criminalizing the willful murder of one's own slaves. Even so, such laws still made exemptions for slave deaths in cases of insurrection or correction. Trials for the murder of slaves did arise in Southern states, and courts did imprison some murderous masters, though usually only in cases in which the master's brutality especially violated his white neighbors' sense of decency. "Almost all homicides of slaves, from the colonial period to the end of slavery, ended in acquittals, or at most in verdicts of manslaughter," one legal scholar writes, noting that "the master–slave relationship was so delicate that it was intruded upon only in extreme or unusual circumstances."[4]

In practice, a slave's life was very much in the master's hands. "I speak advisedly when I say this," Frederick Douglass wrote in his autobiography, "that killing a slave, or any colored person, in Talbot County, Maryland, is not treated as a crime, either by the courts or the community." In 1864, Kentucky slave Patsey Leach suffered the death of her husband, a trooper in the 5th US Colored Cavalry, and nearly died herself at the hands of her master. "When my husband was Killed my master whipped me severely saying my husband had gone into the army to fight white folks," Leach testified, "and he my master would let me know that I was foolish to let my husband go he would 'take it out of my back,' he would 'Kill me by piecemeal' and hoped 'that the last one of the nigger soldiers would be Killed.'" After enduring several whippings, Leach made her escape, taking her baby but forced to leave her other five children behind in her flight for survival. As the colonial Virginia slave code implied, often the best protector of a slave's life was the master's self-interest in not destroying valuable human property, yet among the cruelest masters, even that safeguard had its limits.[5]

Part of the price slave states paid for indulging in the peculiar institution was living with a deep underlying fear that their supposedly docile and contented human property might rise up in violent revolution. Torn between concerns for "justice" and "self-preservation," Thomas Jefferson wrote of the problem of slavery that "we have the wolf by the ear, and we can neither hold him, nor safely let him go." The American colonies and the early republic experienced several isolated slave revolts in places such as New York City, South Carolina, and Louisiana. After the 1790s, the Haitian Revolution, which overthrew the French colonial slave society of Saint-Domingue and claimed the lives of tens of thousands of whites and blacks, loomed large as the archetypal slave uprising in white Southerners' imaginations.[6]

The United States experienced its largest slave revolt in Southampton County, Virginia, in 1831 in the form of Nat Turner's Rebellion. Turner, a slave preacher and mystic, sparked an uprising in which he and his followers slaughtered approximately sixty white men, women, and children, mostly using axes and other ad hoc weapons, before they were suppressed. John Brown's raid in 1859 raised the specter of a slave rebellion incited and aided by radical white abolitionists. The attack on the US Armory and Arsenal at Harpers Ferry, Virginia, featured a strange mix of aggression and restraint. In capturing and holding the town, Brown's white and black raiders killed four civilians and took scores more hostage, yet Brown himself was conspicuously cordial in the treatment of his hostages, even ordering breakfast to be sent over for them from a local hotel. Despite its tactical failure, John Brown's raid heightened Southern paranoia over slave unrest on the eve of the presidential election of 1860, dramatically kindling the fires of secession.

Slave revolts and political violence highlighted the passion and outrage that could bring both black and white opponents of slavery to kill. In Kansas, three years before the Harpers Ferry raid, John Brown and his followers carried out the Pottawatomie Massacre, in which they dragged five proslavery settlers from their cabins in the dead of night, and in front of their families butchered the men with artillery short swords. The incident was only a part of the frontier civil war known to history as Bleeding Kansas, in which proslavery and antislavery settlers fought one another in order to determine whether Kansas would join the Union as a slave or free state. Proslavery propagandists capitalized on antislavery violence as well as radical abolitionist rhetoric, particularly if it betokened more violence. A proslavery book published in 1863 quoted with outrage a Methodist preacher who promised that upon meeting his first Rebel, "I will discharge the contents of my musket through him, and while the blood is weltering from his veins, I will kneel down by his side, and pray God to pardon his sins."[7]

Such was the fear and rage that slave revolts brought forth in white Southerners that in combating such uprisings, they not only met violence measure for measure but also often exceeded it. In the wake of slave violence, blacks could expect vicious reprisals, regardless of whether they had been involved. In the aftermath of Nat Turner's Rebellion, in which some three score whites were killed, authorities executed fifty-six blacks, while approximately another 200 died at the hands of white militias and vigilantes. During the Harpers Ferry raid, raiders who fell into the hands of vengeful townsfolk and local militia met a grisly fate. Dangerfield Newby, a freeman who had tried unsuccessfully to purchase his wife and children out of slavery, fell dead with a shot through the throat. The town's liberators mutilated his corpse by beating it with sticks and cutting off his ears before throwing the body into an alley to be devoured by hogs. White raider William Leeman tried to swim across the Potomac but was shot to death as he climbed onto a rock in the river. Militiamen continued to fire bullets into his lifeless body for sport and target practice until it slipped back into the river. The same anxiety, fury, and outrage that fired white Southerners in the face of slave uprisings would rekindle when Confederate soldiers confronted black soldiers in the Civil War.[8]

Northern whites opposed or held reservations about enlisting blacks as soldiers for many reasons. Those harboring deep racial animosity opposed challenging the racial status quo by making war on slavery and enfranchising the black man by making a soldier of him. "We want you d——d niggers to keep out of this," angry Cincinnati police told freemen who rallied in 1861 to express their willingness to fight. "This is a white man's war." Racial assumptions also caused many Northerners, be they hostile or benign in their attitudes toward blacks, to doubt whether they could make effective soldiers. Much of this speculation concerned whether members of an enslaved and supposedly inferior race could stand the ordeal of combat. Even Abraham Lincoln wondered whether black soldiers could stand and fight, asking if arms issued to them would "in a few weeks . . . be in the hands of the rebels." Others specifically asked if blacks possessed the physical and psychological capacity to kill in combat. Charles Francis Adams Jr., son of the US ambassador to Britain and commander of a black Massachusetts cavalry regiment, insisted that a black soldier "cannot fight for life like a white man." Kentucky congressman Charles A. Wickliffe believed that "a negro is afraid, by instinct or by nature, of a gun." General Benjamin Butler similarly believed blacks were "horrified of firearms." Before the war, as a Massachusetts Democrat, he had asked, "Did not all history show that if armed conflict arose between the races, 'the inferior race, as God has made it, must yield as it ever has yielded?'" Though a lackluster general, to his credit Butler ultimately welcomed black soldiers into his command and celebrated their achievements.[9]

Many white Union soldiers of various racial attitudes reconciled themselves to the use of black soldiers as an effective war measure. Their various rationales reflected competing assumptions about whether the nature of soldiering was to risk one's own life or to take enemy lives. Quite a few white Federals reasoned, on the basis of a rough sense of equality, that a black man could stop a bullet as well as a white; the use of black troops in combat could thus well save their own lives. Irish-born New York officer Charles G. Halpine, writing in comic Irish dialect under the pen name "Private Miles O'Reilly," popularized this view in his song, "Sambo's Right to be Kilt":

> Some tell us 'tis a burnin' shame
> To make the naygers fight;
> An' that the thrade of bein' kilt
> Belongs but to the white:
> But as for me, upon my sowl!
> So liberal are we here,
> I'll let Sambo be murthered instead of myself
> On every day in the year.

As Halpine's ditty concludes in the final two verses, "The right to be kilt we'll divide wid him, / And give him the largest half!" Other Union soldiers expressed the same sentiment in even blunter terms. "The more nigers they get, the better I will be suited for I would rather see a nigers head blowed off than a white mans," a Pennsylvanian wrote. "If any African will stand between me and a rebel bullet," an Iowa sergeant declared, "he is welcome to the honor and the bullet too."[10]

Conversely, other Northerners welcomed black soldiers into the fight not so much because they favored black men being killed but rather because they reckoned such men would make effective killers of Confederates. "I wish they would arm all the slaves there is in the south," opined a Vermonter. "They are ready to go at the rebels like a mess of blood hounds." The *Chicago Tribune* waxed eloquent in favor of raising a black regiment, declaring that Illinois men of color would "stand as much hardship, and fight as desperately, and kill as many rebels in battle, as any equal number of men of the purest Anglo-Saxon blood that have gone to the wars." Even "Sambo's Right to be Kilt" acknowledged the black man's ability to kill Rebels amid the song's racial humor:

> Though Sambo's black as the ace of spades,
> His finger a thrigger can pull,
> And his eye runs sthraight on the barrel-sights
> From undher its thatch of wool.

Whether they mocked him, despised him, or welcomed him in good faith, many white Union soldiers recognized their black comrades' equality in being able to die or kill for their country.[11]

Exploring the motivations of United States Colored Troops (USCT) to enlist and fight, including their attitudes toward killing in combat, is made difficult by the comparative lack of written accounts they left. Widespread illiteracy, the result of slave codes and poverty, chiefly accounts for this lack. Of 186,017 blacks in Federal service, 134,111 came from the slaveholding South, which prohibited or highly restricted teaching blacks to read and write. Writing in 1978, historian Bell Irvin Wiley lamented the "dearth of letters written by the [approximate] 200,000 blacks who donned the blue," explaining that his research "had turned up less than a score of these sources." Happily, historians in recent decades have discovered still more USCT letters, including documents in the National Archives and public correspondence to prominent African American newspapers of the era, enriching our understanding of their experience of the Civil War. Nevertheless, accounts that discuss the idea or the experience of killing are challenging enough to find among white soldiers, and the search for such accounts among the relatively scarce USCT sources yields even fewer results. Rather than describing the psychology of combat, such letters far more often addressed the moral battles waged by black soldiers. Unlike their white comrades, black Federals fought against not only Confederate soldiers but also prejudice within their own army. In addition to reporting the campaigns of their regiments, USCT writers also used their public letters to campaign for causes such as their right to pay equal to that of white soldiers and their eligibility for officer commissions.[12]

Black soldiers' accounts, especially those written by soldier-correspondents for publication in newspapers, most often discussed killing in combat as a rhetorical description of their soldierly duties. Writing for a public audience, soldiers used such references to highlight their units' fighting zeal and readiness for the fray. Celebrating his regiment's receipt of prime Enfield rifle muskets, Corporal James Henry Gooding of the famed 54th Massachusetts assured his hometown newspaper that the army must "intend us to make good use of them; and I doubt not if the opportunity presents itself, they *will* be made good use of." William H. Johnson, who managed to attach himself to the white 8th Connecticut despite being of noticeable African descent, boasted, "We expect to take Secesh, box him up, label him 'dead,' and send him to Bunker Hill, on or before the Fourth of July." Praising his regiment's defense of Wilson's Landing, Virginia, the black chaplain of the 1st USCT extolled "the coolness and cheerfulness of the men, the precision with which they shot, and the vast number of rebels they unmercifully slaughtered." So accurate had been their fire, he wrote, that the Confederate attackers "declared our regiment were sharp-shooters." In 1864, a "National Convention of Colored Men," led by Frederick Douglass, used USCT military service to call for black suffrage, asking, "Are we good enough to use bullets, and not good enough to use ballots?"[13]

If black soldiers offered scant details about killing in their surviving letters, then other sources can be tapped to understand this aspect of their military service. White officers and enlisted men who observed USCT in combat testified to their tenacity and readiness to kill. One Wisconsin cavalryman admitted, "I never believed in niggers before, but by Jesus, they are hell in fighting." At an 1864 action in Marion, Virginia, Colonel James S. Brisbin helped lead a spirited charge by the 6th US Colored Cavalry, which broke the Confederate battle line. Brisbin remembered the sight of one black trooper "fighting with a gun barrel, swinging it about his head like a club"—a man from whom the Rebels precipitously fled. The experience left the colonel marveling, "I never yet saw anything in battle so terrible as an infuriated negro." A captain in a white Vermont regiment paid tribute to the ill-fated black troops who did battle in the Petersburg Crater, remembering "that they fought like heroes and many a rebel bit the dust from their unerring bullets."[14]

Black soldiers themselves left little written record of reluctance or remorse over the killing of Confederate soldiers, men they deemed "the enemies of our country and race." Knowledge of Rebels' proclivity to show them no quarter contributed to the desperation and ferocity with which USCT often fought, as did the specter of enslavement hanging over them if they or the Union cause failed in battle. More so than white Federals, black soldiers could easily imagine the personal consequences of military defeat. Chauncey Cooke, a white Wisconsin soldier who unabashedly supported fighting for emancipation, understood why: "The poor black devils are fighting for their wives and children, yes and for their lives, while we white cusses are fighting for . . . an idea." Sergeant James C. Taylor of the 93rd USCT spoke for many of his comrades when he declared, "But for our race to go back into bondage again, to be hunted by dogs through the swamps and cane-brakes, to be set up on the block and sold for gold and silver, and what is yet meaner (Confederate money) no never; gladly would we die first."[15]

Other media in addition to soldiers' accounts extolled black soldiers' martial prowess and ability to kill in battle. In particular, both blacks and whites celebrated USCT in verse as well as in prose. A song with variants attributed to Sojourner Truth and to Captain Lindley Miller, a white officer in a black regiment, and sung to the same tune as "John Brown's Body" and "The Battle Hymn of the Republic," boasted, "We can hit a Rebel further than a white man ever saw, / As we go marching on." One poem memorialized a soldier of the 1st Kansas Colored Volunteers fallen at the Battle of Poison Spring, having stayed on the battle line loading and firing despite having received a mortal wound:

> His rifle 'gainst the traitor foe
> With deadly aim would ply;
> And, till his life-blood ceased to flow,
> Fight on for liberty.

Visually, the regimental flag of the 22nd USCT represented one of the most dramatic expressions of black soldiers' deadly intent in battle. Painted by black Philadelphia artist David Bustill Bowser, the seal on the silk banner's obverse depicts a black soldier with a fixed bayonet poised at or plunging into the body of a Confederate soldier at bay. A banner above the seal proclaims "Sic Semper Tyrannis" (Thus always to tyrants). Bowser included in the scene a white flag on the ground next to the Confederate's left hand. Whether the artist intended the detail to convey that the enemy soldier has been forced to surrender or that Confederates could expect no quarter is unclear, but nevertheless, the defiant banner seems to speak volumes about the fighting men who were to carry it into battle.[16]

In March 1863, Abraham Lincoln wrote to Andrew Johnson—then the military governor of Tennessee—to encourage his willingness to pursue the policy of recruiting blacks, musing optimistically, "The bare sight of fifty thousand armed and drilled black soldiers on the banks of the Mississippi, would end the rebellion." The introduction of colored troops did elicit a dramatic response from rebellious Southerners—but not the one for which Lincoln hoped. Confederate soldiers and civilians reacted with visceral anger and outrage at the United States' newest fighting men. The policy tapped into their society's deep-seated fears of slave revolt and the destruction of white racial hegemony. "For many Southerners," Dudley Taylor Cornish explained in his seminal work *The Sable Arm*, "it was psychologically impossible to see a black man bearing arms as anything but an incipient slave uprising complete with arson, murder, pillage, and rapine." An Arkansas newspaper editor heartily endorsed the decision in Richmond to treat USCT as insurrectionists, declaring, "It follows irresistibly that we *cannot* treat negroes taken in arms as prisoners of war without a destruction of the social system for which we contend." Because they threatened the "social system" of the South, he insisted, "We *must* claim the full control of all negroes who may fall into our hands, to punish with death, or any other penalty, or remand to their owners. If the enemy retaliate, we must do likewise, and if the *black flag* follows, the blood will be upon their heads."[17]

For many white Southerners, sending armed black men to fight against them constituted nothing less than a war crime, a reaction codified by the Confederate Congress on May 1, 1863. The resolution it passed empowered Jefferson Davis and Confederate forces to treat the use of black Union soldiers as they would a slave insurrection. White officers commanding colored troops could "if captured be put to death or be otherwise punished" by military courts, while black soldiers themselves were to be handed over to local state authorities, who would presumably execute them or reduce them to slavery. To his credit, Abraham Lincoln responded with measures by which the US government would attempt to guarantee "the same protection to all its soldiers," be they white or black. Lincoln threatened the Confederacy with a policy of retaliation if USCT officers and enlisted men were not treated according to the laws of war, declaring that Union forces would execute a Rebel prisoner for every Federal soldier put to death, and would put a Rebel prisoner to hard labor for every USCT soldier who was enslaved. Ostensibly, Lincoln's order forced the Confederates to retreat from their policy, with the result that the two warring governments did not publicly pursue retaliatory acts of executing or subjugating prisoners of war. More accurately, Lincoln's threat managed only to limit the execution and maltreatment of USCT prisoners and to drive it underground. The Lincoln administration lacked the political will and public support to aggressively police and challenge Confederate treatment of captured USCT soldiers. In turn, the Confederate government was essentially able to have its cake and eat it too, because it could count on many of its own troops to execute or otherwise brutalize black soldiers without officially having to order it. As one writer notes, denying quarter to black soldiers "became a de facto policy by default because it was condoned, never punished, and always denied"—a policy that "enjoyed Richmond's tacit approval."[18]

One of the most telling and callous ways in which Confederate soldiers and civilians reacted to the killing of black soldiers in battle was to refer to their monetary value as human chattel. Such expressions not only reflected the pervasiveness of slave society ideology but also served Confederates as a rhetorical means of actively dehumanizing black soldiers whom they deemed unfit military opponents for white Southerners. "Just think how infamous it is that our *gentlemen* should have to go out and fight niggers," fumed one South Carolina woman, "and that every nigger they shoot is a thousand dollars out of their own pockets! Was there ever anything more outrageous?" Recalling the repulse of a Union charge at the Battle of New Market Heights, a Texas soldier wrote, "We killed in our front about a million dollars worth of niggers, at current prices." Another soldier, surveying the aftermath of a skirmish at Natural Bridge, Florida, found "dead Negroes enough around . . . to have made a slave holder rich." For believers in a slaveholders' republic, the killing of black soldiers was less a case of lives taken as it was of valuable property destroyed.[19]

Not all Confederates were blind to black Federals' humanity or their worth as soldiers. Some could objectively appreciate their merits as fellow fighting men. One Confederate veteran who faced black regiments in battle at Olustee, Florida, dispassionately told a newspaper correspondent, "They stood killing d——d well, but they didn't hurt us much." According to what he heard, the reporter concluded, "Train them thoroughly in firing at target until they have confidence in their weapons, and on the whole, are rather anxious to try their effect on human bodies (this is the natural effect of such training), and if they have brave officers they will fight as well as the average of mankind."[20]

The execution and brutalization of black soldiers were not confined to few isolated incidents. A number of recent studies, particularly *Black Flag Over Dixie* and *Confederate Rage, Yankee Wrath*, have conclusively documented that Confederate soldiers across the embattled Confederacy routinely denied quarter and proper treatment to USCT who fell into their hands. In the latter book, George S. Burkhardt writes, "Southern soldiers . . . killed wounded, surrendered, or trapped black Federals as a matter of course, although that practice never became the Confederacy's declared official policy."[21] What follows are vignettes examining some of the best-documented and most significant incidents regarding the killing and murder of black soldiers.

Black soldiers first clashed with Confederate forces in a number of skirmishes in 1862, some fought by the 1st Kansas Colored Volunteers, which had yet to come under Federal military oversight. By and large, however, Americans North and South did not begin to take notice of the performance of such troops until summer 1863, when a series of actions—the assault on Port Hudson, the Battle of Milliken's Bend, and the assault on Fort Wagner—signaled to many observers that black troops could and would fight bravely and acquit themselves well as soldiers. Among these, the defense of Milliken's Bend particularly stands out, marked by a chaotic night battle in which raw, barely trained black soldiers clashed in brutal hand-to-hand fighting with their Confederate foes.[22]

In spring 1863, four black infantry regiments—the 9th, 11th, and 13th Louisiana, African Descent, and the 1st Mississippi, African Descent—began organizing on the west bank of the Mississippi River at Milliken's Bend, Louisiana. Federally recruited from local freed slaves, the four regiments camped along a series of levees had not yet reached full strength and had only just begun drilling with their recently issued Austrian rifles, deemed by one officer who inspected the weapons as "old, defective, and worthless." Rudimentary marksmanship training progressed slowly, to the consternation of regiments' white officers. Meanwhile, General John G. Walker's division of Texans had begun targeting Union outposts along the Mississippi, hoping to interdict Union supply lines as Ulysses Grant maneuvered around and then laid siege to the all-important city of Vicksburg, Mississippi.[23]

Brigadier General Henry E. McCulloch and his four Texas regiments began their attack on Milliken's Bend around 2:30 A.M. on June 7, driving in the Union pickets as they forced their way through a series of Osage orange hedges. Still new to their weapons, most of the black soldiers managed to loose a single volley, which only momentarily checked the onrushing Texans as they charged the Union line atop the levee. Hitting the Federals at an oblique, McCulloch's men first crashed into the enemy left, held by the 9th Louisiana. What the black soldiers lacked in precise loading and firing, they made up for in tenacity as they fought the Texans hand to hand with bayonets and musket butts. Lieutenant David Cornwell witnessed one of his men, six-and-a-half-foot-tall "Big Jack" Jackson, wade into the Confederates with a clubbed musket: "With the fury of a tiger he sprang into that gang and smashed everything before him." When his musket stock shattered, Big Jack continued swinging away with the barrel. Shouts of "Shoot that big nigger, shoot that big nigger" sounded from the Texans' ranks, until finally a shot to the head killed the giant of a soldier.[24]

It is not clear how early the Confederates attacking Milliken's Bend realized they were facing black soldiers, although many managed to recognize the race of their opponents once the fighting became hand to hand. Hermann Lieb, colonel of the 9th Louisiana and acting brigade commander of the four black regiments, heard Rebel shouts of "No quarters for white officers, kill the damned abolitionists, but spare the niggers." This was a notable exception to most encounters between Confederates and black Federals that followed, in which white Union soldiers stood a better chance of being taken alive than their black comrades. Matthew Miller, a lieutenant in Lieb's regiment, also wrote that the attackers shouted "No quarters," presumably because they faced black soldiers. Fifteen-year-old Confederate soldier Henry Dick Lester, writing home to his family how his regiment "fought Bayonet crossing Bayonet for full one minute," proudly recounted his victorious encounter with a black soldier: "My antagonist was a huge Negro who fired and missed me and then clubbed his gun and tried to strike me." Twice Lester bayoneted his opponent before raising his weapon to parry a musket blow to the shoulder "which darn near br[oke] the shoulder blade." Lester once more thrust his bayonet "clear through him and finished fired into him . . . which blew him all to pieces."[25]

For all their tenacity, the black Louisianans and Mississippians forming the Union left and center could not stem the momentum of the Confederate attack and were forced to retreat to the riverbank. Faced with a fleeing enemy, the Texans redoubled their efforts; facing a vulnerable enemy, they could kill all the more easily and prolifically. Once the Federals "stampeded" down the first levee, Texas infantryman Joseph P. Blessington wrote, "Our troops followed after them, bayonetting them by the hundreds." Another Texan, John M. Wright, boasted, "We made it hot for those negroes. There was not one left to tell the tale." A white Union regiment, the veteran 23rd Iowa, disembarked from a nearby troop transport and plunged into the fray. Like their black comrades, the Iowans clashed with the Texans in brutal close-quarters combat, making the levee "a very hot place," until they too had to retreat. Only on the defenders' far right, the strongest portion of the Union position and the last to be hit by the Confederate attacks, did several companies of the 11th Louisiana manage to hold their original position throughout the duration of the battle. The rest of the Union force regrouped behind a second levee, their backs to the Mississippi. McCulloch's brigade pressed the attack and might have captured or destroyed what remained of five regiments, but with dawn lighting the battlefield, Union ironclads opened a relentless fusillade to protect the beleaguered infantrymen. Unable to withstand the naval gunfire, the Confederates eventually withdrew, leaving the bloodied Union brigade in possession of the field.[26]

The Battle of Milliken's Bend was a limited tactical victory for US forces, but for the black soldiers involved, particularly the 9th and 11th Louisiana, it represented a decisive moral victory. For raw, partially trained troops who had faced a sudden attack in the middle of the night, the men of the African Descent regiments had performed reasonably, even extraordinarily, well, especially those who had stood and fought hand to hand after their initial volley failed to stop the Confederate attack. Both Northern and Southern skeptics had doubted black men could stand battle under the best of circumstances, but at Milliken's Bend, they had fought under the most desperate circumstances. The veteran white soldiers of the 23rd Iowa, arriving on the field in the midst of the fighting, had suffered comparable casualties to the aforementioned Louisiana regiments, and they too had been forced back to the second levee. In a letter home to Illinois, Captain Matthew M. Miller of the 9th Louisiana wrote feelingly of the sacrifice made by his men: "I never felt more grieved and sick at heart than when I saw how my brave soldiers had been slaughtered. . . . I never more wish to hear the expression, 'The niggers won't fight.' Come with me 100 yards from where I sit and I can show you the wounds that cover the bodies of 16 as brave, loyal, and patriotic soldiers as ever drew bead on a rebel." News of the battle spread by word of mouth and in print, including newspaper printings of Miller's letter, convincing many Northern soldiers and civilians that black troops truly would fight.[27]

Confederate reactions to Milliken's Bend were far more mixed. Texan survivors of the battle credited the tenacity of their Union opponents, describing the battle as "hard fighting" and a "struggle . . . close and deadly." General Henry McCulloch acknowledged that his attack had been "resisted by the negro portion of the enemy's force with considerable ob-stinacy." Many Confederate civilians met the news that their soldiers had fought armed blacks with shock and disbelief. In nearby Monroe, Louisi-ana, Sarah Wadley wrote, "It is said that . . . the negroes fought desper-ately, and would not give up until our men clubbed muskets upon them. . . . It is terrible to think of such a battle as this, white men and freemen fighting with their slaves, and to be killed by such a hand, the very soul revolts from it." Hearing of a repulse at Milliken's Bend, diarist Kate Stone discounted the notion of a Confederate defeat, finding it "hard to believe that Southern soldiers—and Texans at that—have been whipped by a mon-grel crew of white and black Yankees." The daughter of a wealthy planter family, Stone found the idea that black soldiers had fought bravely and fiercely to be the most unbelievable: "It is said the Negro regiments fought there like mad demons, but we cannot believe that. We know from long experience they are cowards."[28]

Confederate forces at Milliken's Bend do not seem to have indulged in the black flag tactics that characterized the aftermath of other battles with black soldiers, yet the Confederate military response to the battle still re-flected radical proslavery ideology. In fact, General Edmund Kirby Smith, commanding the Trans-Mississippi Department, expressed concern that black soldiers had been taken prisoner instead of being killed outright. Writing to General Richard Taylor, under whose command McCulloch's Texans served, Smith stated, "I have been unofficially informed that some of your troops have captured negroes in arms. I hope this may not be so, and that your subordinates who may have been in command of capturing parties may have recognized the propriety of giving no quarter to armed negroes and their officers. In this way we may be relieved from a disagree-able dilemma." As Smith noted, the Confederate Congress had recently dictated that white officers leading black soldiers were subject to execu-tion, while black soldiers themselves should be turned over to local state authorities, who would then either execute them for insurrection or return them to slavery as they saw fit. With much of Louisiana occupied, how-ever, many Confederate courts were no longer sitting, presumably creating the "disagreeable dilemma" of which Smith wrote. Furthermore, as Linda Barnickel pointedly observes in her history of the battle, Kirby Smith in his dispatch conspicuously referred to the Union combatants at Milliken's Bend as negroes "armed" or "in a state of insurrection," thus confirming their perceived status as rebellious slaves rather than recognizing them as US soldiers.[29]

The perception of black soldiers as human chattel with fungible value, rather than as lawful combatants, extended down the Confederate chain of command. During the fighting at Milliken's Bend, a Confederate musician assisting his regimental surgeon had been captured (along with the surgeon's horse) by a captain and his company of black soldiers forty-nine men strong. The musician managed to trick the captain by leading the company into Confederate lines rather than toward the Union position, resulting in the capture of his captors. General McCulloch proposed rewarding him with "a choice boy from among these fellows to cook and wash for him and his mess during the war, and to work for him as long as the negro lives." McCulloch also suggested that, because the surgeon had lost his horse in the course of the encounter, "another of these fellows might be well and properly turned over to him to compensate for his loss," further underscoring black slaves' status in slaveholders' eyes as a kind of human livestock.[30]

Fought almost a year after the Battle of Milliken's Bend, the fight at Fort Pillow, Tennessee, witnessed another attack on a Union post on the Mississippi River garrisoned by black soldiers. The latter, however, ended not in a Confederate retreat but in a precipitous Union defeat and a wanton massacre of many of the fort's black and white defenders. Tragically, the Battle of Fort Pillow, scene of the Civil War's most notorious atrocity, was arguably a battle that need never have been fought in the first place. Completed by Confederate forces in 1862, Fort Pillow's earthen ramparts sat atop a high bluff overlooking the Mississippi River, some forty miles north of Memphis. That same year, Union advances up the Tennessee and Cumberland rivers threatened to isolate the fort, prompting the Confederate garrison to abandon the post in June 1862. A number of Union units occupied the fort until January 1864, when General William T. Sherman ordered the fort vacated in preparation for his forthcoming campaign against Atlanta, seeking to free up more men for his own army and the protection of outposts protecting his supply lines. General Stephen A. Hurlbut, the Union district commander, initially complied with the order, only to violate it in late March when he ordered it reoccupied by a small garrison under the command of Major Lionel F. Booth. Booth's force, consisting of a detachment from the 2nd US Colored Light Artillery, the 6th US Colored Heavy Artillery, and the 13th Tennessee Cavalry (composed of white Tennessee Unionists), would have the dubious distinction of holding a fort that Sherman as Federal commander in the West had already deemed unnecessary to the war effort.[31]

The reoccupation of Fort Pillow placed Booth's command squarely in the sights of the formidable Confederate cavalry commander Nathan Bedford Forrest. That March, Forrest launched a raid into western Tennessee and Kentucky. It was the kind of operation at which he and other mounted partisans excelled, aimed at capturing vulnerable Federal outposts charged with holding occupied Rebel territory and maintaining Union supply lines. One of Forrest's subordinates successfully bluffed the garrison of Union City, Tennessee, into surrendering. Forrest then turned his attention to Paducah, Kentucky, situated at the junction of the Ohio and Tennessee rivers. There he demanded the surrender of the Federal garrison at nearby Fort Anderson, promising, "If you surrender, you shall be treated as prisoners of war, but if I have to storm your works, you may expect no quarter." Well fortified and backed with gunboats, Fort Anderson successfully rebuffed Forrest, who departed after seizing Union supplies.[32]

It remains unclear how seriously Forrest meant his threat of no quarter and whether a massacre similar to the one at Fort Pillow would have played out at Fort Anderson if the latter had been successfully stormed. On one hand, it was commonplace during the war for Forrest and other Confederates attacking Union outposts to warn enemy commanders that they could not assure the defenders' lives if forced to assault their forts. Fort Pillow stands out as one of a few occasions during the Civil War of an isolated post refusing to surrender and subsequently being taken by storm. On the other hand, Fort Anderson's garrison might well have suffered a fate similar to the Fort Pillow defenders because both comprised both white and black soldiers—the primary motive for the massacre. A Union captain who escaped after the surrender of Union City later testified that he had heard his Rebel captors "say repeatedly that they intended to kill negro troops wherever they could find them." They were prepared to kill any black soldiers they found at Union City (there were none), and they similarly anticipated killing those at Paducah, he reported. Like too many Confederate soldiers, it seems Forrest's men had eagerly resolved to kill black soldiers in Union blue under any circumstances.[33]

Major General Nathan Bedford Forrest, the man whose conduct and responsibility at Fort Pillow dominate the controversy over the battle, was steeped both in violence and the institution of slavery. Born in 1821, Forrest grew up among the hardship and danger of frontier Mississippi. As a young man, he had successfully hunted and killed a cougar that had attacked his mother on the trail. Forrest exemplified the frontier's savage, no-holds-barred brand of Southern honor and violence. He was involved in a number of bloody encounters, including a melee in 1845 when he came to the defense of an uncle being accosted by four planters, killing one and wounding another in the process. Before the war, he also managed to pull himself out of hardscrabble poverty, making his fortune in cotton and slave trading. White observers described him as a kind master and one who allowed slaves in his Memphis slave market great liberty, though notably it was also said that this was made possible because "he had taught them to fear him exceedingly." Certainly Forrest had a vested interest in preserving the South's slave society, and in fact, as a slave trader, was personally more involved in maintaining the institution than some other Confederate general officers. Forrest's racial legacy is further complicated by his early involvement after the war in the Ku Klux Klan as it fought to restore the Old South's racial status quo—to which the enlistment of black soldiers posed such a threat—though biographers debate the extent of his involvement as the Klan became increasingly murderous and terroristic.[34]

As one author notes, though many of Forrest's altercations were cases of self-defense, they also revealed a savage fury. He exhibited a starkly Janus-faced personality: he could be tender and loving toward his family and even benevolent to the slaves in his charge, but those who crossed him would find in Nathan Bedford Forrest a fearsome and implacable enemy. In such encounters, writes Richard Fuchs in his history of Fort Pillow, Forrest displayed "an utter commitment to the complete annihilation of his adversaries—the uncontrolled torrent of rage that could not be satiated short of total destruction of the threat," making him "a seething cauldron who when challenged would erupt with reckless violence and abandon." During the war, a dispute with an artillery officer resulted in the man wounding Forrest with a revolver, after which Forrest stabbed his opponent in the belly with a penknife. Convinced his own wound was mortal, Forrest fetched another revolver and pursued his attacker, determined to kill the man who had killed him, only to be restrained by his subordinates. Even when blood was not shed, Forrest could be fearsome in his wrath. Early biographers claimed that twice during the war he defied superior officers—Generals Braxton Bragg and John Bell Hood—vociferously denouncing each to his face and insisting that neither was man enough to be worth fighting, though the threat of physical harm remained unmistakable. One can easily imagine a man of such violent passions permitting the murder of black soldiers, either presiding over or allowing the massacre at Fort Pillow.[35]

Forrest's mixed force of cavalry and infantry reached Fort Pillow the morning of April 12, ten days after the demonstration at Paducah, and proceeded to invest the Union position. He would bring to bear at least 1,500 men to oppose a garrison less than 600 strong. Throughout the morning and early afternoon, Forrest's men pushed their way toward the Union ramparts. The rugged terrain surrounding Fort Pillow served the defenders poorly; Confederate sharpshooters took advantage of the hills looking down on the defenses and the deep ravines on its approach to pour a deadly fire into the defenders. One sharpshooter's bullet struck Booth squarely in the chest, killing him instantly.[36]

At 3:30 that afternoon, Forrest sent a communiqué of his own to the fort. Praising the conduct of the defenders, he offered to accord the garrison treatment as prisoners of war if they surrendered presently, adding ominously, "Should my demand be refused, I cannot be responsible for the fate of your command." The ranking Union officer, answering in Booth's name, asked for an hour to consider the terms. Forrest allowed him twenty minutes. During the deliberations, Forrest continued maneuvering his men closer to the fort, in flagrant violation of a military parley. Within the twenty minutes' time, he had his answer: Fort Pillow would not surrender.[37]

Shortly after receiving the Union reply, Forrest launched his attack. The Federals lashed out with musketry and artillery, but they could do little to check the attackers. Confederate sharpshooters continued to pepper the fort, making it dangerous for the defenders to expose themselves, and the poorly situated defenses meant that once the Rebel attackers reached a certain point, the Union defenders lacked clear fields of fire. Soon the Confederates were up and over the earthworks, and the real killing could begin.[38]

Having overwhelmed the defenses, the Confederates had the white and black defenders at their mercy. Poet and Lincoln biographer Carl Sandburg luridly described the ensuing frenzy as "a race riot, a mass lynching . . . an orgy of unleashed primitive human animals riding a storm of anger and vengeance directed at their sworn enemy, whom they considered less than human and beyond all laws of civilized war: the negro." Forrest's vengeful men started indiscriminately slaughtering the fort's inhabitants when they tried to surrender or when they fled toward the river. A Confederate sergeant described the bloodbath in a letter home to his sisters:

> The slaughter was awful. Words cannot describe the scene. The poor deluded negroes would run up to our men fall upon their knees and with uplifted hands scream for mercy but they were ordered to their feet and then shot down. The white men fared but little better. Their fort turned out to be a great slaughter pen—blood, human blood stood about in pools and brains could have been gathered up in any quantity.

"I know the colored troops had a great deal the worst of it," one Union lieutenant noted. "I saw several shot after they wounded them; as they were crawling around, the secesh would step up and blow their brains out."[39]

Unlike at Milliken's Bend, there seems to have been no call at Fort Pillow to kill only white Yankees and spare the blacks (as property). At least one of Forrest's officers ordered his men, "Kill all the niggers." Later, when one Confederate officer threatened to arrest soldiers for killing black civilians found in the fort, another overruled him: "Damn it, let them go on; it isn't our law to take any niggers prisoners; kill every one of them." For many of the killers, fury at facing armed members of a perceived subservient race— men their society taught must be their social inferiors—chiefly fueled their wrath. George Shaw, a black recruit in the 6th US Colored Heavy Artillery, begged for his life when confronted by one irate Rebel, who cursed, "Damn you, you are fighting against your master." Shaw's assailant shot him through his open mouth, the bullet exiting the back of his head. Remarkably, he survived the grievous wound, testifying to the congressional inquiry into the battle. Like Shaw, many black participants in the battle only survived because they had been shot and were assumed to be dead by the vengeful attackers.[40]

The black soldiers' white officers and the white Unionists of the 13th Tennessee Cavalry suffered almost as grievously in the massacre as the black troops. Confederate attackers targeted the white Federals in the fort for mixed reasons. Forrest's men, many of them from Tennessee, derided the blue-coated Southerners as "Tennessee Tories," echoing the Patriots' hatred of the loyalists in the Revolutionary War. "The Rebel Tennesseans have about the same bitterness against Tennesseans in the Federals army as against the negroes," observed one Northern newspaperman. The murder of white Federals, however, was inseparable from issues of race and slavery. Many Confederates deemed it nothing short of a war crime to arm blacks to fight against them, and they dealt harshly with white Federals who had the temerity to fight alongside black soldiers. Charles Robinson, a civilian photographer who had joined the defenders wearing a Union coat, described how "our poor fellows . . . surrendered in vain for the rebels now ran down the bank and putting their revolvers right to their heads would blow out their brains or lift them up on bayonets and throw them headlong into the river below." Robinson was sheltering behind a log with a trooper from the 13th when one of the Rebels happened upon them. A point-blank shot from the man's revolver "scatter[ed] the blood & brains" of the cavalryman in Robinson's face. Turning to Robinson, the Confederate placed the pistol's muzzle against his chest, saying, "You'll fight with the niggers again will you? You d——d yankee," and pulled the trigger. The hammer fell on an empty chamber, the Rebel having fired all his shots, allowing Robinson to survive the slaughter. Another Federal survivor remembered his attacker, cursing, "God damn you, you fought with niggers and we will kill the last one of you," before shooting him. Some of the black artillerymen's officers had their surrenders accepted, but upon admitting to their captors what troops they commanded, they were summarily shot.[41]

To their credit, some of Forrest's men wanted no part in the killing of Union soldiers trying to surrender. Samuel H. Caldwell, a surgeon in a Tennessee regiment, wrote his wife of the battle, "It was decidedly the most horrible sight that I have ever witnessed." Some Confederates even tried to end the slaughter. Sergeant Achilles V. Clark, who described the slaughter of "the poor deluded negroes" in his letter home, also related how "I with several others tried to stop the butchery and at one time had partially succeeded." Daniel Stamps, a Tennessee Unionist, was fortunate enough to be taken captive by soldiers willing to abide by the laws of war. Stamps heard one of his guards refuse a mounted officer's order to continue the killing, insisting the Federals must be treated as prisoners of war. "I tell you to kill the last God damned one of them," the officer snapped before he rode off, his order unheeded. What percentage of the attackers participated in the massacre or opposed the wanton killing can never accurately be known. Plenty of the Confederate attackers did give themselves over to the killing—enough to turn Fort Pillow into a slaughterhouse.[42]

Historians continue to debate the role Forrest played in instigating or permitting the Fort Pillow massacre. Two of the previously quoted Confederates who were appalled by the slaughter, both writing days after the battle, left conflicting accounts of their commander's actions. Though he and others tried to stop the killing of Union prisoners, Sergeant Clark told his sisters, "Gen. Forrest ordered them shot down like dogs." Conversely, Surgeon Caldwell wrote, "If General Forrest had not run between our men & the Yanks with his pistol and sabre drawn not a man would have been spared." Clark's and Caldwell's accounts are not necessarily mutually exclusive. Forrest might have permitted, even encouraged, the killing at first, then interceded to end it. Black artilleryman Arthur Coleman testified that "towards evening, General Forrest issued an order not to kill any more Negroes, because he wanted them to help haul the artillery out." If so, Forrest may have stopped the killing less for humanitarian reasons and more to preserve black survivors as useful human property—much the same reasons Confederates at Milliken's Bend had been interested in sparing black soldiers. Forrest himself expressed no regret about the massacre. In an April 13 dispatch, Forrest boasted of the "complete" victory: "The river was dyed with the blood of the slaughter for 200 yards. . . . It is hoped that these facts will demonstrate to the Northern people that negro soldiers cannot cope with Southerners."[43]

Reports of the Fort Pillow massacre shocked the North. Union losses told the terrible tale: almost half of the fort's approximately 580-strong garrison had been killed or mortally wounded. Almost two thirds of the black artillerymen had perished, as had roughly one third of the white 13th Tennessee Cavalry (US). Congress's Joint Committee on the Conduct of the War held an inquiry into the circumstances of the massacre and concluded "that the atrocities committed at Fort Pillow were not the result of passions excited by the heat of conflict, but were the results of a policy deliberately decided upon and unhesitatingly announced." Motivated both by righteous anger and the opportunity to strike a propaganda coup against the Confederacy, the committee's Radical Republicans denounced "the brutality and cruelty of the rebels," men who "seemed to vie with each other in the devilish work." The Republican *Chicago Tribune* declared, "The whole civilized world will be shocked by the great atrocity at Fort Pillow," and insisted such behavior was endemic to the institution of slavery. True abolitionists wholeheartedly agreed that slaveholding fostered such barbarism: "In no other school could human beings have been trained to such readiness for cruelties like these. . . . Accustomed to brutality and bestiality all their lives, it was easy for them to perpetuate the atrocities."[44]

Outrage over the Fort Pillow massacre manifested itself among white Union soldiers. At the Battle of Resaca, Robert Hale Strong and his comrades in the 105th Illinois overran a line of Confederate artillery, killing the gunners who resisted and taking prisoner those who gave themselves up. One bare-chested artilleryman, emerging from under a gun carriage and begging for quarter, bore a tattoo reading on one arm "Fort Pillow." "As soon as the boys saw the letters on his arm, they yelled, 'No quarter for you!' and a dozen bayonets went into him and a dozen bullets were shot into him," Strong reported. "I shall never forget his look of fear." Strong's account does not specify exactly why his comrades exacted retribution for Fort Pillow. Did the Illinois soldiers only resent that fellow white soldiers had been massacred by Forrest's men? Or did they also have a sense of solidarity with the black soldiers as comrades in arms wearing the uniform of the United States? At the very least, Strong implied his comrades decided in the moment that an enemy who celebrated black flag tactics did not deserve quarter himself.[45]

In the initial aftermath of Fort Pillow, Confederate society at large celebrated what Forrest's men had wrought. The letter of one soldier-correspondent to a Southern newspaper proclaimed, "The sight of negro soldiers stirred the bosoms of our soldiers with courageous madness." A soldier in Lee's army, having incorrectly heard that Forrest had "killed everyone" of the fort's black soldiers, deemed it "the best thing he ever done in his life." "Good for him," opined one East Tennessee woman, "I think that he did exactly right." According to a North Carolina plantation mistress, the crime of arming black men merited such treatment: "If they will steal our slaves & lead them on to murder & rapine, they must take the consequences."[46]

As Northern outrage over the Fort Pillow atrocities mounted during the war, and later, as Southern whites sought to foster the Lost Cause and protect the reputation of leaders like Forrest, supposed justifications for the killing emerged. Confederates and ex-Confederates emphasized that some Union soldiers kept on fighting after the fort had been overrun. There is indeed strong evidence to suggest that some Federals continued to resist even as others tried to surrender. The speed with which the fort fell and the chaotic aftermath precluded any kind of formal Federal surrender. Furthermore, the fact that many Confederates were predisposed not to show quarter must also have convinced some of the defenders to sell their lives dearly rather than be killed trying to surrender. Some Confederates blamed continued Union resistance on drunkenness among the defenders, a claim that most historians today reject as baseless.[47]

Still other apologists looked to the nature and history of human behavior in battle to explain the attackers' behavior. A sound argument can be made that soldiers keyed up to face the danger of combat and flushed with adrenaline can have difficulty "coming down" from such a high and distinguishing between active enemies to be fought and passive enemies to be shown quarter. Thomas Jordan, a Forrest biographer and a Confederate general who was not present at Fort Pillow, suggested that "as always happens in places taken by storm, unquestionably some whites, as well as negroes, who had thrown down their arms, and besought quarter, were shot down under the *insania beli* which invariably rages on such occasions." Historically, military law and custom had made special allowances for troops facing the terrible prospect of storming an enemy fortress. As late as the 1700s, European texts justified showing no quarter to a garrison that continued to resist beyond a certain point (such as after a "practicable" breach in the walls had been achieved)—a custom echoed in some of the surrender demands issued in the Civil War, including at Fort Pillow. However, by the 1860s, such a practice was being relegated to the past by Western armies and was scarcely part of the American military tradition.[48]

Most recent scholarship rejects Confederate apologia for the Fort Pillow massacre. Richard Fuchs dismisses Jordan's invocation of *insania beli,* countering that "there are no other reported happenings of wanton killing during the Civil War whose justification was measured by historical precedent." Likewise, continued resistance by some of the garrison cannot entirely exonerate the attackers. "The charge of unyielding resistance, the strongest part of the Confederate argument, would hold great weight," John Cimprich explains in *Fort Pillow, a Civil War Massacre, and Public Memory,* "except that several Confederates admitted the occurrence of a massacre." Most damning of all, multiple Union and Confederate accounts plainly reveal that anger and hatred toward threats to Southern slave society—armed black ex-slaves, whites who would fight alongside them, white Tennessee Unionists—overwhelmingly fueled the wanton killing at Fort Pillow.[49]

If the slaughter of black soldiers at Fort Pillow was the Civil War's most notorious racial atrocity, then the lesser-known Saltville Massacre must rank as one of the most blatant of the conflict. In contrast to Forrest's men, who had killed their opponents in the immediate aftermath of storming the fort, the Confederate victors at Saltville, Virginia, continued to murder black soldiers the day after the battle. "Murder it was," writes George Burkhardt, "done in the cool of the morning, many hours removed from the heat and the adrenaline rush of battle." Because the killing at the Virginia fight had been more unambiguously unlawful, historian Bell I. Wiley even suggests, "It appears that Saltville deserves more than Fort Pillow to be called a massacre."[50]

In fall 1864, Union forces planned a raid on Saltville in the southwestern corner of Virginia, targeting the strategically valuable saltworks that gave the mountain town its name. On the evening of October 1, many among the mixed force of Confederate soldiers and local militia already knew that the next day they would confront Union troops that included black soldiers (specifically the 5th US Colored Cavalry), a prospect that many of them welcomed with fierce relish. "My men tell me the Yanks have a lot of nigger soldiers along," Brigadier General Alfred E. Jackson announced to a colonel and his assembled Virginia militia. "Do you think your reserves will fight niggers?" Jackson asked. "Fight 'em?" the colonel earnestly replied, "by ——, Sir, they'll eat 'em up! No! Not eat 'em up! That's too much! By ——, Sir, we'll cut 'em up!" The militiamen evidently shared their commander's enthusiasm; the next day, shortly before they pitched into the fray, they could be seen "sighting their guns and showing how they would shoot a nigger, if they had the chance."[51]

The next day, October 2, saw seesaw fighting as Union troops crossed branches of the Holston River to attack Confederates dug in on the hills out-side Saltville. As in other battles, word spread among the Rebels that they faced black soldiers—news that outraged and galvanized them. "We surely slew negroes that day," one Confederate cavalryman proudly recalled. White Union soldiers testified to the bravery of their black comrades. A cavalry of-ficer from Kentucky confessed that he "never thought they would fight," yet that day "never saw troops fight like they did." Colonel Brisbin of the 5th United States Colored Cavalry boasted, "I have seen white troops fight in twenty-seven battles and I never saw any fight better" than his own men. Despite the tenacity of Brisbin's black troopers, however, the Federals failed to overcome the Confederate defenders, instead quitting the field that night.[52]

The retreat left both the battlefield and Union wounded in Confederate hands. Early the next morning, Private George Dallas Mosgrove of the 4th Kentucky Cavalry (CS) heard gunfire that "swelled to the volume of that of a skirmish line," which he first took to be the sound of a renewed Yan-kee attack. Upon further investigation, he found the persistent firing came from Confederate comrades from Tennessee gunning down wounded black troopers:

> I cautiously rode forward and came upon a squad of Tennesseeans, mad and excited to the highest degree. They were shooting every wounded negro they could find. Hearing firing on other parts of the field, I knew that the same awful work was going on all about me. It was horrible, most horrible. Robertson's and Dibbrell's brigades had lost many good men and officers, probably shot by these same ne-groes, and they were so exasperated that they could not be deterred from their murderous work. Very many of the negroes standing about in groups were only slightly wounded, but they soon went down be-fore the unerring pistols and rifles of the enraged Tennesseeans.

Mosgrove came to a small cabin in the middle of the battlefield, inside of which he found "seven or eight slightly wounded negroes standing with their backs against the walls." Suddenly, a young man that the Kentuckian guessed to be sixteen came into view, a revolver in each hand, and began gunning down the wounded prisoners. Mosgrove himself barely had time to get out of the deadly teenager's line of fire. "In less time than I can write it, the boy had shot every negro in the room," the Kentucky trooper wrote. "Every time he pulled a trigger a negro fell dead."[53]

Others on the Saltville battlefield testified to the killings. Captain Ed-ward O. Guerrant, another Kentucky Rebel, recorded in his October 3 diary entry how the resounding gunshots "sung the death knell of many a poor negro who was unfortunate enough not to be killed yesterday. Our men took no negro prisoners. Great numbers of them were killed yesterday and today." Private Harry Shocker, a wounded Ohio cavalryman, witnessed notorious Confederate guerrilla Champ Ferguson murder white and black Federals—and lived to tell the tale. Ferguson's behavior suggests that the fact that white Yankees had fought alongside blacks played a significant role in his motive for murder. Shocker saw the guerrilla chief berate one of his wounded comrades, asking "why he came up there to fight with the damn niggers" and whether he wanted to be shot in the back or his face. Despite the Ohioan's pleas to spare his life, Ferguson shot Shocker's comrade dead. Fittingly, Union forces executed the bloody-handed Ferguson shortly after the war, having convicted him on fifty-three counts of murder, although the massacre of black troopers at Saltville played little role in his trial.[54]

Some Confederates at Saltville did attempt to stop the slaughter of black soldiers. Private Mosgrove recounted that John C. Breckinridge, the Confederate department commander, tried to restore order when he arrived on the field: "General Breckinridge, with blazing eyes and thunderous tones, ordered that the massacre should be stopped. He rode away and—the shooting went on. The men could not be restrained." The murder of black soldiers appalled Mosgrove as well, but he insisted it could not be helped, writing, "I pitied them from the bottom of my heart and would have interposed in their behalf had I not known that any effort to save them would be futile." If a Confederate general could not halt the killing, what hope could a young cavalry private have? To his credit, John C. Breckinridge seems to have tried to hold several Confederate officers accountable for the killings, but the war ended before anything could come of the matter.[55]

Confederate newspapers added insult to injury by gleefully celebrating the slaughter of black soldiers in their reportage. Historian Thomas D. Mays exposes how the Richmond *Enquirer* "proudly ran a segregated casualty list" for the Battle of Saltville:

| | |
|---|---|
| Killed, (Yankee Whites) | 106 |
| Negroes, | 150 |
| Wounded, (Whites) | 80 |
| Negroes, | 6 |

The vastly disproportionate ratio of killed to wounded Union soldiers, both black and white, testified starkly to postbattle slaughter that had taken place. The Richmond *Dispatch* similarly chortled over the defeat of the so-called Yankee blackbirds, stating, "The country has since been infested with birds of the same color, but greater respectability. They are turkey-buzzards this time, and they come in quest of Yankee carcasses."[56]

The Battles of Milliken's Bend, Fort Pillow, and Saltville were all minor battles in obscure corners of the Civil War, primarily remembered for the presence of black soldiers and their treatment at the hands of their Confederate opponents. By contrast, the engagement after the detonation of the Petersburg mine, known as the Battle of the Crater, represented a major clash between elements of the Army of the Potomac and the Army of Northern Virginia, a battle with the potential to decide the course of both the Siege of Petersburg and the war in the eastern theater. However, the operation that could have ended the war nine months early resulted instead in a bloody debacle for Union forces, and a battle in which the USCT might have played a decisive role in bringing about such victory instead witnessed the largest slaughter of black soldiers yet. Not without reason have historians deemed the Crater the largest massacre of the Civil War.[57]

Engineered by coal miners of the 48th Pennsylvania, the Union plan involved tunneling under a projecting Confederate battery known as Elliott's Salient, only about 100 yards from Union siege lines. Underground galleries dug beneath the Rebels would be packed with gunpowder and then exploded, blasting a gap in Confederate lines through which Union forces could attack. If successful, the operation could potentially break the Siege of Petersburg, sever the rail lines critical to linking Richmond with what remained of the Confederacy, and capture a sizable portion of Robert E. Lee's army. General Ambrose Burnside, whose Ninth Corps included the troops that had masterminded the mine and those that would conduct the assault, approved the plan.

In selecting which units would spearhead the attack, Burnside passed over the battle-weary First, Second, and Third Divisions of his corps and instead chose the fresh, unbloodied Fourth Division, composed entirely of USCT regiments. As the Pennsylvania coal miners labored beneath the earth, Burnside's black troops trained rigorously in maneuvers designed to best exploit the breach. Two days before the battle, however, Army of the Potomac commander George G. Meade gave orders that threatened to derail Burnside's preparations. There was already little love lost between the two generals, and Meade, skeptical of the operation's feasibility, had begrudged the Ninth Corps the necessary tools and the full load of explosives that Burnside's men had requested. Now, Meade directed that veteran white troops should lead the attack instead of the untested but specially trained black Fourth Division. Burnside appealed to General in Chief Ulysses Grant, but Meade convinced Grant not to allow the black division to be sent first, lest the assault fail and it appear that the army had used the black soldiers as cannon fodder. Burnside was left to alter his attack plans accordingly.[58]

On July 30th, at 4:44 A.M., the Pennsylvanians detonated 8,000 pounds of gunpowder beneath Elliott's Salient, blowing the fort and much of its garrison skyward. The blast left a crater measuring roughly 200 feet long, sixty feet wide, and thirty feet deep, plus a temporary breach of abandoned defenses about 500 yards long. After an artillery bombardment and a fifteen-minute delay, James Ledlie's First Division started for the breach, followed by Orlando Wilcox's Third Division and Robert Potter's Second Division. While the black soldiers of the Fourth Division had been prepared to deploy around the crater, the initial wave of white troops found themselves drawn into the gaping, steep-sloped hole in the earth. The further delay limited the attackers' ability to exploit the breach and gave the rattled Confederates valuable time to recover. Meanwhile, Brigadier General Stephen Elliott rallied what remained of his brigade of South Carolinians to resist the attack while nearby regiments from Virginia and North Carolina rushed to their aid. With the Union advance stalled, Burnside heeded orders from Meade to reinforce the attack and at 8:00 A.M. sent in Edward Ferrero's Fourth Division.[59]

The two USCT brigades of Ferrero's division managed to clear the next line of Rebel trenches beyond the crater, but this marked the furthest extent of the Union breakthrough. Chaos and poor Federal generalship blunted the effectiveness of the operation; now the arrival of Confederate reinforcements sealed the fate of Union soldiers in and around the Crater. Brigadier General William Mahone had personally led two brigades from his division to seal the breach, one of Georgians and another of Virginians (many of them Petersburg natives). At about 9:30, Mahone threw them forward in a madcap bayonet charge that crashed into the Yankees. Vicious hand-to-hand fighting ensued in the dense honeycomb of trenches and bombproofs surrounding the crater as the counterattack forced back Union soldiers. With the tide turning in the Confederates' favor, the battle began degenerating into a massacre. Based on the progress of the fighting that followed, historians have actually identified four separate massacres of black soldiers in the course of the Battle of the Crater—four distinct opportunities for Confederate soldiers to brutalize black Federals wounded or trying to surrender. The first occurred as Mahone's men recaptured the trenches taken by the USCT, the second as they then scoured those works for blacks who had sought shelter, the third as helpless black prisoners were hustled to the rear, and the fourth when black soldiers trapped in the crater itself tried to surrender.[60]

A number of factors primed Confederate soldiers at the Crater to massacre their black opponents. As with other soldiers across the embattled South, the prejudices and fears instilled by the ideology of a slave society and the hostile policy of their own government had readied men from Lee's army to show no quarter to soldiers of color. "Our men, who were always made wild by having negroes sent against them . . . were utterly frenzied with rage," recorded artillery officer John C. Haskell. Compounding this, many soldiers in the USCT regiments, burning to avenge the outrages inflicted on their comrades, had entered the battle shouting battle cries of "Remember Fort Pillow!" and vows to give no quarter to the Rebels. Such threats were not lost on Confederate soldiers, resulting in a redoubling of their willingness to show no mercy to an already despised enemy. According to Virginia private Henry Van Lewenigh Bird, "The negro's charging cry of 'No quarter' was met with the stern cry of 'amen' and without firing a single shot we closed with them." Some USCT continued their shouts of defiance in the face of the Rebel counterattack. Georgia infantryman Dorsey Binion wrote, "When we got to the works it was filled with negroes and they were crying out No quarter when a hand to hand conflict ensued with the breach of our Guns and Bayonets and you may depend we did not show much quarters but slayed them." Binion added with apparent regret that some black soldiers escaped their vengeance: "Some few negroes went to the rear as we could not kill them as fast as they past us."[61]

Confederate officers also played a critical role in inciting their men to kill and show no mercy. William Mahone in particular made sure his men knew of the threats black soldiers had made. Lieutenant P. M. Vance of Saunders's brigade of Alabamians remembered, "Gen. Mahone had told the soldiers of the brigade that negro troops were in possession of the Crater and had come in yelling, 'No quarter for the Rebels!' He did not say 'Show no quarter,' but Saunders's men decided that point." According to another Alabamian, however, the general expressly did give such an order. "General Mahone . . . told us that the negroes in the Crater had holloed 'Remember Fort Pillow! No Quarter!' He said it was a life and death struggle, and for us not to take any of them, but to load our guns, fix bayonets, and . . . go in among them, and give them h——; and we tried to obey orders," veteran B. F. Phillips remembered. "Just before the job was completed General Mahone sent orders to us not to kill quite all of them." Apparently as the battle wound down, Mahone decided some of the USCT would be more useful as living laborers than as dead soldiers.[62]

As Mahone's men hunted through the trenches and bombproofs for USCT survivors, the 12th Virginia's George Bernard witnessed the particularly brutal murder of a black soldier, a sight which "made my blood run cold," the twenty-six-year-old private later wrote.

> Just about the outer end of the ditch by which I had entered stood a negro soldier . . . begging for his life of two Confederate soldiers who stood by him, one of them striking the poor wretch with a steel ramrod, the other holding a gun in his hand, with which he seemed to be trying to get a shot at the negro. The man with the gun fired at the negro, but did not seem to seriously injure him, as he only clapped his hand to his hip, when he appeared to have been shot, and continued to beg for his life. The man with the ramrod continued to strike the negro therewith, whilst the fellow with the gun deliberately reloaded it, and, placing its muzzle close against the stomach of the poor negro, fired, at which the latter fell limp and lifeless at the feet of the two Confederates. It was a brutal, horrible act.

What Bernard described appears all the more appalling if one carefully considers the details of his account. Even for men in the frenzy of combat, the two killers' actions required no small amount of ruthlessness. The second soldier shot his victim not once but twice, "deliberately" reloading his single-shot musket, a process that would take about 20 seconds. This he did while the first Confederate used a ramrod to beat the helpless black soldier as he begged for his life. Such prolonged cruelty suggests not killing in the heat of the moment but instead cold-blooded murder.[63]

The Confederate counterattack drove the Federals, both black and white troops, into the crater, which soon turned into a death trap. Rebels lined the rim of the pit and fired into the blue-coated mass of humanity. Some took spare muskets with fixed bayonets and threw them down like spears into the tightly packed mob. Artillerymen brought up small coehorn mortars, which lobbed exploding shells amid the trapped Union soldiers. At about 1 P.M., the Confederates began charging into the crater itself, once more engaging in vicious hand-to-hand combat. "We went rite in . . . on them and Bayoneted them," wrote one North Carolinian. Seventeen-year-old John S. Wise of Virginia recoiled at how "our men, inflamed to relentless vengeance by their presence, disregarded the rules of warfare which restrained them in battle with their own race, and brained and butchered the blacks until the slaughter was sickening." As the Rebels stormed into the crater, Captain Frank Kenfield of the 17th Vermont remembered, "I heard the order given 'save the white men but kill the damn niggers.' And I saw them run their bayonets through many a colored man showing him no mercy."[64]

Adding to the horror of the hellish climax to the Battle of the Crater, the killing in some cases became fratricidal as some white Federals turned on their black comrades. Even with Confederates urging their comrades to kill the blacks but spare the white Yankees, many white Union soldiers feared that the enemy would exact retribution on them as well for having been caught fighting alongside blacks, as had infamously occurred at Fort Pillow. "It was believed among the whites that the enemy would give no quarter to negroes, or to whites taken with them, and so to be shut up with blacks in the crater was equal to a doom of death," wrote George L. Kilmer, a private in the 14th New York Heavy Artillery. Even before the Confederate counterattack, according to Kilmer, some white Federals had objected to continuing the advance once the black Fourth Division joined the battle for just this reason. Now, trapped in the crater and motivated by fear, hatred, and desperation, a number of Union soldiers did the unthinkable and murdered their own black comrades in arms. "It has been positively asserted that white men bayoneted blacks who fell back into the crater. This was in order to preserve the whites from Confederate vengeance," George Kilmer reported. "Men boasted in my presence that blacks had been thus disposed of, particularly when the Confederates came up."[65]

Ultimately, physical exhaustion brought the killing, or at least the battle, to an end. An exasperated officer in the 8th Alabama called out to the Yankees trapped in the crater, "Why in the h—— don't you fellows surrender?" An aggrieved Union colonel snapped back, "Why in the h—— don't you let us?" In the chaos in and around the Crater, and amid the enraged Confederates' killing frenzy, bringing the battle to a close was no easy task. Shortly after the exchange, however, another Union officer waved a white handkerchief in token of surrender, and once both sides had ceased fire, Confederate soldiers began collecting Union survivors as prisoners. The safety of those prisoners was far from certain, however, especially for the black soldiers. Triumphant Rebels murdered some of the USCT wounded, and the lives of USCT being marched back through Confederate lines were in similar peril.[66]

While some Confederate soldiers were appalled by the carnage of the battle and the atrocities committed by their comrades, others in the Army of Northern Virginia endorsed the slaughter of black Federals. Lieutenant Colonel William Pegram, one of Lee's artillery commanders, observed, "It seems cruel to murder them in cold blood, but I think the men who did it had very good cause for doing so." Incredibly, Captain John Featherston of the 9th Alabama felt compelled to apologize for how many USCT had survived. "All that we had not killed surrendered, and I must say we took some of the negroes prisoners," he wrote his wife. "But we will not be held culpable for this when it is considered the numbers we had already slain."[67]

Once again, the casualty count betrays a battlefield massacre. The nine black infantry regiments in the Ninth Corps, having begun the battle 4,300 strong, tallied their total casualties as 219 killed, 681 wounded, and 410 missing. On the basis of the pension records for the 410 missing USCT soldiers, researcher Bryce Suderow found that 205 of these were killed, while fewer than 100 were taken alive as prisoners. The Confederates claimed to have taken 200 black soldiers prisoner, so if both their estimates and the pension records are accurate, more than half of these men might have been murdered after being taken prisoner, some perhaps even after they had been marched away from the fighting. On the basis of such calculations, the Fourth Division lost at least 423 men killed by day's end on July 30. George Burkhardt, taking into account men who probably died of their wounds, increases the estimated death toll for black soldiers to 900 or more and suggests that more than half of these were massacred.[68]

Confederate policy and proclivity to show no quarter to black soldiers, exemplified by the massacres at Fort Pillow and the Petersburg Crater, remain a notorious part of Civil War history. Less well known is the retribution that black soldiers tried to exact on the battlefield to avenge these atrocities. Provoked by an enemy who all too often refused to show mercy to men of their race, many black soldiers elected to respond in kind and give no mercy to their Rebel foes. Objectively examining racial reprisals by black Federals proves challenging to an extent, given their sympathetic role in the war. Soldiers from black state regiments and the USCT represent some of the most admirable figures of the Civil War, fighting to free themselves and their posterity from slavery and battling Northern as well as Southern racism. Understandable as it is for fighting men of any race or background to seek to retaliate in kind when faced by enemies who refuse to show them any mercy or quarter, it does not necessarily justify resorting to those same practices. When Union soldiers, black or white, vowed to adopt the same black flag tactics as the Confederates, they strayed into violating the same rules of warfare as their enemies and thus further endangered the lives of themselves and their comrades.

It is open to speculation whether black soldiers would have denied quarter to Confederate opponents had they not first been outraged and provoked by sensational massacres of USCT such as Fort Pillow and the Crater. Soldiers and human beings in general find it easier to kill or murder fellow humans from whom they are socially detached, those who have a quality of otherness. Certainly the racial divide between black Federals and white Confederates and the viscerally painful legacy of slavery might have induced some black soldiers to show no quarter to the soldiers of a white slaveholders' republic.

Conversely, prior Confederate atrocities seem significantly to have motivated a collective desire to retaliate among many USCT. Historians have aptly compared the intense enmity and resulting atrocities between Confederate soldiers and black Federals to the brutal and often merciless fighting between US and Japanese forces in the Pacific Theater of World War II. Conventional wisdom attributes the willingness to kill and the unwillingness to offer quarter between the combatants in the Pacific to race-motivated hatred. Strong scholarship, however, suggests that cultural differences between the Americans and Japanese may have played as strong, if not stronger, a role in defining the nature of the combat. The new military history has emphasized that military forces reflect the cultures and societies from which they spring and for whom the fight. As historian John A. Lynn points out, such forces reflect cultural expectations for how combat should rightly be conducted. Furthermore, fighting men who encounter opponents from a culture that does not recognize those same rules often react in outrage by lowering their own standards in retaliation, thereby opening the door to battlefield atrocity. In the case of the Pacific Theater, the Japanese military code treated the willingness to surrender as contemptible, whereas American servicemen affirmed a Western tradition that allowed for honorable surrender and mercy toward an enemy and that deemed unnecessary killing barbaric. With each side loathing key elements of the other side's martial culture, the two became some of the bitterest enemies of World War II. Just as many American servicemen might have held less enmity toward the warriors of imperial Japan had it not been for their propensity to brutalize prisoners, many black soldiers in the Civil War might have been less prone to retaliation had not the Confederacy's soldiers, government, and society treated the very act of black men bearing arms as a capital war crime.[69]

That black soldiers who would offer no quarter to Confederates who showed them none might seem like a straightforward, eye-for-an-eye act of retaliation, and doubtless many USCT saw it as such. However, some USCT viewed adopting their own black flag tactics as a just military reprisal—a deterrent to teach the Rebels the hard way not to treat them as anything less than honorable fighting men. In one instance in which a Union officer protected Confederate prisoners from vengeful black soldiers, the enlisted men insisted that the Rebels "killed us wherever they could find us, and we were going to change the game." A different USCT officer defended the take-no-prisoners attitude of his men, declaring, "We can bayonet the enemy to terms on this matter of treating colored soldiers as prisoners of war, far sooner than the authorities can bring him to it by negotiation." George E. Stephens, a sergeant in the famed 54th Massachusetts, expressed similar frustration with the Lincoln administration's inability to take Confederates to task: "When shall this weakness and folly on the part of our authorities cease? and when shall these atrocities be met with that vengeance and retaliation they so justly merit?"[70]

White officers in black regiments offered conflicting attitudes toward showing quarter to Confederate soldiers. As commissioned officers, their military and moral authority gave them considerable power alternatively to legitimize or prevent the killing of wounded and surrendering Confederates. A number of officers intervened, sometimes still in the heat of battle, to stay the hands of their men and spare enemy soldiers from retaliatory killing. Others, such as Charles Francis Adams Jr., adopted a more ambivalent stance. As colonel of the 5th Massachusetts Colored Volunteer Cavalry, the Boston blueblood condescendingly doubted the practicality of holding black soldiers to the same conduct as white troops: "Of course, our black troops are not subject to any of the rules of civilized warfare. If they murder prisoners, as I hear they did, it is to be lamented and stopped, but they can hardly be blamed."[71]

Officers shared the outrage of their men at the notorious massacres of USCT, and some publicly voiced a desire to retaliate measure for measure. "I often ask myself the question, 'Shall we, as officers and men of colored regiments, ever be found with prisoners in our possession?'" a 55th USCT lieutenant wrote to an African American newspaper in the wake of Fort Pillow. "I can only answer for myself; I would be tempted in such circumstances to mow the infernal rebels to the ground, as I would mow the grass before my scythe." Others endorsed such a policy more decisively. In a ceremony at Chicago honoring the newly raised 29th USCT, an Illinois colonel declared in his speech, "These colored troops should take no prisoners until the massacre at Fort Pillow is avenged." Some officers even led by example when it came to killing Rebels hors de combat. A lieutenant in the 23rd USCT recorded how during the Battle of the Crater, his colonel had ordered a captured enemy officer to help one of the regiment's wounded men. When the "Confederate with an oath said he would not help carry any negro . . . the colonel whipped out his revolver and shot him dead."[72]

Black soldiers exacted violent retribution on a number of battlefields for atrocities done to their comrades. After a skirmish in Marianna, Florida, in 1864, a surgeon with the 2nd Maine Cavalry wrote,

> When the colored troops came up they went into the fight like mad men—their rallying cry, *Remember Fort Pillow:* giving no quarter, and answering, "Your men give us no quarter when they take us; now it is our turn." A fitting retribution for the barbarities exercised toward them. All who witnessed this engagement say that the negro troops *will fight* and woe to the rebel who is unfortunate to fall into their hands.

For the black soldiers present, "it did not make any difference to them about the Rebs surrendering," reported a trooper in the same regiment. "They would shoot them down, the officers had hard work to stop them from killing all the prisoners." Still other killings seem to have occurred when white and black troops successfully stormed Fort Blakely outside Mobile, Alabama, in April 1865. "The niggers did not take a prisoner," wrote a lieutenant in the 51st USCT. "They killed all they took to a man." Confederate prisoners made similar claims, including one survivor who declared, "Blakely was the Yankee Fort Pillow." Other USCT officers either denied such charges or tried to mitigate them, such as the chaplain of the 51st, who insisted that "no extravagances were committed beyond those incident to every charge." A number of historians conclude that a small number of surrendering or captured Rebels were indeed killed—a number kept low because the Confederate garrison's precipitous flight kept many of them out of harm's way.[73]

Other white Federals testified to the danger that vengeful USCT sometimes posed to captured Confederates. "The Rebel prisoners are very fearful of being left to the charge of the colored troops as they fear their own acts of inhumanity will be repaid," wrote a New Jersey colonel. "The Nigs are all anxious to kill but not to take prisoners, and their cry is Ft. Pillow." At times white Union guards forcefully had to fend off black soldiers in order to protect Confederate prisoners. Lone soldiers or small groups could be brazen in their attacks on guarded prisoners. "I didn't see but one [prisoner] killed. . . . A great bushy Nigger came up to him, knocked him down, and ran his bayonet through his heart," a New Yorker recounted. "Our boys turned on the Niggers and kept them back."[74]

Shouts of "Remember Fort Pillow!" and acting out on the urge to retaliate for such atrocities could come back to haunt USCT, often in the same battle when the tide turned against them. At the Battle of Brice's Crossroads, black soldiers once again battled forces under Nathan Bedford Forrest and, not surprisingly, invoked Fort Pillow as their battle cry. In the wake of what turned out to be another Union debacle, "Forrest and his men again slew black soldiers wholesale, but this time as something of a sporting event," one historian notes, creating another massacre that somehow "lacked the drama and sensational publicity" of Fort Pillow. As previously discussed, Confederates at the Battle of the Crater, capitalizing on black soldiers' words and deeds, resolved that indeed no quarter should be asked or given, turning the "horrid pit" into another racial atrocity. "I never felt more like fighting in my life," fumed Lieutenant Colonel William H. Stewart of the 61st Virginia. "Our comrades had been slaughtered in a most inhuman and brutal manner, and slaves were trampling over their mangled and bleeding corpses. Revenge must have fired every heart, and strung every arm with nerves of steel, for the herculean task of blood." Of course, at such battles, black soldiers' threats and actual reprisals served only as a pretext for the racial atrocities inflicted on them, not to mention a boon for Rebel propaganda. As Stewart's own words and those of his comrades betrayed, for many Confederates, the "outrage" of facing armed black men in combat was all the excuse they needed to kill in battle and even afterward. Moreover, black soldiers' shouts of "Remember Fort Pillow" did not always signal a call to take no prisoners, although often it did. Some USCT officers and men continued the battle cry even in the final terrible stage of the Crater when they were in the Rebels' power and not the other way around. In such cases, invoking Fort Pillow reminded black soldiers of the price of defeat, acting as a call to victory or death. Unfortunately for the USCT, when it came to victory or death at battles such as Brice's Crossroads and the Crater, they faced an enemy all too capable of denying them the former and giving them the latter.[75]

As a matter of perspective, black soldiers were essentially more sinned against than sinning in terms of battlefield atrocities. In all likelihood, far more hors de combat USCT were killed by Confederates than vice versa. Partially this was a function of where and when black troops served. Many garrisoned isolated outposts behind Union lines, thereby freeing veteran white units for the front, but also leaving USCT at places such as Fort Pillow vulnerable to wrathful Confederates. Black regiments became part of major field armies such as the Army of the Potomac late in the war when they were engaged in offensive operations, as at Petersburg. As such, much of their fighting consisted of frontal assaults on fortified positions. Although black regiments scored impressive victories in this capacity, particularly at New Market Heights, many other times they were repulsed without closing with the enemy. Under such circumstances, black soldiers simply lacked the opportunity to retaliate against the Confederates, whether they sought to or not. In addition, the Union officer corps exercised greater command and control than their Rebel counterparts when it came to preventing or stopping battlefield atrocities. Although some USCT officers expressed ambivalence or approval of denying quarter to the enemy, still others actively intervened to restrain their men. Outside USCT regiments, white Union officers and men often could be counted on to protect Rebel prisoners from retaliation, sometimes up to and beyond the threat of force. Nothing among Federal forces could compare with the systematic approval and even encouragement among the Confederates of murdering and brutalizing USCT officers and men.

Just as it brought about the war itself, the problem of slavery left its mark on Civil War combat. The peculiar institution tainted the South with a legacy of violence, contempt, and fear in terms of matters of race. As a result, many Confederates responded with those qualities when their slaveholders' republic was challenged on the battlefield by members of an enslaved race. For many throughout the Confederate government, the Confederate army, and Confederate society, the entrance into the war of armed black men, wearing the uniform of the United States, represented a threat and an outrage not to be tolerated. Fighting men in butternut and gray across the rebellious South responded by showing little mercy to such opponents, resulting in the most notorious acts of wanton killing in the Civil War. Such brutality at the hands of men who would kill or enslave them only fired the resolve of the Union's black fighting men all the more. At times, it even tempted them into transgressing the same rules of war and denying their enemies the quarter denied them. Battles between the two pitted racial animosity against righteous anger, making whites in Confederate gray and blacks in Union blue some of the war's deadliest of enemies and the readiest to kill.

# Epilogue

The Civil War did not officially end on April 15, 1865. There were still skirmishes to be fought, Confederate armies in the field that had yet to surrender, even a commerce raider on the high seas, the CSS *Shenandoah,* that had yet to strike its colors. Yet after hundreds of thousands of Americans had been killed on battlefields from Pennsylvania to New Mexico Territory, one particular killing rocked the broken nation, symbolically ending a tragic conflict on one last tragic note. On April 14, Good Friday, John Wilkes Booth slipped into the presidential box at Ford's Theatre, and, using a Deringer pistol, fired a .44-caliber ball into the back of Abraham Lincoln's head. The next morning, in a boardinghouse across the street, Lincoln died, the first US president to be murdered by an assassin.

Booth, on the run from the greatest manhunt the nation had ever seen, eagerly checked the newspapers to see how his countrymen were reacting to his deed. He did not like what he read. The *Baltimore Clipper,* published in a city Booth had called home—one that Lincoln's advisors had feared traveling through and that had stoned and killed Union soldiers—branded him a murderer and an assassin. The paper condemned the work of Booth and his conspirators as "fiendish acts . . . cowardly and vile," insisting that "whilst we shrink from horror at the contemplation of atrocity so fearful and startling, the thought will occur of the utter madness that could have prompted the authors of these crimes." He expected to be heralded as a Brutus who slew a tyrannical American Caesar, yet he had been marked as a bloody-handed coward. "I struck boldly and not as the papers say," an outraged Booth scribbled in his diary, trying to justify himself. The celebrated actor had tried to cast himself in the role of a heroic tyrannicide but found himself "looked upon as a common cutthroat."[1]

Most of Booth's fellow Americans would have none of his delusions. Instinctively they found nothing to admire about a conspirator who crept in on a man in a theater and shot him from behind. Booth's deed hardly resembled the killing of the past four years, in which Union and Confederate soldiers had battled one another across fields and forests, towns and trenches, hazarding their own lives in the process.

More killing followed Lincoln's assassination, beyond simply the death of Booth, who was mortally wounded in a Virginia tobacco barn by a Union cavalryman, as well as those of four more convicted conspirators, hanged at Old Arsenal Penitentiary. Union soldiers had suffered the murder of their commander in chief, and some were angry enough to kill anyone who had the temerity to celebrate that murder. "Every soldier's heart was fired with indignation," Sergeant Coe of the 19th Michigan wrote in his diary. "Every man that rejoiced over the news was doomed to death on the spot. Some were shot, others bayonetted, others mauled to death. At this writing I learn of six or seven that have thus met their doom." George W. Squier from Indiana, a captain at war's end, blamed "not only the fiend who has rob[b]ed us of our leader," but also "the whole class of both North and South who are rejoiced at our loss." Believing Booth's plot originated in the highest echelons of the Confederacy, Squier raged, "Let a hundred lives of our 'erring Brethren' be sacrificed for every drop of blood which has been so ruthlessly spilled."[2]

Some Union soldiers especially wanted Jefferson to die in retribution for the murder of Lincoln. The erstwhile Confederate president was fortunate that he was not captured until "after the excitement and anger at Lincoln[']s assassination had died down," wrote Iowa veteran William Barker; otherwise, the soldiers' verse "'We'll hang Jeff Davis on a sour apple tree' . . . might have had a literal fulfilment." As Barker recounted decades afterward, "And from the temper of that army—as I personally saw it—and felt it, too—Davis ran a narrow escape."[3]

For Samuel D. Buck, late captain in the 13th Virginia, his postassassination remarks almost resulted in a one-sided gunfight. Having surrendered and returned to the Shenandoah Valley, Buck encountered a Union scout who was talking down the Confederacy's soldiers in a Winchester hotel bar. Buck jumped into the conversation and managed to make a laughingstock of the scout, who managed to retort that at least "we have that lovely President of yours in prison." Buck snapped back, "We got yours first," saying it more in anger than out of any ill will toward Lincoln. Regretting his words, Buck quickly added that Lincoln's assassination "was the worst thing that could have happened to the South." The two went their separate ways, at least for the time being.

Later Buck learned that the scout had fetched his pistols and had come looking to shoot him, only to be delayed by some local citizens. The Confederate veteran, having survived four years fighting Federals, decided he was not about to run from one hotheaded Yankee. Having surrendered his weapons, Buck found a hatchet and went to face down the scout at the same hotel bar. There, with hatchet in one hand, Buck maneuvered himself close enough to the scout at the bar so that the man would have a hard time drawing his revolvers before Buck brought down his hatchet. Staring each other down, the scout dared Buck to repeat his previous comments. Buck repeated what he said. The scout evidently thought better of making a fight of it, for he muttered that he had not realized that Buck regretted Lincoln's death and then walked out. The scout tried to intimidate Buck in an encounter a few days later, but the ex-Confederate had seen that the man was all bark and no bite, and afterward heard no more of the matter.[4]

Despite the sometimes murderous passions unleashed by Lincoln's murder, the process of reconciliation had already begun. On April 9, five days before the assassination, Robert E. Lee surrendered his army to Ulysses Grant at Appomattox Courthouse, a beginning to the end of the Civil War. The Union general celebrated in the North as "Unconditional Surrender" Grant not only offered the enemy generous terms but also ordered that his own army begin issuing rations to Lee's hungry men. Even before the quartermasters could begin doling out fresh rations to the Confederates, Union soldiers began sharing food out of their own haversacks with men who had been their mortal enemies only hours before. Elisha Hunt Rhodes, colonel of the 2nd Rhode Island, noted that his men "cheerfully" divided their three days' rations with the "half starved" Rebels, even though it meant temporarily subsisting on half rations themselves. In their joy at the war's end, the Rhode Islanders evidently shared in the generosity of spirit with which their colonel marked the surrender in his diary: "Glory to God in the highest. Peace on earth, good will to men!"[5]

In the days after the surrender, officers and enlisted men from the rival armies enthusiastically intermingled and conversed with one another, an outgrowth of the readiness to fraternize with the foe they had demonstrated even when they had been at war. Other episodes seemed to indicate that once deadly enemies were ready to reconcile as fellow countrymen. During the formal surrender ceremony of the Army of Northern Virginia on April 12, in one of the most cherished stories from Appomattox, General Joshua L. Chamberlain ordered his Union soldiers to "carry arms" as the Confederates marched by, offering them a kind of "marching salute." Leading the Confederate column, General John B. Gordon recognized the gesture and, gracefully wheeling his horse to face Chamberlain, lowered his sword tip to his stirrup to return the salute. It was, in Chamberlain's words, "honor answering honor."[6]

Comforting as such accounts are to Americans celebrating the healing of the sectional divide, reconciliation did not come easily to all the Civil War's surviving combatants. The passion and hatred that had animated men to try to destroy one another on the battlefield still smoldered in some men's hearts. As one historian reminds us, Joshua Chamberlain experienced a less brotherly encounter with another Confederate officer after the formal surrender. Admiring the bravery his erstwhile enemies had shown, Chamberlain observed that "brave men may become good friends." The Confederate would have none of it. "You're mistaken, sir," he replied. "You may forgive us but we won't be forgiven. There is a rancor in our hearts which you little dream of. We hate you, sir."[7]

Eventually a spirit of reconciliation did triumph, reuniting the national bond between Northerners and Southerners. Reconciliation also came at a price. White Southerners felt especially welcome in the Union after Rutherford B. Hayes pulled Federal troops from the former Rebel states, removing the chief safeguard of black Southerners' civil rights and essentially ending Reconstruction. Especially conciliatory Northerners celebrated reconciliation by downplaying the considerable ideological differences that had fostered the war, some agreeing to disagree, others falling under the sway of the Rebels' version of the conflict.

Former Confederates went to work framing the history of the Civil War to put the Southern rebellion in the best possible light, giving lie to the old chestnut that history is always written by the winners. Before 1865 had passed, they had already begun crafting the Lost Cause narrative, espousing the notion that the Confederate cause had been essentially right and noble (usually downplaying or whitewashing the importance of slavery in the process) and insisting that Confederate forces never could have triumphed in the face of overwhelming Northern manpower and resources. Many Northerners, especially Union veterans, remained resolute in their conviction that fighting to save the Union by putting down the rebellion had been a worthy cause, and that emancipation had been a noble means of subduing that rebellion. Still, by 1877, many Northerners lacked the political will and racial empathy to continue a military occupation of the

South, and thus allowed the cause of civil rights to be delayed by almost a century.

Just as Civil War soldiers expressed diverse attitudes toward killing during the war, as postwar veterans, they still reflected a diversity of opinion. The war's outcome seemed to vindicate the decision of Union men to fight, apparently proving, as their martyred president had hoped, that right made might. Alternatively, Union veterans who had been reluctant or refused to kill could take comfort that their cause had prevailed, and they had dutifully played their parts, regardless of the choices they made in actual combat. For Confederates, reunion was more complicated. If they had come back into the American fold, what had been the purpose of a war between the states in which Americans had killed one another? Some men hoped they had not been the cause of others' deaths. "I fired a cannon," an aged Tennessean said of his military service. "I hope I never killed anyone." Some former Confederates, pleased or content that the Unites States had remained whole, could even find purpose in the material destruction that had helped end the war and the killing. "Which is the worst in war," asked Virginia cavalryman John Opie in his memoir, "to burn a barn, or kill a fellow man?"[8]

Not all Confederate veterans regretted or felt compelled to apologize for having fought—or killed. The song "Good Old Rebel," based on a poem by one of J. E. B. Stuart's staff officers and popularized during Reconstruction, must have spoken for many an "unreconstructed" Rebel. In one line the speaker declares, "I killed a chance of Yankees, and I wish I killed some mo'!" The next stanza doubles down on the deadly sentiment:

> Three hundred thousand Yankees is dead in Southern dust,
> We got three hundred thousand before they conquered us;
> They died of Southern fever, of Southern steel and shot—
> I wish they was three million instead of what we got.

Other Confederate veterans thought they could reconcile reunion with the North without having to apologize for having fought as Rebels. Texas veteran William Fletcher professed his thankfulness "that during the war and since, I carried no hatred against the victorious foe." He had proved a formidable warrior in the battle line and on the skirmish line, yet Fletcher also understood that both he and his Union opponents had given their all in fighting for their respective causes and "performed it as one of their most sacred duties."[9]

When Americans look back on the Civil War, they tend to remember that millions of men from North and South had been willing to risk their lives on behalf of their respective causes. Over 600,000 Americans— perhaps over 700,000—did lose their lives, whether they died on battlefields or in hospitals, from bullets or sickness, giving what Abraham Lincoln called "the last full measure of devotion." They also understand it as a war in which Americans fought Americans, sometimes brother against brother. Sometimes these two realities seem disconnected, as if the Civil War had come as some great historical storm that had swept away the thousands of lives, as if battle had been a chaotic tempest into which soldiers marched, hoping to come through alive. In some ways that was true, but the Civil War's combat dead did not die by impersonal forces but by the hands of fellow Americans. We speak rather euphemistically of soldiers fighting for their country, but Nathan Bedford Forrest, that most ruthless of Civil Warriors, spoke of a harsher, starker truth. War means fighting, and fighting means killing.

Millions of American citizen-soldiers confronted that reality in the Civil War. Moreover, the weight of evidence indicates that the great many accepted killing as part of their martial duty. As individuals, they reflected a great diversity of opinion in their attitudes toward killing. This spectrum ranged from enthusiastic killers to reluctant killers to soldiers who would take extreme measures to avoid killing. Most soldiers fell somewhere along this spectrum: they would fight as effectively as possible, including killing, regardless of whether they had resolved their feelings on the matter. Many, it appears, believed that killing the enemy in battle represented a positive good, both for their respective causes and the survival of themselves and their comrades. History tells us that many soldiers experience an innate resistance to killing their fellow man, but the record that Civil War soldiers left us suggests that the majority of Federals and Confederates overcame this resistance in the course of their service.

Culture and society in both North and South had primed Americans for civil war. The hatred, fears, and acrimony of the sectional crisis, marked and exacerbated by flash points of outright political violence, had fitted Americans to see one another as enemies. In varying degrees, attitudes toward war, firearms, violence, and death brought future volunteer soldiers steps closer toward legitimizing and normalizing what they would be asked to do as Federals and Confederates. Of all elements of antebellum culture, Christian teachings and ethics offered the single greatest stumbling block to the generation of Americans who went to war against one another. For a significant minority of soldiers, the King James Bible's injunction "Thou shalt not kill" troubled them in heart and mind. Yet for still more soldiers for whom faith also mattered, religious reasoning fortified their sense of mission, even to the point of killing the enemy.

Once at war, many factors helped Civil War soldiers endure the challenge of killing. Some of those factors encouraged fighting lethally. The tactics by which they fought commanded and controlled their firing, adding moral force to their conduct in battle. Fighting elbow to elbow in line of battle provided a sense of group solidarity. If a given soldier numbered among the majority of men who expressed political and ideological motivations for fighting, then this potentially strengthened his sense of purpose in battle. He also hailed from a society that largely supported his mission, celebrating his actions as fulfilling a patriotic and even sacred duty. In addition, the nature of battle often helped shield him from the full rigor of knowingly killing the enemy. Firing at often distant enemies through clouds of gun smoke and with hundreds of his comrades' weapons discharging around him, a soldier who harbored reservations about killing could often take refuge in the anonymity and uncertainty of the Civil War battlefield.

Civil War accounts reveal soldiers' attitudes not only in the feelings they expressly described but also in the words they used. Fighting men could speak bluntly of killing the enemy, or they could draw from a rich vocabulary of slang and euphemism for killing. Whether they spoke of "good execution," "deliberate aim," "murderous fire," or used still more varied and colorful expressions, this language of killing tells its own story. Soldiers unnerved by having to take human life could distance themselves from the uncomfortable reality of killing. For combatants who accepted or affirmed killing in battle, these turns of phrase gave voice to the attitudes of professionalism, enthusiasm, and even humor with which they faced combat and allowed them to frame those viewpoints to outsiders.

Some soldiers naturally proved more adept at killing than others. Men with the greatest marksmanship skills and confidence in those skills took on the role of sharpshooters, able to shoot accurately and kill from afar. While some troops condemned sharpshooters as wicked, unprincipled murderers, history may have exaggerated just how many Civil War soldiers thought so. Many soldiers not necessarily trained or equipped as sharpshooters still aspired to their skills and emulated their role in battle. Union and Confederate armies treated sharpshooters as ethically legitimate and tactically beneficial. Behind the lines, the civilian world largely celebrated the accomplishments of their side's sharpshooters, heralding them as successors to past generations of American marksmen.

With the passions loosed by the Civil War, some men took the killing too far, taking enemy lives in ways not sanctioned by the laws of war. On both sides, some men would show no quarter to a foe who tried to surrender after killing one of their own. Among Union soldiers, many of the most passionately motivated men spoke openly of killing civilians at home whom they believed threatened the success of the war effort. Most Federals lacked the means during the war to make good on these threats, though during the vengeful response to Lincoln's assassination some did take the lives of dissidents who openly celebrated the murder. Confederates had greater opportunity to commit atrocity killings. Outraged by the invasion and desolation of the South, Confederate regular and irregular forces routinely murdered Union foragers, often leaving their mangled bodies as ghastly warnings. Most scandalous of all, Rebel troops massacred black Federals on numerous battlefields across the Confederacy, both in the heat of battle and in cold blood. Denied quarter by a slave society that denied their people liberty, the Union's black troops decided that in battle with Confederates, they in turn would neither ask for nor give quarter.

Despite a general readiness to kill among soldiers and the war's worst excesses of killing, decided limits to soldiers' willingness to kill stands out in counterpoint. Even the bravest of troops dreaded engaging the enemy in deadly hand-to-hand combat. Melee fighting occurred relatively rarely during the Civil War not only because the weaponry of the day made it difficult to close with the enemy but also because many soldiers hesitated to plunge themselves into combat so dangerous and unnerving, though when Union and Confederate soldiers did meet in close combat it resulted in some of fiercest killing of the war. More proactively, soldiers also illustrated the limits of killing in their acts of mercy and forbearance. Even in the frenzy of battle, many soldiers showed great willingness to take prisoners. In pointed contrast to the bitter fighting, Federals and Confederates famously enjoyed talking and trading with one another between the lines as fellow fighting men and fellow Americans. Perhaps most incredibly, during extended campaigns many soldiers alternated between fighting and fraternizing with seeming effortlessness.

Whether war's end found them reveling in the victory of the Stars and Stripes or tearfully surrendering tattered Rebel banners, Civil War soldiers could find reason for relief and joy in 1865. Whether that end brought them victory or defeat, it meant that they had survived the great struggle. For four bloody years, Americans from North and South had fought and killed one another to decide the future of the republic and of their own lives. At the end of those years, the Union had survived and slavery had died. During that time, Abraham Lincoln, himself a casualty of the Civil War, had contemplated the fact that the two warring peoples in America both read the same Bible and prayed to the same God. At war's end, many Federal and Confederate veterans may well have turned their thoughts to a well-remembered passage in Ecclesiastes describing the ebb and flow of the human condition: "To every thing there is a season, and a time to every purpose under the heaven. . . . A time to kill, and a time to heal . . . a time of war, and a time of peace" (3:1, 3, 8). After four years of civil war, it was time for peace. After four years of Americans killing Americans, it was time to heal.

## Prologue

1. Adam Goodheart, *1861: The Civil War Awakening* (New York: Knopf, 2011), 282–285; "Death of Francis Edwin Brownell," *New York Times*, March 16, 1894.

2. Goodheart, *1861*, 284–285; "Death of Francis Edwin Brownell," *New York Times*.

3. *Life of James W. Jackson, the Alexandria Hero, and the Slayer of Ellsworth* (Richmond, VA: West & Johnston, 1862), 22; Goodheart, *1861*, 284.

4. Goodheart, *1861*, 285; "Death of Francis Edwin Brownell," *New York Times*.

5. All excerpts (with the exception of the House quotation and the envelope) are from the Elmer E. Ellsworth Archival Collection, Civil War Museum (Kenosha, WI); House, quoted in Charles A. Ingraham, *Elmer E. Ellsworth and the Zouaves of '61* (Chicago: University of Chicago Press, 1927), 150–152; "Commemorative Envelope, circa 1861," Colonel Elmer Ephraim Ellsworth Collection, 1860–1861, Archives of Lake Forest Academy and Ferry Hall (Lake Forest, IL), *Illinois Digital Archives*, http://www.idaillinois.org/.

6. *Life of James W. Jackson*, 1, 10, 32–38, 45–46.

## Introduction

1. Bernard Cornwell, foreword to *Sword and Honor: Thrilling Battle Stories of Courage and Victory*, ed. Mike Ashley (New York: Fall River Press, 2011), x.

2. Ian Tuttle, "The Demonization of Chris Kyle," *National Review*, January 20, 2015, http://www.nationalreview.com/.

3. Robert E. Bonner, *The Soldier's Pen: Firsthand Impressions of the Civil War* (New York: Hill & Wang, 2006), 5.

## Chapter 1. The Things They Carried: Influences on Civil War Soldiers and Killing

1. Thomas Chandler Haliburton, *The Letter-bag of the Great Western, or Life in a Steamer* (Paris: Baudry's European Library, 1840), 100.

2. Quoted in Kingsley Martin, *The Crown and the Establishment* (Harmondsworth, UK: Penguin, 1962), 106.

3. Martin, *The Crown and the Establishment*, 106.

4. Maury Klein, *Days of Defiance: Sumter, Secession, and the Coming of the Civil War* (New York: Vintage Books, 1999), 60.

5. David Herbert Donald, *Lincoln* (New York: Simon & Schuster, 1995), 277–278; James M. McPherson, *Battle Cry of Freedom: The Civil War Era* (New York: Oxford University Press, 1988), 285.

6. Drew Gilpin Faust, *This Republic of Suffering: Death and the American Civil War* (New York: Knopf, 2008), 34–35.

7. Bell I. Wiley, *The Life of Billy Yank: The Common Soldier of the Union* (Indianapolis, IN: Bobbs-Merrill, 1952), 39–40; Gerald F. Linderman, *Embattled Courage: The Experience of Combat in the American Civil War* (New York: Free Press, 1987), 2; James M. McPherson, *For Cause and Comrades: Why Men Fought in the Civil War* (New York: Oxford University Press, 1997), 91, 100–101, 168.

8. Quoted in Robert E. Bonner, *The Soldier's Pen: Firsthand Impressions of the Civil War* (New York: Hill & Wang, 2006), 151; Jason Phillips, "A Brothers' War? Exploring Confederate Perceptions of the Enemy," in *The View from the Ground: Experiences of Civil War Soldiers*, ed. Aaron Sheehan-Dean (Lexington: University Press of Kentucky, 2007), 76; William A. Fletcher, *Rebel Private: Front and Rear* (1908; repr., New York: Dutton, 1995), 151.

9. Robert A. Moore, *A Life for the Confederacy: As Recorded in the Pocket Diaries of Pvt. Robert A. Moore*, ed. James W. Silver (1959; repr., Wilmington, NC: Broadfoot, 1987), 28; Chauncey H. Cooke, *A Badger Boy in Blue: The Civil War Letters of Chauncey H. Cooke*, ed. William H. Mulligan Jr. (Detroit: Wayne State University Press, 2007), 86.

10. W. G. Bean, "A House Divided: The Civil War Letters of a Virginia Family," *Virginia Magazine of History and Biography* 59, no. 4 (October 1951): 401; Saxon DeWolf (6th MI Heavy Artillery), quoted in McPherson, *For Cause and Comrades*, 18.

11. John W. Ames to "My dear Mother," November 12, 1861, John W. Ames Papers, US Army Heritage and Education Center (Carlisle, PA) (USAHEC); Cooke, *Badger Boy*, 75.

12. Bell I. Wiley, *The Life of Johnny Reb: The Common Soldier of the Confederacy* (1943; repr., Garden City, NY: Doubleday, 1971), 20; John D. Wright, *The Language of the Civil War* (Greenwood, CT: Oryx, 2001), 177; "Leo," quoted in William B. Styple, ed., *Writing and Fighting the Civil War: Soldier Correspondence to the New York Sunday Mercury*, 2nd rev. ed. (Kearny, NJ: Belle Grove, 2004), 280.

13. Quoted in Styple, *Writing and Fighting the Civil War*, 194; John F. Brobst, *Well, Mary: Civil War Letters of a Wisconsin Volunteer*, ed. Margaret Brobst Roth (Madison: University of Wisconsin Press, 1960), 38; "Curse to Confederate President Jeff Davis, written by one of the 1863 Federal prisoners," Old Courthouse Civil War Museum (Winchester, VA).

14. Mark A. Noll, *The Civil War as a Theological Crisis* (Chapel Hill: University of North Carolina Press, 2006), 28. See also Steven E. Woodworth, *While God Is Marching On: The Religious World of Civil War Soldiers* (Lawrence: University Press of Kansas, 2001), 3–26.

15. James O. Lehman and Steven M. Nolt, *Mennonites, Amish, and the American Civil War* (Baltimore, MD: Johns Hopkins University Press, 2011), 58.

16. Woodworth, *While God Is Marching On*, 216; Matthew Henry, "Commentary: Exodus 20:12–17," *Bible Gateway*, https://www.biblegateway.com/.

17. Quoted in McPherson, *For Cause and Comrades*, 71; Hugh G. Bailey, ed., "An Alabamian at Shiloh: The Diary of Liberty Independence Nixon," *Alabama Review* 11, no. 2 (April 1958): 152.

18. Paul Hubbard and Christine Lewis, eds., "'Give yourself no trouble about

me': The Shiloh Letters of George W. Lennard," *Indiana Magazine of History* 76, no. 1 (March 1980): 26.

19. John Keegan, *The Face of Battle* (1976; repr., New York: Penguin, 1978), 320; Dave Grossman, *On Killing: The Psychological Cost of Learning to Kill in War and Society*, rev. ed. (New York: Bay Back Books, 2009), xxxi–xxxvi.

20. McPherson, *For Cause and Comrades*, 63.

21. David W. Rolfs, "'No nearer heaven now but rather farther off': The Religious Compromises and Conflicts of Northern Soldiers," in *The View from the Ground: Experiences of Civil War Soldiers*, ed. Aaron Sheehan-Dean (Lexington: University Press of Kentucky, 2007), 122–123; Woodworth, *While God Is Marching On*, 216–217; Bailey, "Alabamian at Shiloh," 152.

22. Daniel I. Dreher, "A Sermon Delivered by Rev. Daniel I. Dreher . . . ," *Documenting the American South*, http://docsouth.unc.edu/; "G.E." (9th NY), quoted in Styple, *Writing and Fighting the Civil War*, 30; quoted in Mitchell G. Klingenberg, "'Without the shedding of blood there can be no remission': The War Theology of Horace Bushnell and the Meaning of America, 1861 to 1866," *Connecticut History* 51, no. 2 (Fall 2012): 169. I am grateful to Klingenberg for calling my attention to this valuable anecdote.

23. Valerius Cincinnatus Giles, *Rags and Hope: The Recollections of Val C. Giles, Four Years with Hood's Brigade, Fourth Texas Infantry, 1861–1865*, ed. Mary Lasswell (New York: Coward-McCann, 1961), 81.

24. Charles A. Stevens, *Berdan's United States Sharpshooters in the Army of the Potomac, 1861–1865* (St. Paul, MN: Price-McGill, 1892), 275–276; Wyman S. White, *The Civil War Diary of Wyman S. White, First Sergeant of Company F, 2nd United States Sharpshooter Regiment, 1861–1865*, ed. Russell C. White (Baltimore, MD: Butternut & Blue, 1993), 205; "Brooklyn," quoted in Styple, *Writing and Fighting the Civil War*, 122.

25. Lorien Foote, *The Gentlemen and the Roughs: Manhood, Honor, and Violence in the Union Army* (New York: New York University Press, 2010), 59, 69–79.

26. Michael C. C. Adams, *Fighting for Defeat: Union Military Failure in the East, 1861–1865* (Lincoln: University of Nebraska Press, 1992), vii, 72; John G. Nicolay, *With Lincoln in the White House: Letters, Memoranda, and Other Writings of John G. Nicolay, 1860–1865*, ed. Michael Burlingame (Carbondale: Southern Illinois University Press, 2006), 69.

27. Glennys Howarth, *Death and Dying: A Sociological Introduction* (Cambridge: Polity Press, 2007), 30–31; Faust, *This Republic of Suffering*, xii, 7–11; Grossman, *On Killing*, xxviii–xxix; Mark S. Schantz, *Awaiting the Heavenly Country: The Civil War and America's Culture of Death* (Ithaca, NY: Cornell University Press, 2008), 2, 8–15.

28. Earl J. Hess, *The Rifle Musket in Civil War Combat: Myth and Reality* (Lawrence: University Press of Kansas, 2008), 61–71.

29. Clayton E. Cramer, *Armed America: The Remarkable Story of How and Why Guns Became as American as Apple Pie* (Nashville, TN: Nelson Current, 2006), 209; Cooke, *Badger Boy*, 79.

30. Washington Ives, *Civil War Journal and Letters of Serg. Washington Ives, 4th Florida CSA*, ed. Jim R. Cabaniss (Tallahassee, FL: J. R. Cabaniss, 1987), 29; quoted

in *Eyewitnesses at the Battle of Franklin*, comp. David R. Logsdon, 3rd ed. (Nashville, TN: Kettle Mills Press, 1991), 37.

31. Benjamin F. McGee, *History of the 72nd Indiana Volunteer Infantry of the Mounted Lightning Brigade*, 2nd ed. (Huntington, WV: Blue Acorn Press, 1995), 678; Hess, *Rifle Musket*, 83–84. Hess considers these numbers of purchases "relatively" small, but a figure of approximately one in ten Union veterans choosing to buy back their arms seems like a significant percentage. One factor that may have limited purchases was that an army-issue rifle musket was ill suited to civilian purposes as a result of its length and large caliber, which would require more powder and lead than a civilian arm. Notably, a number of veterans "sporterized" their muskets, having their barrels and stocks cut down to make them handier. Some even had the rifling bored out to convert them into shotguns, a more practical arm than a .58-caliber rifle.

32. Kenneth Lyftogt, *Blue Mills to Columbia: Cedar Falls and the Civil War* (Ames: Iowa State University Press, 1993), 71.

33. Ives, *Civil War Journal*, 67; Lyman S. Widney, *Campaigning with Uncle Billy: The Civil War Memoirs of Sgt. Lyman S. Widney, 34th Illinois Volunteer Infantry*, ed. Robert I. Girardi (Bloomington, IN: Trafford, 2008), 219.

34. Theodore F. Upson, *With Sherman to the Sea: The Civil War Letters, Diaries, and Reminiscences of Theodore F. Upson*, ed. Oscar Osburn Winther, 2nd ed. (Bloomington: Indiana University Press, 1956), 102–107; *Henry's Repeating Rifle 1865: Henry Co. Catalogue* (Brighton, MI: Cornell Publishing, 2005), 21–23.

35. George H. Lewis (1st USSS) to "Dear Sister," May 16, 1862, George H. Lewis letters, Wisconsin Historical Society, Madison (WHS); *Henry's Repeating Rifle 1865*, 17–18.

36. Wiley Sword, *The Historic Henry Rifle: Oliver Winchester's Famous Civil War Repeater* (Lincoln, RI: Andrew Mowbray, 2002), 14; Upson, *With Sherman to the Sea*, 107, 157–158; Maj. William Ludlow, quoted in Andrew L. Bresnan, "The Henry Repeating Rifle," *RareWinchesters.com*, http://www.rarewinchesters.com/.

37. Fletcher, *Rebel Private*, 3; James Cooper Nisbet, *Four Years on the Firing Line*, ed. Bell Irvin Wiley (Wilmington, NC: Broadfoot, 1991), 20.

38. William Young Warren Ripley, *Vermont Riflemen in the War for the Union, 1861–1865: A History of Company F, First United States Sharp Shooters* (Rutland, VT: Tuttle, 1883), 4; Rudolph Aschmann, *Memoirs of a Swiss Officer in the American Civil War*, ed. Heinz K. Meier (Bern: Herbert Lang, 1972), 30.

39. Quoted in Adrian Gilbert, *Stalk and Kill: The Thrill and Danger of the Sniper Experience* (New York: St. Martin's Press, 1997), 104; William L. Nugent, *My Dear Nellie: The Civil War Letters of William L. Nugent to Eleanor Smith Nugent*, ed. William M. Cash and Lucy Somerville Howorth (Jackson: University Press of Mississippi, 1977), 32.–4

40. Cooke, *Badger Boy*, 14.

41. Widney, *Campaigning with Uncle Billy*, 27; Samuel W. Hankins, quoted in Hess, *Rifle Musket*, 65.

42. Quoted in William B. Styple, ed., *Writing and Fighting from the Army of Northern Virginia: A Collection of Civil War Soldier Correspondence* (Kearny, NJ: Belle Grove,

2003), 29; George W. Squier, *This Wilderness of War: The Civil War Letters of George W. Squier, Hoosier Volunteer,* ed. Julie A. Doyle, John David Smith, and Richard M. McMurry (Knoxville: University of Tennessee Press, 1998), 11.

43. Samuel D. Buck, *With the Old Confeds: Actual Experiences of a Captain in the Line* (Baltimore, MD: H. E. Houck, 1925), 123.

44. Grossman, *On Killing,* xxviii; Steven E. Woodworth and Kenneth J. Winkle, *Atlas of the Civil War* (Oxford: Oxford University Press, 2004), 364.

45. Preston Lafayette Ledford, *Reminiscences of the Civil War, 1861–1865* (Thomasville, NC: News Printing House, 1909), 54.

46. Relevant verses include 1 Peter 1:18–19, Colossians 1:20, and 1 John 1:7. Squier, *This Wilderness of War,* 85; William Pitt Chambers, *Blood and Sacrifice: The Civil War Journal of a Confederate Soldier,* ed. Richard A. Baumgartner (Huntington, WV: Blue Acorn Press, 1994), 194.

47. Quoted in Styple, *Writing and Fighting from the Army of Northern Virginia,* 29; R. L. Murray, ed., *Letters from Berdan's Sharpshooters* (Wolcott, NY: Benedum Books, 2005), 87. Quoted in Linderman, *Embattled Courage,* 150.

48. John Hill Ferguson, *On to Atlanta: The Civil War Diaries of John Hill Ferguson, Illinois Tenth Regiment of Volunteers,* ed. Janet Correll Ellison (Lincoln: University of Nebraska Press, 2001), 38; "J.B." (1st WI), quoted in Styple, *Writing and Fighting the Civil War,* 31; Ledford, *Reminiscences,* 40–41.

49. John A. Lynn, *Battle: A History of Combat and Culture,* rev. ed. (Philadelphia: Basic Books, 2008), 229.

50. Duncan Emrich, ed., "Songs and Ballads of American History and of the Assassination of Presidents," *Library of Congress,* http://www.loc.gov/; Ray Mathis, *In the Land of the Living: Wartime Letters by Confederates from the Chattahoochee Valley of Alabama and Georgia* (Troy, AL: Troy State University Press, 1981), 10; John O. Casler, *Four Years in the Stonewall Brigade* (1906; repr., Columbia: University of South Carolina Press, 2005), 25; Aurelia Austin, *Georgia Boys with "Stonewall" Jackson: James Thomas Thompson and the Walton Infantry* (Athens: University of Georgia Press, 1967), 5; Ellen E. Hodges and Stephen Kerber, eds., "'Rogues and Black Hearted Scamps': Civil War Letters of Winston and Octavia Stephens, 1862–1863," *Florida Historical Quarterly* 57, no. 1 (July 1978): 61.

51. Thomas Morgan, Wisconsin Veterans Reminiscences, WHS; William C. Catlin to "Mr. A. Smyth," November 21, 1861, in Ohio, *Message and Reports to the General Assembly and Governor of the State of Ohio for the Year 1861,* part 1 (Columbus, OH: Richard Nevins, 1862); William R. Ray, *Four Years with the Iron Brigade: The Civil War Journal of William Ray, Company F, Seventh Wisconsin Volunteers,* ed. Lance Herdegen and Sherry Murphy (Cambridge, MA: Da Capo Press, 2009), 11; Luther H. Cowan to Harriet Cowan, February 1–2, 1862, Civil War letters and diary of Luther H. Cowan, WHS.

52. Anderson Chappell, ed., *Dear Sister: Civil War Letters to a Sister in Alabama* (Huntsville, AL: Branch Springs Publishing, 2002), 111; Styple, *Writing and Fighting from the Army of Northern Virginia,* 29; quoted in McPherson, *For Cause and Comrades,* 95–96.

53. Nugent, *My Dear Nellie,* 46, 74.

54. Joseph Plumb Martin, *Memoir of a Revolutionary Soldier: The Narrative of Joseph Plumb Martin* (Mineola, NY: Dover, 2006), 10.

## Chapter 2. Seeing the Elephant: Killing and the Face of Battle

1. S. L. A. Marshall, *Men Against Fire: The Problem of Battle Command in Future War* (1947; repr., Gloucester, MA: Peter Smith, 1978), 23, 64–75; William E. Persons, Oliver S. Wood, Joseph Plassmeyer, Paul V. Kellogg, and John E. McCammon, *Military Science and Tactics* (Columbia: University of Missouri, 1921), 3:196; John H. Allspaugh, "Mission Ridge: The Story of the Charge Told by an Enlisted Man," *National Tribune*, June 2, 1887, 2.

2. Paddy Griffith, *Battle Tactics of the Civil War* (New Haven, CT: Yale University Press, 1989), 86–89; Edward O. Lord, *History of the Ninth Regiment New Hampshire Volunteers in the War of the Rebellion* (Concord, NH: Republican Press Association, 1895), 71.

3. Widney, *Campaigning with Uncle Billy*, 24.

4. Hess, *Rifle Musket*, 68–71; Ives, *Civil War Journal*, 7; Louis Leon, *Diary of a Tar Heel Confederate Soldier* (Charlotte, NC: Stone, 1913), 59.

5. "J.S.H.," quoted in Styple, *Writing and Fighting the Civil War*, 114; Richard Crane (7th WI) Diary, January 28, 1864, Richard Crane Papers, WHS; Simon Bolivar Hulbert, *One Battle Too Many: An American Civil War Chronicle: The Writings of Simon Bolivar Hulbert, Private, Company E, 100th Regiment, New York State Volunteers, 1861–1864*, ed. Richard P. Galloway (Gaithersburg, MD: Olde Soldier, 1987), 76, 131.

6. Hulbert, *One Battle Too Many*, 76, 141–142.

7. Almeron W. Stillwell Diary, June 6, 1864, A. W. Stillwell Diary, WHS; Widney, *Campaigning with Uncle Billy*, 212.

8. Grossman, *On Killing*, xviii–xix, 252–257.

9. Claud E. Fuller, *The Rifled Musket* (Harrisburg, PA: Stackpole Books, 1958), 59–128; Hans Busk, *Hand-Book for Hythe* (1860; repr., Brighton, MI: Cornell Publications, ca. 2003), frontispiece, 96.

10. Grossman, *On Killing*, 58.

11. Hulbert, *One Battle Too Many*, 75; Ledford, *Reminiscences*, 64; quoted in John J. Hennessy, *The First Battle of Manassas: An End to Innocence, July 18–21, 1861*, rev. ed. (Mechanicsburg, PA: Stackpole Books, 2015), 18.

12. Edward Simonton, "Recollections of the Battle of Fredericksburg," *MOLLUS* 27 (1890): 254.

13. Ray, *Four Years with the Iron Brigade*, 58; R[alph] H. Rea to Horace E. Allen, July 8, 1863, 7th Michigan File, Gettysburg National Military Park (Gettysburg, PA) (GNMP).

14. Franks Potts, Diary, 34, Library of Virginia (Richmond, VA).

15. Henry O. Dwight, "The Affair on the Raymond Road," *New York Daily Tribune*, November 21, 1886, 11.

16. Grossman, *On Killing*, 173; Sam R. Watkins, *"Co. Aytch," Maury Grays, First Tennessee Regiment, or A Side Show of the Big Show* (1882; repr., Wilmington, NC: Broadfoot, 1990), 55.

17. Private Roland E. Bowen (15th MA), quoted in Marion V. Armstrong Jr., *Un-*

*furl Those Colors! McClellan, Sumner, and the Second Army Corps in the Antietam Campaign* (Tuscaloosa: University of Alabama Press, 2008), 188; Watkins, *Co. Aytch*, 55.

18. Edwin W. Smith, "Battle of Ezra Church: A Coffee-Cooler's Experience," *National Tribune*, July 5, 1888, 3.

19. Quoted in Otis F. R. Waite, *New Hampshire in the Great Rebellion* (Claremont, NH: Tracy, Chase, 1870); 266; Private T. N. Rownsdale (14th IN), quoted in Armstrong, *Unfurl Those Colors!*, 218.

20. Don Troiani, *Don Troiani's Civil War: Infantry* (Mechanicsburg, PA: Stackpole Books, 2002), 8; Stephen W. Sears, *To the Gates of Richmond: The Peninsula Campaign* (New York: Ticknor & Fields, 1992), 237; Osborn H. Oldroyd, "The Diary of Osborn H. Oldroyd," May 12, 1863, *Battle of Raymond, Mississippi*, http://www.battleofraymond.org/oldroyd.htm.

21. Reynold M. Kirby (Richmond Howitzers), quoted in Time-Life Books, *First Manassas* (Alexandria, VA: Time-Life, 1997), 51; Thomas G. Murphey, quoted in Armstrong, *Unfurl Those Colors!*, 212.

22. Rufus R. Dawes, *Service with the Sixth Wisconsin Volunteers* (Marietta, OH: E. R. Alderman & Sons, 1890), 90–91.

23. James T. Holmes, *52d OVI: Then and Now* (Columbus, OH: Berlin, 1898), 256; quoted in Bonner, *Soldier's Pen*, 79; William E. Bevens, *Reminiscences of a Private: William E. Bevens of the First Arkansas Infantry, CSA*, ed. Daniel E. Sutherland (Fayetteville: University of Arkansas Press, 1992), 137.

24. Buck, *With the Old Confeds*, 62; Seymour Dexter, *Seymour Dexter, Union Army: Journal and Letters of Civil War Service in Company K, 23rd New York Volunteer Regiment of Elmira, with Illustrations*, ed. Carl A. Morrell (Jefferson, NC: McFarland, 1996), 80–81.

25. Quoted in James D. McCabe Jr., *The Grayjackets: And How They Lived, Fought, and Died, for Dixie* (Richmond, VA: Jones Brothers, 1867), 180–181; Wilbur F. Crummer, *With Grant at Fort Donelson, Shiloh, and Vicksburg* (Oak Park, IL: E. C. Crummer, 1915), 37–38.

26. Griffith, *Battle Tactics*, 112; S. M. H. Byers, "How Men Feel in Battle," *American History Illustrated* 22 (April 1987): 12; Rice C. Bull, *Soldiering: The Civil War Diary of Rice C. Bull, 123rd New York Volunteer Infantry*, ed. K. Jack Bauer (1977; repr., Navato, CA: Presidio Press, 1995), 56; Simonton, "Recollections," 254.

27. Quoted in D. Scott Hartwig, "'I dread the thought of the place': The Iron Brigade at Antietam," in *Giants in Their Tall Black Hats: Essays on the Iron Brigade*, ed. Alan T. Nolan and Sharon Eggleston Vipond (Bloomington: Indiana University Press, 1998), 43; Hugh C. Perkins to Herbert E. Frisbie, September 21, 1862, Manuscript Archive, USAHEC; Ives, *Civil War Journal*, 36.

28. Frank Holsinger, "How Does One Feel Under Fire?," *MOLLUS* 15 (1892): 294.

29. C. Calvin Smith, ed., "The Duties of Home and War: The Civil War Letters of John G. Marsh (A Selection)," *Upper Ohio Valley Historical Review* 8 (1979): 11.

30. Nugent, *My Dear Nellie*, 185–186.

31. Oliver Willcox Norton, *Army Letters, 1861–1865* (Chicago: O. L. Deming, 1903), 107; Brobst, *Well, Mary*, 87; Cooke, *Badger Boy*, 109

32. Bevens, *Reminiscences of a Private*, 69.

33. Quoted in Lyftogt, *Blue Mills to Columbia*, 111; Mary J. S. Callaway, quoted in Joshua K. Callaway, *The Civil War Letters of Joshua K. Callaway*, ed. Judith Lee Hallock (Athens: University of Georgia Press, 1997), 34.

34. Stephen Pierson, "From Chattanooga to Atlanta in 1864—A Personal Reminiscence," *Proceedings of the New Jersey Historical Society* 16 (1931): 343; George L. Wood, *The Seventh Regiment: A Record* (New York: James Miller, 1865), 129–130.

35. Wilbur F. Hinman, *The Story of the Sherman Brigade: The Camp, the March, the Bivouac, the Battle; and How "The Boys" Lived and Died during Four Years of Active Field Service* (Alliance, OH, 1897), 374; Captain Matthew T. Nunnally (11th GA), quoted in Austin, *Georgia Boys*, 13; Ferguson, *On to Atlanta*, 104; Brobst, *Well, Mary*, 91–92.

36. Widney, *Campaigning with Uncle Billy*, 271.

37. Henry E. Handerson, *Yankee in Gray: The Civil War Memoirs of Henry E. Handerson, with a Selection of His Wartime Letters* (Cleveland, OH: Press of Western Reserve University, 1962), 95; Richard Robert Crowe to "Dear Mommy," July 18, 1864, Richard Robert Crowe letters, WHS.

38. Thomas Benton Reed, *A Private in Gray* (Camden, AR: T. B. Reed, 1905), 42; Hulbert, *One Battle Too Many*, 259.

39. John Will Dyer, *Reminiscences, or Four Years in the Confederate Army: A History of the Experiences of the Private Soldier in Camp, Hospital, Prison, on the March, and on the Battlefield, 1861 to 1865* (Evansville, IN: Keller, 1898), 184; Cooke, *Badger Boy*, 92.

40. Dyer, *Reminiscences*, 183; Hamlin Alexander Coe, *Mine Eyes Have Seen the Glory: Combat Diaries of Union Sergeant Hamlin Alexander Coe*, ed. David Coe (Cranbury, NJ: Fairleigh Dickinson University Press, 1975), 125.

41. Joseph Wendel Muffly, ed., *The Story of Our Regiment: A History of the 148th Pennsylvania Vols* (Des Moines, IA: Kenyon Printing & Mfg. Co., 1904), 537.

42. Giles, *Rags and Hope*, 208.

43. David E. Holt, *A Mississippi Rebel in the Army of Northern Virginia: The Civil War Memoirs of Private David Holt*, ed. Thomas D. Cockrell and Michael B. Ballard (Baton Rouge: Louisiana State University Press, 1995), 147.

44. Grossman, *On Killing*, 23–24.

45. Grossman, *On Killing*, 27–28.

46. Carol A. Reardon, *With a Sword in One Hand and Jomini in the Other: The Problem of Military Thought in the Civil War North* (Chapel Hill: University of North Carolina Press, 2012), 114.

47. Cooke, *Badger Boy*, 41; Private William C. Littlefield (14th IA) to mother, April 15, 1864, W. C. Littlefield Letters, Abraham Lincoln Presidential Library and Museum (Springfield, IL).

48. Giles, *Rags and Hope*, 181–183.

49. Brent Nosworthy, *The Bloody Crucible of Courage: Fighting Methods and Combat Experience of the Civil War* (New York: Carroll & Graf, 2003), 580–581.

50. Lieutenant Samuel C. Hodgman to "Dear Father," November 17, 1862, "'Gone a sogerine': The Civil War Experiences of Samuel Chase Hodgman, Seventh Michigan Volunteer Infantry Regiment, May 27, 1861–Januray 4, 1864," 7th Michigan Infantry File, GNMP; Lieutenant Eugene Carter (3rd US), quoted in Robert G. Carter, "Four Brothers in Blue," *Maine Bugle* 3, no. 4 (October 1896): 311.

51. Herbert T. Ezekiel, "Pickett's Last Man," *Richmond Times-Dispatch*, June 28, 1936. Readers should note that a number of sources incorrectly date this article as September 28, but it is definitely June 28, 1936.

52. Grossman, *On Killing*, 5–9.

53. Quoted in Gary G. Lash, *"Duty Well Done": The History of Edward Baker's California Regiment (71st Pennsylvania Infantry)* (Baltimore, MD: Butternut & Blue, 2001), 343.

54. John M. King, *Three Years with the 92d Illinois: The Civil War Diary of John M. King*, ed. Claire E. Swedberg (Mechanicsburg, PA: Stackpole Books, 1999), 171–172.

55. Marion Hill Fitzpatrick, *Letters to Amanda: The Civil War Letters of Marion Hill Fitzpatrick, Army of Northern Virginia*, ed. Jeffrey C. Lowe and Sam Hodges (Macon, GA: Mercer University Press, 1998), 25; Orlando T. Hanks, *History of Captain B. F. Benton's Company, Hood's Texas Brigade, 1861–1865* (Austin, TX: Morrison Books, 1984), 16–17.

56. Quoted in Wiley Sword, *Courage Under Fire: Profiles in Bravery from the Battlefields of the Civil War* (New York: St. Martin's Griffin, 2007), 164–165.

57. Quoted in Scott C. Patchan, "The Battle of Piedmont, June 5, 1864," *Shenandoah 1864*, June 4, 2010, https://shenandoah1864.wordpress.com/.

58. Grossman, *On Killing*, 97–98; Samuel T. Foster, *One of Cleburne's Command: The Civil War Reminiscences and Diary of Capt. Samuel T. Foster, Granbury's Texas Brigade, CSA*, ed. Norman D. Brown (Austin: University of Texas Press, 1980), 62, emphasis added.

59. Earl J. Hess, *Kennesaw Mountain: Sherman, Johnston, and the Atlanta Campaign*, Civil War America (Chapel Hill: University of North Carolina Press), 131–135; Watkins, *Co. Aytch*, 156–157.

60. Watkins, *Co. Aytch*, 159.

61. Grossman, *On Killing*, 127–129.

62. Quoted in Hartwig, "I dread the thought of the place," 42; Joseph Boyce, "Missourians in the Battle of Franklin," *Confederate Veteran* 24 (1916): 102–103; Foster, *One of Cleburne's Command*, 92.

63. Keegan, *Face of Battle*, 190, 322.

64. Buck, *With the Old Confeds*, 82, 112–112, emphasis added; Nisbet, *Four Years*, 103; Eugene Blackford memoirs, 175, Civil War Miscellaneous Collection, USAHEC; Chambers, *Blood and Sacrifice*, 146.

65. *Official Records* (US War Department, *The War of the Rebellion: Official Records of the Union and Confederate Armies*, 128 vols. [Washington, DC: Government Printing Office, 1881–1901] [hereafter *OR*]), vol. 11, part 1, p. 731; United States Army Center of Military History, "Medal of Honor Recipients: American Civil War (A–L)," *US Army Center of Military History*, http://www.history.army.mil/; Thomas F. Wildes, *Record of the One Hundred and Sixteenth Regiment Ohio Volunteers in the War of the Rebellion* (Sandusky, OH: I. F. Mack & Bros., 1884), 207; Harris H. Beecher, *Record of the 114th Regiment, NYSV: Where It Went, What It Saw, and What It Did* (Norwich, NY: J. F. Hubbard Jr., 1866), 446.

66. Widney, *Campaigning with Uncle Billy*, 70, 250; White, *Civil War Diary*, 162.

67. Eugene Kingman, *Tramping Out the Vintage: The Civil War Diaries and Letters*

of *Eugene Kingman*, ed. Helene C. Phelan (Almond, NY: Helene C. Phelan, 1983), 105; A. C. McPherson, quoted in Styple, *Writing and Fighting from the Army of Northern Virginia*, 30; Casler, *Four Years in the Stonewall Brigade*, 89.

68. R. Pressley Boyd, quoted in *The Boys of Diamond Hill: The Lives and Civil War Letters of the Boyd Family of Abbeville County, South Carolina*, ed. J. Keith Jones (Jefferson, NC: McFarland, 2011), 50–51; quoted in Mathis, *In the Land of the Living*, 37.

69. James Longstreet, "The Battle of Fredericksburg," in *Battles and Leaders of the Civil War*, ed. Robert Underwood Johnson and Clarence Clough Buel, 4 vols. (New York: Century, 1887–1888), 3:81–82; Lee, quoted in John Esten Cooke, *A Life of Gen. Robert E. Lee* (New York: D. Appleton, 1871), 184; Alexander Hunter, *Johnny Reb and Billy Yank* (New York: Neale, 1905), 316; Charles S. Powell, Charles S. Powell Memoirs, Duke University (Durham, NC), 17.

70. Orsell Cook Brown [44th NY] to Olivia A. Brown, September 18, 1862, Orsell Cook Brown Papers, Manuscripts and Special Collections, New York State Library (Albany, NY); quoted in James Durkin, ed., *This War Is an Awful Thing: Civil War Letters of the National Guards, the 19th and 90th Pennsylvania Volunteers* (Glenside, PA: J. Michael Santarelli, 1994), 165; Widney, *Campaigning with Uncle Billy*, 73.

71. Michael H. B. Cunningham (18th WI) to "My Dear" (Hannah Cunningham), October 9, 1863, Michael Hayes Branniger Cunningham Letters, WHS; Coe, *Mine Eyes Have Seen the Glory*, 154; Benjamin Borton, *On the Parallels, or Chapters of Inner History; a Story of the Rappahannock* (Woodstown, NJ: Monitor-Register Print, 1903), 65.

72. John Williams Green, *Johnny Green of the Orphan Brigade: The Journal of a Confederate Soldier*, ed. A. D. Kirwan (Lexington: University Press of Kentucky, 1956), 163; Alexander R. Thain to Sue Smith, January 9, 1865, Minto Family papers, 95.45.415, Lake County History Archives (Wauconda, IL).

73. James A. Sexton, "The Observations and Experiences of a Captain of Infantry at the Battle of Franklin, November 30, 1864," *MOLLUS* 13 (1907): 478–479; Watkins, *Co. Aytch*, 220–222.

74. Brobst, *Well, Mary*, 61; quoted in Austin, *Georgia Boys*, x, 42.

75. "Tivoli," quoted in Styple, *Writing and Fighting from the Army of Northern Virginia*, 177; George M. Neese, *Three Years in the Confederate Horse Artillery* (New York: Neale, 1911), 90.

### Chapter 3. Good Execution: The Language of Killing

1. Quoted in Styple, *Writing and Fighting the Civil War*, 132; Perry Mayo, *The Civil War Letters of Perry Mayo*, ed. Robert W. Hodge (East Lansing: Michigan State University Press, 1967), 243; William Wiley, *The Civil War Diary of a Common Soldier: William Wiley of the 77th Illinois Infantry*, ed. Terrence J. Winschel (Baton Rouge: Louisiana State University Press, 2001), 153.

2. Horatio Staples, "Reminiscences of Bull Run," *MOLLUS* 18 (1908): 134.

3. Chappell, *Dear Sister*, 103; Joseph L. Cornet, "28th Penn'a at Antietam," *Grand Army Scout and Soldiers' Mail*, September 22, 1883, 2; "rub out," Dictionary.com, http://www.dictionary.com/; Wright, *Language of the Civil War*, 33, 46, 256, 326. One of the earliest appearances of the phrase "bite the dust" can be found in 1748.

The phrase may have its earliest origins in the 1611 King James Bible. See Corinne Cunard, "The Origins of 'Another One Bites the Dust,'" *Daily Bruin*, October 15, 2010, http://dailybruin.com/.

4. Leon, *Diary of a Tar Heel;* "The Battle of Piedmont, June 5, 1864," quoted in Scott C. Patchan, "The Battle of Piedmont, June 5, 1864," *Shenandoah 1864*, June 4, 2010, https://shenandoah1864.wordpress.com/.

5. H. Howard Sturgis, "Hard Fighting by Lookout Mountain," *Confederate Veteran* 17 (March 1909): 121; Henry H. Orendorff, G. M. Armstrong, Newton Ellis, M. V. D. Voorhees, S. R. Quigley, C. F. Matteson, and A. J. Stutes, *Reminiscences of the Civil War from the Diaries of Members of the 103d Illinois Volunteer Infantry* (Chicago: Press of J. F. Leaming, 1904), 28.

6. Kingman, *Tramping Out the Vintage*, 185, 190, 207.

7. William James Harriss Bellamy Diary, June 6–10, 1862, Bellamy Papers, Southern Historical Collection, University of North Carolina, Chapel Hill. Because Bellamy's father and maternal grandfather were physicians, and he himself became a doctor after the war, this would seem to account for the anatomical detail of Bellamy's account.

8. Silas S. Canfield, *History of the 21st Regiment Ohio Volunteer Infantry in the War of the Rebellion* (Toledo, OH: Vrooman, Anderson & Bateman, 1893), 73; Kingman, *Tramping Out the Vintage*, 190–191; Reed, *Private in Gray*, 79.

9. Charles I. Wickersham, "Personal Recollections of the Cavalry at Chancellorsville," *MOLLUS* 48:461–462.

10. Wickersham, "Personal Recollections," 461–462.

11. According to US Army surgeons, small arms accounted for 94 percent of recorded wounds, compared to 5.5 percent for artillery and less than 0.4 percent for edged weapons. George Washington Adams, *Doctors in Blue: The Medical History of the Union Army in the Civil War* (1996; repr., Baton Rouge: Louisiana State University Press, 1952), 113; Canfield, *History of the 21st Regiment*, 79; Salem Dutcher, "Williamsburg: A Graphic Story of the Battle of May 5, 1862," *Southern Historical Society Papers* 17 (1889): 415–416.

12. Webb B. Garrison, *The Encyclopedia of Civil War Usage: An Illustrated Compendium of the Everyday Language of Soldiers and Civilians* (Nashville, TN: Cumberland House, 2001), 85; Brobst, *Well, Mary*, 45; quoted in Lyftogt, *Blue Mills to Columbia*, 56; "HIGH PRIVATE" (31st NY), quoted in Styple, *Writing and Fighting the Civil War*, 101.

13. Dawes, *Service with the Sixth Wisconsin Volunteers*, 61; Moore, *Life for the Confederacy*, 28; James B. Thomas, *The Civil War Letters of First Lieutenant James B. Thomas, Adjutant, 107th Pennsylvania Volunteers*, ed. Mary Warner Thomas and Richard A. Sauers (Baltimore, MD: Butternut & Blue, 1995), 16; Robert T. Coles, *From Huntsville to Appomattox: R. T. Coles's History of 4th Regiment, Alabama Volunteer Infantry, CSA, Army of Northern Virginia*, ed. Jeffrey D. Stocker (Knoxville: University of Tennessee Press, 1996), 21; H. Seymour Hall. "A Volunteer at the First Bull Run," *MOLLUS* 15 (1892): 155; Thompson, quoted in Styple, *Writing and Fighting from the Army of Northern Virginia*, 104.

14. Joseph E. Worcester, *A Comprehensive Dictionary of the English Language* (Boston: Swan, Brewer, and Tileston, 1860), 179; John Longmuir, *Walker and Webster*

Combined in a Dictionary of the English Language (London: William Tegg, 1864), 155–156.

15. Worcester, Comprehensive Dictionary, 430; Longmuir, Walker and Webster, 469; quoted in Styple, Writing and Fighting from the Army of Northern Virginia, 104.

16. Washington B. Crumpton, "In the Atlanta Campaign," Confederate Veteran 29 (October 1921): 381; Conrad Wise Chapman, Ten Months in the "Orphan Brigade": Conrad Wise Chapman's Civil War Memoir, ed. Ben L. Bassham (Kent, OH: Kent State University Press, 1999), 69.

17. William H. Andrews, "Tige Anderson's Brigade at Sharpsburg," Confederate Veteran 16 (1908): 579.

18. J[ohn] H. D[onovan], "Details of the Battle of Fredericksburg. By an Officer of the Irish Brigade," New York Irish-American, January 3, 1863; quoted in Canfield, History of the 21st Regiment, 137; John K. Duke, History of the Fifty-third Regiment Ohio Volunteer Infantry, during the War of the Rebellion, 1861 to 1865 (Portsmouth, OH: Blade, 1900), 137–138; Edmund E. Nutt, "Twentieth Ohio at Atlanta," Ohio Soldier and National Picket Guard 7, no. 21 (July 28, 1894): 1.

19. Ferguson, On to Atlanta, 45; Worcester, Comprehensive Dictionary, 297; Longmuir, Walker and Webster, 293.

20. Giles, Rags and Hope, 151; James A. Connolly, Three Years in the Army of the Cumberland: The Letters and Diary of Major James A. Connolly, ed. Paul M. Angle (1959; repr., Bloomington: Indiana University Press, 1987), 247; R. K. Charles, "Events in Battle of Fredericksburg," Confederate Veteran 14 (1906): 67; Durkin, This War Is an Awful Thing, 163.

21. John Banks, "Letter from Antietam: 'Nothing but murder to place us there,'" John Banks' Civil War Blog, August 7, 2015, http://john-banks.blogspot.com/.

22. Francis E. Pierce to Edward D. Chapin, December 17, 1862, in "Civil War Letters of Francis Edwin Pierce of the 108th New York Volunteer Infantry," Rochester in the Civil War, ed. Blake McKelvey (Rochester, NY: Rochester Historical Society, 1944), 163; Connolly, Three Years, 247; Foster, One of Cleburne's Command, 151.

23. Allspaugh, "Mission Ridge," 2.

24. Daniel H. Hill, "McClellan's Change of Base and Malvern Hill," in Johnson and Buel, Battles and Leaders, 2:394; Evander M. Law, "From the Wilderness to Cold Harbor," in Johnson and Buel, Battles and Leaders, 4:142; William T. Sherman, Memoirs of General William T. Sherman (New York: D. Appleton, 1876), 2:194.

25. Hill, "McClellan's Change of Base," 394–395.

### Chapter 4. With Bayonet and Clubbed Musket: Killing in Hand-to-Hand Combat

1. Sgt. Francis Moran (73rd NY), quoted in Styple, Writing and Fighting the Civil War, 72; Handerson, Yankee in Gray, 91; Durkin, This War Is an Awful Thing, 59.

2. Alan H. Archambault, The Confederate Infantryman: A Sketchbook (Gretna, LA: Pelican, 2014), 41; Reed, Private in Gray, 42; Orlando T. Hanks, History of Captain B. F. Benton's Company, Hood's Texas Brigade, 1861–1865 (Austin, TX: Morrison Books, 1984), 2.

3. Mark K. Christ, ed., *Getting Used to Being Shot At: The Spence Family Civil War Letters* (Fayetteville: University of Arkansas Press, 2002), 9.

4. Alan H. Archambault, *The Union Infantryman: A Sketchbook* (Gretna, LA: Pelican, 2014), 24; Widney, *Campaigning with Uncle Billy*, 8, 13–14.

5. Martin A. Haynes, *A History of the Second Regiment, New Hampshire Volunteer Infantry, in the War of the Rebellion* (Lakeport, NH, 1896), 131–132.

6. Archambault, *Confederate Infantryman*, 40; Archambault, *Union Infantryman*, 24.

7. Marcus B. Toney, *The Privations of a Private: Campaigning with the First Tennessee, CSA, and Life Thereafter*, ed. Robert E. Hunt (Tuscaloosa: University of Alabama Press, 2005).

8. Theodore F. Upson, *With Sherman to the Sea: Civil War Letters, Diaries, and Reminiscences of Theodore F. Upson*, ed. Oscar Osburn Winther (Bloomington: Indiana University Press, 1958), 50–52.

9. Nosworthy, *Bloody Crucible*, 598–599.

10. Henry T. Childs, "The Battle of Seven Pines," *Confederate Veteran* 25 (1917): 20; *OR*, vol. 27, pt. 1, p. 624; Henry Morton Stanley, *The Autobiography of Sir Henry Morton Stanley*, ed. Dorothy Stanley (Boston: Houghton Mifflin, 1909), 190–191. Private Stanley, later Sir Henry Morton Stanley, gained fame after the Civil War as the leader of the African expedition to find the Christian missionary David Livingstone, upon whose discovery Stanley allegedly offered the greeting, "Dr. Livingstone, I presume?"

11. Perhaps the most notable work in the rifle-as-game-changer school is Grady McWhiney and Perry D. Jamieson's *Attack and Die: Civil War Military Tactics and the Southern Heritage* (Tuscaloosa: University of Alabama Press, 1984). For critiques of this interpretation, see Griffith, *Battle Tactics*, 189–192; Hess, *Rifle Musket*, 1–8; Earl J. Hess, *Civil War Infantry Tactics: Training, Combat, and Small-Unit Effectiveness* (Baton Rouge: Louisiana State University Press, 2015), xi–xx.

12. Nosworthy, *Bloody Crucible*, 597–598.

13. Quoted in Nosworthy, *Bloody Crucible*, 595; Fletcher, *Rebel Private*, 71; quoted in Larry M. Strayer and Richard A. Baumgartner, eds., *Echoes of Battle: The Atlanta Campaign* (Huntington, WV: Blue Acorn Press, 1991), 280.

14. J. K. Merrifield, "Opdyke's Brigade at Franklin," *Confederate Veteran* 13 (December 1905): 564; J. D. Remington, Statement of, in *History of the Seventy-Third Illinois*, 450; W. M. Crook, "W. M. Crook's Heroism at Franklin," *Confederate Veteran* 5 (June 1897): 303.

15. Hess, *Civil War Infantry Tactics*, 70; Pete Kautz, "The American Training Bayonet, 1858–1912," *Alliance Martial Arts*, http://www.alliancemartialarts.com/; George B. McClellan, *Manual of Bayonet Exercise: Prepared for the Use of the Army of the United States* (Philadelphia: Lippincott, Grambo, 1852), vi–viii; R. Milton Cary, *Skirmishers' Drill and Bayonet Exercise as Now Used in the French Army with Suggestions for the Soldier in Actual Conflict* (Richmond: West & Johnston, 1861), title page.

16. McClellan, *Manual of Bayonet Exercise*, 1–4.

17. "Improved Bayonet Guard," *Scientific American* 7, no. 13 (September 27, 1862): 200.

18. Dan Emmett, *Within Arm's Length: A Secret Service Agent's Definitive Inside Account of Protecting the President* (New York: St. Martin's Press, 2014), 23; Stephen Trask, "British Bayonet Tactics for US Army," *Arms and the Man* 62, no. 10 (June 2, 1917): 192.

19. Kingman, *Tramping Out the Vintage*, 263–264; John J. Berney, "To all at Home," April 4, 1863, John J. Barney Papers, WHS; Louis J. Lamson, *The Civil War Diary of Louis J. Lamson, Corporal, Company A, 30th Wisconsin Infantry Regiment Including a Complete Roster of the 30th Wisconsin Infantry Regiment, Volunteers,* comp. Richard N. Larsen, August 26, 1863, Wisconsin Veterans Museum, Madison.

20. Ogden Greenough to "Dear Ma," October 31, 1861, Ogden Greenough Letters, Civil War Museum (Kenosha, WI).

21. Lucius B. Swift to John Bigelow, April 18, 1913, John Bigelow Papers, Library of Congress (Washington, DC). Swift's letter includes an extract from his unpublished paper "An Enlisted Man in the Chancellorsville Campaign."

22. Wilbur F. Hinman, *Corporal Si Klegg and His "Pard": How They Lived and Talked, and What They Did and Suffered, While Fighting for the Flag,* 10th ed. (1887; repr., Cleveland: N. G. Hamilton, 1895), 90–91.

23. Grossman, *On Killing*, 120–122.

24. Bob McKenna, quoted in Grossman, *On Killing*, 121.

25. *OR*, vol. 31, pt. 1, p. 101; Sherman, *Memoirs*, 2:394.

26. Grossman, *On Killing*, 120–123.

27. Grossman, *On Killing*, 120.

28. Nosworthy, *Bloody Crucible*, 597–599.

29. Earl J. Hess, *Trench Warfare under Grant and Lee: Field Fortifications in the Overland Campaign* (Chapel Hill: University of North Carolina Press, 2007), xiv–xv; Richard S. Tuthill, "An Artilleryman's Recollections of the Battle of Atlanta," *MOLLUS* 10 (1891): 304–305.

30. Winfield S. Hancock, quoted in McWhiney and Jamieson, *Attack and Die*, 92

31. "Banners of Glory," *Civil War Journal*, American History in Video, dir. Craig Haffner (New York: A&E Television, 1993).

32. Isaac H. Elliott, *History of the Thirty-third Illinois Veteran Volunteer Infantry in the Civil War* (Gibson City, IL: Regimental Association of the Thirty-third Illinois, 1902), 62.

33. Steven E. Woodworth, *Nothing but Victory: The Army of the Tennessee, 1861–1865* (New York: Knopf, 2005), 13–14; Wiley, *Life of Johnny Reb,* 21. The two speeches cited here concerned flag presentations to individual companies (ten companies typically made up a Civil War infantry regiment). Notably, company flags were often locally made, whereas regimental colors tended to be professionally made. Because regiments typically only carried colors representing the entire regiment, most company flags were sent home instead of being used in the field. Nevertheless, the sentiments expressed in presentations of company flags can reasonably be inferred to apply to regimental colors as well.

34. Troiani, *Don Troiani's American Battles: The Art of the Nation at War, 1754–1865* (Mechanicsburg, PA: Stackpole Books, 2006), 150–152; James Houghton, "Journal

of James Houghton," trans. George Wilkinson, *4thMichigan.com*, http://www.4th michigan.com/.

35. John Cheeves Haskell, *The Haskell Memoirs*, ed. Gilbert E. Govan and James W. Livingood (New York: G. P. Putnam's Sons, 1960), 32–34.

36. George N. Carpenter, *History of the Eighth Regiment Vermont Volunteers, 1861–1865* (Boston: Press of Deland & Barta, 1886), 215; S. E. Howard, "The Morning Surprise at Cedar Creek," *MOLLUS* 53 (1900): 419.

37. Joseph Tyler Butts, ed., *A Gallant Captain of the Civil War, Being the Extraordinary Adventures of Friedrich Otto Baron von Fritsch* (New York: F. Tennyson Neely, 1902), 77.

38. Sexton, "Observations and Experiences," 478; Merrifield, "Opdyke's Brigade at Franklin," 563; William J. K. Beaudot, *The 24th Wisconsin Infantry in the Civil War: The Biography of a Regiment* (Mechanicsburg, PA: Stackpole Books, 2003), 337–338.

39. Stephen Z. Starr, *The Union Cavalry in the Civil War: From Fort Sumter to Gettysburg, 1861–1863* (Baton Rouge: Louisiana State University Press, 1979), 136.

40. Gregory J. W. Urwin, *The United States Cavalry: An Illustrated History* (Poole, UK: Blandford Press, 1983), 96, 107–133.

41. Starr, *Union Cavalry*, 136; Thomas Crofts, *History of the Service of the Third Ohio Veteran Volunteer Cavalry in the War for the Preservation of the Union from 1861–1865* (Columbus, OH: Stoneman Press, 1910), 18.

42. John S. Mosby, *The Memoirs of Colonel John S. Mosby* (Boston: Little, Brown, 1917), 30; *Documenting the American South*, http://docsouth.unc.edu/; quoted in Nosworthy, *Bloody Crucible*, 299.

43. Crofts, *History of the Service*, 18–19; Captain Frederick Whittaker (6th NY Cav), quoted in Gervasse Phillips, "Sabre versus Revolver: Mounted Combat in the American Civil War," *Academia.edu*, http://www.academia.edu/, 1.

44. Arthur Fremantle, *Three Months in the Southern States: April, June, 1863* (Mobile, AL: S. H. Goetzel, 1864), 143.

45. Phillips, "Sabre versus Revolver," 6–7.

46. Wickersham, "Personal Recollections," 461–462.

47. Myron Beaumont and Frank M. Myers, quoted in Eric J. Wittenberg, *The Battle of Brandy Station: North America's Largest Cavalry Battle* (Charleston, SC: History Press, 2010), 124, 89; "TYPO," quoted in Styple, *Writing and Fighting from the Army of Northern Virginia*, 230–231.

48. "Incidental Tools of the Artilleryman," *Washington Artillery of New Orleans—5th Company and the 6th Massachusetts Light Artillery*, http://www.oocities.org /heartland/woods/3501/newpage61.htm; Joseph Roberts, *The Hand-Book of Artillery, for the Service of the United States (Army and Militia)* (New York: D. Von Nostrand, 1860), 49. Although in civilian usage "gun" can refer to any firearm, in military terminology, it usually applies exclusively to artillery. In this chapter I follow the latter usage, in which "gun" refers to a cannon.

49. Griffith, *Battle Tactics*, 172–175; Nosworthy, *Bloody Crucible*, 423–424; Pegram, quoted in A. S. Drewry, "The Purcell Battery from Richmond, VA: Its Gallant Conduct at the Battle of Cedar Run," *Southern Historical Society Papers* 27 (1899): 91;

William J. Wray, *History of the Twenty-third Pennsylvania Volunteer Infantry, Birneys Zouaves* (Philadelphia, 1904), 401.

50. Louis Sherfesee, "Reminiscences of a Color-Bearer," in *Memoirs of the Stuart Horse Artillery Battalion: Moorman's and Hart's Batteries*, ed. Robert J. Trout (Knoxville: University of Tennessee Press, 2008), 324; Augustus C. Buell, *The Cannoneer: Recollections of Service in the Army of the Potomac* (Washington, DC: National Tribune, 1890), 288; Lieutenant Aaron P. Baldwin (6th OH Light Artillery) in *OR*, vol. 45, pt. 1, p. 334. Historians have called into question the reliability of Buell's writings, including his Civil War remembrances, based on a number of inconsistencies and falsehoods, such as claiming to have fought at Gettysburg six weeks before his actual enlistment. The remarks cited here do, however, square with other accounts from Cedar Creek and those of other Civil War artillerymen in general. For a critique of Buell's veracity, see Milton W. Hamilton, "Augustus C. Buell: Fraudulent Historian," *Pennsylvania Magazine of History and Biography* 80, no. 4 (October 1956): 478–492.

51. Quoted in Robert K. Krick, *Conquering the Valley: Stonewall Jackson at Port Republic* (Baton Rouge: Louisiana State University Press, 2002), 412; David E. Holt, quoted in Gordon C. Rhea, *The Battles for Spotsylvania Court House and the Road to Yellow Tavern, May 7–12, 1864* (Baton Rouge: Louisiana State University Press, 2005), 271; James Dinkins, quoted in Eric A. Jacobson and Richard A. Rupp, *For Cause and for Country: A Study of the Affair at Spring Hill and the Battle of Franklin* (Franklin, TN: O'More, 2007), 323; George W. Patten, Statement of, in *History of the Seventy-third Illinois* (Springfield, IL: 1890), 462.

### Chapter 5. Hunters of Men: Sharpshooters and Killing

1. Modern militaries have since adopted the term "sniper," a word also well known in the civilian world. The use of "sniper" was virtually unknown in Civil War America (although some veterans did use it in their postwar memoirs). As a result, I have opted to use the more period-correct term "sharpshooter" throughout this chapter, with the exception of using variations of the verb "snipe" to refer to the act of picking off individual soldiers in combat.

2. Hess, *Rifle Musket*, 176.

3. *OR*, vol. 7, p. 887; William S. Dunlop, *Lee's Sharpshooters, or The Forefront of Battle: A Story of Southern Valor That Never Has Been Told* (Little Rock, AR: Tunnam & Pittard, 1899), 75; quoted in Murray, *Letters from Berdan's Sharpshooters*, 136.

4. Hess, *Rifle Musket*, 14–16; Fred L. Ray, *Shock Troops of the Confederacy: The Sharpshooter Battalions of the Army of Northern Virginia* (Asheville, NC: CFS Press, 2006), 4–5; Philipp Elliot-Wright, *Rifleman: Elite Soldiers of the Wars against Napoleon* (London: Publishing News, 2000), 12–33.

5. Philip Katcher, *Sharpshooters of the American Civil War, 1861–65* (Oxford: Osprey, 2002), 6–7, 30–31.

6. *Harper's Weekly*, October 5, 1861, 625, 636.

7. Stevens, *Berdan's United States Sharpshooters*, 10–11.

8. Murray, *Letters from Berdan's Sharpshooters*, 28; Stevens, *Berdan's United States Sharpshooters*, 42, 399–400.

9. Irving Buck, *Cleburne and His Command*, 102–103, 224–225; Hess, *Rifle Musket*, 184–185.

10. White, *Civil War Diary*, 7–8; Luke Emerson Bicknell, "The Sharpshooters," 3, Massachusetts Historical Society (Boston, MA); Ray, *Shock Troops*, 46; Walter R. Montgomery, *Georgia Sharpshooter: The Civil War Diary and Letters of Walter Rhadamanthus Montgomery, 1839–1906* (Macon, GA: Mercer University Press, 1997), 84, 98.

11. Ripley, *Vermont Riflemen*, 35.

12. Quoted in Gilbert, *Stalk and Kill*, 104; Ripley, *Vermont Riflemen*, 179.

13. Grossman, *On Killing*, 171–174; Ray, *Shock Troops*, 23.

14. Quoted in Ray, *Shock Troops*, 146–147; Dunlop, *Lee's Sharpshooters*, 249; Murray, *Letters from Berdan's Sharpshooters*, 8, 23; White, *Civil War Diary*, 260.

15. Dunlop, *Lee's Sharpshooters*, 262; White, *Civil War Diary*, 260.

16. Berry Benson, *Berry Benson's Civil War Book: Memoir of a Confederate Scout and Sharpshooter*, ed. Susan Williams Benson (Athens: University of Georgia Press, 1962), 68; Dunlop, *Lee's Sharpshooters*, 49.

17. Henry Uptmore, quoted in *Eyewitnesses at the Battle of Fort Donelson*, comp. David R. Logsdon (Nashville, TN: Kettle Mills Press, 1998), 23.

18. Charles F. Hubert, *History of the Fiftieth Regiment, Illinois Volunteer Infantry in the War for the Union* (Kansas City, MO: Western Veteran, 1894), 77–78.

19. Daniel Boyd (7th SC) in Jones, *Boys of Diamond Hill*, 124.

20. Hubert, *History of the Fiftieth Regiment*, 77–78; Henry Uptmore, quoted in Logsdon, *Fort Donelson*, 23; Mensendike, quoted in Hubert, *History of the Fiftieth Regiment*, 78.

21. Justin S. Solonick, *Engineering Victory: The Union Siege of Vicksburg* (Carbondale: Southern Illinois University Press, 2015), 133–137; William Reid diary, June 10, 1863, 15th Illinois Infantry, Diaries and Letters Files, Vicksburg National Military Park (VNMP), Vicksburg, MS; George Ditto Diary, June 6, 1863, Abraham Lincoln Presidential Library and Museum (Springfield, IL); Osborn H. Oldroyd, *A Soldier's Story of the Siege of Vicksburg* (Springfield, IL, 1885), 34.

22. Edward N. Potter diary, June 6, 1863, Wisconsin Veterans Museum, Madison.

23. Robert F. Ward, quoted in Dunlop, *Lee's Sharpshooters*, 421; quoted in Murray, *Letters from Berdan's Sharpshooters*, 34; Aschmann, *Memoirs of a Swiss Officer*, 125–126; John Mason Memoir, Gregory A. Coco Collection, GNMP.

24. Dunlop, *Lee's Sharpshooters*, 53; quoted in Gilbert, *Stalk and Kill*, 36–37, 41.

25. Ripley, *Vermont Riflemen*, 24–25.

26. White, *Civil War Diary*, 235–236.

27. White, *Civil War Diary*, 291.

28. Quoted in Christopher Kent Wilson, "Marks of Honor and Death: *Sharpshooter* and the Peninsular Campaign of 1862," in *Winslow Homer: Paintings of the Civil War*, ed. Marc Simpson (San Francisco, CA: Fine Arts Museums of San Francisco, 1988), 38.

29. Robert Stiles, *Four Years under Marse Robert* (New York: Neale, 1910), 290; Frank Wilkeson, *Recollections of a Private Soldier in the Army of the Potomac* (New York: G. P. Putnam's Sons, 1887), 120–121.

30. Wilson, "Marks of Honor and Death," 37; Earl J. Hess, *The Union Soldier in*

Battle: Enduring the Ordeal of Combat (Lawrence: University Press of Kansas, 1997), 107; Bruce Catton, A Stillness at Appomattox (Garden City, NY: Doubleday, 1953), 167; Briton Cooper Busch, Bunker Hill to Bastogne: Elite Forces and American Society (Washington, DC: Potomac Books, 2006), 72.

31. Wilson, "Marks of Honor and Death," 37.

32. Quoted in Gilbert, Stalk and Kill, 37.

33. Ray, Shock Troops, 119.

34. Frank Elliot, "A June Evening before Atlanta: Cothran's Battery and Knipe's Brigade Repulses Stevenson's Division," National Tribune, October 26, 1905, 3.

35. Gilbert, Stalk and Kill, 103; Ed Porter Thompson, History of the Orphan Brigade (Louisville, KY: Lewis N. Thompson, 1898), 243; quoted in William B. Green, Letters from a Sharpshooter: The Civil War Letters of William B. Green, The Civil War Letters of Private William B. Greene, Co. G, 2nd United States Sharpshooters (Berdan's) Army of the Potomac, 1861–1865, comp. William H. Hastings (Belleville, WI: Historic Publications, 1993), 290; Stevens, Berdan's United States Sharpshooters, 340.

36. S. Millett Thompson, Thirteenth Regiment of New Hampshire Volunteer Infantry in the War of the Rebellion, 1861–1865: A Diary Covering Three Years and a Day (Boston: Houghton, Mifflin, 1888), 144; Anonymous in Styple, Writing and Fighting from the Army of Northern Virginia, 293.

37. Quoted in Styple, Writing and Fighting the Civil War, 86; John A. Edmiston to William T. Rigby, March 8, 1902, 20th Illinois Regimental File, VNMP; Green, Johnny Green, 127–128.

38. Murray, Letters from Berdan's Sharpshooters, 34; quoted in Styple, Writing and Fighting from the Army of Northern Virginia, 104; John Mason Memoir, Gregory A. Coco Collection, GNMP; Fletcher, Rebel Private, 15; quoted in Stevens, Berdan's United States Sharpshooters, 462–463.

39. Aschmann, Memoirs of a Swiss Officer, 125–126; Dunlop, Lee's Sharpshooters, 163.

40. White, Civil War Diary, 240–241.

41. Aschmann, Memoirs of a Swiss Officer, 170–172.

42. Ripley, Vermont Riflemen, 190; White, Civil War Diary, 198–199.

43. White, Civil War Diary, 229; Upson, With Sherman to the Sea, 159.

44. Quoted in Gilbert, Stalk and Kill, 50.

### Chapter 6. Murder and Mercy: The Extremes of Killing

1. Styple, Writing and Fighting the Civil War, 34; Colonel Henry Dougherty, quoted in Daniel N. Rolph, My Brother's Keeper: Union and Confederate Soldiers' Acts of Mercy during the Civil War (Mechanicsburg, PA: Stackpole Books, 2002), 50.

2. Dean S. Thomas, Round Ball to Rimfire: A History of Civil War Small Arms Ammunition (Gettysburg, PA: Thomas, 1997), 220–221, 237; Hess, Rifle Musket, 77–79.

3. Crook, "W. M. Crook's Heroism at Franklin," 303; Mayo, Civil War Letters, 208.

4. McPherson, Battle Cry of Freedom, 311.

5. Woodworth, Nothing but Victory, 590; Ferguson, On to Atlanta, 24; Adin Ballou Underwood, The Three Years' Service of the Thirty-third Mass. Infantry Regiment,

1862–1865: And the Campaigns and Battles of Chancellorsville, Beverley's Ford, Gettysburg, Wauhatchie, Chattanooga, Atlanta, the March to the Sea and through the Carolinas, in which It Took Part (Boston: A. Williams, 1881), 271.

6. Widney, Campaigning with Uncle Billy, 354–355.

7. Lee Kennett, Marching through Georgia: The Story of Soldiers and Civilians during Sherman's Campaign (New York: HarperCollins, 1995), 263–264; Woodworth, Nothing but Victory, 626; Jeffry D. Wert, Mosby's Rangers (New York: Simon & Schuster, 1990), 211; E.D.J. to "Dear Parents," December 18, 1864, Galveston Weekly News, 1865, http://apps.uttyler.edu/.

8. Casler, Four Years in the Stonewall Brigade, 242; Steven E. Woodworth, e-mail message to author, October 17, 2014.

9. OR vol. 43, pt. 2, p. 202; OR vol. 39, pt. 3, pp. 713–714; Mark Grimsley, The Hard Hand of War: Union Military Policy toward Southern Civilians, 1861–1865 (Cambridge: Cambridge University Press, 1995), 175; Mark E. Neely Jr., The Civil War and the Limits of Destruction (Cambridge, MA: Harvard University Press, 2007), 117–120.

10. Kennett, Marching through Georgia, 304–307.

11. OR vol. 47, pt. 2, pp. 546, 596; OR vol. 39, pt. 2, p. 422.

12. OR vol. 47, pt. 2, pp. 546, 597; Joseph T. Glatthaar, The March to the Sea and Beyond: Sherman's Troops in the Savannah and Carolinas Campaigns (New York: New York University Press, 1985), 72–74; Kennett, Marching through Georgia, 304–307.

13. Woodworth, Nothing but Victory, 618–622.

14. Works that argue for the relative restraint of Union hard war policy and rarity of crimes toward Southern civilians include Glatthaar, March to the Sea; Grimsley, Hard Hand of War; Kennett, Marching through Georgia; Edward Caudill and Paul Ashdown, Sherman's March in Myth and Memory (Lanham, MD: Rowman & Littlefield, 2008); Neely, Civil War.

15. Henry Kyd Douglas, I Rode with Stonewall, Being Chiefly the War Experiences of the Youngest Member of Jackson's Staff from the John Brown Raid to the Hanging of Mrs. Surratt (Chapel Hill: University of North Carolina Press, 1940), 315.

16. Quoted in Timothy J. Orr, "'A viler enemy in our rear': Pennsylvania Soldiers Confront the North's Antiwar Movement," in The View from the Ground: Experiences of Civil War Soldiers, ed. Aaron Sheehan-Dean (Lexington: University Press of Kentucky, 2007), 178–179, 180; Cooke, Badger Boy, 49.

17. Quoted in Orr, "A viler enemy in our rear," 172; Ferguson, On to Atlanta, 24.

18. Quoted in Bonner, Soldier's Pen, 146; Mayo, Civil War Letters, 229; Hulbert, One Battle Too Many, 218.

19. Quoted in Orr, "A viler enemy in our rear," 179; Cooke, Badger Boy, 179; Brobst, Well, Mary, 72, 93.

20. Mark E. Neely Jr., Lincoln and the Triumph of the Nation: Constitutional Conflict in the American Civil War (Chapel Hill: University of North Carolina Press, 2011), 154–155.

21. Orr, "A viler enemy in our rear," 174, 189.

22. Orr, "A viler enemy in our rear," 180, 189.

23. OR, vol. 43, pt. 1, p. 811; Jay W. Simson, Custer and the Front Royal Executions of 1864 (Jefferson, NC: McFarland, 2009), 11–19, 82–85.

24. Kevin H. Siepel, *Rebel: The Life and Times of John Singleton Mosby* (Lincoln: University of Nebraska Press, 2008), 128–130.

25. *OR*, vol. 43, pt. 2, p. 920; Siepel, *Rebel*, 30.

26. Woodworth, *Nothing but Victory*, 626–627; A[lvan] E. Sample, *A History of Company "A," 30th Illinois Infantry* (Lyons, KS, 1907), 7.

27. Burke Davis, *Sherman's March* (New York: Random House, 1980), 204; Clint Johnson, *Touring the Carolinas' Civil War Sites* (Winston-Salem, NC: John F. Blair, 1996), 334.

28. Mathis, *In the Land of the Living*, 9–10, 115.

29. John Mason Memoir, Gregory A. Coco Collection, GNMP.

30. Steven E. Woodworth, *Beneath a Northern Sky: A Short History of the Gettysburg Campaign* (Lanham, MD: Rowman & Littlefield, 2008), 60–61; Dawes, *Service with the Sixth Wisconsin Volunteers*, 167–169.

31. J. M. Weiser, "Trigg's Brigade at Chickamauga," *Confederate Veteran* 34 (December 1926): 453.

32. Sword, *Courage under Fire*, 164.

33. Rutherford B. Hayes, "Incidents at the Battle of Cedar Creek," *MOLLUS* 4 (1896): 239.

34. Green, *Johnny Green*, 160; Sexton, "Observations and Experiences," 478–479.

35. Enos Bloom to "Dear Father," July 12, 1862, "Enos Bloom Writes Home," *PA-Roots,* http://www.pa-roots.com/.

36. A. R. Gibbons, *The Recollections of an Old Confederate Soldier* (Shelbyville, MO: Herald Print, ca. 1931), 8; Crumpton, "In the Atlanta Campaign," 1921): 381.

37. Quoted in Charles Carleton Coffin, *Redeeming the Republic: The Third Period of the War of the Rebellion, in the Year 1864* (New York: Harper & Brothers, 1889), 194–196; Jacobson and Rupp, *For Cause and for Country*, 342–343.

38. Quoted in James I. Robertson Jr., *Stonewall Jackson: The Man, the Soldier, the Legend* (New York: Macmillan, 1997), 424, 866. Robertson, Jackson's preeminent modern biographer, observes that this anecdote "appears at various times and in slightly altered versions throughout Jackson studies." In some variations, Jackson advises to "kill the brave ones" because "they lead on the others." I have chosen to follow Robertson's example and accept the account told by Colonel John M. Patton, 21st Virginia, who described it as an exchange between Jackson and himself.

39. Tuthill, "Artilleryman's Recollections," 308.

40. Giles, *Rags and Hope*, 201.

41. W. T. Barnes, "An Incident of Kenesaw Mountain," *Confederate Veteran* 30 (1922): 49.

42. Joseph B. Kershaw, "Richard Kirkland, the Humane Hero of Fredericksburg," *Southern Historical Society Papers* 8 (1880): 186–188; Rolph, *My Brother's Keeper,* 34–36.

43. Kershaw, "Richard Kirkland," 188; Rolph, *My Brother's Keeper,* 36–37.

44. Mayo, *Civil War Letters*, 234; Logsdon, *Fort Donelson*, 52.

45. Mathis, *In the Land of the Living*, 77; Thomas F. Galwey, quoted in Linderman, *Embattled Courage*, 72; Newt Bosworth Diary, January 27, 1864, GNMP.

46. Linderman, *Embattled Courage*, 72; August V. Kautz, *The 1865 Customs of Ser-*

vice for Non-Commissioned Officers and Soldiers, 2nd ed. (Mechanicsburg, PA: Stackpole Books, 2001), 47–50.

47. Richard A. Baumgartner and Larry M. Strayer, eds., *Echoes of Battle: The Struggle for Chattanooga* (Huntington, WV: Blue Acorn Press, 1996), 234; R. M. Collins, *Chapters from the Unwritten History of the War between the States, or The Incidents in the Life of a Confederate Soldier in Camp, on the March, in the Great Battles, and in Prison* (St. Louis, MO: Nixon-Jones, 1893), 168.

48. Anonymous soldier-correspondent, quoted in Styple, *Writing and Fighting from the Army of Northern Virginia*, 299–300.

49. Ferguson, *On to Atlanta*, 53, 76.

50. Malcolm Brown and Shirley Seaton, *Christmas Truce* (New York: Hippocrene Books, 1984), 39–40, 198.

51. Cooke, *Badger Boy*, 105; Chambers, *Blood and Sacrifice*, 78.

52. Chauncey C. Baker, "And a Little Child Shall Lead Them," *Confederate Veteran* 28 (1928): 446.

53. James King Newton, *A Wisconsin Boy in Dixie: Selected Letters of James K. Newton*, ed. Stephen E. Ambrose (Madison: University of Wisconsin Press, 1961), 72.

54. George W. Gore to *Taylors Falls Reporter*, January 12, 1862, Civil War Letters, WHS; quoted in Rolfs, "No nearer heaven now," 122.

55. Joseph Bowker Diary, June 8, 1863, 42nd Ohio Regimental File, VNMP; Robert D. Smith, *Confederate Diary of Robert D. Smith*, ed. Jill K. Garrett (Columbia, TN: Captain James Madison Sparkman Chapter, United Daughters of the Confederacy, 1997), 143; Holmes, *52d OVI*, 183.

56. Wiley, *Life of Billy Yank*, 357; Wiley, *Civil War Diary*, 53; Coe, *Mine Eyes Have Seen the Glory*, 174; Ripley, *Vermont Riflemen*, 181.

57. Styple, *Writing and Fighting the Civil War*, 280.

58. Orson Young to "Dear Parents," June 6, 1864, Orson Young Letters, 92.33.67, Lake County History Archives (Wauconda, IL); quoted in Strayer and Baumgartner, *Echoes of Battle: The Atlanta Campaign*, 132.

59. Leon, *Diary of a Tar Heel*, 49; Brobst, *Well, Mary*, 80.

60. Brobst, *Well, Mary*, 80, 87, 91–92.

### Chapter 7. Killing in Black and White: Race, Combat, and Hate

1. Abraham Lincoln, "Reply to Emancipation Memorial Presented by Chicago Christians of All Denominations," September 13, 1862, and Abraham Lincoln, "Address on Colonization to a Deputation of Negroes," August 14, 1862, both in "The Collected Works of Abraham Lincoln," *Abraham Lincoln Association*, http://quod.lib.umich.edu/l/lincoln/.

2. Peter Kolchin, *American Slavery, 1619–1877* (New York: Hill and Wang, 1993), 18–24, 120–127.

3. Kolchin, *American Slavery*, 121–122; Theodore Dwight Weld, *American Slavery as It Is: Testimony of a Thousand Witnesses* (New York: American Anti-slavery Society), 62–63, 77; Stephen B. Oates, *To Purge This Land with Blood: A Biography of John Brown*, 2nd ed. (Amherst: University of Massachusetts Press, 1984), 12.

4. Thomas D. Morris, *Southern Slavery and the Law, 1619–1860* (Chapel Hill: University of North Carolina Press, 1996), 161–181.

5. Frederick Douglass, *Narrative of the Life of Frederick Douglass, an American Slave,* 24, *Documenting the American South,* http://docsouth.unc.edu/; quoted in Noah Andre Trudeau, *Like Men of War: Black Troops in the Civil War, 1862–1865* (Boston: Little, Brown, 1998), 275.

6. Thomas Jefferson to John Holmes, April 22, 1820, *Library of Congress,* http://www.loc.gov/; Linda Barnickel, *Milliken's Bend: A Civil War Battle in History and Memory* (Baton Rouge: Louisiana State University Press, 2013), 1–2, 13.

7. John Bell Robinson, *Pictures of Slavery and Anti-slavery: Advantages of Negro Slavery and the Benefits of Negro Freedom. Morally, Socially, and Politically Considered* (Philadelphia, 1863), 110.

8. Oates, *To Purge This Land,* 294–295.

9. Trudeau, *Like Men of War,* 8; Lincoln, "Reply to Emancipation Memorial"; Charles F. Adams Jr. to Charles F. Adams Sr., November 2, 1864, in *A Cycle of Adams Letters, 1861–1865,* ed. Worthington C. Ford (Boston: Houghton Mifflin, 1920), 2:217; quoted in John David Smith, "Let Us All Be Grateful That We Have Colored Troops That Will Fight," in *Black Soldiers in Blue: African American Troops in the Civil War Era,* ed. John David Smith (Chapel Hill: University of North Carolina Press, 2002), 10; quoted in Trudeau, *Like Men of War,* 24; quoted in Murray M. Horowitz, "Ben Butler and the Negro: 'Miracles Are Occurring.'" *Louisiana History* 17, no. 2 (Spring 1976): 159.

10. J[ames] C. Derby, *Fifty Years among Authors, Books, and Publishers* (New York: G. W. Carleton, 1884), 428–430; quoted in George S. Burkhardt, *Confederate Rage, Yankee Wrath: No Quarter in the Civil War* (Carbondale: Southern Illinois University Press, 2007), 25.

11. "An Illinois Colored Regiment," *Chicago Tribune,* June 15, 1863, 1; quoted in Burkhardt, *Confederate Rage,* 22; Derby, *Fifty Years,* 429–430.

12. Quoted in Edwin S. Redkey, ed., *A Grand Army of Black Men: Letters from African-American Soldiers in the Union Army, 1861–1865* (Cambridge: Cambridge University Press, 1992), ix; for black soldiers' emphasis on equality in the US Army, see chaps. 6, 7, and 8.

13. James Henry Gooding, *On the Altar of Freedom: A Black Civil War Soldier's Letters from the Front,* ed. Virginia Matzke Adams (Amherst: University of Massachusetts Press, 1991), 16; Redkey, *Grand Army,* 14, 97–98, 207.

14. Quoted in Allen C. Guelzo, *Fateful Lightning: A New History of the Civil War and Reconstruction* (Oxford: Oxford University Press, 2012), 184; quoted in Joseph Thomas Wilson, *The Black Phalanx: A History of the Negro Soldiers of the United States in the Wars of 1775–1812, 1861–'65* (Hartford, CT: American, 1890), 311; Frank Kenfield, "Captured by Rebels: A Vermonter at Petersburg, 1864," *Vermont History* 36, no. 4 (Autumn 1968): 233.

15. Cooke, *Badger Boy,* 81; Redkey, *Grand Army,* 145, 147–148.

16. David Walls, "Marching Song of the First Arkansas Colored Regiment: A Contested Attribution," *Arkansas Historical Quarterly* 66, no. 4 (Winter 2007): 401, 409. Miller's version of the song, "Marching Song of the First Arkansas Colored

Regiment," was associated with his own regiment, later designated the 46th USCT. Sojourner Truth's version, "The Valiant Soldiers," was associated with the 1st Michigan Colored Infantry (102nd USCT). William Wells Brown, *The Negro in the American Rebellion: His Heroism and His Fidelity* (Boston: Lee & Shepard, 1867), 234; "Sic semper tyrannis—22th Regt. US Colored Troops," photographic print, Prints and Photographs Online Catalog, *Library of Congress,* http://www.loc.gov/.

17. Dudley Taylor Cornish, *The Sable Arm: Black Troops in the Union Army, 1861–1865,* 2nd ed. (Lawrence: University Press of Kansas, 1987), 160; quoted in Gregory J. W. Urwin, "'We Cannot Treat Negroes . . . as Prisoners of War': Racial Atrocities and Reprisals in Civil War Arkansas," in *Black Flag Over Dixie: Racial Atrocities and Reprisals in the Civil War,* ed. Gregory J. W. Urwin (Carbondale: Southern Illinois University Press, 2004), 140.

18. Cornish, *Sable Arm,* 161–162, 168–169; Burkhardt, *Confederate Rage,* 1.

19. Quoted in Burkhardt, *Confederate Rage,* 39; D. H. Hamilton, *History of Company M: First Texas Volunteer Infantry, Hood's Brigade, Longstreet's Corps, Army of the Confederate States of America* (Waco, TX: W. M. Morrison, 1962), 62; quoted in Trudeau, *Like Men of War,* 371.

20. Quoted in Arthur W. Bergeron Jr., "The Battle of Olustee," in Smith, *Black Soldiers in Blue,* 146.

21. Burkhardt, *Confederate Rage,* 1.

22. Trudeau, *Like Men of War,* 3–6; Richard Lowe, "Battle on the Levee: The Fight at Milliken's Bend," in Smith, *Black Soldiers in Blue,* 107.

23. Lowe, "Battle on the Levee," 108–113; Barnickel, *Milliken's Bend,* 79–80.

24. Barnickel, *Milliken's Bend,* 87–91; Lowe, "Battle on the Levee," 117–122.

25. Barnickel, *Milliken's Bend,* 90; Richard P. Sevier, comp., "Battle of Milliken's Bend, Madison Parish, LA June 7, 1863," *RootsWeb,* http://www.rootsweb.ancestry.com/.

26. Barnickel, *Milliken's Bend,* 91–96; Lowe, "Battle on the Levee," 121–124.

27. Barnickel, *Milliken's Bend,* 103–104, 167; Lowe, "Battle on the Levee," 126–128.

28. Lowe, "Battle on the Levee," 128; Barnickel, *Milliken's Bend,* 108.

29. *OR,* ser. 2, vol. 6, pp. 21–22; Barnickel, *Milliken's Bend,* 112–115.

30. Barnickel, *Milliken's Bend,* 96.

31. Trudeau, *Like Men of War,* 157–161.

32. Richard L. Fuchs, *An Unerring Fire: The Massacre at Fort Pillow* (Rutherford, NJ: Fairleigh Dickinson University Press, 1994), 38–43.

33. Captain Thomas P. Gray reached Union-held Memphis by way of Fort Pillow, where he had informed Maj. Booth that he had not heard anything from the Confederates indicating a planned attack on Fort Pillow. John Gauss, *Black Flag! Black Flag! The Battle at Fort Pillow* (Lanham, MD: University Press of America, 2003), 46–48.

34. Fuchs, *Unerring Fire,* 26–32.

35. Fuchs, *Unerring Fire,* 32–36.

36. Fuchs, *Unerring Fire,* 51–52; Trudeau, *Like Men of War,* 160–163.

37. Fuchs, *Unerring Fire,* 56–57.

38. Fuchs, *Unerring Fire,* 57–58; Trudeau, *Like Men of War,* 164–166.

39. Carl Sandburg, *Abraham Lincoln: The Prairie Years and the War Years* (Pleasantville, NY: Reader's Digest, 1970), 421; Trudeau, *Like Men of War*, 110, 112.

40. US Congress, *Report of the Joint Committee on the Conduct of the War on the Fort Pillow Massacre and on Returned Prisoners*, 38th Cong., 1st sess., Rep. Com. 63 and 68, 1864, 25–27.

41. Trudeau, *Like Men of War*, 160–161; George Bodnia, ed. "Fort Pillow 'Massacre': Observations of a Minnesotan," *Minnesota History Magazine*, Minnesota Historical Society, http://collections.mnhs.org/MNHistoryMagazine/articles/43/v43 i05p186-190.pdf; Burkhardt, *Confederate Rage*, 111–113; US Congress, *Report of the Joint Committee*, 94.

42. Burkhardt, *Confederate Rage*, 110, 113; Trudeau, *Like Men of War*, 167.

43. Trudeau, *Like Men of War*, 167–168; US Congress, *Report of the Joint Committee*, 96; *OR*, vol. 32, pt. 1, p. 610.

44. Trudeau, *Like Men of War*, 168; Burkhardt, *Confederate Rage*, 116–117; US Congress, *Report of the Joint Committee*, 1–4; Derek W. Frisby, "'Remember Fort Pillow!': Politics, Atrocity Propaganda, and the Evolution of Hard War," in Urwin, *Black Flag Over Dixie*, 118–119.

45. Robert Hale Strong, *A Yankee Private's Civil War*, ed. Ashley Halsey (Chicago: Henry Regnery, 1961), 16.

46. Quoted in Burkhardt, *Confederate Rage*, 110, 122.

47. For refutation of drunkenness among the Federals, see Gauss, *Black Flag*, 130–131; John Cimprich, *Fort Pillow, a Civil War Massacre, and Public Memory* (Baton Rouge: Louisiana State University Press, 2005), 111–112.

48. Fuchs, *Unerring Fire*, 109; Cimprich, *Fort Pillow*, 112.

49. Fuchs, *Unerring Fire*, 109; Cimprich, *Fort Pillow*, 112–113.

50. Burkhardt, *Confederate Rage*, 195; Wiley, quoted in Thomas D. Mays, "The Battle of Saltville," in Smith, *Black Soldiers in Blue*, 200.

51. Trudeau, *Like Men of War*, 271; Mays, "Battle of Saltville," 208, 211.

52. Thomas D. Mays, *The Saltville Massacre* (Abilene, TX: McWhiney Foundation Press, 1998), 55; Mays, "Battle of Saltville," 208–211.

53. George Dallas Mosgrove, *Kentucky Cavaliers in Dixie, or The Reminiscences of a Confederate Cavalry Man*, ed. Bell I. Wiley (Jackson, TN: McCowat-Mercer Press, 1957), 206–207.

54. Mays, "Battle of Saltville," 212; Mays, *Saltville Massacre*, 58–59.

55. Mosgrove, *Kentucky Cavaliers*, 207.

56. Mays, *Saltville Massacre*, 66.

57. Bryce A. Suderow, "The Battle of the Crater: The Civil War's Worst Massacre," in Urwin, *Black Flag Over Dixie*, 203; Burkhardt, *Confederate Rage*, 160.

58. Alan Axelrod, *The Horrid Pit: The Battle of the Crater, the Civil War's Cruelest Mission* (New York: Carroll & Graf, 2007), 91–99.

59. Trudeau, *Like Men of War*, 236–238; Axelrod, *Horrid Pit*, 123; Suderow, "Battle of the Crater," 203–204.

60. Axelrod, *Horrid Pit*, 179–187; Suderow, "Battle of the Crater," 204–206.

61. Haskell, *Haskell Memoirs*, 77; Dorsey N. Binion to "Dear Sister," August 1, 1864, Michael P. Musick Collection, USAHEC.

62. P. M. Vance, "Incidents of the Crater Battle," *Confederate Veteran* 14 (April 1906): 178; B. F. Phillips, "Wilcox's Alabamians in Virginia," *Confederate Veteran* 15 (November 1907): 490.

63. George S. Bernard, "The Battle of the Crater, July 30, 1864," 12, *Civil War Times Illustrated* Collection, USAHEC.

64. Quoted in Burkhardt, *Confederate Rage*, 168; John S. Wise, *The End of an Era* (Boston: Houghton, Mifflin, 1901), 366; Kenfield, "Captured by Rebels," 233.

65. George L. Kilmer, "The Dash into the Crater," *Century Magazine*, September 1887, 775–776.

66. George Clark, "Alabamians in the Crater Battle," *Confederate Veteran* 3 (1895): 69; Richard Slotkin, *No Quarter: The Battle of the Crater, 1864* (New York: Random House, 2009), 292–293.

67. Slotkin, *No Quarter*, 293–294; John C. Featherston, "Graphic Account of Battle of Crater," *Southern Historical Society Papers* 33 (1905): 373.

68. Suderow argues that forty-two soldiers from the Fourth Division were incorrectly (perhaps prematurely) counted as missing, so he gives the two USCT brigades an MIA count of 368 instead of 410. Burkhardt lists 658 MIA, but it is not clear from the text or his sources how he arrived at this figure. Suderow, "Battle of the Crater," 207–208; Burkhardt, *Confederate Rage*, 172.

69. Lynn, *Battle*, 231–251.

70. Burkhardt, *Confederate Rage*, 146–147; Redkey, *Grand Army*, 46.

71. Burkhardt, *Confederate Rage*, 238; Charles F. Adams Jr. to Charles F. Adams Sr., June 19, 1864, in Ford, *Cycle of Adams Letters*, 2:154.

72. W. A. Price, quoted in Trudeau, *Like Men of War*, 169; Colonel F. A. Eastman, quoted in Edward A. Miller Jr., *The Black Civil War Soldiers of Illinois: The Story of the Twenty-ninth US Colored Infantry* (Columbia: University of South Carolina Press, 1998), 38–39; William Baird, quoted in Burkhardt, *Confederate Rage*, 163.

73. Trudeau, *Like Men of War*, 268–269, 406–407; Burkhardt, *Confederate Rage*, 238–239.

74. Richard S. Thompson, *While My Country Is in Danger: The Life and Letters of Lieutenant Colonel Richard S. Thompson, Twelfth New Jersey Volunteers*, ed. Gerry Harder Poriss and Ralph Gibbs Poriss (Hamilton, NY: Edmonston, 1994), 109; Burkhardt, *Confederate Rage*, 146.

75. Quoted in Wilson, *Black Phalanx*, 422.

### Epilogue

1. Edward Steers, *Blood on the Moon: The Assassination of Abraham Lincoln* (Lexington: University Press of Kentucky, 2005), 162.

2. Coe, *Mine Eyes Have Seen the Glory*, 224; Squier, *This Wilderness of War*, 104.

3. William H. H. Barker (3rd IA Cavalry), "Memories of the Civil War, 1926," 142, *Civil War Times Illustrated* Collection, USAHEC.

4. Buck, *With the Old Confeds*, 134–137.

5. Elisha Hunt Rhodes, *All for the Union: The Civil War Diary and Letters of Elisha Hunt Rhodes*, ed. Robert Hunt Rhodes (New York: Orion Books, 1991), 229–230.

6. Joshua L. Chamberlain, *The Passing of the Armies: An Account of the Final Cam-*

paign of the Army of the Potomac, Based upon Personal Reminiscences of the Fifth Army Corps (1915; repr., Gettysburg, PA: Stan Clark Military Books, 1994), 258–261.

7. Phillips, "Brothers' War," 67–68; Chamberlain, *Passing of the Armies*, 267–268.

8. John Mason, quoted in James I. Robertson Jr., *The Civil War's Common Soldier* (Fort Washington, PA: Eastern National, 2006), 51; John N. Opie, *A Rebel Cavalryman with Lee, Stuart, and Jackson* (Chicago: W. B. Conkey, 1899), 255.

9. John A. Lomax and Alan Lomax, *American Ballads and Folk Songs* (1934; repr., New York: Dover, 1994), 535–539; Christian McWhirter, *Battle Hymns: The Power and Popularity of Music in the Civil War* (Chapel Hill: University of North Carolina Press, 2012), 175–176; Fletcher, *Rebel Private*, 194–195.

## Abbreviations

GNMP    Gettysburg National Military Park, Gettysburg, PA

MOLLUS  *Papers of the Military Order of the Loyal Legion of the United States.* 56 vols., various publishers and dates; reprint, Wilmington, NC: Broadfoot, 1994

OR    *Official Records* (US War Department, *The War of the Rebellion: Official Records of the Union and Confederate Armies,* 128 vols. [Washington, DC: Government Printing Office, 1881–1901]; except as otherwise noted, all references are to series 1)

USAHEC  US Army Heritage and Education Center, Carlisle, PA

VNMP    Vicksburg National Military Park, Vicksburg, MS

WHS    Wisconsin Historical Society, Madison

## Unpublished Primary Sources

**Abraham Lincoln Presidential Library and Museum (Springfield, IL)**
    George Ditto Diary
    W. C. Littlefield Letters

**Civil War Museum (Kenosha, WI)**
    Elmer E. Ellsworth Archival Collection
        Ogden Greenough Letters

**Duke University (Durham, NC)**
    David M. Rubenstein Rare Book and Manuscript Library
        Charles S. Powell Memoirs

**Gettysburg National Military Park (Gettysburg, PA)**
    7th Michigan Infantry File
        Samuel C. Hodgman, "'Gone a Sogerine': The Civil War Experiences of Samuel Chase Hodgman, Seventh Michigan Volunteer Infantry Regiment, May 27, 1861–Januray 4, 1864"
        Ralph H. Rea letter
    Gregory A. Coco Collection
        Private Newt Bosworth, Co. F, 31st VA IN Letters and Diary, 1861–1865
        Corporal John Mason, Co. A, 9th AL IN Memoir, 1861–1864

**Lake County History Archives (Wauconda, IL)**
Minto Family Papers
Alexander R. Thain letter
Orson Young Letters

**Library of Congress (Washington, DC)**
John Bigelow Papers
Lucius B. Swift letter

**Library of Virginia (Richmond, VA)**
Frank Potts Diary

**Massachusetts Historical Society (Boston, MA)**
Luke Emerson Bicknell, "The Sharpshooters"

**New York State Library (Albany, NY)**
Manuscripts and Special Collections
Orsell Cook Brown Papers

**US Army Heritage and Education Center (Carlisle, PA)**
John W. Ames Papers
Civil War Miscellaneous Collection
Eugene Blackford Memoirs
*Civil War Times Illustrated* Collection
William H. H. Barker, "Memories of the Civil War, 1926"
George S. Bernard, "The Battle of the Crater, July 30, 1864"
Manuscript Archive
Hugh C. Perkins Letters
Michael P. Musick Collection
Dorsey N. Binion Letter

**University of North Carolina at Chapel Hill**
Documenting the American South
Southern Historical Collection
William James Harriss Bellamy Papers

**Vicksburg National Military Park (Vicksburg, MS)**
20th Illinois Regimental File
John A. Edmiston letter
42nd Ohio Regimental File
Joseph Bowker Diary
Diaries and Letters Files
William Reid Diary

**Wisconsin Historical Society (Madison, WI)**
    John J. Barney Papers
    Civil War Letters
    Civil War letters and diary of Luther H. Cowan
    Richard Crane Papers
    Richard Robert Crowe Letters
    Michael Hayes Branniger Cunningham Letters
    George H. Lewis Letters
    Almeron W. Stillwell Diary
    Wisconsin Veterans Reminiscences

**Wisconsin Veterans Museum (Madison, WI)**
    Louis J. Lamson Diary
    Edward N. Potter Diary

## References

Adams, George Washington. *Doctors in Blue: The Medical History of the Union Army in the Civil War.* 1996. Reprint, Baton Rouge: Louisiana State University Press, 1952.

Adams, Michael C. C. *Fighting for Defeat: Union Military Failure in the East, 1861–1865.* Lincoln: University of Nebraska Press, 1992.

Andrews, William H. "Tige Anderson's Brigade at Sharpsburg." *Confederate Veteran* 16 (November 1908): 578–580.

Archambault, Alan H. *The Confederate Infantryman: A Sketchbook.* Gretna, LA: Pelican, 2014.

———. *The Union Infantryman: A Sketchbook.* Gretna, LA: Pelican, 2014.

Armstrong, Marion V., Jr. *Unfurl Those Colors! McClellan, Sumner, and the Second Corps in the Antietam Campaign.* Tuscaloosa: University of Alabama Press, 2008.

Aschmann, Rudolph. *Memoirs of a Swiss Officer in the American Civil War.* Edited by Heinz K. Meier. Bern: Herbert Lang, 1972.

Austin, Aurelia. *Georgia Boys with "Stonewall" Jackson: James Thomas Thompson and the Walton Infantry.* Athens: University of Georgia Press, 1967.

Axelrod, Alan. *The Horrid Pit: The Battle of the Crater, the Civil War's Cruelest Mission.* New York: Carroll & Graf, 2007.

Bailey, Hugh G., ed. "An Alabamian at Shiloh: The Diary of Liberty Independence Nixon." *Alabama Review* 11, no. 2 (April 1958): 144–155.

Baker, Chauncey C. "And a Little Child Shall Lead Them." *Confederate Veteran* 28 (December 1928): 446.

"Banners of Glory." *Civil War Journal.* American History in Video. Directed by Craig Haffner. New York: A&E Television, 1993.

Barnes, W. T. "An Incident of Kenesaw Mountain." *Confederate Veteran* 30 (February 1922): 48–49.

Barnickel, Linda. *Milliken's Bend: A Civil War Battle in History and Memory.* Baton Rouge: Louisiana State University Press, 2013.

Baumgartner, Richard A., and Larry M. Strayer, eds. *Echoes of Battle: The Struggle for Chattanooga.* Huntington, WV: Blue Acorn Press, 1996.

Bean, W. G. "A House Divided: The Civil War Letters of a Virginia Family." *Virginia Magazine of History and Biography* 59, no. 4 (October 1951): 397–422.

Beaudot, William J. K. *The 24th Wisconsin Infantry in the Civil War: The Biography of a Regiment*. Mechanicsburg, PA: Stackpole Books, 2003.

Beecher, Harris H. *Record of the 114th Regiment, NYSV: Where It Went, What It Saw, and What It Did*. Norwich, NY: J. F. Hubbard Jr., 1866.

Benson, Berry. *Berry Benson's Civil War Book: Memoir of a Confederate Scout and Sharpshooter*. Edited by Susan Williams Benson. Athens: University of Georgia Press, 1962.

Bergeron, Arthur W., Jr. "The Battle of Olustee." In Smith, *Black Soldiers in Blue*, 136–149.

Bevens, William E. *Reminiscences of a Private: William E. Bevens of the First Arkansas Infantry, CSA*. Edited by Daniel E. Sutherland. Fayetteville: University of Arkansas Press, 1992.

Bodnia, George, ed. "Fort Pillow 'Massacre': Observations of a Minnesotan." *Minnesota History Magazine*. Minnesota Historical Society. http://collections.mnhs.org/MNHistoryMagazine/articles/43/v43i05p186-190.pdf.

Bonner, Robert E. *The Soldier's Pen: Firsthand Impressions of the Civil War*. New York: Hill & Wang, 2006.

Borton, Benjamin. *On the Parallels, or Chapters of Inner History; a Story of the Rappahannock*. Woodstown, NJ: Monitor-Register Print, 1903.

Boyce, Joseph. "Missourians in the Battle of Franklin." *Confederate Veteran* 24 (March 1916): 101–103.

Brobst, John F. *Well, Mary: Civil War Letters of a Wisconsin Volunteer*. Edited by Margaret Brobst Roth. Madison: University of Wisconsin Press, 1960.

Brown, Malcolm, and Shirley Seaton. *Christmas Truce*. New York: Hippocrene Books, 1984.

Brown, William Wells. *The Negro in the American Rebellion: His Heroism and His Fidelity*. Boston: Lee & Shepard, 1867.

Buck, Samuel D. *With the Old Confeds: Actual Experiences of a Captain in the Line*. Baltimore, MD: H. E. Houck, 1925.

Buell, Augustus C. *The Cannoneer: Recollections of Service in the Army of the Potomac*. Washington, DC: National Tribune, 1890.

Bull, Rice C. *Soldiering: The Civil War Diary of Rice C. Bull, 123rd New York Volunteer Infantry*. Edited by K. Jack Bauer. 1977. Reprint, Navato, CA: Presidio Press, 1995.

Burkhardt, George S. *Confederate Rage, Yankee Wrath: No Quarter in the Civil War*. Carbondale: Southern Illinois University Press, 2007.

Busch, Briton Cooper. *Bunker Hill to Bastogne: Elite Forces and American Society*. Washington, DC: Potomac Books, 2006.

Busk, Hans. *Hand-Book for Hythe*. 1860. Reprint, Brighton, MI: Cornell Publications, ca. 2003.

Butts, Joseph Tyler, ed. *A Gallant Captain of the Civil War, Being the Extraordinary Adventures of Friedrich Otto Baron von Fritsch*. New York: F. Tennyson Neely, 1902.

Byers, S. M. H. "How Men Feel in Battle." *American History Illustrated* 22 (April 1987): 10–17.

Callaway, Joshua K. *The Civil War Letters of Joshua K. Callaway*. Edited by Judith Lee Hallock. Athens: University of Georgia Press, 1997.

Canfield, Silas S. *History of the 21st Regiment Ohio Volunteer Infantry in the War of the Rebellion*. Toledo, OH: Vrooman, Anderson & Bateman, 1893.

Carpenter, George N. *History of the Eighth Regiment Vermont Volunteers, 1861–1865*. Boston: Press of Deland & Barta, 1886.

Carter, Robert G. "Four Brothers in Blue." *Maine Bugle* 3, no. 4 (October 1896): 306–314.

Cary, R. Milton. *Skirmishers' Drill and Bayonet Exercise as Now Used in the French Army with Suggestions for the Soldier in Actual Conflict*. Richmond, VA: West & Johnston, 1861.

Casler, John O. *Four Years in the Stonewall Brigade*. 1906. Reprint, Columbia: University of South Carolina Press, 2005.

Catton, Bruce. *A Stillness at Appomattox*. Garden City, NY: Doubleday, 1953.

Caudill, Edward, and Paul Ashdown. *Sherman's March in Myth and Memory*. Lanham, MD: Rowman & Littlefield, 2008.

Chamberlain, Joshua L. *The Passing of the Armies: An Account of the Final Campaign of the Army of the Potomac, Based upon Personal Reminiscences of the Fifth Army Corps*. 1915. Reprint, Gettysburg, PA: Stan Clark Military Books, 1994.

Chambers, William Pitt. *Blood and Sacrifice: The Civil War Journal of a Confederate Soldier*. Edited by Richard A. Baumgartner. Huntington, WV: Blue Acorn Press, 1994.

Chapman, Conrad Wise. *Ten Months in the "Orphan Brigade": Conrad Wise Chapman's Civil War Memoir*. Edited by Ben L. Bassham. Kent, OH: Kent State University Press, 1999.

Chappell, Frank Anderson, ed. *Dear Sister: Civil War Letters to a Sister in Alabama*. Huntsville, AL: Branch Springs, 2002.

Charles, R. K. "Events in Battle of Fredericksburg." *Confederate Veteran* 14 (February 1906): 65–68.

Childs, Henry T. "The Battle of Seven Pines." *Confederate Veteran* 25 (January 1917): 19–20.

Christ, Mark K., ed. *Getting Used to Being Shot At: The Spence Family Civil War Letters*. Fayetteville: University of Arkansas Press, 2002.

Cimprich, John. *Fort Pillow, a Civil War Massacre, and Public Memory*. Baton Rouge: Louisiana State University Press, 2005.

Clark, George. "Alabamians in the Crater Battle." *Confederate Veteran* 3 (March 1895): 68–70.

Coe, Hamlin Alexander. *Mine Eyes Have Seen the Glory: Combat Diaries of Union Sergeant Hamlin Alexander Coe*. Edited by David Coe. Cranbury, NJ: Fairleigh Dickinson University Press, 1975.

Coffin, Charles Carleton. *Redeeming the Republic: The Third Period of the War of the Rebellion, in the Year 1864*. New York: Harper & Brothers, 1889.

Coles, Robert T. *From Huntsville to Appomattox: R. T. Coles's History of 4th Regiment, Alabama Volunteer Infantry, CSA, Army of Northern Virginia*. Edited by Jeffrey D. Stocker. Knoxville: University of Tennessee Press, 1996.

Collins, R. M. *Chapters from the Unwritten History of the War between the States, or The Incidents in the Life of a Confederate Soldier in Camp, on the March, in the Great Battles, and in Prison*. St. Louis, MO: Nixon-Jones, 1893.

Connolly, James A. *Three Years in the Army of the Cumberland: The Letters and Diary of Major James A. Connolly*. Edited by Paul M. Angle. 1959. Reprint, Bloomington: Indiana University Press, 1987.

Cooke, Chauncey H. *A Badger Boy in Blue: The Civil War Letters of Chauncey H. Cooke*. Edited by William H. Mulligan Jr. Detroit, MI: Wayne State University Press, 2007.

Cooke, John Esten. *A Life of Gen. Robert E. Lee*. New York: D. Appleton, 1871.

Cornish, Dudley Taylor. *The Sable Arm: Black Troops in the Union Army, 1861–1865*. 2nd ed. Lawrence: University Press of Kansas, 1987.

Cornwell, Bernard. Foreword to *Sword and Honor: Thrilling Battle Stories of Courage and Victory*. Edited by Mike Ashley. New York: Fall River Press, 2011.

Cramer, Clayton E. *Armed America: The Remarkable Story of How and Why Guns Became as American as Apple Pie*. Nashville, TN: Nelson Current, 2006.

Crofts, Thomas. *History of the Service of the Third Ohio Veteran Volunteer Cavalry in the War for the Preservation of the Union from 1861–1865*. Columbus, OH: Stoneman Press, 1910.

Crook, W. M. "W. M. Crook's Heroism at Franklin." *Confederate Veteran* 5 (June 1897): 303–304.

Crummer, Wilbur F. *With Grant at Fort Donelson, Shiloh, and Vicksburg*. Oak Park, IL: E. C. Crummer, 1915.

Crumpton, Washington B. "In the Atlanta Campaign." *Confederate Veteran* 29 (October 1921): 381–383.

Davis, Burke. *Sherman's March*. New York: Random House, 1980.

Dawes, Rufus R. *Service with the Sixth Wisconsin Volunteers*. Marietta, OH: E. R. Alderman & Sons, 1890.

Derby, J[ames] C. *Fifty Years among Authors, Books, and Publishers*. New York: G. W. Carleton, 1884.

Dexter, Seymour. *Seymour Dexter, Union Army: Journal and Letters of Civil War Service in Company K, 23rd New York Volunteer Regiment of Elmira, with Illustrations*. Edited by Carl A. Morrell. Jefferson, NC: McFarland, 1996.

Donald, David Herbert. *Lincoln*. New York: Simon & Schuster, 1995.

Douglas, Henry Kyd. *I Rode with Stonewall, Being Chiefly the War Experiences of the Youngest Member of Jackson's Staff from the John Brown Raid to the Hanging of Mrs. Surratt*. Chapel Hill: University of North Carolina Press, 1940.

Drewry, A. S. "The Purcell Battery from Richmond, VA: Its Gallant Conduct at the Battle of Cedar Run." *Southern Historical Society Papers* 27 (1899): 89–92.

Duke, John K. *History of the Fifty-third Regiment Ohio Volunteer Infantry, during the War of the Rebellion 1861 to 1865*. Portsmouth, OH: Blade, 1900.

Dunlop, William S. *Lee's Sharpshooters, or The Forefront of Battle: A Story of Southern Valor That Never Has Been Told*. Little Rock, AR: Tunnam & Pittard, 1899.

Durkin, James, ed. *This War Is an Awful Thing: Civil War Letters of the National Guards, the 19th and 90th Pennsylvania Volunteers*. Glenside, PA: J. Michael Santarelli, 1994.

Dutcher, Salem. "Williamsburg: A Graphic Story of the Battle of May 5, 1862." *Southern Historical Society Papers* 17 (1889): 409–419.

Dyer, John Will. *Reminiscences, or Four Years in the Confederate Army: A History of the Experiences of the Private Soldier in Camp, Hospital, Prison, on the March, and on the Battlefield, 1861 to 1865.* Evansville, IN: Keller, 1898.

Elliott, Isaac H. *History of the Thirty-third Illinois Veteran Volunteer Infantry in the Civil War.* Gibson City, IL: Regimental Association of the Thirty-third Illinois, 1902.

Elliot-Wright, Philipp. *Rifleman: Elite Soldiers of the Wars against Napoleon.* London: Publishing News, 2000.

Emmett, Dan. *Within Arm's Length: A Secret Service Agent's Definitive Inside Account of Protecting the President.* New York: St. Martin's Press, 2014.

Faust, Drew Gilpin. *This Republic of Suffering: Death and the American Civil War.* New York: Knopf, 2008.

Featherston, John C. "Graphic Account of Battle of Crater." *Southern Historical Society Papers* 33 (1905): 358–374.

Ferguson, John Hill. *On to Atlanta: The Civil War Diaries of John Hill Ferguson, Illinois Tenth Regiment of Volunteers.* Edited by Janet Correll Ellison. Lincoln: University of Nebraska Press, 2001.

Fitzpatrick, Marion Hill. *Letters to Amanda: The Civil War Letters of Marion Hill Fitzpatrick, Army of Northern Virginia.* Edited by Jeffrey C. Lowe and Sam Hodges. Macon, GA: Mercer University Press, 1998.

Fletcher, William A. *Rebel Private: Front and Rear.* 1908. Reprint, New York: Dutton, 1995.

Foote, Lorien. *The Gentlemen and the Roughs: Manhood, Honor, and Violence in the Union Army.* New York: New York University Press, 2010.

Ford, Worthington C., ed. *A Cycle of Adams Letters, 1861–1865.* Vol. 2. Boston: Houghton Mifflin, 1920.

Foster, Samuel T. *One of Cleburne's Command: The Civil War Reminiscences and Diary of Capt. Samuel T. Foster, Granbury's Texas Brigade, CSA.* Edited by Norman D. Brown. Austin: University of Texas Press, 1980.

Fremantle, Arthur. *Three Months in the Southern States: April, June, 1863.* Mobile, AL: S. H. Goetzel, 1864.

Frisby, Derek W. "'Remember Fort Pillow!': Politics, Atrocity Propaganda, and the Evolution of Hard War." In Urwin, *Black Flag Over Dixie,* 104–131.

Fuchs, Richard L. *An Unerring Fire: The Massacre at Fort Pillow.* Rutherford, NJ: Fairleigh Dickinson University Press, 1994.

Fuller, Claud E. *The Rifled Musket.* Harrisburg, PA: Stackpole Books, 1958.

Garrison, Webb B. *The Encyclopedia of Civil War Usage: An Illustrated Compendium of the Everyday Language of Soldiers and Civilians.* Nashville, TN: Cumberland House, 2001.

Gauss, John. *Black Flag! Black Flag! The Battle at Fort Pillow.* Lanham, MD: University Press of America, 2003.

Gibbons, A. R. *The Recollections of an Old Confederate Soldier.* Shelbyville, MO: Herald Print, ca. 1931.

Gilbert, Adrian. *Stalk and Kill: The Thrill and Danger of the Sniper Experience.* New York: St. Martin's Press, 1997.

Giles, Valerius Cincinnatus. *Rags and Hope: The Recollections of Val C. Giles, Four Years with Hood's Brigade, Fourth Texas Infantry, 1861–1865.* Edited by Mary Lasswell. New York: Coward-McCann, 1961.

Glatthaar, Joseph T. *The March to the Sea and Beyond: Sherman's Troops in the Savannah and Carolinas Campaigns.* New York: New York University Press, 1985.

Goodheart, Adam. *1861: The Civil War Awakening.* New York: Knopf, 2011.

Gooding, James Henry. *On the Altar of Freedom: A Black Civil War Soldier's Letters from the Front.* Edited by Virginia Matzke Adams. Amherst: University of Massachusetts Press, 1991.

Green, John Williams. *Johnny Green of the Orphan Brigade: The Journal of a Confederate Soldier.* Edited by A. D. Kirwan. Lexington: University Press of Kentucky, 1956.

Greene, William B. *Letters from a Sharpshooter: The Civil War Letters of Private William B. Greene, Co. G, 2nd United States Sharpshooters (Berdan's) Army of the Potomac, 1861–1865.* Compiled by William H. Hastings. Belleville, WI: Historic Publications, 1993.

Griffith, Paddy. *Battle Tactics of the Civil War.* New Haven, CT: Yale University Press, 1989.

Grimsley, Mark. *The Hard Hand of War: Union Military Policy toward Southern Civilians, 1861–1865.* Cambridge: Cambridge University Press, 1995.

Grossman, Dave. *On Killing: The Psychological Cost of Learning to Kill in War and Society.* Rev. ed. New York: Bay Back Books, 2009.

Guelzo, Allen C. *Fateful Lightning: A New History of the Civil War and Reconstruction.* Oxford: Oxford University Press, 2012.

Haliburton, Thomas Chandler. *The Letter-bag of the Great Western, or Life in a Steamer.* Paris: Baudry's European Library, 1840.

Hall, H. Seymour. "A Volunteer at the First Bull Run." *MOLLUS* 15 (1892): 143–159.

Hamilton, D. H. *History of Company M: First Texas Volunteer Infantry, Hood's Brigade, Longstreet's Corps, Army of the Confederate States of America.* Waco, TX: W. M. Morrison, 1962.

Hamilton, Milton W. "Augustus C. Buell: Fraudulent Historian." *Pennsylvania Magazine of History and Biography* 80, no. 4 (October 1956): 478–492.

Handerson, Henry E. *Yankee in Gray: The Civil War Memoirs of Henry E. Handerson, with a Selection of His Wartime Letters.* Cleveland, OH: Press of Western Reserve University, 1962.

Hanks, Orlando T. *History of Captain B. F. Benton's Company, Hood's Texas Brigade, 1861–1865.* Austin, TX: Morrison Books, 1984.

Hartwig, D. Scott. "'I dread the thought of the place': The Iron Brigade at Antietam." In *Giants in Their Tall Black Hats: Essays on the Iron Brigade,* edited by Alan T. Nolan and Sharon Eggleston Vipond, 30–52. Bloomington: Indiana University Press, 1998.

Haskell, John Cheeves. *The Haskell Memoirs.* Edited by Gilbert E. Govan and James W. Livingood. New York: G. P. Putnam's Sons, 1960.

Hayes, Rutherford B. "Incidents at the Battle of Cedar Creek." *MOLLUS* 4 (1896): 235–245.

Haynes, Martin A. *A History of the Second Regiment, New Hampshire Volunteer Infantry, in the War of the Rebellion.* Lakeport, NH, 1896.

Hennessy, John J. *The First Battle of Manassas: An End to Innocence, July 18–21, 1861.* Rev. ed. Mechanicsburg, PA: Stackpole Books, 2015.

*Henry's Repeating Rifle 1865: Henry Co. Catalogue.* 1865. Reprint, Brighton, MI: Cornell Publishing, 2005.

Hess, Earl J. *Civil War Infantry Tactics: Training, Combat, and Small-Unit Effectiveness.* Baton Rouge: Louisiana State University Press, 2015.

———. *Kennesaw Mountain: Sherman, Johnston, and the Atlanta Campaign.* Chapel Hill: University of North Carolina Press, 2013.

———. *The Rifle Musket in Civil War Combat: Myth and Reality.* Lawrence: University Press of Kansas, 2008.

———. *Trench Warfare under Grant and Lee: Field Fortifications in the Overland Campaign.* Chapel Hill: University of North Carolina Press, 2007.

———. *The Union Soldier in Battle: Enduring the Ordeal of Combat.* Lawrence: University Press of Kansas, 1997.

Hill, Daniel H. "McClellan's Change of Base and Malvern Hill." In *Battles and Leaders of the Civil War,* edited by Robert U. Johnson and Clarence C. Buel, 2:383–395. New York: Century, 1887.

Hinman, Wilbur F. *Corporal Si Klegg and His "Pard": How They Lived and Talked, and What They Did and Suffered, While Fighting for the Flag.* 10th ed. 1887. Reprint, Cleveland, OH: N. G. Hamilton, 1895.

———. *The Story of the Sherman Brigade: The Camp, the March, the Bivouac, the Battle; and How "The Boys" Lived and Died during Four Years of Active Field Service.* Alliance, OH, 1897.

Hodges, Ellen E., and Stephen Kerber, eds. "'Rogues and Black Hearted Scamps': Civil War Letters of Winston and Octavia Stephens, 1862–1863." *Florida Historical Quarterly* 57, no. 1 (July 1978): 54–82.

Holmes, James T. *52d OVI: Then and Now.* Columbus, OH: Berlin, 1898.

Holsinger, Frank. "How Does One Feel Under Fire?" *MOLLUS* 15 (1892): 290–304.

Holt, David E. *A Mississippi Rebel in the Army of Northern Virginia: The Civil War Memoirs of Private David Holt.* Edited by Thomas D. Cockrell and Michael B. Ballard. Baton Rouge: Louisiana State University Press, 1995.

Horowitz, Murray M. "Ben Butler and the Negro: 'Miracles Are Occurring.'" *Louisiana History* 17, no. 2 (Spring 1976): 159–186.

Howard, S. E. "The Morning Surprise at Cedar Creek." *MOLLUS* 53 (1900): 415–424.

Howarth, Glennys. *Death and Dying: A Sociological Introduction.* Cambridge: Polity Press, 2007.

Hubbard, Paul, and Christine Lewis, eds. "'Give yourself no trouble about me': The Shiloh Letters of George W. Lennard." *Indiana Magazine of History* 76, no. 1 (March 1980): 21–53.

Hubert, Charles F. *History of the Fiftieth Regiment, Illinois Volunteer Infantry in the War for the Union.* Kansas City, MO: Western Veteran, 1894.

Hulbert, Simon Bolivar. *One Battle Too Many: An American Civil War Chronicle: The Writings of Simon Bolivar Hulbert, Private, Company E, 100th Regiment, New York State Volunteers, 1861–1864.* Edited by Richard P. Galloway. Gaithersburg, MD: Olde Soldier, 1987.

Hunter, Alexander. *Johnny Reb and Billy Yank.* New York: Neale, 1905.

Ingraham, Charles A. *Elmer E. Ellsworth and the Zouaves of '61.* Chicago: University of Chicago Press, 1927.

Ives, Washington. *Civil War Journal and Letters of Serg. Washington Ives, 4th Florida CSA.* Edited by Jim R. Cabaniss. Tallahassee, FL: J. R. Cabaniss, 1987.

Jacobson, Eric A., and Richard A. Rupp. *For Cause and for Country: A Study of the Affair at Spring Hill and the Battle of Franklin.* Franklin, TN: O'More, 2007.

Johnson, Clint. *Touring the Carolinas' Civil War Sites.* Winston-Salem, NC: John F. Blair, 1996.

Johnson, Robert U., and Clarence C. Buel, eds. *Battles and Leaders of the Civil War.* 4 vols. New York: Century, 1884–1888.

Jones, J. Keith, ed. *The Boys of Diamond Hill: The Lives and Civil War Letters of the Boyd Family of Abbeville County, South Carolina.* Jefferson, NC: McFarland, 2011.

Katcher, Philip. *Sharpshooters of the American Civil War, 1861–65.* Oxford: Osprey, 2002.

Kautz, August V. *The 1865 Customs of Service for Non-Commissioned Officers and Soldiers.* 2nd ed. Mechanicsburg, PA: Stackpole Books, 2001.

Keegan, John. *The Face of Battle.* 1976. Reprint, New York: Penguin, 1978.

Kenfield, Frank. "Captured by Rebels: A Vermonter at Petersburg, 1864." *Vermont History* 36, no. 4 (Autumn 1968): 230–235.

Kennett, Lee. *Marching through Georgia: The Story of Soldiers and Civilians during Sherman's Campaign.* New York: HarperCollins, 1995.

Kershaw, Joseph B. "Richard Kirkland, the Humane Hero of Fredericksburg." *Southern Historical Society Papers* 8 (1880): 186–188.

Kilmer, George L. "The Dash into the Crater." *Century Magazine,* September 1887, 774–776.

King, John M. *Three Years with the 92d Illinois: The Civil War Diary of John M. King.* Edited by Claire E. Swedberg. Mechanicsburg, PA: Stackpole Books, 1999.

Kingman, Eugene. *Tramping Out the Vintage: The Civil War Diaries and Letters of Eugene Kingman.* Edited by Helene C. Phelan. Almond, NY: Helene C. Phelan, 1983.

Klein, Maury. *Days of Defiance: Sumter, Secession, and the Coming of the Civil War.* New York: Vintage Books, 1999.

Klingenberg, Mitchell G. "'Without the shedding of blood there can be no remission': The War Theology of Horace Bushnell and the Meaning of America, 1861 to 1866." *Connecticut History* 51, no. 2 (Fall 2012): 147–171.

Kolchin, Peter. *American Slavery, 1619–1877.* New York: Hill & Wang, 1993.

Krick, Robert K. *Conquering the Valley: Stonewall Jackson at Port Republic.* Baton Rouge: Louisiana State University Press, 2002.

Lash, Gary G. *"Duty Well Done": The History of Edward Baker's California Regiment (71st Pennsylvania Infantry).* Baltimore, MD: Butternut & Blue, 2001.

Ledford, Preston Lafayette. *Reminiscences of the Civil War, 1861–1865.* Thomasville, NC: News Printing House, 1909.

Lehman, James O., and Steven M. Nolt. *Mennonites, Amish, and the American Civil War.* Baltimore, MD: Johns Hopkins University Press, 2011.

Leon, Louis. *Diary of a Tar Heel Confederate Soldier.* Charlotte, NC: Stone, 1913.

*Life of James W. Jackson, the Alexandria Hero, and the Slayer of Ellsworth.* Richmond, VA: West & Johnston, 1862.

Lincoln, Abraham. "The Collected Works of Abraham Lincoln." *Abraham Lincoln Association,* http://quod.lib.umich.edu/l/lincoln/.

Linderman, Gerald F. *Embattled Courage: The Experience of Combat in the American Civil War.* New York: Free Press, 1987.

Logsdon, David R., comp. *Eyewitnesses at the Battle of Fort Donelson.* Nashville, TN: Kettle Mills Press, 1998.

———. *Eyewitnesses at the Battle of Franklin.* 3rd ed. Nashville, TN: Kettle Mills Press, 1991.

Lomax, John A., and Alan Lomax. *American Ballads and Folk Songs.* 1934. Reprint, New York: Dover, 1994.

Longmuir, John. *Walker and Webster Combined in a Dictionary of the English Language.* London: William Tegg, 1864.

Longstreet, James. "The Battle of Fredericksburg." In *Battles and Leaders of the Civil War,* edited by Robert Underwood Johnson and Clarence Clough Buel, 3:70–85. New York: Century, 1887–1888.

Lord, Edward O. *History of the Ninth Regiment New Hampshire Volunteers in the War of the Rebellion.* Concord, NH: Republican Press Association, 1895.

Lowe, Richard. "Battle on the Levee: The Fight at Milliken's Bend." In Smith, *Black Soldiers in Blue,* 107–135.

Lyftogt, Kenneth. *Blue Mills to Columbia: Cedar Falls and the Civil War.* Ames: Iowa State University Press, 1993.

Lynn, John A. *Battle: A History of Combat and Culture.* Rev. ed. Philadelphia: Basic Books, 2008.

Marshall, S. L. A. *Men Against Fire: The Problem of Battle Command in Future War.* 1947. Reprint, Gloucester, MA: Peter Smith, 1978.

Martin, Joseph Plumb. *Memoir of a Revolutionary Soldier: The Narrative of Joseph Plumb Martin.* Mineola, NY: Dover, 2006.

Martin, Kingsley. *The Crown and the Establishment.* Harmondsworth, UK: Penguin, 1962.

Mathis, Ray. *In the Land of the Living: Wartime Letters by Confederates from the Chattahoochee Valley of Alabama and Georgia.* Troy, AL: Troy State University Press, 1981.

Mayo, Perry. *The Civil War Letters of Perry Mayo.* Edited by Robert W. Hodge. East Lansing: Michigan State University Press, 1967.

Mays, Thomas D. "The Battle of Saltville." In Smith, *Black Soldiers in Blue,* 200–226.

———. *The Saltville Massacre.* Abilene, TX: McWhiney Foundation Press, 1998.

McCabe, James D., Jr. *The Grayjackets: And How They Lived, Fought, and Died, for Dixie.* Richmond, VA: Jones Brothers, 1867.

McClellan, George B. *Manual of Bayonet Exercise: Prepared for the Use of the Army of the United States*. Philadelphia: Lippincott, Grambo, 1852.

McGee, Benjamin F. *History of the 72nd Indiana Volunteer Infantry of the Mounted Lightning Brigade*. 2nd ed. Huntington, WV: Blue Acorn Press, 1995.

McKelvey, Blake, ed. *Rochester in the Civil War*. Rochester, NY: Rochester Historical Society, 1944.

McPherson, James M. *Battle Cry of Freedom: The Civil War Era*. New York: Oxford University Press, 1988.

———. *For Cause and Comrades: Why Men Fought in the Civil War*. New York: Oxford University Press, 1997.

McWhiney, Grady, and Perry D. Jamieson. *Attack and Die: Civil War Military Tactics and the Southern Heritage*. Tuscaloosa: University of Alabama Press, 1984.

McWhirter, Christian. *Battle Hymns: The Power and Popularity of Music in the Civil War*. Chapel Hill: University of North Carolina Press, 2012.

Merrifield, J. K. "Opdyke's Brigade at Franklin." *Confederate Veteran* 13 (December 1905): 563–564.

Miller, Edward A., Jr. *The Black Civil War Soldiers of Illinois: The Story of the Twenty-ninth US Colored Infantry*. Columbia: University of South Carolina Press, 1998.

Montgomery, Walter R. *Georgia Sharpshooter: The Civil War Diary and Letters of Walter Rhadamanthus Montgomery, 1839–1906*. Macon, GA: Mercer University Press, 1997.

Moore, Robert A. *A Life for the Confederacy: As Recorded in the Pocket Diaries of Pvt. Robert A. Moore*. Edited by James W. Silver. 1959. Reprint, Wilmington, NC: Broadfoot, 1987.

Morris, Thomas D. *Southern Slavery and the Law, 1619–1860*. Chapel Hill: University of North Carolina Press, 1996.

Mosgrove, George Dallas. *Kentucky Cavaliers in Dixie, or The Reminiscences of a Confederate Cavalry Man*. Edited by Bell I. Wiley. Jackson, TN: McCowat-Mercer Press, 1957.

Muffly, Joseph Wendel, ed. *The Story of Our Regiment: A History of the 148th Pennsylvania Vols*. Des Moines, IA: Kenyon Printing & Mfg. Co., 1904.

Murray, R. L., ed. *Letters from Berdan's Sharpshooters*. Wolcott, NY: Benedum Books, 2005.

Neely, Mark E., Jr. *The Civil War and the Limits of Destruction*. Cambridge, MA: Harvard University Press, 2007.

———. *Lincoln and the Triumph of the Nation: Constitutional Conflict in the American Civil War*. Chapel Hill: University of North Carolina Press, 2011.

Neese, George M. *Three Years in the Confederate Horse Artillery*. New York: Neale, 1911.

Newton, James King. *A Wisconsin Boy in Dixie: Selected Letters of James K. Newton*. Edited by Stephen E. Ambrose. Madison: University of Wisconsin Press, 1961.

Nicolay, John G. *With Lincoln in the White House: Letters, Memoranda, and Other Writings of John G. Nicolay, 1860–1865*. Edited by Michael Burlingame. Carbondale: Southern Illinois University Press, 2006.

Nisbet, James Cooper. *Four Years on the Firing Line.* Edited by Bell Irvin Wiley. Wilmington, NC: Broadfoot, 1991.

Noll, Mark A. *The Civil War as a Theological Crisis.* Chapel Hill: University of North Carolina Press, 2006.

Norton, Oliver Willcox. *Army Letters, 1861–1865.* Chicago: O. L. Deming, 1903.

Nosworthy, Brent. *The Bloody Crucible of Courage: Fighting Methods and Combat Experience of the Civil War.* New York: Carroll & Graf, 2003.

Nugent, William L. *My Dear Nellie: The Civil War Letters of William L. Nugent to Eleanor Smith Nugent.* Edited by William M. Cash and Lucy Somerville Howorth. Jackson: University Press of Mississippi, 1977.

Nutt, Edmund E. "Twentieth Ohio at Atlanta." *Ohio Soldier and National Picket Guard* 7, no. 21 (July 28, 1894): 1–2.

Oates, Stephen B. *To Purge This Land with Blood: A Biography of John Brown.* 2nd ed. Amherst: University of Massachusetts Press, 1984.

Ohio. *Message and Reports to the General Assembly and Governor of the State of Ohio for the Year 1861, part 1.* Columbus, OH: Richard Nevins, 1862.

Oldroyd, Osborn H. *A Soldier's Story of the Siege of Vicksburg.* Springfield, IL, 1885.

Opie, John N. *A Rebel Cavalryman with Lee, Stuart, and Jackson.* Chicago: W. B. Conkey, 1899.

Orendorff, Henry H., G. M. Armstrong, Newton Ellis, M. V. D. Voorhees, S. R. Quigley, C. F. Matteson, and A. J. Stutes. *Reminiscences of the Civil War from the Diaries of Members of the 103d Illinois Volunteer Infantry.* Chicago: Press of J. F. Leaming, 1904.

Orr, Timothy J. "'A viler enemy in our rear': Pennsylvania Soldiers Confront the North's Antiwar Movement." In *The View from the Ground: Experiences of Civil War Soldiers,* edited by Aaron Sheehan-Dean, 171–198. Lexington: University Press of Kentucky, 2007.

Persons, William E., Oliver S. Wood, Joseph Plassmeyer, Paul V. Kellogg, and John E. McCammon. *Military Science and Tactics.* Vol. 3. Columbia: University of Missouri, 1921.

Phillips, B. F. "Wilcox's Alabamians in Virginia." *Confederate Veteran* 15 (November 1907): 490.

Phillips, Jason. "A Brothers' War? Exploring Confederate Perceptions of the Enemy." In *The View from the Ground: Experiences of Civil War Soldiers,* edited by Aaron Sheehan-Dean, 67–90. Lexington: University Press of Kentucky, 2007.

Pierson, Stephen. "From Chattanooga to Atlanta in 1864—A Personal Reminiscence." *Proceedings of the New Jersey Historical Society* 16 (1931): 324–356.

Ray, Fred L. *Shock Troops of the Confederacy: The Sharpshooter Battalions of the Army of Northern Virginia.* Asheville, NC: CFS Press, 2006.

Ray, William R. *Four Years with the Iron Brigade: The Civil War Journal of William Ray, Company F, Seventh Wisconsin Volunteers.* Edited by Lance Herdegen and Sherry Murphy. Cambridge, MA: Da Capo Press, 2009.

Reardon, Carol A. *With a Sword in One Hand and Jomini in the Other: The Problem of Military Thought in the Civil War North.* Chapel Hill: University of North Carolina Press, 2012.

Redkey, Edwin S., ed. *A Grand Army of Black Men: Letters from African-American Soldiers in the Union Army, 1861–1865.* Cambridge: Cambridge University Press, 1992.

Reed, Thomas Benton. *A Private in Gray.* Camden, AR: T. B. Reed, 1905.

Rhea, Gordon C. *The Battles for Spotsylvania Court House and the Road to Yellow Tavern, May 7–12, 1864.* Baton Rouge: Louisiana State University Press, 2005.

Rhodes, Elisha Hunt. *All for the Union: The Civil War Diary and Letters of Elisha Hunt Rhodes.* Edited by Robert Hunt Rhodes. New York: Orion Books, 1991.

Ripley, William Young Warren. *Vermont Riflemen in the War for the Union, 1861–1865: A History of Company F, First United States Sharp Shooters.* Rutland, VT: Tuttle, 1883.

Roberts, Joseph. *The Hand-Book of Artillery, for the Service of the United States (Army and Militia).* New York: D. Von Nostrand, 1860.

Robertson, James I., Jr. *The Civil War's Common Soldier.* Fort Washington, PA: Eastern National, 2006.

———. *Stonewall Jackson: The Man, the Soldier, the Legend.* New York: Macmillan, 1997.

Robinson, John Bell. *Pictures of Slavery and Anti-slavery: Advantages of Negro Slavery and the Benefits of Negro Freedom. Morally, Socially, and Politically Considered.* Philadelphia, 1863.

Rolfs, David W. "'No nearer heaven now but rather farther off': The Religious Compromises and Conflicts of Northern Soldiers." In *The View from the Ground: Experiences of Civil War Soldiers,* edited by Aaron Sheehan-Dean, 121–144. Lexington: University Press of Kentucky, 2007.

Rolph, Daniel N. *My Brother's Keeper: Union and Confederate Soldiers' Acts of Mercy during the Civil War.* Mechanicsburg, PA: Stackpole Books, 2002.

Sample, A[lvan] E. *A History of Company "A," 30th Illinois Infantry.* Lyons, KS, 1907.

Sandburg, Carl. *Abraham Lincoln: The Prairie Years and the War Years.* Pleasantville, NY: Reader's Digest, 1970.

Schantz, Mark S. *Awaiting the Heavenly Country: The Civil War and America's Culture of Death.* Ithaca, NY: Cornell University Press, 2008.

Sears, Stephen W. *To the Gates of Richmond: The Peninsula Campaign.* New York: Ticknor & Fields, 1992.

Sexton, James A. "The Observations and Experiences of a Captain of Infantry at the Battle of Franklin, November 30, 1864." *MOLLUS* 13 (1907): 466–484.

Sherman, William T. *Memoirs of General William T. Sherman.* New York: D. Appleton, 1876.

Siepel, Kevin H. *Rebel: The Life and Times of John Singleton Mosby.* Lincoln: University of Nebraska Press, 2008.

Simonton, Edward. "Recollections of the Battle of Fredericksburg." *MOLLUS* 27 (1890): 245–266.

Simson, Jay W. *Custer and the Front Royal Executions of 1864.* Jefferson, NC: McFarland, 2009.

Slotkin, Richard. *No Quarter: The Battle of the Crater, 1864.* New York: Random House, 2009.

Smith, C. Calvin, ed. "The Duties of Home and War: The Civil War Letters of John G. Marsh (A Selection)." *Upper Ohio Valley Historical Review* 8 (1979): 7–20.

Smith, John David. *Black Soldiers in Blue: African American Troops in the Civil War Era.* Chapel Hill: University of North Carolina Press, 2002.

———. "Let Us All Be Grateful That We Have Colored Troops That Will Fight." In Smith, *Black Soldiers in Blue,* 1–77.

Smith, Robert D. *Confederate Diary of Robert D. Smith.* Edited by Jill K. Garrett. Columbia, TN: Captain James Madison Sparkman Chapter, United Daughters of the Confederacy, 1997.

Solonick, Justin S. *Engineering Victory: The Union Siege of Vicksburg.* Carbondale: Southern Illinois University Press, 2015.

Squier, George W. *This Wilderness of War: The Civil War Letters of George W. Squier, Hoosier Volunteer.* Edited by Julie A. Doyle, John David Smith, and Richard M. McMurry. Knoxville: University of Tennessee Press, 1998.

Stanley, Henry Morton. *The Autobiography of Sir Henry Morton Stanley.* Edited by Dorothy Stanley. Boston: Houghton Mifflin, 1909.

Staples, Horatio. "Reminiscences of Bull Run." *MOLLUS* 18 (1908): 126–138.

Starr, Stephen Z. *The Union Cavalry in the Civil War: From Fort Sumter to Gettysburg, 1861–1863.* Baton Rouge: Louisiana State University Press, 1979.

Steers, Edward. *Blood on the Moon: The Assassination of Abraham Lincoln.* Lexington: University Press of Kentucky, 2005.

Stevens, Charles A. *Berdan's United States Sharpshooters in the Army of the Potomac, 1861–1865.* St. Paul, MN: Price-McGill, 1892.

Stiles, Robert. *Four Years under Marse Robert.* New York: Neale, 1910.

Strayer, Larry M., and Richard A. Baumgartner, eds. *Echoes of Battle: The Atlanta Campaign.* Huntington, WV: Blue Acorn Press, 1991.

Strong, Robert Hale. *A Yankee Private's Civil War.* Edited by Ashley Halsey. Chicago: Henry Regnery, 1961.

Sturgis, H. Howard. "Hard Fighting by Lookout Mountain." *Confederate Veteran* 17 (March 1909): 121.

Styple, William B., ed. *Writing and Fighting from the Army of Northern Virginia: A Collection of Civil War Soldier Correspondence.* Kearny, NJ: Belle Grove, 2003.

———. *Writing and Fighting the Civil War: Soldier Correspondence to the New York Sunday Mercury.* 2nd rev. ed. Kearny, NJ: Belle Grove, 2004.

Suderow, Bryce A. "The Battle of the Crater: The Civil War's Worst Massacre." In Urwin, *Black Flag Over Dixie,* 203–209.

Sword, Wiley. *Courage Under Fire: Profiles in Bravery from the Battlefields of the Civil War.* New York: St. Martin's Griffin, 2007.

———. *The Historic Henry Rifle: Oliver Winchester's Famous Civil War Repeater.* Lincoln, RI: Andrew Mowbray, 2002.

Thomas, Dean S. *Round Ball to Rimfire: A History of Civil War Small Arms Ammunition.* Gettysburg, PA: Thomas, 1997.

Thomas, James B. *The Civil War Letters of First Lieutenant James B. Thomas, Adjutant, 107th Pennsylvania Volunteers.* Edited by Mary Warner Thomas and Richard A. Sauers. Baltimore, MD: Butternut & Blue, 1995.

Thompson, Ed Porter. *History of the Orphan Brigade.* Louisville, KY: Lewis N. Thompson, 1898.

Thompson, Richard S. *While My Country Is in Danger: The Life and Letters of Lieutenant Colonel Richard S. Thompson, Twelfth New Jersey Volunteers*. Edited by Gerry Harder Poriss and Ralph Gibbs Poriss. Hamilton, NY: Edmonston, 1994.

Thompson, S. Millett. *Thirteenth Regiment of New Hampshire Volunteer Infantry in the War of the Rebellion, 1861–1865: A Diary Covering Three Years and a Day*. Boston: Houghton, Mifflin, 1888.

Time-Life Books. *First Manassas*. Alexandria, VA: Time-Life, 1997.

Toney, Marcus B. *The Privations of a Private: Campaigning with the First Tennessee, CSA, and Life Thereafter*. Edited by Robert E. Hunt. Tuscaloosa: University of Alabama Press, 2005.

Trask, Stephen. "British Bayonet Tactics for US Army." *Arms and the Man* 62, no. 10 (June 2, 1917): 187, 190, 192.

Troiani, Don. *Don Troiani's American Battles: The Art of the Nation at War, 1754–1865*. Mechanicsburg, PA: Stackpole Books, 2006.

———. *Don Troiani's Civil War: Infantry*. Mechanicsburg, PA: Stackpole Books, 2002.

Trout, Robert J., ed. *Memoirs of the Stuart Horse Artillery Battalion: Moorman's and Hart's Batteries*. Knoxville: University of Tennessee Press, 2008.

Trudeau, Noah Andre. *Like Men of War: Black Troops in the Civil War, 1862–1865*. Boston: Little, Brown, 1998.

Tuthill, Richard S. "An Artilleryman's Recollections of the Battle of Atlanta." *MOLLUS* 10 (1891): 293–309.

Underwood, Adin Ballou. *The Three Years' Service of the Thirty-third Mass. Infantry Regiment, 1862–1865: And the Campaigns and Battles of Chancellorsville, Beverley's Ford, Gettysburg, Wauhatchie, Chattanooga, Atlanta, the March to the Sea and through the Carolinas, in which It Took Part*. Boston: A. Williams, 1881.

Upson, Theodore F. *With Sherman to the Sea: Civil War Letters, Diaries, and Reminiscences of Theodore F. Upson*. Edited by Oscar Osburn Winther. Bloomington: Indiana University Press, 1958.

Urwin, Gregory J. W., ed. *Black Flag Over Dixie: Racial Atrocities and Reprisals in the Civil War*. Carbondale: Southern Illinois University Press, 2004.

———. *The United States Cavalry: An Illustrated History*. Poole, UK: Blandford Press, 1983.

———. "'We cannot treat Negroes . . . as prisoners of war': Racial Atrocities and Reprisals in Civil War Arkansas." In Urwin, *Black Flag Over Dixie*, 132–152.

US Congress. *Report of the Joint Committee on the Conduct of the War on the Fort Pillow Massacre and on Returned Prisoners*. 38th Cong., 1st sess., Rep. Com. 63 and 68. 1864.

Vance, P. M. "Incidents of the Crater Battle." *Confederate Veteran* 14 (April 1906): 178–179.

Waite, Otis F. R. *New Hampshire in the Great Rebellion*. Claremont, NH: Tracy, Chase, 1870.

Walls, David. "Marching Song of the First Arkansas Colored Regiment: A Contested Attribution." *Arkansas Historical Quarterly* 66, no. 4 (Winter 2007): 401–421.

Watkins, Sam R. *"Co. Aytch," Maury Grays, First Tennessee Regiment, or A Side Show of the Big Show*. 1882. Reprint, Wilmington, NC: Broadfoot, 1990.

Weiser, J. M. "Trigg's Brigade at Chickamauga." *Confederate Veteran* 34 (December 1926): 452–453.

Weld, Theodore Dwight. *American Slavery as It Is: Testimony of a Thousand Witnesses.* New York: American Anti-slavery Society, 1839.

Wert, Jeffry D. *Mosby's Rangers.* New York: Simon & Schuster, 1990.

White, Wyman S. *The Civil War Diary of Wyman S. White, First Sergeant of Company F, 2nd United States Sharpshooter Regiment, 1861–1865.* Edited by Russell C. White. Baltimore, MD: Butternut & Blue, 1993.

Wickersham, Charles I. "Personal Recollections of the Cavalry at Chancellorsville." *MOLLUS* 48 (1903): 453–462.

Widney, Lyman S. *Campaigning with Uncle Billy: The Civil War Memoirs of Sgt. Lyman S. Widney, 34th Illinois Volunteer Infantry.* Edited by Robert I. Girardi. Bloomington, IN: Trafford, 2008.

Wildes, Thomas F. *Record of the One Hundred and Sixteenth Regiment Ohio Volunteers in the War of the Rebellion.* Sandusky, OH: I. F. Mack & Bros., 1884.

Wiley, Bell I. *The Life of Billy Yank: The Common Soldier of the Union.* Indianapolis, IN: Bobbs-Merrill, 1952.

———. *The Life of Johnny Reb: The Common Soldier of the Confederacy.* 1943. Reprint, Garden City, NY: Doubleday, 1971.

Wiley, William. *The Civil War Diary of a Common Soldier: William Wiley of the 77th Illinois Infantry.* Edited by Terrence J. Winschel. Baton Rouge: Louisiana State University Press, 2001.

Wilkeson, Frank. *Recollections of a Private Soldier in the Army of the Potomac.* New York: G. P. Putnam's Sons, 1887.

Wilson, Christopher Kent. "Marks of Honor and Death: *Sharpshooter* and the Peninsular Campaign of 1862." In *Winslow Homer: Paintings of the Civil War,* edited by Marc Simpson, 25–45. San Francisco, CA: Fine Arts Museums of San Francisco, 1988.

Wilson, Joseph Thomas. *The Black Phalanx: A History of the Negro Soldiers of the United States in the Wars of 1775–1812, 1861–'65.* Hartford, CT: American, 1890.

Wise, John S. *The End of an Era.* Boston: Houghton, Mifflin, 1901.

Wittenberg, Eric J. *The Battle of Brandy Station: North America's Largest Cavalry Battle.* Charleston, SC: History Press, 2010.

Wood, George L. *The Seventh Regiment: A Record.* New York: James Miller, 1865.

Woodworth, Steven E. *Beneath a Northern Sky: A Short History of the Gettysburg Campaign.* Lanham, MD: Rowman & Littlefield, 2008.

———. *Nothing but Victory: The Army of the Tennessee, 1861–1865.* New York: Knopf, 2005.

———. *While God Is Marching On: The Religious World of Civil War Soldiers.* Lawrence: University Press of Kansas, 2001.

Woodworth, Steven E., and Kenneth J. Winkle. *Atlas of the Civil War.* Oxford: Oxford University Press, 2004.

Worcester, Joseph E. *A Comprehensive Dictionary of the English Language.* Boston: Swan, Brewer, and Tileston, 1860.

Wray, William J. *History of the Twenty-third Pennsylvania Volunteer Infantry, Birney's Zouaves.* Philadelphia, 1904.

Wright, John D. *The Language of the Civil War.* Greenwood, CT: Oryx, 2001.

abolition, Union motivation to fight and, 18
Adams, Charles Francis, Jr., 194, 222
Adams, John, 174
Alabama regiments
  4th, 174
  5th, 70
  8th, 219
  44th, 78–79
Allatoona Pass, Battle of, 31
Allspaugh, Jacob H., 87
*American Slavery as It Is* (Dwight), 190
*American Sniper* (film), 6
ammunition
  fears of poisoned bullets, 153
  soldiers' vocabulary for, 81
Andrews, William H., 84
Andrews Sharpshooters, 124
animal slaughtering and butchering, 34–35
antebellum period
  attitudes toward violence, 25–27
  politics and violence in, 14–15
  views of death, 27
  views of the military and militarism,
    24–25
Antietam, Battle of
  accounts of taking "deliberate aim," 84
  choosing a target in battle, 47–48
  impact of officers on killing in battle, 70
  officers blamed for reckless killing, 86
  retreating enemy as targets, 69
  searching to find the bodies of slain
    enemies, 66
  soldiers' attitudes toward the reality of
    war and, 73
  soldiers' language of killing, 78
  soldiers on the loss of comrades, 74–75
  target attractiveness, 50, 51
  volume of fire, 64
Antietam Campaign, 35
antiwar Northerners, 160–165
Appomattox Courthouse, 228–229
Arkansas Post, Battle of, 66–67
Arkansas regiments
  1st, 52
  6th, 97

"Arkansas toothpick," 92
Army of Northern Virginia
  Battle of the Crater, 215–220
  foraging by, 157
  Malvern Hill, 87–88
  sharpshooters, 132
  surrender at Appomattox, 228–229
Army of Tennessee, 123. *See also* Ezra
    Church, Battle of; Franklin, Battle of;
    Overland Campaign
*Army of the Potomac—A Sharp-Shooter on Picket
    Duty, The* (Homer), 132–133, 134
Army of West Virginia, 172
artillerymen
  attitudes toward sharpshooters, 133,
    134–135
  distancing from the reality of killing,
    135–136
  hand-to-hand combat, 116–118
  skilled gunnery likened to sharpshooting,
    136–137
Aschmann, Rudolph, 130, 139, 140
Aschmann, William, 32
Atlanta Campaign
  accounts of "murderous fire," 85
  alternating states of friendliness and
    fighting on picket lines, 185–186
  hand-to-hand combat, 107
  mercy in battle and sparing the enemy, 175
  officers blamed for reckless killing, 87
  revenge as a motivation for killing in
    battle, 54
  skill gunnery likened to sharpshooting,
    136–137
  Union shelling of Atlanta, 158
*Atlanta Southern Confederacy*, 33–34
atrocities
  Battle of the Crater, 215–220
  battle viewed as a continuum, 152–153
  factors tempering, 187–188
  fears of and propagandizing about, 153
  Fort Pillow, 204–212
  overview and summary, 233
  Pottawatomie Massacre, 193
  retaliatory executions, 165–168

atrocities, *continued*
    retaliatory violence against Confederates
        by black Union soldiers, 220–224
    retaliatory violence in the Pacific Theater
        in World War II, 221
    Saltville Massacre, 212–215
    surrender executions, 153–154
    Union hostility toward Copperheads,
        160–165
authority figures, 42–43

Baker, Chauncey C., 182
Ballard, Alfred, 134
Baltimore, Maryland, 15–16, 19
*Baltimore Clipper*, 226
Barber, Lorenzo, 24
Barker, William, 227
Barnes, William T., 176
Barnickel, Linda, 203
Barr, George W., 156
battlefield truces, 175–176, 179–181, 182–184
battle flags
    company flags, 110–111, 248n33
    hand-to-hand combat and, 109–112
    regimental flags of United States Colored
        Troops, 197–198
    significance of, 110–111
    target attractiveness and, 50
"Battle Hymn of the Republic" (Howe), 35
bayonets
    charges, 96–98
    fencing, 99–100
    fights, 96, 97, 98
    soldiers' preference for clubbed muskets
        over, 103–106
    training, 98–102, 105
    types and uses of, 95–96
Bellamy, William, 79
Belmont, Battle of, 153
belt guns, 94
belt knives, 92–94
Benson, Berry, 127
Bentonville, Battle of, 141
Berdan, Hiram, 29, 46, 121–122, 123, 124
Berdan's Sharpshooters
    accounts of killing, 126
    desensitization to death and killing, 71
    on the duty to kill, 36
    formation of, 121–122
    at Gettysburg, 71, 137
    Lincoln's endorsement of, 122

    notions about legitimate conduct on the
        battlefield, 139–140
    rifles used by, 29–30
    Siege of Petersburg, 131, 137
    Siege of Yorktown, 123, 134
    Winslow Homer and, 132–133, 134
    *See also* US sharpshooter regiments
Bernard, George, 218
Bethune, J. D., 139
Bevens, William, 52
Bicknell, Luke Emerson, 124
Bierce, Ambrose, 96
Bigbie, Thomas, 178
Binion, Dorsey, 217
Bird, Henry Van Lewenigh, 217
Birge's Western Sharpshooters, 33, 129
"bite the dust," 78, 173, 244n3
Blackburn's Ford, 48
*Black Flag Over Dixie*, 200
Blackford, Eugene, 70
Black Republicans, 18
black Union soldiers. *See* United States
    Colored Troops
Blair, Frank, 167
Bleeding Kansas, 15, 193
Blessington, Joseph P., 201
Bliss, Zenas, 71
Bloody Angle (Spotsylvania), 118
Bloody Lane (Antietam), 50
Bloom, Enos, 173
Boone, Daniel, 26
Booth, John Wilkes, 226–227
Booth, Lionel F., 204, 207
Borcke, Heros von, 98
Border Ruffians, 15
Borton, Benjamin, 73
Bosworth, Newt, 178
Bowen, Roland, 49–50
Bowie knife, 92, 93
Bowker, Joseph, 184
Bowser, David Bustill, 197–198
Boyce, Joseph, 69–70
Boyd, Pressley, 72
Bragg, Braxton, 206
Brandy Station, Battle of, 116, 117
Branscomb, James, 38–39
Branscomb, Lewis, 78
Brawner's Farm, Battle of, 82
Breckinridge, John C., 214
breechloading rifles, 29, 30, 45. *See also* Sharps
    breechloading rifles

Brethren, 20
Brice's Crossing, Battle of, 223–224
Brisbin, James S., 196, 213
Brobst, John, 54, 56, 74, 162, 186
Brooks, Preston, 15
Brown, John, 15, 191, 192, 193
Brown, J. Smith, 130
Brownell, Francis E., 2, 3, 4
Buck, Samuel D., 34, 52, 70, 227–228
Bucktails Brigade, 33
Buell, Augustus, 117–118
Bull, Rice C., 53
bullets, poisoned, 153
Burdette, Robert, 36
Burkhardt, George S., 200, 212
"Burning, the" (destruction of the Lower
    Shenandoah Valley), 155, 156, 159–160,
    165–167
Burnside, Ambrose, 86–87, 215–216
Bushnell, Reverend Horace, 24
butchering, 34–35
butcher knives, 92–94
Butler, Benjamin, 194
Buzzell, Lewis, 138
Byers, Samuel, 53

Caldwell, Samuel H., 209
Callaway, Mary, 55
Camp Randall, 101
Canfield, Silas S., 79, 81
Cannoneer, The (Buell), 117–118
cartridges, 81
Casler, John O., 38, 72, 155, 156
Catton, Bruce, 134
cavalry and cavalry charges, 113–116
Cedar Creek, Battle of, 34, 71, 112, 117–118,
    172
Cedar Mountain, Battle of, 55, 75
Cemetery Hill (Cedar Creek), 117–118
Cemetery Ridge (Gettysburg), 64–65
Chamberlain, Joshua L., 97, 229
Chambers, Bob, 182
Chambers, William Pitt, 36, 70, 182
Chancellorsville, Battle of, 53, 80–81, 116
Chantilly, Battle of, 77
Chapman, Conrad Wise, 84
Chattanooga Campaign, 104, 179–180, 182
Cherokee Lincoln Killers, 19
Chicago Tribune, 195, 210
Chickamauga, Battle of, 52, 58–59, 85,
    170–171, 175

Childs, Henry T., 97
Christianity
    motivation to kill in combat and, 20–24
    notions of sacrifice and, 35, 36
    See also religion
Christmas Truce (World War I), 181
Churchill, James O., 177
Cimprich, John, 212
Civil War
    Confederate Lost Cause narrative and, 229
    Lee's surrender at Appomattox, 228–229
    notions of a soldier's duty as sacrifice and/
        or killing, 35–37
    overview of factors affecting and
        legitimizing killing in battle, 39–40
    personal attitudes of soldiers toward
        killing, 37–39
    political ideology and the motivation to
        fight, 13–20
    reconciliation and healing in the aftermath
        of, 228–229, 230, 233–234
    religion and the motivation to fight,
        20–24, 231–232
    total casualties in, 230
    writings and accounts of killing in war,
        9–10, 11
    See also killing in battle; killing in the Civil
        War
Clark, Achilles V., 209
Clausewitz, Carl von, 69
Cleburne, Patrick, 123, 135
clergy, 23–24
clubbed muskets, 103–106
Co. Aytch (Watkins), 50
Cockerill, John, 28
coded language, 76–77
Coe, Hamlin Alexander, 58, 73, 184, 227
coffee, 179, 180
Cold Harbor, Battle of, 61–62, 88, 126, 174
Coleman, Arthur, 209
Collins, Robert M., 180
color bearers, 50
colors. See battle flags
Colt, Samuel, 94
Colt revolving rifles, 29–30
Columbia, Battle of, 158–159
Commando Order, 159
company flags, 110–111, 248n33
company officers, duties of, 43
Confederate Congress, 198, 203
Confederate flag, 110

*Confederate Rage, Yankee Wrath* (Burkhardt),
    200
Confederate soldiers
    desertions, 180–181
    hostility toward black Union soldiers, 10,
        190, 200–220 (*see also* United States
        Colored Troops)
    Lost Cause narrative, 229
    pacifist Christians, 20–21
    political ideology and the motivation to
        fight, 16–17, 18–19
    postwar issues of reunion and
        reconciliation, 229
    reactions to black Union soldiers, 198–200
    reactions to Lincoln's assassination,
        227–228
    religion and the motivation to kill in
        combat, 20–24
    responses to the Fort Pillow massacre,
        210–212
    responses to Union foraging, 154–161
    retaliatory violence against, by black
        Union soldiers, 220–224
    slavery and the motivation to fight, 16–17,
        18–19
    Southern honor and, 26
    *See also* killing in battle; killing in the Civil
        War; Southern civilians
Confederate sympathizers, 160–165
Connecticut regiments
    8th, 196
    16th, 86
Connolly, James A., 86
Cooke, Chauncey
    on antiwar Northerners, 161, 162
    attitude toward killing in battle, 57, 58
    on casualties and firepower, 62
    on fighting by black Union soldiers, 197
    on fraternization between the two sides,
        182
    on guns and pioneer life, 28
    on hunting, 33
    on revenge as the motivation to kill in
        battle, 54
    view of emancipation, 18
Copperheads, 160–165
Corinth, Battle of, 53
Cornet, Joseph L., 78
Cornfield (Antietam), 51
Cornish, Dudley Taylor, 198
Cornwell, Bernard, 6

Cornwell, David, 201
*Corporal Si Klegg and His "Pard"* (Hinman), 102
cover, hand-to-hand combat and, 107
Cowan, Luther H., 38
Crater, Battle of the, 138, 197, 215–220
Crockett, David, 26
Crofts, Thomas, 114
Crook, W. M., 98, 154
Cross, Edward, 50
Crowe, Richard Robert, 57
Crummer, William F., 52
Crumpton, Washington Bryan, 84
Cunningham, Michael, 73
Cusac, Isaac, 85
Custer, George Armstrong, 166
*Customs of Service for Non-Commissioned Officers
    and Soldiers* (Kautz), 178

Davis, Jefferson, 18, 19–20, 198, 227
Dawes, Rufus, 51, 82, 170, 171
Dead Angle (Kennesaw Mountain), 68–69
death, antebellum views of, 27
death lotteries, 166, 167
De Forest, John, 91, 133
Delaware, 1st Regiment, 51
"deliberate aim," 83–84
DeLong, Harrison, 120
Dent, S. H., 38, 72, 168
Dernten, J. A., 183
desensitization, 71–72
desertions, 180–181
Devil's Den (Gettysburg), 137
DeWolf, Saxon, 18
Dexter, Seymour, 52
Dicus, Joshua, 157
dilemma of the discarded weapons, 60, 61–62
Donovan, John H., 85
Douglas, Henry Kyd, 159–160
Douglass, Frederick, 191–192, 196
Duke, John K., 85
Dunlop, William S., 120, 126, 127, 128, 131,
    139
du Picq, Ardant, 69
Dutcher, Salem, 81
duty, as sacrifice and/or killing, 35–37
Dwight, Henry, 49, 98
Dwight, Theodore, 190
Dyer, John Will, 57, 58

Edward VIII (duke of Windsor), 14
Elliot, Frank, 136–137

Elliott, Stephen, 216
Elliott's Salient (Petersburg), 215, 216
Ellsworth, Elmer E., 1–4
emancipation, Union motivation to fight and, 18
Emancipation Proclamation, 189
Enfield rifles, 29, 30
execution
    "good," 82–83
    military, 168–169
    retaliatory, 165–168
    surrender, 153–154
    "terrible," 83
*Exposition of the Old and New Testaments* (Henry), 21
Ezra Church, Battle of, 50, 56, 86, 87

*Face of Battle, The* (Keegan), 22
Faust, Drew Gilpin, 8
Featherston, John, 219–220
Ferguson, Champ, 214
Ferguson, John H., 37, 85, 155–156, 162, 180–181
Ferrero, Edward, 216
fighting knives, 92–94
firearms
    "deliberate aim," 83–84
    dilemma of the discarded weapons, 60, 61–62
    loading and firing single-shot muzzleloaders, 41–42
    overshooting, 63–65
    posturing, 65–66
    revolvers and pistols, 94–95
    soldiers' affinity for and shooting prowess, 27–32
    soldiers' vocabulary for ammunition, 81
    training and target practices, 43–46
fire control, 42
Fire Zouaves, 1–4, 92
firing squads, 167–169
First Bull Run, Battle of. *See* First Manassas, Battle of
First Manassas, Battle of
    exposure and desensitization to death, 72
    fears of atrocities, 153
    hand-to-hand combat with knives, 92
    hunting compared to killing in battle, 33–34
    overshooting, 64
    rhetoric of hand-to-hand combat, 91

soldiers' attitudes toward killing in, 36, 39
soldiers' language of killing, 77
soldiers on the loss of comrades, 74
transformation experienced by combatants, 52
Zouave uniforms as targets, 51
First US Division, 216
Fitzpatrick, Marion Hill, 66
Fletcher, William A., 17, 31, 98, 139, 229
Florida, 4th Regiment, 53
Foote, Lorien, 26
foraging
    Army of Northern Virginia and, 157
    Union hard war policy and Confederate responses, 154–161, 164–165
*For Cause and Comrades* (McPherson), 11, 16
Forrest, Nathan Bedford, 5, 204–206, 207, 209–210, 224, 230
Fort Anderson, 205
Fort Blakely, 223
Fort Donelson, 26, 52, 128–129, 177
fortifications, hand-to-hand combat and fighting "across the works," 106–109
Fort Pillow
    Battle of, 204–212
    as a rallying cry of black Union soldiers, 222, 223, 224
*Fort Pillow, a Civil War Massacre* (Cimprich), 212
Fort Wagner, Battle of, 200
Foster, Samuel T., 68, 70, 87
4th US Artillery, 133
Fourth US Division, 215–216, 219
Franklin, Battle of
    hand-to-hand combat, 98, 106, 107, 108, 113, 118
    mercy in battle and sparing the enemy, 174
    posturing, 65
    retreating enemy as targets, 69–70
    soldiers' mourning of dead comrades, 74
    surrender executions and, 154
    taking of prisoners and, 172, 173
Franklin, James H., 174
fraternization
    alternating states of friendliness and fighting, 183–187, 188
    battlefield truces, 175–176, 179–181, 182–184
    desertion by Confederate soldiers and, 180–181
    development of sentiments about ending the war, 182–183

fraternization, *continued*
  friendly picket line interactions, 179–181
  impact on a soldier's ability to fight,
    181–182
  in World War I, 181
Fredericksburg, Battle of
  accounts of "murderous fire," 85–86
  hand-to-hand combat, 107
  impact of officers on killing in battle, 71
  officers blamed for reckless killing, 86–87
  Richard Kirkland and the "Angel of
    Marye's Heights," 176–177
  soldiers' ambivalence about killing, 59–60
  soldiers' attitudes toward the reality of
    war and, 72–73
  soldiers' experiences of battle, 53
  visibility on the battlefield, 47
Fremantle, Arthur, 115
French and Indian War, 121
Fritsch, Friedrich von, 112–113
frontier/civilization conflict, 26–27
frontier riflemen, 120
Front Royal, Battle of, 56, 166–167
Fuchs, Richard, 212

Gaines Mill, Battle of, 50–51, 54, 111
*Galveston Weekly News*, 156
Galwey, Thomas, 178
Gaust, Drew Gilpin, 16
generals, blamed for reckless killing, 86–87
Georgia regiments
  1st, 84
  2nd, 139
  4th, 131
  11th, 74
  28th, 82
  45th, 66
Germanic immigrants, 32
Gettysburg, Battle of
  bayonet charges, 97
  desensitization to killing, 71
  dilemma of the discarded weapons, 60
  fierceness of fighting at Little Round Top,
    62–63
  fighting for battle flags, 111
  hand-to-hand combat, 112–113, 117
  overshooting and Pickett's Charge, 64–65
  physical and emotional effects of battle,
    51–52
  posturing, 65
  sharpshooters, 137

soldiers' ambivalence about killing, 57, 58
soldiers who refused to kill, 58, 59
  taking of prisoners, 170, 171
Gibbons, Alfred, 173–174
Giles, Val, 24, 58–59, 85–86, 175
*gladius hispaniensis*, 104
Glendale, Battle of, 173
Gomard, Antonin, 99
"good execution," 82–83
Gooding, James Henry, 196
"Good Old Rebel" (song), 229
Gordon, John B., 229
Gore, George W., 183
Gould, John, 73, 86
Grant, Ulysses S.
  Battle of the Crater and, 215–216
  campaigns of 1864 and, 187
  on deactivated soldiers retaining their
    arms, 29
  disgust at the sight of blood, 34
  Lee's surrender at Appomattox, 228
  retaliatory executions and, 166
  Sheridan's burning of the Shenandoah
    Valley and, 155
  use of sharpshooters at Vicksburg, 130
Green, Johnny, 73, 138
Greenough, Ogden, 101
Griffith, Paddy, 53, 97
Grossman, Dave
  on animal slaughtering and butchering, 34
  on Civil War linear tactics, 42
  on Civil War soldiers avoiding killing,
    60–61
  on hand-to-hand combat, 102, 103, 104, 105
  on human resistance to killing as innate,
    22
  on killing and physical proximity to the
    enemy, 67
  on killing in battle as a stressor, 8
  on killing indirectly, 46
  on killing the retreating enemy, 69
  "posturing" concept, 65
  on target attractiveness, 49
group absolution, 43
"Guerillas, The" (poem), 17
Guerrant, Edward O., 213–214

Haliburton, Thomas Chandler, 14
Halpine, Charles G., 194–195
Hammon, James Henry, 15
Hampton, Wade, 156, 157–158, 159

*Handbook of Artillery* (Roberts), 117
Handerson, Henry E., 56, 91
hand-to-hand combat
    bayonets, 95–98
    bayonet training, 98–102
    circumstances necessary for, 106–112
    defense of regimental battle flags, 109–112
    defined, 90–91
    fighting "across the works," 108–109
    fighting by artillerymen, 116–118
    fighting by cavalry, 113–116
    fighting by officers, 112–113
    media portrayals of, 91
    overview and summary, 233
    preference for clubbed muskets versus
        bayonets, 103–106
    psychological nature of, 90, 102–103, 118
    rarity of, 90, 97, 98, 118
    sidearms, 91–95
    soldiers' descriptions of, 118
    in soldiers' wartime rhetoric, 91
hangings, 166–167
Hankins, Samuel, 33
Hanks, Orlando T., 66, 92
hard war policy, Union foraging and
        Confederate responses, 154–161,
        164–165
Harn, Isaac, 79
Harner, Edward B., 156
Harpers Ferry raid, 15, 192, 193
*Harper's Monthly*, 98
*Harper's Weekly*, 122, 132–133
Haskell, John Cheves, 111, 217
Hayes, Rutherford B., 172, 229
Hays, Alexander, 123
Hayward, Henry, 162, 163
Henry, Matthew, 21
Henry repeating rifles, 30, 31
Hess, Earl J., 8, 28, 97, 134
Hill, Daniel Harvey, 87–88
Hinman, Wilbur F., 102
Hitler, Adolf, 159
Holsinger, Frank, 53
Holt, David E., 59–60
Homer, Winslow, 132–133, 134
Hood, John Bell, 87, 206
horse pistols, 94
House, E. H., 3
Howard, S. E., 112
"How Does One Feel under Fire?"
    (Holsinger), 53

Howe, Julia Ward, 35
Hubert, Charles F., 128–129
Hughes, William A., 68
Hulbert, Simon Bolivar, 24, 44–45, 47, 57, 58
Hunter, Alexander, 47, 73
hunting experience / skills
    killing in battle and, 32–34
    sharpshooters and, 125–126
Hurlburt, Stephen A., 204

Illinois, Copperheads and, 162, 163
Illinois regiments
    7th, 31
    10th, 37, 56, 85, 155–156, 162, 180–181
    11th, 177
    30th, 101, 167–168
    34th, 30, 43–44, 56, 93, 156
    45th, 52
    47th, 36
    50th, 128–129
    65th, 174
    66th, 33, 129
    73rd, 98
    77th, 184
    88th, 98
    92nd, 66
    96th, 73–74, 185
    103rd, 79
    105th, 210
Indiana regiments
    44th, 34
    57th, 22
    72nd, 29
    100th, 141
Indian wars, 25
Iowa regiments
    5th, 53
    23rd, 202
    31st, 29
Irish Brigade, 85
Iron Brigade, 44, 47–48, 69
irregular guerrillas, 10–11
Ives, Washington, 28, 30, 53

Jackson, Alfred E., 212
Jackson, Andrew, 120
Jackson, "Big Jack," 201
Jackson, James W., 2, 3–4
Jackson, Thomas J. "Stonewall," 24, 174–175
Japanese military, 221
Jarmon, Robert, 179

Jefferson, Thomas, 192
Jeffords, Harrison, 111
Jesus Christ, 21–22
Johnson, Andrew, 198
Johnson, William H., 196
Joint Committee on the Conduct of the War,
    210
Jonesboro, Battle of, 172–173, 186
Jordan, Thomas, 211
just war theory, 21

Kansas
    1st Colored Volunteers, 197, 200
    slavery and political violence, 14–15
Kautz, August, 178
Keegan, John, 22, 70
Kelly's Ford, 140
Kenfield, Frank, 218–219
Kennesaw Mountain, Battle of, 68–69, 176,
    180–181, 184
Kentucky regiments
    4th Cavalry, 213
    9th, 173
Kentucky rifles, 120
Kernstown, First Battle of, 54
Kerr rifles, 123, 137, 138
Kershaw, Joseph, 176, 177
killing, versus murder, 21–22
killing in battle ("seeing the elephant")
    ambivalent or regretful feelings toward,
        56–63
    attitudes of black Union soldiers toward,
        195–198
    battlefield visibility and, 46–47
    Dave Grossman on soldiers avoiding
        killing, 60–61
    desensitization, 71–72
    dilemma of the discarded weapons, 60,
        61–62
    extremes of killing and not killing,
        152–153, 232–233 (see also atrocities;
        mercy in battle)
    feelings about having slain an enemy,
        48–49
    impact of officers on, 70–71
    influence of race on, 189–190, 224–225 (see
        also United States Colored Troops)
    linear tactics, 42–43
    loading and firing single-shot
        muzzleloaders, 41–42
    meaning of "seeing the elephant," 41

    military training and target practice, 43–46
    overshooting, 63–65
    physical and emotional effects of, 51–54
    physical proximity to the enemy and,
        67–69
    posturing, 65–66, 108
    retreating enemy as targets, 69–70
    revenge as motivation, 54–56
    searching to find the bodies of slain
        enemies, 66–67
    soldiers' attitudes toward the reality of
        war, 72–75
    soldiers who refused to kill, 58–59
    target attractiveness, 49–51
    target selection, 47–48
killing in the Civil War
    antebellum attitudes toward violence,
        25–27
    antebellum views of death, 27
    antebellum views of the military, 24–25
    differences between Confederate and
        Union soldiers, 10
    diversity of soldiers' experiences, 6–7
    factors enabling, 7
    familiarity with firearms and shooting
        prowess, 27–32
    historical sources and the focus of study,
        9–11
    hunting experience and, 32–34
    influence of race on, 189–190, 224–225 (see
        also United States Colored Troops)
    key historians on, 8
    Nathan Bedford Forrest on, 5
    new military history approach to, 8–9
    notions of duty as sacrifice and/or killing,
        35–37
    overview of factors affecting and
        legitimizing, 39–40, 231–232
    political ideology and the motivation to
        fight, 13–20
    religion and the motivation to fight,
        20–24, 231–232
    soldiers' acceptance of, 230
    soldiers' personal attitudes toward killing,
        37–39
    soldiers' writings and accounts of, 9–10, 11
    value of studying, 12
killing in war
    Dave Grossman on, 8 (see also Grossman,
        Dave)
    Nathan Bedford Forrest on, 5

public attitudes toward, 5–6
S. L. A. Marshall's study of, 7–8
Kilmer, George L., 219
King, John M., 66
King James Bible, 21–22
Kingman, Eugene, 72, 79–80, 101
Kirkland, Richard, 176–177
knives, 92–94
Knowlton, Daniel C., 71
Ku Klux Klan, 206
Kyle, Chris, 6

land mines, 88, 139. *See also* Crater, Battle of
language of killing
    coded language for killing, 76–77
    "deliberate aim," 83–84
    "good execution," 82–83
    murder and "murderous fire," 84–88
    significance of, 76, 88–89, 232
    vocabulary, slang, and euphemisms for
        killing, 77–81
    vocabulary for ammunition, 81
lashing, of slaves, 190–191
Law, Evander, 88
Law's Brigade, 111
Leach, Patsey, 192
Ledford, Preston Lafayette, 37, 47
Ledlie, James, 216
Lee, Robert E., 72–73, 157, 228
Leeman, William, 193
Lennard, George W., 22
Leon, Louis, 44, 78, 186
Lester, Henry Dick, 201
Lewis, George H., 30
Lieb, Hermann, 201
Lightning Brigade, 29, 30, 66
Lincoln, Abraham
    assassination of, 226–228
    on black Union soldiers, 194, 198
    on common American identity, 169,
        233–234
    Confederate animosity toward, 18–19
    Emancipation Proclamation, 189
    endorsement of sharpshooters, 122
    on the fighting ability of Westerners,
        26–27
    first inaugural address, 13
    hard war policy and, 164–165
    "last full measure of devotion," 230
    on the loss of comrades in battle, 74
    Marshall House incident and, 1, 4

notion of redemptive sacrifice and, 35
passage through Baltimore in 1861, 15, 19
on the rebellion and religion, 23
reckless view of personal safety, 19
response to Confederate threats against
    black Union soldiers, 198–199
on slavery and the rebellion, 189
Linderman, Gerald, 16
linear tactics, 42–43
line of battle, 42–43
Little Round Top (Gettysburg), 62–63, 97
livestock slaughtering and butchering, 34–35
Longstreet, James, 72
Louisiana regiments
    9th, 56
    9th, African Descent, 200, 201, 202
    11th, African Descent, 200, 202
    13th, African Descent, 200
Lynn, John A., 221

MacArthur, Arthur, 113
Mahone, William, 216, 217
Maine regiments
    2nd, 77
    2nd Cavalry, 223
    12th, 79, 101
    20th, 47, 97
Malvern Hill, Battle of, 74, 87–88
Manson, Henry, 127
March to the Sea, 155–159, 167–168
marksmanship, 44–46, 232
marksmen, 31–32. *See also* sharpshooters
Marsh, John G., 54
Marshall, S. L. A., 7–8, 42, 60
Marshall House incident, 1–4
Marye's Heights (Fredericksburg), 47, 72–73,
        85–87, 176–177
Mason, John, 168–169
Massachusetts regiments
    5th Colored Volunteer Cavalry, 222
    6th, 15–16
    33rd, 156
    34th, 67, 78
    54th, 196, 222
Matson, John S. B., 66–67
Mayo, Perry, 77, 162, 177
Mays, Thomas D., 214
McClellan, George B., 99, 101
McCulloch, Henry E., 200, 202–203, 204
McFarland, George Fisher, 161, 164
McPherson, A. Campbell, 39, 72

McPherson, James M., 8, 11, 16, 23
Meade, George G., 215–216
Mennonites, 20, 21
Mensendike, Fred, 129
mercy in battle
    alternating states of friendliness and
        fighting, 183–187
    battlefield truces, 175–176, 179–181,
        182–184
    battle viewed as a continuum, 152–153
    factors tempering, 187–188
    mercy toward wounded enemies, 177
    one-man acts of mercy, 176–177
    overview and summary, 233
    picket line interactions and fraternization
        between sides, 178–183 (see also
        fraternization)
    sparing the enemy, 174–175
    taking of prisoners, 169–173
Merrifield, James K., 98
Metcalf, George, 24
Mexican War, 25
Meyer, Henry, 58
Michigan regiments
    2nd, 77
    4th, 111
    7th, 48
    19th, 227
military and militarism, views of in the
        antebellum period, 24–25
military executions, 168–169
military training, 43–46
Miller, Isaac, 172
Miller, Lindley, 197
Miller, Matthew M., 201, 202
Milliken's Bend, Battle of, 200–204
mines, 88, 139. See also Crater, Battle of the
Minnich, J. W., 141
Missionary Ridge, 55, 68, 87
Mississippi regiments
    1st, African Descent, 200
    2nd, 33
    16th, 59–60
    17th, 17
    28th Cavalry, 54
    37th, 84
    46th, 70
Mississippi Squadron, 30
Missouri Brigade, 69–70
Mitchell, Reid, 8
Montgomery, W. R., 124

Moore, Robert A., 17, 82
Morgan, Daniel, 120
Morgan, Thomas, 38
Morse, Nathan, 127
Mosby, John S., 114, 156, 166–167
Mosby's Rangers, 114, 166–167
Mosgrove, George Dallas, 213, 214
Moys, Battle of, 106
Mule Shoe (Spotsylvania), 106, 107–108
murder
    killing in battle compared to murder or
        "murderous fire," 84–88
    of slaves, 191
    versus killing, 21–22
muzzleloaders
    British, 45
    dilemma of the discarded weapons, 60,
        61–62
    loading and firing, 41–42

"National Convention of Colored Men," 196
Nat Turner's Rebellion, 192, 193
Neely, Mark, 163
Neese, George, 75
Nelson, Frank, 64–65
Newby, Dangerfield, 193
New Hampshire regiments
    2nd, 93
    5th, 50
    9th, 43
    13th, 138
New Jersey regiments
    1st Cavalry, 116
    12th, 51–52
    24th, 73
    33rd, 55
new military history, 8–9
New Testament, 21–22, 35
Newton, James K., 183
New York regiments
    1st Light Artillery, 136–137
    11th Volunteers (Fire Zouaves), 1–4, 92
    12th State Militia, 44
    14th Brooklyn, 24, 170
    14th Heavy Artillery, 219
    16th, 50–51
    40th, 77
    44th, 71
    68th, 112–113
    89th, 162
    95th, 170

100th, 44–45
108th, 86–87
114th, 71
123rd, 53
154th, 185–186
*New York Sunday Mercury*, 19
*New York Tribune*, 3
Nicholson, Bill, 174
Ninth US Corps, 215
Nisbet, James Cooper, 31, 70
Nixon, Liberty Independence, 22, 23
Noll, Mark, 20
North Carolina regiments
    1st, 186
    4th, 73
    18th, 79
Norton, Oliver, 54
Nosworthy, Brent, 96, 98
Nugent, William L., 32, 39, 54
Nunnally, Matthew T., 74
Nutt, Edmund N., 85

officers
    as authority figures, 42–43
    blamed for reckless killing, 86–87
    endorsement of sharpshooters, 122–123
    fighting in hand-to-hand combat, 112–113
    friendly picket line interactions and,
        179–180
    as high-value targets, 49–50
    impact on soldiers and killing in battle,
        70–71
    *See also* Union officers of black soldiers
Ohio regiments
    3rd Cavalry, 114
    20th, 49, 51, 85
    21st, 79, 81, 85
    29th, 54
    31st, 87
    46th, 30
    53rd, 85
    54th, 50
    68th, 156–157
    93rd, 172
    116th, 71
    120th, 66–67
    175th, 172
"Old Red Shirt" (Confederate sharpshooter),
    128–129
Oldroyd, Osborn, 51, 130
Old Testament, 21

Olustee, Battle of, 199
*On Killing* (Grossman), 8, 60–61
Opdycke, Emerson, 113
Opie, John, 229
Orphan Brigade, 73, 84, 137, 138
Overland Campaign
    accounts of "murderous fire," 86
    alternating states of friendliness and
        fighting, 184
    hand-to-hand combat, 107
    sharpshooters, 131–132
    soldiers' attitudes toward the reality of
        war and, 73
    soldiers' language of killing, 80
overshooting, 63–65

pacifist Christians, 20–21
Peace Democrats, 161. *See also* Copperheads
Peachtree Creek, Battle of, 84, 174
Pegram, William "Willy," 117, 219
Peninsula Campaign, 70, 82, 137, 139
Pennsylvania Bucktails, 173
Pennsylvania regiments
    8th Cavalry, 80–81, 116
    28th, 78, 162, 163
    48th, 215, 216
    71st, 65
    83rd, 54
    90th, 86
    148th, 58
percussion revolvers, 114–115
Perkins, Hugh, 53, 69
"Personal Recollections of the Cavalry at
        Chancellorsville" (Wickersham), 80–81
Petersburg, Siege of
    Battle of the Crater, 138, 197, 215–220
    fraternization between the two sides, 180
    mines, 139
    sharpshooters, 126–127, 129, 130, 131, 137,
        139, 140
*Philadelphia Inquirer*, 161
Phillips, B. F., 217
physical proximity, killing in battle and, 67–69
picket lines
    alternating states of friendliness and
        fighting, 185–186
    purpose of and regulations about, 178–179
pickets, sharpshooters and, 132
Pickett, George E., 180
Pickett's Charge, 64–65
Piedmont, Battle of, 67, 78

Pierce, Francis E., 86–87
Pierson, Stephen, 55
Pine Knob, 55
pistols, 94–95
Pleasant Hill, 62
pocket guns, 94
Pohanka, Brian, 110
poisoned bullets, 153
Poison Spring, Battle of, 197
politics/political ideology
    antebellum violence and, 14–15
    soldiers' attitudes toward war and, 13–20
Porter, Fitz John, 122–123
Port Hudson, Siege of, 79, 133, 200
posturing, 65–66, 108
Pottawatomie Massacre, 193
Potter, Robert, 216
Potter, William, 130
Potts, Frank, 48
Powell, Ben, 127–128
Powell, Charles S., 73
prisoners
    deceiving enemies willing to offer quarter,
        173
    mercy and the taking of, 169–173
    refusals to take, 172
    resistance and escape by, 173–174
    retaliatory executions, 165–168
    surrender executions, 153–154
"Private Miles O'Reilly," 194–195

Quakers, 20

race, influence on killing in the Civil War,
    189–190, 224–225. See also United
    States Colored Troops
Ragin, James, 131
rape, 158
Rath, John and George, 55
Ray, William R., 38, 47–48
Raymond, Battle of, 49, 51
Raymond, Bud, 95
Rea, Ralph, 48
Reed, Thomas Benton, 57, 58, 80, 92
regimental chaplains, 24
regimental flags
    hand-to-hand combat and, 109–112
    significance of, 110–111
    of United States Colored Troops, 197–
        198
Reid, William, 130

religion
    just war theory and, 21
    motivation to kill in combat and, 20–24,
        231–232
    notions of sacrifice and, 35, 36
    soldiers' attitudes toward war and, 13
repeating rifles
    Henry rifles, 30, 31
    posturing and, 65–66
    Spencer rifles, 29, 66
Resaca, Battle of, 57, 58, 210
retaliatory executions, 165–168
retreating enemy, 69–70
revenge, as the motivation to kill in battle,
    54–56
Revolutionary War, 25, 96, 120
revolvers
    of artillerymen, 116–117
    cavalry melees, 114–115, 116
    in hand-to-hand combat, 94–95
Rhode Island regiments
    2nd, 228
    7th, 71
Rhodes, Elisha Hunt, 228
Rhodes, William C., 167
Rice, James C., 71
Richmond Dispatch, 214–215
Richmond Enquirer, 214
rifle matches, 28
rifles
    clubbed muskets in hand-to-hand combat,
        103–106
    dilemma of the discarded weapons, 60,
        61–62
    overshooting, 63–65
    posturing, 65–66
    Sharps breechloader rifles, 29, 30, 45,
        124–125
    sharpshooters and, 123, 124–125
    soldiers' affinity for and shooting prowess,
        27–32
    See also muzzleloaders; repeating rifles
Ripley, William, 31–32, 124, 125, 140, 184
Roberts, Joseph, 117
Robinson, Charles, 208
Rolfs, David, 23
roughs, 26
Ruchs, Richard, 206

sabers, 113, 114, 115, 116
Sable Arm, The (Cornish), 198

sacrifice, notion of duty as, 35–37
Saltville Massacre, 212–215
"Sambo's Right to Be Kilt" (song), 194–195
Sandburg, Carl, 207
Schantz, Mark S., 27
*Scientific American*, 99–100, 114
Scott, Winfield, 121
Second Manassas, Battle of, 66, 93
Second US Division, 216
Sedgwick, John, 127–128
sergeants, duties of, 43
Seven Pines, Battle of, 78
Sexton, James, 74, 113, 173
Sharps breechloading rifles, 29, 30, 45, 124–125
sharpshooters
    claiming credit for high-profile kills,
        127–128
    combat roles, 124
    endorsements of, 122–123
    fighting the enemy's sharpshooters,
        130–132
    formation of units, 121–122
    at Fort Donelson, 128–129
    at Fort Pillow, 206–207
    hunting skills and, 125–126
    incentives for enlisting as, 124–126
    language of killing in the accounts of,
        126–127
    notions about legitimate conduct on the
        battlefield, 139–140
    officers as high-value targets, 49
    overview and history of, 119–121, 232
    reactions of civilians to, 132–133, 141, 232
    Siege of Petersburg, 126–127, 129, 130,
        131, 137, 139, 140
    skilled gunnery likened to, 136–137
    soldiers' attitudes toward, 129–130,
        133–139, 141, 232
    tactical benefits of, 128–129
    targeting pickets, 132
Shaw, George, 208
Shenandoah Valley
    1862 campaign, 174–175
    Battle of Piedmont, 67, 78
    Battle of Toms Brook, 115
    "Burning," 155, 156, 159–160, 165–167
Sheridan, Phil, 155, 156, 157
Sherman, William T.
    campaigns of 1864 and, 187
    on clubbing and bayoneting in hand-to-
        hand combat, 104

Fort Pillow and, 204
    March to the Sea, 155–159
    on murder in war, 88
Shiloh, Battle of, 22, 23, 28, 34, 55, 97
Shocker, Harry, 214
shooting prowess, 31–32
Shore, Clifford, 125
short sword, 104
sidearms
    of artillerymen, 116–117
    of cavalrymen, 113–116
    hand-to-hand combat and, 91–95
siege operations
    alternating states of friendliness and
        fighting on picket lines, 185–186, 187
    Port Hudson, 79, 133, 200
    Yorktown, 122–123, 130, 134, 138
    *See also* Petersburg, Siege of; Vicksburg,
        Siege of
Simonton, Edward, 47, 53
single-shot muzzleloaders. *See* muzzleloaders
six-shooters, 94, 114
Sixth Commandment, 21–22
slain enemies, searching to find the bodies of,
    66–67
slaughtering, 34–35
slave codes, 190, 191, 192
slave revolts
    fears of, 192–193
    Nat Turner's Rebellion, 192, 193
    reprisals following, 193
slavery
    Confederate motivation to fight and, 17
    Mexican War and, 25
    Nathan Bedford Forrest and, 205–206
    roles of violence and power in, 190–192
    as root cause of the Civil War, 189
    Union motivation to fight and, 18
    violence by opponents of, 193
slave trade, 190
Smith, David, 51–52
Smith, Edmund Kirby, 203
Smith, Edwin M., 50
Smith, Richard Penn, 65
Smith, Walter, 86
Smith-Dorrien, Sir Horace, 181
smoothbore rifles, 29
snipers. *See* sharpshooters
Snyder, Henry, 91
socket bayonets, 95
Soldier Jim, 33–34, 36

South Carolina regiments
    2nd, 176–177
    12th, 127–128
    15th, 126
Southern civilians
    animosity toward Lincoln, 18–19
    Lost Cause narrative, 229
    pacifist Christians, 20–21
    postwar issues of reunion and
      reconciliation, 229
    responses to the Fort Pillow massacre,
      210–211
    responses to the Saltville Massacre,
      214–215
    Union hard war policy and, 157–159,
      164–165
Southern honor, 26
"Southern Soldier, The" (song), 37–38
South Mountain, Battle of, 43
Spence, Alexander, 92
Spencer repeating rifles, 29, 66
spike bayonets, 95
Spofford, Edwin F., 16
Spotsylvania, Battle of
    hand-to-hand combat, 106, 107–108, 118
    posturing, 65
    sharpshooters and the killing of John
      Sedgwick, 127–128
    skill gunnery likened to sharpshooting,
      136
Springfield rifles, 30
Squier, George W., 34, 36, 227
Stamps, Daniel, 209
Stanley, Henry, 97
Staples, Horatio, 77
Steinbaugh, Jacob, 118
Stephens, George E., 222
Stephens, Winston, 38
Stevens, Charles A., 122, 123
Stewart, William H., 224
Stiles, Robert, 133
Stillness at Appomattox, A (Catton), 134
Stillwell, Almeron, 45
Stone, Kate, 203
Stonewall Brigade, 38
Strong, Robert Hale, 210
Sturgis, H. Howard, 78–79
Sumner, Charles, 15
Sunday Mercury, 153
surrender executions, 153–154
Swift, Lucius B., 102

sword bayonets, 95
swords
    cavalry sabers, 113, 114, 115, 116
    of infantry officers, 112, 113

targets
    human-looking, 46
    target attractiveness, 49–51
    target practice, 44–46
    target selection, 47–48
Taylor, James C., 197
Taylor, Richard, 203
Tennessee regiments
    1st, 68–69, 94
    13th, 98
    13th Cavalry, 204, 208, 210
Tenyson, John, 30
Texas Brigade, 24, 66, 87, 175
Texas Rangers, 156
Thain, Alexander, 73–74
Third US Division, 216
Thompson, James T., 38
Thompson, John Edgar, 82, 83
Tillotson, George, 162
tobacco, 179, 180
Toms Brook, Battle of, 115
Toney, Marcus, 94
torpedoes, 88
trench warfare, picket lines and, 185–186, 187
Trigg, Robert C., 170
Truth, Sojourner, 197
Tunnel Hill, 79
Turner, Nat, 192
Tuthill, Richard S., 107, 175

uniforms
    target attractiveness and, 50–51
    wearing captured uniforms, 156
Union City, 205
Union officers of black soldiers
    Confederate threats against, 198, 203
    views of retaliatory violence, 222
Union Soldier in Battle, The (Hess), 134
Union soldiers
    animosity toward Jefferson Davis, 18,
      19–20
    black (see United States Colored Troops)
    foraging, hard war policy, and Confederate
      responses, 154–161, 164–165
    political ideology and the motivation to
      fight, 15–16, 17–18, 19–20

reactions to Lincoln's assassination, 227–228

religion and the motivation to kill in combat, 20–24

roughs, 26

slavery as a motivation to fight, 18

*See also* killing in battle; killing in the Civil War

United States Colored Troops

attitudes of white Union soldiers toward, 194–195

attitudes toward killing in battle, 195–198

Battle of Milliken's Bend, 200–204

Battle of the Crater, 215–220

Confederate dehumanizing of, 199, 203–204

Emancipation Proclamation and, 189

Fort Pillow, 204–212

hostility of Confederate soldiers toward, 10, 190, 200–220

Northern views of, 193–194

overview of the influence of race on killing in battle, 189–190, 224–225

prejudice in the Union Army and, 196

reactions of Confederate civilians and soldiers to, 198–200

retaliatory violence against Confederates, 220–224

Saltville Massacre, 212–215

United States Colored Troops regiments

1st, 196

2nd Light Artillery, 204

5th Cavalry, 212, 213

6th Cavalry, 196

6th Heavy Artillery, 204, 208

22nd, 197–198

23rd, 222

29th, 222

51st, 223

55th, 222

93rd, 197

Upson, Theodore, 30, 31, 95, 141

Uptmore, Henry, 129

US Congress

antebellum politics and violence in, 15

Joint Committee on the Conduct of the War, 210

US flag, 110

US sharpshooter regiments

1st, 31–32, 122, 124, 130, 137, 139

2nd, 24, 124, 126–127, 137

*See also* Berdan's Sharpshooters

Vallandigham, Clement, 161–162

Vance, P. M., 217

vedettes (mounted sentries), 178

Vermont regiments

8th, 112

17th, 218–219

Vicksburg, Siege of

alternating states of friendliness and fighting, 184

battlefield truces, 183

fraternization between the two sides, 182

sharpshooters, 129–130, 138

Victorian age

attitudes toward violence, 25–27

views of death, 27

Virginia

Nat Turner's Rebellion, 192, 193

slave codes, 191, 192

Virginia regiments

1st, 48

7th, 81

12th, 23, 218

13th, 34, 70, 227–228

54th, 170–171

56th, 64–65

61st, 224

Virginia Cavalry, 43rd Battalion, 166–167

(*see also* Mosby's Rangers)

visibility on the battlefield, 46–47

Voltaire, 32

von Borcke, Heros, 98

Walker, John G., 200

Warner, Lewis D., 185–186

War of 1812, 25, 120

Watkins, Sam, 49, 50, 68–69, 74

Wauhatchie, Battle of, 78–79

Weiser, James M., 170–171

Welsh, James L., 18

West, John, 131

Westerners, Lincoln on the fighting ability of, 26–27

Western Sharpshooters, 33, 129

West Woods (Antietam), 84

Wheatfield (Gettysburg), 111

Wheat's Tigers, 19

Wheeler, Joseph, 156

whipping, of slaves, 190–191

White, William, 140–141

White, Wyman, 71, 124, 126–127, 131–132, 139–140

Whitworth rifles, 123
"Who Wouldn't Be a Fire Zouave" (poem),
    91
Wickersham, Charles I., 80–81, 116
Wickliffe, Charles A., 194
Widney, Lyman S., 30, 33, 43–44, 45, 56, 71,
    73, 93
Wilcox, Orlando, 216
Wilder, John T., 30
Wiley, Bell Irvin, 8, 16, 184, 195, 212
Wiley, William, 77, 184
Wilkeson, Frank, 133, 135, 138
Williams, Elijah D., 153
Williamsburg, Battle of, 81
Wilson's Landing, 196
Wisconsin regiments
    1st Heavy Artillery, 182, 183
    5th, 45
    6th, 51, 82, 170, 171
    7th, 38, 53, 69, 82
    14th, 183

24th, 113
25th, 17
29th, 101, 130
30th, 101
32nd, 57
Wise, John S., 218
Womack, James, 39
women, regimental battle flags and, 110–111
"Woodstock Races," 115
World War I, 181
World War II, 7–8, 60, 159, 221
Wright, John M., 201

Yates, Richard, 162
Yorktown, Siege of, 122–123, 130, 134, 138
Young, Orson, 185, 187

Zouave regiments
    bayonet training, 100–101
    Fire Zouaves, 1–4, 92
    uniforms and target attractiveness, 51

Printed in the USA
CPSIA information can be obtained
at www.ICGtesting.com
CBHW030222210724
11886CB00006B/475